Defeating Mau Mau, Creating Kenya

Counte

This book details the devastating Mau Mau civil war fought in Kenya during the 1950s and the legacies of that conflict for the post-colonial state. There were as many Kikuyu who fought with the colonial government as there were loyalists who joined the Mau Mau rebellion. Focusing on the role of those loyalists, the book examines the ways in which residents of the country's Central Highlands sought to navigate a path through the bloodshed and uncertainty of civil war. It explores the instrumental use of violence, changes to allegiances, and the ways in which cleavages created by the war informed local politics for decades after the conflict's conclusion. Moreover, the book moves toward a more nuanced understanding of the realities and effects of counter-insurgency warfare. Based on archival research in Kenya and the United Kingdom and insights from literature from across the social sciences, the book reconstructs the dilemmas facing members of a society at war with itself and its colonial ruler.

Daniel Branch is currently Assistant Professor in African History at the University of Warwick. Previously, he taught at the University of Exeter and was a Fellow of the Macmillan Center for International and Area Studies at Yale University. His articles have appeared in a number of journals, including *African Affairs,* the *Journal of African History, Africa Today*, and the *Review of African Political Economy*. He is currently working on two forthcoming book projects and is co-editing (with Nicholas Cheeseman) a volume on Kenyan politics since 1950.

AFRICAN STUDIES

The *African Studies Series*, founded in 1968, is a prestigious series of monographs, general surveys, and textbooks on Africa covering history, political science, anthropology, economics, and ecological and environmental issues. The series seeks to publish work by senior scholars as well as the best new research.

A list of books in this series will be found at the end of this volume.

Defeating Mau Mau, Creating Kenya

Counterinsurgency, Civil War, and Decolonization

DANIEL BRANCH

University of Warwick

CAMBRIDGE
UNIVERSITY PRESS

CAMBRIDGE UNIVERSITY PRESS
Cambridge, New York, Melbourne, Madrid, Cape Town, Singapore,
São Paulo, Delhi, Dubai, Tokyo

Cambridge University Press
32 Avenue of the Americas, New York, NY 10013-2473, USA

www.cambridge.org
Information on this title: www.cambridge.org/9780521130905

First published 2009

Printed in the United States of America

A catalog record for this publication is available from the British Library.

Library of Congress Cataloging in Publication data

Branch, Daniel, 1978–
Defeating Mau Mau, creating Kenya : counterinsurgency, Civil War, and decolonization /
Daniel Branch. – 1st ed.
    p.   cm. – (African studies ; 111)
Includes bibliographical references and index.
ISBN 978-0-521-11382-3 (hardback) – ISBN 978-0-521-13090-5 (pbk.)
1. Kenya – History – Mau Mau Emergency, 1952–1960.   2. Mau Mau – History – 20th
century.   I. Title.   II. Series.
DT433.577.B73   2009
967.62′03 – dc22   2009013028

ISBN 978-0-521-11382-3 Hardback
ISBN 978-0-521-13090-5 Paperback

For my parents

In times of peace and prosperity, both cities and individuals can have lofty ideals because they have not fallen before the force of overwhelming necessity. War, however, which robs us of our daily needs, is a harsh teacher and absorbs most people's passions in the here and now.
Thucydides, *The Peloponnesian War*, 3.81.5.

'Now', I said, 'there is no need for you to speak,
You filthy traitor; for now, and to your shame,
I will take back a true report of you.'
Dante, *Inferno*, XXXII 109

Contents

Preface

'Contemporary history,' writes Eric Hobsbawm, 'is useless unless it allows emotion to be recollected in tranquillity.'[1] Unfortunately, tranquillity has not been a luxury afforded to this book. The research and writing of it has coincided with a tremendous reawakening of the public memory in Kenya and Britain of the Mau Mau war of 1952–1960. The history of the anti-colonial rebellion was largely silenced in national debate in Kenya during the presidencies of Jomo Kenyatta (1963–1978) and Daniel arap Moi (1978–2002).[2] The war was too contradictory to be claimed by the new nation-state as one of national liberation after independence in 1963. Lacking a clearly defined nationalist ideology and restricted to the hills of the Kikuyu-dominated Central Province, the Mau Mau insurgents were not explicitly national in either intellectual or operational scope. Furthermore, those who clung to the memory of the insurgency as a tool of political mobilisation after 1963 were those unwelcome in the state institutions of post-colonial Kenya: the poor, the landless, and the opponents of the capitalist development path followed by successive post-colonial regimes. Most significantly, the war was not the neat conflict of the nationalist imagination.[3]

[1] Eric Hobsbawm, 'Could It Have Been Different?' *London Review of Books* 28 (2006).
[2] Marshall Clough, 'Mau Mau and the Contest for Memory,' in *Mau Mau and Nationhood: Arms, Authority and Narration*, eds. Elisha Stephen Atieno Odhiambo and John Lonsdale (Oxford, 2003).
[3] Elisha Stephen Atieno Odhiambo, '*Matunda ya Uhuru*, Fruits of Independence: Seven Theses on Nationalism in Kenya,' in *Mau Mau and Nationhood: Arms, Authority and Narration*, eds. Elisha Stephen Atieno Odhiambo and John Lonsdale (Oxford, 2003).

The war did not simply pit oppressive British forces against noble Kenyan nationalist rebels. Instead, it took the form of a civil war within Kikuyu society as so-called loyalists from among that community forged alliances with the colonial government and turned on their fellow Kikuyu Mau Mau within the ranks of the insurgency. As many Kikuyu fought with the colonial government as did those against it. It was the success of that process of alliance-building that allowed some of these loyalists to assume key positions of power within the state before and after the British departure. And it was the post-independence presence of these loyalists within the ruling party, the Kenya African National Union (KANU), the civil service, the boardrooms of the private sector, and Kenyatta's inner circle of advisers that required Mau Mau to be buried as a subject for public discussion. Precisely because of this attempt to silence an inconvenient past, the history of the Mau Mau war became embraced by opposition figures after independence. Politicians, novelists, academics, and pro-democracy activists turned to an ever more stylised and heroic Mau Mau to critique the elitist focus of Kenyatta and Moi. In the rebellion's history, these critics found a mirror to hold up against the growing prevalence of official corruption and the declining opportunities to express discontent within formal political institutions. Within this alternative and politicised rendering of the past, loyalists were represented as colonial quislings and the betrayers of the nation.

It is no surprise, therefore, that what appeared at the time to be a triumph for the forces for democracy in 2002, at which point KANU were removed from power, was accompanied by an explosion of interest in the Mau Mau war. Although the government of Mwai Kibaki proved to be no more interested in promoting democracy and ending corruption than its predecessors, it enthusiastically supported this rediscovery of the past.[4] For example, a task force was formed to investigate the viability of a truth and reconciliation commission to examine crimes committed by the state during the colonial and post-colonial period. The group's findings, though, were largely ignored.[5] At times, this effort by the state has assumed the form of farce. In 2003, for example, senior figures within the government were happy to welcome to Kenya Lemna Ayamu, an Ethiopian farmer claimed by two Kenyan journalists to be another of

4 Parselelo Kantai, 'Death of the Kenya Dream?' *East African*, 31 July 2006.
5 Government of Kenya, *Report of the Task Force on the Establishment of a Truth, Justice and Reconciliation Commission* (Nairobi, 2003).

Mau Mau's leaders, Stanley Mathenge.[6] Mathenge was, in Mau Mau's mythology, claimed to have fled north to independent Ethiopia during the war to escape the British. Most likely, he died like thousands of his followers, in the forests of Central Kenya. Needless to say, once the hoax was exposed shortly after the arrival of Ayamu in Nairobi in mid-2003, the government quickly washed its hands of the affair. Other efforts by the government to encourage Mau Mau's renaissance were of far greater significance and longevity. Between 2003 and 2007, the government legalised the Mau Mau organisation itself and assisted efforts by victims of atrocities committed in colonial detention camps to seek compensation from the British government.[7] A statue of Dedan Kimathi, unveiled with great ceremony, was erected in 2007 by the government in downtown Nairobi.[8]

The politics of this reclaiming of Mau Mau by the state is only now becoming apparent. Although billed as a democratisation of the past, more instrumental motives can be identified on the part of the government. First, mirroring Kenyatta's consolidation of power within an inner circle of advisers from his own Kiambu district, Kibaki swiftly became reliant on what is often termed a 'Mount Kenya mafia' of key supporters. Reminding Kenyans more generally of a presumed debt to Central Kenya derived from the sacrifices Mau Mau supporters made for independence served as a crude ideological justification for this regionalistation of power. Second, celebrating Mau Mau's memory was also an attempt to snatch the legacy of the rebellion from the group known as Mungiki, part criminal gang, part Kikuyu cultural revival movement, and part private political army. Mungiki, which means 'multitude' in the Kikuyu language, is a group made up of discontented, unemployed youth from Nairobi and the towns of the Central Highlands. Mungiki has periodically clashed with state security forces, resulting in significant fatalities. The group's leaders see in Mau Mau a precedent for violent protest against the Kikuyu elite who have failed to redistribute wealth and opportunity among the ethnic community the Kikuyu elite claim authority

---

[6] Mburu Mwangi & Tigist Kassa, 'The Puzzle Remains as 'Gen Mathenge' Comes Home,' *Daily Nation*, 31 May 2003.

[7] Chris McGreal, 'Mau Mau Veterans to Sue Britain Over Torture and Illegal Killings in Kenya,' *The Guardian*, 6 October 2006.

[8] Wanyiri Kihoro, 'Kimathi's Battle for Recognition Finally Won,' *The Standard*, 14 March 2007.

over.[9] By appropriating the legacy of Mau Mau, leading figures within
the government sought to delegitimise Mungiki, thus participating in a
broader effort to retain Kikuyu support for Kibaki's government and
to silence the intense class tensions that have marked the politics of the
Central Highlands over the past century.

Within this new wave of public memorialisation of the conflict, the role
of loyalists has once again been silenced. Mau Mau has finally become
the war of national liberation, as foreseen at independence by Mazrui,
with the contradictions of such a representation simply ignored.[10] The
public depiction of the war now matches that held privately by many
in Kenya. Although what follows here overwhelmingly relies on archival
sources, memories of countless conversations with Kenyans held during
the research and writing of this book between 2002 and 2007 will remain
vivid for years to come. Whether in conversations with Mau Mau veterans, former loyalists, or the elderly relatives of friends, discussions about
this research project principally took the form of stories of suffering,
pride, and, above all, pain. Despite enthusiastically volunteering their
most personal memories and opinions of the 1950s, few Kenyans outside
of academic institutions agreed with the topic of this book. Nearly all,
even former loyalists, thought it more important to record the memories
of those who had fought the hardest against British colonialism and had
lost the most as a result.

It was into this intensely charged political atmosphere that Caroline
Elkins released her *Imperial Reckoning* – published in Britain as *Britain's
Gulag* – in early 2005.[11] Echoing the nationalist representation of the
Mau Mau war, Elkins focused on the British response to what she portrayed as unified Kikuyu insurgency. Loyalists were barely considered
within the book. Elkins repeated claims of torture in detention camps,
similar to those found in the voluminous number of memoirs written by
Mau Mau veterans. However, she went further than even those authors
by arguing Britain had overseen an 'incipient genocide'[12] that claimed

---

9 David Anderson, 'Vigilantes, Violence and the Politics of Public Order in Kenya,' *African
   Affairs* 101 (2001); Peter Kagwanja, 'Facing Mount Kenya or Facing Mecca? The
   Mungiki, Ethnic Violence and the Politics of the Moi Succession in Kenya, 1987–2002,'
   African Affairs 102 (2003).
10 Ali Mazrui, 'On Heroes and Uhuru-Worship,' *Transition* 11 (1963).
11 Caroline Elkins, *Imperial Reckoning: The Untold Story of Britain's Gulag in Kenya*
   (New York, 2005).
12 Ibid., 49.

the lives of 'perhaps hundreds of thousands.'[13] Such allegations garnered much attention, and the book received a Pulitzer Prize in 2006. Among academics, the book has been less well received. The methodology behind some of the most contentious claims has been called into question.[14] Moreover, respected figures from within the fields of imperial and African history have fiercely criticised Elkins's arguments.[15] The use by the Kibaki government of Elkins's work as an intellectual prop during the reclaiming of Mau Mau's history is an additional matter of concern. Although Elkins's intentions have never been anything other than worthy, the wisdom of allowing her book's launch in Nairobi to become an official event at which both the justice and constitutional affairs minister, Kiraitu Murungi, and vice-president, Moody Awori, spoke is questionable.[16] Both were subsequently named in investigations into gross corruption overseen by the Kibaki regime and have proved to be among the president's closest allies.[17]

The controversy created by Elkins has ensured tremendous interest in every setting at which the preliminary findings of this research project have been presented. The study of Mau Mau has benefited immeasurably from the interest of a talented cadre of scholars, from both Kenya and beyond. Few such tightly defined periods of time in the history of such a small area of the world can have been subjected to such intensive scrutiny as Kenya's Central Highlands for the years between the end of World War II and independence in 1963. Historians, anthropologists, and political scientists have explored the roots of the Mau Mau insurgency within the colonial political economy of Kenya, detailed the movement's members, described the events of the 1950s, and considered the tortured position of memories of the rebellion within the politics of the post-colonial state. To them, and particularly to David Anderson and John Lonsdale, I owe a tremendous intellectual debt. Yet, this book hopes to stimulate new lines of thinking about Mau Mau by placing

[13] Ibid., xvi.
[14] John Blacker, 'The Demography of Mau Mau: Fertility and Mortality in Kenya in the 1950s, a Demographer's Viewpoint,' *African Affairs* 106 (2007).
[15] Susan Carruthers, 'Being Beastly to the Mau Mau,' *Twentieth Century British History* 16 (2005); Bethwell A. Ogot, 'Britain's Gulag,' *Journal of African History* 46 (2005); Derek Peterson, 'The Intellectual Lives of Mau Mau Detainees,' *Journal of African History* 48 (2008).
[16] *The Nation*, 'Kenya Wants Apology From UK Over Colonial Evils,' 4 March 2005.
[17] Andrew Teyie, 'A Case to Answer,' *The Standard*, 31 March 2006.

the insurgents' indigenous opponents and the violence of the conflict at the heart of the analysis. It attempts to do so by engaging with literature concerned with similar events outside of Kenya.

The reception given to Elkins's book, and to that of David Anderson, whose *Histories of the Hanged*[18] was published on the same day, has much to do with a revived interest in imperialism, detention, and torture. This trend can be attributed to the revelations of the treatment of detainees at Abu Ghraib, the use of detention without trial at Guantánamo Bay, and the misadventures of the United States and Britain in Iraq and Afghanistan. Britain's experience in Kenya and during its other late colonial wars was proffered by both critics and supporters of American foreign policy variously as a warning or lesson from history on the conduct of counterinsurgency campaigns on the global periphery.[19] Again driven by current events, similar figures have turned their attention to another related field of study. Over the past decade, civil war has emerged from the margins of academic research to assume a central position within the study of political violence in the modern world. But explaining these conflicts presents a very different challenge to scholars than explaining international war, which previously dominated the attention of social scientists. This book is underpinned by a belief, encouraged by the work of Stathis Kalyvas, that civil wars are defined by their ambiguity.[20] Definite divisions between combatants, such as that between loyalists and Mau Mau, are the product of these wars, not their catalysts.

This book was written and researched during political and academic firestorms that relate immediately to what is written herein. The arguments of the book attempt to engage directly with these current debates surrounding the questions of the place of the history of Mau Mau within Kenyan politics, the lessons of imperialism, the nature of contemporary warfare, and the dynamics of civil wars. The main purposes of the book are, first, to describe the ambiguity that characterised the war's early stages and to explain how from it the cleavage between Mau Mau supporters and loyalists emerged. The book then considers the significance

---

[18] David Anderson, *Histories of the Hanged: Britain's Dirty War in Kenya and the End of Empire* (London, 2005).
[19] See, for example, Caroline Elkins, 'The Wrong Lesson,' *The Atlantic Monthly* 296 (2005); Michael Howard, 'What's in a Name? How to Fight Terrorism,' *Foreign Affairs* 81 (2002); John Nagl, *Learning to Eat Soup With a Knife: Counterinsurgency Lessons From Malaya and Vietnam* (Chicago, 2005).
[20] Stathis Kalyvas, *The Logic of Violence in Civil War* (Cambridge, 2006).

of violence as a force in directing the trajectory of the war. The final objective is to explore the legacies of the conflict.

Kenya after 1963, or at least its Central Highlands, needs to be understood as much as a post-conflict as a post-colonial society. The two great abstractions of modern African politics, the nation and the ethnic group, have been allowed to distract us from examining the fractious divides within Kikuyu society that were created in the 1950s and exist up to the present. Underpinning so much of political debate since, the divides of the Mau Mau war continue to resurface in contemporary affairs.

Any attempt to write about a civil war fought within living memory necessarily engages with memories of hard-won struggles and bitter loss, whether they be found in letters and reports in the archive or in the words and behaviour of informants. Trying to dispassionately peel back these layers of emotion to answer research questions formulated in distant offices is the biggest challenge facing any academic attempting to understand and explain civil war violence. Although that emotion is unquestionably more immediate and all-enveloping while conflicts are still raging or have only recently concluded, 50 years is clearly insufficient time for it to have dissipated. Whether Hobsbawm was right to argue that renders what follows as useless is for the reader to decide.

Acknowledgements

This book would not have been written without the support of a great number of individuals and institutions. The original research was funded by the Arts and Humanities Research Council. Additional funding was provided by St. Peter's College, Oxford, the Royal Historical Society, and the British Institute in Eastern Africa. The writing began while I was a postdoctoral Fellow at the Macmillan Centre for International and Area Studies at Yale University, as a Fellow of the Mellon Foundation and National History Center's decolonization seminar, as a lecturer at the University of Exeter, and as a visiting Fellow of the African Studies Centre in Oxford. The finishing touches were applied at the University of Warwick. Throughout the writing of this book, I have benefited greatly from colleagues generous with their time and advice.

A great many people have generously provided their assistance and comments on the contents of this book during its transition from doctoral thesis to monograph. The publishers of *Journal of African History* and *Africa Today* both gave permission to reproduce material published in those journals in Chapters 4 and 5. Wambui Kamiru, Wm. Roger Louis, Joseph Miller, and Marilyn Young all provided helpful comments on drafts of chapters. In Nairobi, John Gitau Kariuki has been an unfailing friend and has provided invaluable assistance over the years. Gerald Murithi and the Muhoya family were also extremely helpful during fieldwork. At the British Institute in Eastern Africa, Paul Lane, Andrew Burton, Justin Willis, and Stephanie Wynn-Jones were never anything other than approachable, helpful, and friendly. And fellow researchers Cosmos Obote, Amrik Heyer, Miatta Fahnbulleh, Laragh Larsen, Gerard McCann, Matt Carotenuto, Gabrielle Lynch, Kate Luongo, Paul

Ocobock, and Rob Pringle were great company and help during my time in Kenya. So, too, were Natalia Sobrevilla Perea and Steffen Prauser at Yale. In Oxford, Judith Brown, Gavin Williams, and Jan-Georg Deutsch provided much help and advice in the initial stages of the research, while Alex Walsham, Andrew Thorpe, and various colleagues at Exeter were greatly supportive during the completion of this book. Special mention must also go to students in my courses on Mau Mau in 2006–7 and civil war in 2007–8, who greatly helped clarify my thoughts on many of the issues contained within this book. Eric Crahan and Emily Spangler, at Cambridge University Press, and Shana Meyer, at Aptara, Inc., were supportive and encouraging during the editorial process.

A few people deserve particularly heartfelt thanks. First, all the staff at the Kenya National Archives in Nairobi made the archival research an efficient, rewarding, and extremely enjoyable time. Gregg McClymont and Bruce Thomson have been great friends and a source of support throughout the research and writing of the book. As a fellow researcher, friend, and coauthor on several occasions, Nic Cheeseman has helped shape a great many of my ideas of Kenyan politics and history. Jennie Castle patiently put up with me and my interest in Kenyan history during the final stages of writing this book. John Lonsdale, Stathis Kalyvas, and David Anderson have all provided great practical assistance at different times during the writing of this book. Moreover, the intellectual debt I owe to each is evident throughout the book. As a supervisor and a friend, David, in particular, has been critical to the completion of this book, from our first discussions about it in 2001 up to the present. Finally, my parents have been unfaltering in their support of me throughout.

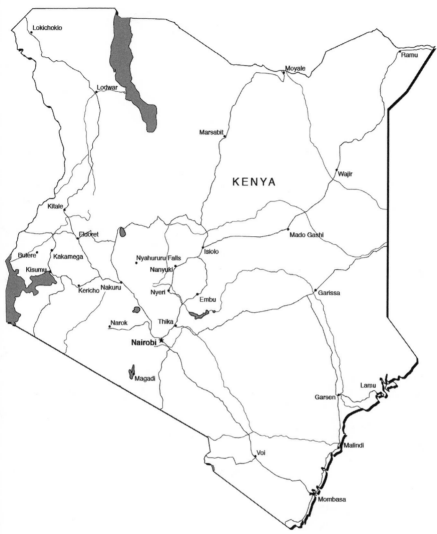

FIGURE 1. Map of Kenya.

Introduction

Understanding Loyalism in Kenya's Civil War

'You Can Have Your Wealth'

Colonialism in tropical Africa was announced by a battleship senselessly 'firing into a continent.'[1] In Kenya, at least, the retreat from empire looked little different. Early in March 1955, Jeremiah Nyagah, one of the indigenous opponents of the anti-colonial Mau Mau insurgency, attended the consecration of a new church in the Embu district. 'Not far from where we were,' Nyagah wrote, 'the Lancaster bombers were pounding the forest and the Mau Mau hideouts.' Despite the dropping of ordnance on to Mount Kenya in an attempt to flush out the bedraggled remnants of Mau Mau's insurgents, 'the noise of the exploding bombs did not mar the beauty of the solemn divine service.'[2] As the bombs fell on the last guerrillas sheltering in the mountain forests of Central Kenya, the attempts to forcibly equate might and right in the minds of colonial subjects and metropolitan citizens were no more comprehensible than they had even been. What had changed was the division of the African population of Kenya's Central Highlands into two definite camps – those like Nyagah watching the infliction of violence on the insurgents from afar and those in the forests targeted by the bombers. Over the duration of colonial Kenya's civil war, which had begun in 1952, the peoples of the Mount Kenya region had been forced by the course of the violence into one of two camps: loyalist or Mau Mau.

---

[1] Joseph Conrad, *Heart of Darkness* (New York, 1999), 16.
[2] Rhodes House Library, Oxford (RHL) Mss Afr s 1727, Foote papers, J. J. Nyagah to M. Foote, 12 March 1955.

Loyalists, such as Nyagah, were drawn from the same one-million-strong members of the Kikuyu, Embu, and Meru ethnic groups from which the Mau Mau rebellion sprang. Indeed, loyalists hailed from the same families, clans, and neighbourhoods as those who became their bitter rivals during the Mau Mau war that engulfed the Central Highlands between 1952 and 1956. The neat division between loyalists and Mau Mau implied by Nyagah's distance from the fighting in its latter stages was a product of the conflict rather than a cause or catalyst of the violence. Initially, that violence was more ambiguous and intimate than it later became. The case of one of the war's very first victims, Matari Muthamia, amply supports that observation.

After dark on an evening in mid-October 1952, a fortnight before Kenya's British rulers declared a State of Emergency, Matari, her sister, four other women, and the children of each were gathered together in a hut in the Meru district. Unlike Nyagah, who was the son and son-in-law of chiefs in the Embu district and later, after independence in 1963, a prominent politician and founder of a political dynasty, Matari was a relatively anonymous figure. A poor widow with a young child, dependent on the generosity of her sister and brother-in-law for her existence, Matari existed on the periphery of society. Together with her companions, and in common with tens of thousands elsewhere in Central Kenya at this time, Matari was summoned to the hut to be secretly oathed and to pledge her support for the movement that had come to be known as Mau Mau.

Oathing was a method of mobilisation and, as discussed in Chapter 1, an attempt to ensure the silence of the general population while the insurgents went about their business in localities. However, the use of oathing paraphernalia drawn from Kikuyu religion, such as raw goat meat, led to wildly exaggerated accusations of witchcraft and bestiality by the colonial regime, who outlawed the practice, and the mission churches. The denunciations of oathing by the latter led to some Christians refusing the oath and thus risking being killed by oath administrators fearful of those same individuals becoming police informers. A combination of secrecy and a willingness to use violence against recalcitrant individuals on the part of oath administrators enabled militant political figures at the head of what became Mau Mau to oath the vast majority of the population of the Central Highlands by the end of 1952 without significant interference from the state.

Matari's oathing ceremony was no different in form from most other similar events. It was held at night, in secret, and at the behest of a figure close to the intended initiates. The clandestine meeting's convener was Matari's brother-in-law, Mugwongo Ruria, with whom the widow sat down to eat dinner every night. Fatefully, Matari was a Christian, and when her turn arrived to pledge her allegiance to the insurgents, she refused. The oathers ordered her to leave the hut to face the punishment for disobedience. As she exited the building, Matari handed her small child to Mugwongo and announced to the assembled group, 'I leave you, you can have your wealth.'[3] Outside the hut she was killed by her brother-in-law, who eventually went to the gallows.

Interrogating the reasons for Matari's death is not a simple exercise. The predominant explanation within Kenyan popular memory for the violence of Mau Mau's insurgents, that it was driven by a nationalist spirit that denied expression in more peaceful forms, explains little about either this specific case or the thousands of Kikuyu killed by one another during the conflict. A more subtle explanation is needed. Petersen is right to warn that in such conditions of conflict, 'the extraordinary is inextricably linked to the ordinary.'[4] Obviously, Matari's faith impacted on her actions, but she acted not just as a convert to Christianity disowning what she saw as the paganism of her family members. Her final words, 'you can have your wealth,' critiqued the actions and motivations of her eventual killers with what is commonly termed 'moral ethnicity,' the interrogative and contested code of behaviour governing the conduct of those who imagined themselves to belong to the same ethnic community.[5] And in killing his sister-in-law, Mugwongo apparently felt he had to do so to protect himself, the other participants, and local activists from the potential consequences of Matari's refusal to respect the code of silence necessary for the incubation of an insurrection. Finally, although we have no knowledge of the nature of the relations between Matari and Mugwongo, it seems reasonable to assume that all was not well within the household. The death of Matari in October 1952 can therefore only be adequately understood when placed within this complex matrix of causation. To explain the violence within the communities of the Central Highlands during the Mau Mau war, an understanding of political economy,

---

[3] Kenya National Archive (KNA) MLA/1/625, CC198/1953, 'Muthuri Gatwankure & 10 Others.' See especially evidence of Raeli Nyagara and Karimi Mugwongo, 2–3 & 8 of proceedings.

[4] Roger Petersen, *Resistance and Rebellion: Lessons From Eastern Europe* (Cambridge, 2001), 1.

[5] John Lonsdale, 'The Moral Economy of Mau Mau: Wealth, Poverty and Civic Virtue in Kikuyu Political Thought,' in *Unhappy Valley: Conflict in Kenya and Africa*, eds. Bruce Berman and John Lonsdale (Oxford, 1992), 463, 466–8.

household relations, the cosmologies of actors, and the demands placed on them by their living in a time of intense conflict must all be given due consideration.

Although historians have long attempted to explain why hundreds of thousands supported the cause of armed rebellion in late-colonial Kenya, rather less attention has been given to those like Matari, who at various times opposed the Mau Mau insurgency. Loyalism is a lacuna in the otherwise substantial literature on the war. Loyalists are all too frequently depicted in this literature as a few, wealthy Christian individuals, who acted in the service of colonial masters in the pursuit of self-interest or as the unconscious agents of "divide and rule" polices.[6] Such arguments significantly underestimate the number of loyalists, deny their agency, and assume that the division between opponents and supporters of the insurgency were determined by prior social, political, or economic cleavages within Kikuyu society. The few brief studies of loyalism make similar assumptions of the distinctiveness of loyalists.[7]

This book in the first instance attempts to answer the question posed by Matari's actions on that night in October 1952; why, despite the plentiful grievances with colonial rule and the manifest populism of Mau Mau's cause, did tens of thousands of Kikuyu, Embu, and Meru at one time or another oppose the insurgency? In so doing, the arguments below differ from the existing literature on three points of significance. First, loyalists were a far more important component of the conflict than readers of other accounts of the Mau Mau war would otherwise surmise. Second, it is not the difference between loyalists and insurgents that demands explanation but instead the similarities shared between the two factions that are most notable. Finally, the motivations of loyalists were far more

[6] See, for example, Bruce Berman, *Control and Crisis in Colonial Kenya: The Dialectic of Domination* (London, 1990), 357; Robert Edgerton, *Mau Mau: An African Crucible* (London, 1990), 82; Elkins, *Imperial*, 28–9, 49, 118, 246; Wunyabari Maloba, *Mau Mau and Kenya: An Analysis of a Peasant Revolt* (Oxford, 1998), 88–9; D. Makaru Ng'ang'a, 'Mau Mau, Loyalists and Politics in Murang'a 1952–70,' *Kenya Historical Review* 5 (1977), 368–9; Cora Ann Presley, *Kikuyu Women, the Mau Mau Rebellion, and Social Change in Kenya* (Boulder CO, 1992). 126; Carl Rosberg and John Nottingham, *The Myth of 'Mau Mau': Nationalism in Kenya* (New York, 1966), 292 & 295.

[7] Ng'ang'a, 'Loyalists and Politics'; Bethwell A. Ogot, 'Revolt of the Elders: An Anatomy of the Loyalist Crowd in the Mau Mau Uprising 1952–1956,' in *Hadith 4: Politics and Nationalism in Colonial Kenya*, ed. Bethwell A. Ogot (Nairobi, 1972); Mordechai Tamarkin, 'The Loyalists in Nakuru During the Mau Mau Revolt and Its Aftermath, 1953–1963,' *Asian and African Studies* 12 (1978).

complex than too often assumed. Loyalists opposed Mau Mau because the rebellion posed a variety of threats unconnected to that against the incumbent regime. When opposition to Mau Mau arose, it initially drew on specific, local histories before later becoming a product of the cycle of violence that overwhelmed the Central Highlands through the first half of the 1950s. Mau Mau's anti-colonial rebellion thus developed rapidly into a civil war, a set of circumstances observable elsewhere.[8]

Mau Mau

Over the course of the four years following Matari's death, the anti-colonial rebellion and civil war claimed the lives of approximately 25,000 Kenyan Africans as a direct result of the violence. The vast majority of these fatalities were real or suspected Mau Mau activists.[9] One hundred seventy African members of the official armed forces and at least 1,800 African opponents of the insurgents lost their lives.[10] In contrast, 32 European settlers were murdered, and a further 63 European combatants were killed during the war.[11] Allies recruited from among the indigenous population of Central Kenya were then critical to the counterinsurgency campaign, inflicting 50 percent of Mau Mau casualties by the end of 1954.[12] By providing a numerically significant, temporary, irregular force financed by non-military sources, the militia known as the Home Guard swiftly and cheaply made up a shortfall in military manpower.[13] In all, more than 90 percent of the officially acknowledged casualties of the war

---

[8] See, for example, Ted Swedenberg's study of the 1936–9 rebellion against British rule in Palestine, which similarly transmuted into a conflict between Palestinians, Ted Swedenberg, *Memories of Revolt: The 1935–39 Rebellion and the Palestinian National Past* (Fayetteville AR, 2003), and Peter Hart's study of the Irish Republican Army (IRA) in Cork during the War of Independence and subsequent civil war in Ireland Peter Hart, *The I.R.A. and Its Enemies: Violence and Community in Cork, 1916–1923* (Oxford, 1998).

[9] Blacker, 'Demography of Mau Mau.'

[10] Colony & Protectorate of Kenya, *The Origins and Growth of Mau Mau: An Historical Survey* (Nairobi, 1960), 316.

[11] Elisha Stephen Atieno Odhiambo and John Lonsdale, 'Introduction,' in *Mau Mau and Nationhood: Arms, Authority and Narration*, eds. Elisha Stephen Atieno Odhiambo and John Lonsdale (Oxford, 2003), 3.

[12] RHL Mss Afr s 1580, File III, Hinde to Chief of Staff, 11 December 1954.

[13] David Percox, 'Mau Mau and the Arming of the State,' in *Mau Mau and Nationhood: Arms, Authority and Narration*, eds. Elisha Stephen Atieno Odhiambo and John Lonsdale (Oxford, 2003), 123 & 130.

were Kikuyu, most in all likelihood killed by their fellow inhabitants of Kenya's Central Highlands.[14]

The trigger for this violence was (of course) the intense grievances felt by Mau Mau's insurgents and the reaction of the colonial regime to the growing radicalisation of the colony's politics. The insurgency emerged from a triangle of discontent. The southernmost point was the colony's capital, Nairobi, where an underemployed, largely Kikuyu labour force was housed in the squalid neighbourhoods of the city's African quarters. Urban unrest was channelled towards militant politics by figures closely connected to the trade union movement and the city's criminal underworld. To the north of the city, on the slopes of Mount Kenya and the Aberdares range, lay the Native Reserves of Central Province. The internal boundaries between the districts of Central Province reflected the colonial mind, neatly delineated according to the assumed ethnic origin of the population within. So Embu belonged to the Embu district and Meru to the Meru district. Kikuyu were divided between the three districts of Kiambu, Fort Hall (later known as Murang'a), and Nyeri. In truth, the Kikuyu, Embu, and Meru have more in common culturally, linguistically, economically, and historically than markers of difference. For that reason, all three are referred to collectively here as Kikuyu except when explicitly stated otherwise.

Land was in short supply by 1945 in these overcrowded districts. The poor were thus forced off their holdings and cut adrift by the Kikuyu elites. To the west in the Rift Valley Province and along the rest of the White Highlands, another wave of dispossession swept through the colony in the post-war period. With the mechanisation of the large European farms, the Kikuyu squatter labour forces were rendered redundant and an unwanted burden on the white farmers. Their steady expulsion back to Nairobi and Central Province induced an ethnic solidarity among the Kikuyu population against their colonial oppressors. But this sense of common grievance was insufficiently strong to silence either the contradictions within Kikuyu society or disquiet with its eventual manifestation of militant and violent political action that became known as Mau Mau.

Mau Mau's rebels lacked coherence and organisation after its leadership, real and imagined, was decapitated by the arrests that marked the onset of the Emergency on 20 October 1952. Large numbers of known and suspected activists were detained and British and imperial troops deployed to the colony. Initially, the movement was tied together

---

[14] Atieno Odhiambo and Lonsdale, 'Introduction,' 3.

by the lines of communication created by decades of labour migration from smallholdings in the Native Reserves to the settler farms and the city of Nairobi. Coordination of thought, word, and deed was, however, disturbed by the violence, mass detentions, and forced removals of population that followed in the wake of the colonial state's declaration of war. In response, thousands of dissidents fearing capture took to the forests of Mount Kenya and the Abderdare Mountains in the final weeks of 1952. From there, they launched their guerrilla campaign. Mau Mau's recourse to insurgency was not at a time of its choosing but instead a reaction to the commencement of the Emergency. Beyond a vague and ill-defined commitment to land and freedom, Mau Mau's own discussions of aim, purpose, and legitimacy of violence were therefore left unresolved. The forests became the location for debate, factionalism, and contestation rather than the base for a unified rebel army.[15]

The insurgency must be partly explained by one of the most profound contradictions of colonialism – the establishment by European rulers of modernity as the benchmark for citizenship while restricting the ability of colonised peoples to attain that standard.[16] Denied access to education, land, state institutions, and public services, Kenya's African communities were socially alienated, economically marginalised, and politically disenfranchised. Exacerbated by the proximity to European settlers, the legitimate grievances that ultimately manifested themselves in Mau Mau were more keenly felt after World War II than previously. But the anti-colonial agitation only superficially masked significant competition and contradictions within those same communities. Debates over land tenure, the status of poor and wealthy, patron–client relations, and the reciprocal responsibilities demanded of both were the very stuff of Central Kenya's political debates over the previous five decades at least. The Central Highlands had been increasingly beset by social conflict prior to the civil war of the 1950s. Neighbours and relatives took one another to court to protect their access to the scarce and valuable commodity of land. The wealthy lamented the poor for their unwillingness to work, while the poor accused the wealthy of failing in their duties as patrons to provide sufficient land to labour on. The position of Christianity and its adherents

---

[15] John Lonsdale, 'Authority, Gender and Violence: The War Within Mau Mau's Fight for Land and Freedom,' in *Mau Mau and Nationhood: Arms, Authority and Narration*, eds. Elisha Stephen Atieno Odhiambo and John Lonsdale (Oxford, 2003).

[16] John Comaroff, 'Government, Materiality, Legality, Modernity: On the Colonial State in Africa,' in *African Modernities: Entangled Meanings in Current Debate*, eds. Jan-Georg Deutsch, Peter Probst and Heike Schmidt (Oxford, 2002).

within Kikuyu society was hotly debated. Husbands and wives accused each other of failing in their marital duties.[17] In the context of violent anti-colonial rebellion led by some of the most vociferous and divisive participants in those preexisting internal political and social contests, it is not surprising that many others formed alliances with the colonial government to access the resources necessary to settle these more immediate and pressing disputes.

Loyalism and Civil War

The Mau Mau war is most usefully conceptualised as a helix, with the strands of anti-colonial and civil war violence intertwined. The first strand has dominated the attention of historians and Kenyan public alike. Within the attempts to depict Mau Mau in the broad strokes of 'atavistic tribalism,' 'militant nationalism,' 'peasant war,'[18] or, more recently, 'incipient genocide,'[19] loyalists appear as peripheral figures. Whenever the Mau Mau war is understood as one between Africans and Europeans, the internal aspect is set to one side and loyalists relegated in importance. It is, therefore, the second strand of the helix, that of the civil war, that is discussed in this book. Mau Mau rebels found themselves opposed by a growing body of loyalist opponents prepared to use fair means and foul to challenge the insurgency. As an 'armed conflict within the boundaries of a recognised sovereign entity between parties subject to a common authority at the outset of the hostilities,' Kenya in the 1950s experienced an irregular civil war.[20] Many within and outside of Kenya would contend that the label of civil war is inappropriate for an anti-colonial rebellion on the basis of the asymmetric nature of the violence.[21] Unquestionably,

---

[17] For further discussion of these aspects see Anderson, *Histories*, 9–53 & 139–51; Greet Kershaw, *Mau Mau From Below* (Oxford, 1997); Lonsdale, 'Wealth, Poverty and Civic Virtue,' 263–314; Derek Peterson, *Creative Writing: Translation, Bookkeeping, and the Work of Colonial Imagination* (Portsmouth NH, 2004).

[18] Bruce Berman, 'Nationalism, Ethnicity, and Modernity: The Paradox of Mau Mau,' *Canadian Journal of African Studies* 25 (1991), 196.

[19] Elkins, *Imperial*, 49.

[20] Kalyvas, *Logic of Violence*, 5. Kenya in the 1950s is considered to have experienced a civil war by the quantitative definitions used in much current literature (1000 fatalities killed during military combat with at least 100 on average per year over the duration of the conflict and a minimum of 100 fatalities on both sides). See Jeremy Weinstein, *Inside Rebellion: The Politics of Insurgent Violence* (Cambridge, 2007), 16.

[21] See, for example, Michael Chege, 'Britain's Gulag: Critics Got Facts Wrong,' *Daily Nation*, 17 March 2005.

a significant majority of those killed in the war were, at the time of their death, suspected or actual supporters of the insurgency. But most were killed by loyalists.

It is these all-too-often misunderstood Kikuyu allies of the colonial state that are the subject of this book. The term loyalist is not used to imply any sympathy for colonial rule on the part of Kikuyu opponents of Mau Mau. In such contexts, almost every term used to describe actors and conflicts is contentious. 'The politics of naming' was as much a part of the Mau Mau war as any other.[22] Because of the discrepancy between the commonly accepted meaning of the term loyalist – a pro-imperial actor – and its actual operational definition in the Kenyan context – an opponent of Mau Mau – it is clear that it is a noun that has the potential to misrepresent rather than explain actions. However, loyalist is persevered with here as, first, the label that is commonly used within the historiography on Mau Mau to denote a Kikuyu opponent of the insurgency and, second, the term that those opponents would themselves recognise. Moreover, alternatives to loyalist are not readily forthcoming or satisfactory. The label of surrogacy, a term used by Anderson, implies that the motivations for Kikuyu opponents wishing to see Mau Mau were not independent of those of the colonial government.[23] Although encouraging and frequently cajoling, colonial masters did not impose alliances on a pliant set of individuals.[24] Collaboration is a long-used term within the field of imperial history in such contexts, particularly in relation to the period of the colonial conquest. However, it is clear that collaboration is analytically problematic as readers coming to such debates from outside of that intellectual tradition so commonly understand the term pejoratively. For those reasons, loyalism is retained here to describe the series of alliances forged between Kikuyu opponents of the Mau Mau insurgency and the colonial government, albeit with unequal distributions of power.

These alliances between individual Kikuyu and the colonial regime were largely a product of the violence of the war itself. Initially temporary arrangements, the alliances assumed a degree of permanence only during

---

[22] Mahmood Mamdani, 'The Politics of Naming: Genocide, Civil War, Insurgency,' *London Review of Books* 29 (2007).

[23] David Anderson, 'Surrogates of the State: Collaboration and Atrocity in Kenya's Mau Mau War,' in *The Barbarisation of Warfare*, ed. George Kassimeris (London, 2006).

[24] The arguments advanced here have much in common with those made for Nyeri in Derek Peterson, 'The Home Guard in Mau Mau's Moral War' (paper presented at the African Studies Association annual meeting, Boston 2003).

a division of Kikuyu society that took place after the war had broken out.[25] At different stages of the war, most Kikuyu were both supporters of Mau Mau and allies of the government, sometimes even simultaneously. The conflict between loyalists and insurgents was not fought by two easily identifiable adversaries.[26] In the first instance, violence within local communities broke out along political, economic, and social faultlines produced during the decades prior to the insurgency. However, once initiated in those local communities, a distinctive cycle of violence was triggered. Entrepreneurs sought to exploit the prevailing conditions of war, individuals sought revenge, and the majority of the population of the Central Highlands simply looked to survive the conflict. Behaviour was thus informed by the ever-changing endogenous dynamics of the conflict, 'the logic of violence,' as much as by Mau Mau's long and well-known prehistory.[27] These complex dynamics produced new groups of actors and temporary allegiances that cut across the prior cleavages, with rich and poor, men and women, young and old represented within the two predominant factions of loyalist and Mau Mau. Although the intellectual roots of both had common origins in the moral economy of colonial Central Kenya,[28] these allegiances were, it must be stressed, not determined in conditions other than duress and coercion.

The Micro-Foundations of Violence

Such arguments have been significantly informed by theoretical and comparative studies of similar episodes. As an asymmetric, irregular civil war fought between a state and a rebel group, the conflict in Kenya is far from exceptional. The tens of thousands of Kenyan fatalities of the 1950s number among the 16 million or so killed in civil wars fought globally since the end of World War II.[29] Like Mau Mau, the majority of rebel groups

[25] Greet Kershaw, 'Mau Mau From Below: Fieldwork and Experience, 1955–57 and 1962,' *Canadian Journal of African Studies* 25 (1991), 288–9.
[26] Derek Peterson, 'Writing in Revolution: Independent Schooling and Mau Mau in Nyeri,' in *Mau Mau and Nationhood: Arms, Authority and Narration*, eds. Elisha Stephen Atieno Odhiambo and John Lonsdale (Oxford, 2003), 93.
[27] Kalyvas, *Logic of Violence*.
[28] John Lonsdale, 'The Moral Economy of Mau Mau: The Problem,' in *Unhappy Valley: Conflict in Kenya and Africa*, eds. Bruce Berman and John Lonsdale (Oxford, 1992), 266.
[29] James Fearon and David Laitin, 'Ethnicity, Insurgency, and Civil War,' *American Political Science Review* 97 (2003), 75–90.

involved in those conflicts, 56 percent by one calculation, have sought to contest control of a state with an incumbent regime.[30] Moreover, in common with most rebel groups involved in civil wars since 1945, Mau Mau relied on guerrilla tactics.[31] Yet, while acknowledging that the occurrence and nature of the Mau Mau war is part of broader historical trends, it is important to not lose sight of the fact that all wars are local, even global conflicts. An understanding of how armies are recruited and provisioned, an appreciation of motivation and behaviour, and an adequate measure of the impact of violence on societies all demand interrogation of specific local contexts of conflicts and the various points of interaction between the local, state, and global levels of each war.[32] Actors operating at these different levels of a conflict have different motivations, and thus interpretations of any one war depend on the level of analysis. In the case of Kenya, as with many other similar irregular civil wars, examination of specific, micro-histories of violence such as Matari's murder suggests that the conflict was a good deal more complex than suggested by the definite categories preferred by those ostensibly adopting a broader perspective.

Accounts of the civil war in Kenya have long suffered from an assumption that the war within Kikuyu communities pitted existing factions against one another throughout the conflict. This book suggests that such cleavages were only significant in the very first instance of violence in a local community. Which cleavages were considered most salient was dependent on the specific local histories of the communities concerned. These social, political, or economic cleavages were militarised, but as soon as the violence began, a profound shift in the political alignments occurred. This realignment was caused by the logic of violence, discussed in more detail later. Other writers have used numerous paradigms to examine the Mau Mau conflict, ranging from good and evil,[33] through gender,[34] nationalism,[35] Marxist revolution,[36] social

---

[30] Weinstein, *Inside Rebellion*, 17.
[31] Dylan Balch-Lindsay, Paul Huth, and Benjamin Valentino, 'Draining the Sea: Mass Killing and Guerrilla Warfare,' *International Organization* 58 (2004), 386, also quoted in Weinstein, *Inside Rebellion*, 28–9.
[32] Anna Simons, 'War: Back to the Future,' *Annual Review of Anthropology* 28 (1999), 92.
[33] See, for example, albeit with very different interpretations of who should be considered to represent good and evil, Elkins, *Imperial*; Kenya, *Origins and Growth*.
[34] Presley, *Kikuyu Women*.
[35] Rosberg and Nottingham, *Myth of Mau Mau*.
[36] Maina wa Kinyatti, *Mau Mau: A Revolution Betrayed* (New York, 1991).

conflict,[37] institutionalism,[38] and religion,[39] to the most recent study that relies on hegemony to attempt to explain the war.[40] But the lenses of such studies have simply been set too wide. Assuming that the violence followed the pattern of pre-war societal-level cleavages is a hypothesis that 'tends to conceal more than it reveals.'[41] The vast bulk of the individual acts of violence, such as Matari's murder, simply do not fit such delineated categories. Four observations of the nature and conceptualisation of the violence of the Mau Mau war reveal the weaknesses of such a macro-level approach: the geographical distribution, its intimacy, the frequent retrospective attribution of ideology by actors of non-ideologically driven acts of violence, and underestimation of the extent to which the civil war profoundly altered the conduct of political competition within local communities.

If the violence of the civil war could be explained through reference only to preexisting societal-level cleavages common to the entire Central Highlands, one would reasonably expect to observe an even distribution of violence across the region. In reality, however, topographies of civil wars commonly resemble, in Danner's words, a 'crazy-quilt map.'[42] Kenya in the 1950s was no different. Ogot has already noted that not every location in Central Kenya was the site of an atrocity.[43] Some areas were peaceful, others extremely bloody. The war was made up of a patchwork of local narratives stitched untidily together by an unequally distributed fear and lived experience of violence. In Tumutumu in Nyeri district, the politics of the East African Revival partially determined the course of events.[44] At Lari in Kiambu, it was the alienation of the poorest sections of society and exploitation of land resettlement schemes that played that role.[45] In Fort Hall, it was the forced labour during soil

[37] Ng'ang'a, 'Loyalists and Politics,' 365–84.
[38] Robert Bates, *Beyond the Miracle of the Market: The Political Economy of Agrarian Development in Kenya* (Cambridge, 2005), 11–44.
[39] David Sandgren, *Christianity and the Kikuyu: Religious Divisions and Social Conflict* (New York, 1989).
[40] S. M. Shamsul Alam, *Rethinking Mau Mau in Colonial Kenya* (Basingstoke, 2007).
[41] David Keen, *Conflict and Collusion in Sierra Leone* (Oxford, 2005), 2.
[42] Mark Danner, *The Massacre at El Mozote: A Parable of the Cold War* (London, 2005), 17.
[43] Ogot, 'Revolt of the Elders,' 145.
[44] Derek Peterson, 'Wordy Women: Gender Trouble and the Oral Politics of the East African Revival in Northern Gikuyuland,' *Journal of African History* 42 (2001), 469–89.
[45] Anderson, *Histories*, 119–80.

conservation schemes.[46] At Githumu, the schism between various denominational groups was significant.[47] What is more, there were substantial differences in the local political economies of the Native Reserves of Central Province, Nairobi, and the districts reserved for European-owned farms. The nature and scale of loyalism, and thus the nature of violence, in the so-called settled districts of the White Highlands and Nairobi was very different than in Central Province.[48] Extrapolating a rule from any one specific location at any given moment to explain the violence across Central Kenya for the entire period is futile. Instead, it is widely divergent incidents of violence, even within very small geographical areas, that demand explanation.

Similarly, if violence were the product of broader cleavages, one would again expect the specific identities of victims and perpetrators to reflect those divisions. Yet, where violence did occur, as we can see from the case of Matari, it was often disconcertingly intimate. The perpetrators and victims of violence were both in large part to be both found within the Kikuyu peasantry, again exposed to the same societal-level forces in roughly equal measures. The most simplistic explanation of the civil war – that of it being an embryonic class war – is particularly flawed in this regard. Lonsdale is right to reject the unproven assumption that the division between Mau Mau and loyalists reflects that between the wealthy and poor or any other social cleavage in pre-war Central Kenya.[49] Studies of such conflicts repeatedly show that there is no simple linkage between poverty and violent unrest.[50] Instead, the population of Central Kenya eventually found themselves divided into two opposing camps, often lined up against neighbours and kinfolk, with little apparent regard for social status or previous political allegiance.

Furthermore, scholars explaining the Mau Mau war have often failed to grasp the significance of Kershaw's study of immediate post-conflict

---

[46] David Throup, *Economic and Social Origins of Mau Mau 1945–53* (London, 1988), 139–70.
[47] Sandgren, *Christianity*, 157.
[48] For discussions of loyalism in the White Highlands, see Frank Furedi, 'The Social Composition of the Mau Mau Movement in the White Highlands,' *Journal of Peasant Studies* 1 (1974), 497–8; Frank Furedi, *The Mau Mau War in Perspective* (London, 1989); Tabitha Kanogo, *Squatters and the Roots of Mau Mau* (London, 1987); Mordechai Tamarkin, 'Mau Mau in Nakuru,' *Journal of African History* 17 (1976), 119–34; Tamarkin, 'Loyalists in Nakuru.'
[49] Lonsdale, 'The Problem,' 295.
[50] Mahmood Mamdani, *When Victims Become Killers: Colonialism, Nativism, and the Genocide in Rwanda* (Princeton New Jersey (NJ), 2001), 198.

memories and explanations of actions by those who participated in the conflict. Kershaw suggests that it was that violence and its aftermath that retrospectively produced the identities of Mau Mau and loyalist, and not those identities or earlier variants thereof that drove the conflict.[51] Individual Kikuyu became loyalist or Mau Mau because of the violence and its consequences. Kershaw's observation has equal applicability elsewhere. Participants in civil wars commonly seek to explain their 'strategic nonideological action' by creating an ideologically based explanation that may be more socially acceptable in a post-conflict situation.[52] This process is further obfuscated by a simultaneous formation of more solid identities from temporary and unstable wartime allegiances. This crystallisation of identity occurs by the polarisation of preexisting social cleavages, making violent previously non-violent divisions and creating new cleavages driven by fear and the need for security. Civil wars thus produce new identities, which are in turn institutionalised by the combatants or by settlements between the warring parties.[53] In other words, identity is frequently endogenous to civil war.[54]

The assumption that the violence throughout the Mau Mau war can be explained with reference solely to preconflict cleavages can be finally undermined by identifying the mistaken assumptions implicit within such an understanding of violence. This approach overlooks the changes to the political sphere enforced by the onset of violence. The civil war was not simply a continuation of preconflict politics by other means. Instead, its violence initiated profound realignments in political structures and allegiances, as described in Chapter 2. Actors on both sides, Dedan Kimathi would be one example, skilled in the use of violence, were promoted, thus enforcing a reshuffling of local hierarchies of power. The unpredictability of this process and the uncertain outcome of the conflict in its early stages placed a premium on the adoption of soluble allegiances. The great mass of the Kikuyu population was initially therefore neither loyalist nor Mau Mau. They dealt in the currency of survival rather than ideology, lending the civil war its chief characteristic: ambiguity. Commonly observed in such settings but rarely explained, 'ambiguity is fundamental rather than incidental to civil wars, a matter of structure rather than noise.'[55] It is

---

[51] Kershaw, 'Fieldwork,' 288–90.
[52] Kalyvas, *Logic of Violence*, 38–46.
[53] Ibid., 78–80.
[54] Ibid., 46–7.
[55] Stathis Kalyvas, 'The Ontology of 'Political Violence': Action and Identity in Civil Wars,' *Perspectives on Politics* 1 (2003), 475.

precisely that ambiguity that has escaped capture by many studies of the Mau Mau conflict, but which must be properly understood if the civil war is to be adequately explained.

The violence of the Mau Mau war needs to be understood both as an outcome of historical processes and as a trigger mechanism for new developments and directions in that conflict. Rather than pre-war political affinities, personal ideology, or post-war identity, Kalyvas finds control to be a far more accurate indicator of an individual's wartime allegiance. Control of an area by one warring party or the other is likely to engender support for that party from the local population.[56] We should pay greater attention to what Kalyvas terms the privatisation of politics. There is only limited evidence of the ability of warring parties in Kenya or elsewhere to politicise individuals sufficiently so as to act violently against relatives and neighbours. In other words, and while acknowledging that support for warring parties may vary from individual to individual, macro-level cleavages fail to co-opt people to kill members of rival groups per se. Instead, individuals appear more successful in co-opting resources from representatives of those macro-level cleavages to serve their own locally rooted purposes. Violence is thus a co-production by both the representatives of the macro-level cleavages and local actors, or an alliance:

Alliance entails a transaction between supralocal and local actors, whereby the former supply the latter with external matter, thus allowing them to win decisive local advantage; in exchange, supralocal actors recruit and motivate supporters at the local level. Viewed from this perspective, violence is a key selective benefit that produces collective action and support on the ground.[57]

Several critical factors flow from this argument. First, we need to examine how support for Mau Mau and for loyalism fluctuated in response to both changes in local balances of power and the experience of violence. Second, precisely because civil war violence is the result of an alliance, we need to consider the strong possibility that Kikuyu acted for very different reasons than may be inferred from their allegiance to a particular group. Third, the significance of individual actions to the overall shape of the conflict should again alert us to the futility of searching for singular explanations for the Mau Mau war. There are as many causes of violence as individual participants.[58] It is these

---

[56] Kalyvas, *Logic of Violence*, 113–31.
[57] Ibid., 365.
[58] Ana Arjona and Stathis Kalyvas, 'Preliminary Results of a Survey of Demobilized Combatants in Colombia' (2006); Macartan Humphreys and Jeremy Weinstein, 'What the Fighters Say: A Survey of Ex-Combatants in Sierra Leone June-August 2003' (Freetown, 2004); Kalyvas, *Logic of Violence*, 364–5.

micro-foundations of violence at the level of the individual, household, and extended family that explain the considerable variation in experience of civil war.[59]

The Moral Economy of Civil War

Kalyvas' insistence that studies of civil war violence interrogate its local roots overlaps neatly with the work on Mau Mau of Kershaw, Lonsdale, and Peterson. These authors all suggest that we should turn to the moral economy of the Central Highlands if we are to accurately understand the violence of the 1950s. In particular, they stress that analysis should be located at the level of the household. The Kikuyu home had been transformed in the years encompassing the onset of colonial rule. It became the location for measuring virtue through assessments of the ability of men to harness the productive power of the household to beget wealth.[60] Profitable control of the homestead demonstrated the authority required to speak in public on matters of political importance. Wealth empowered and poverty silenced.[61] The virtue exhibited by the wealthy was *wiathi*, self-mastery.[62] It was they who demonstrated 'the contested understanding of how to attain the moral maturity of working for oneself.'[63] Their wealth had allowed them to marry and thus attain adulthood, to progress through the various hierarchical social strata towards senior elderhood, and to own sufficient land to allow landless clan members to labour towards their own wealth. Wealth thus earned the authority necessary for social and political leadership.[64] That leadership was accepted by the young and poor in return for the access to land that would allow them to follow in the footsteps of their patron towards self-mastery. The desire to achieve self-mastery thus encompassed the aspirations to be wealthy, politically influential, a man, a father, and an elder. But the path to self-mastery also governed the conduct of patron–client relations

---

[59] Petersen, *Resistance*, 10.
[60] Amrik Heyer, "Nowadays They Can Even Kill You for That Which They Feel Is Theirs': Gender and Production of Ethnic Identity in Kikuyu-Speaking Central Kenya,' in *Violence and Belonging: The Quest for Identity in Post-Colonial Africa*, ed. Vigdis Broch-Due (Abingdon, 2005), 41.
[61] Peterson, 'Wordy Women,' 473.
[62] Although a Kikuyu term, *wiathi* was common to Embu and Meru peoples as well (Lonsdale, 'Wealth, Poverty and Civic Virtue,' 347–8).
[63] Lonsdale, 'The Problem,' 295.
[64] John Lonsdale, 'Mau Maus of the Mind: Making Kenya Mau Mau and Remaking Kenya,' *Journal of African History* 31 (1990), 418.

between those in possession of land and those wanting access to that critical resource. During the civil war, although not providing a rubric by which individual Kikuyu could make their decision of which side to support, self-mastery was a powerful sustaining mechanism once those decisions had been made.

By the late 1930s, the circle of reciprocity linking patron and client had been broken. Dissent was provoked by land shortages, the failure of elder-led political action to extend access to land, and attempts by the same group to reform land tenure to exclude landless clients. The abandonment of the landless and failure to be effective political leaders meant patrons had abdicated their right to authority. They demonstrated the tyranny of wealth rather than its virtue. The landless no longer felt constrained by the demands for honourable labour and political silence. But they remained poor and their radical methods of political action promised, to others it appeared, only disorder and violence. It was in this context that armed resistance to colonial rule emerged.

The moral sphere of insurgents and counterinsurgents alike was a critical component of the violence during colonial Kenya's civil war. Shame, dignity, honour, and respect have been identified as powerful motivations of action during civil wars elsewhere.[65] 'Through rebelling,' Wood writes of El Salvador, 'insurgent *campasinos* asserted, and thereby constituted in their own eyes, their dignity in the face of condescension, repression, and indifference.' Actors in civil wars can be 'motivated in part by the value they put on being part of the making of history.'[66] This was certainly the case in Kenya during the 1950s. Lonsdale's study unfurls from the explanation of one Mau Mau fighter for his support of the insurgency: 'Sam Thebere, a former guerrilla, answered the question "Why did you join Mau Mau?" with the twofold reply: "to regain stolen lands and to become an adult."'[67] Thebere was expressing frustration with a political system that required land-based wealth as a qualification for participation, an economic system devoid of opportunity for acquiring land, and a social system that demanded land as a condition for marriage and thus adulthood. Thebere and thousands like him lacked the means to exist as a polity and as a man. Thebere explained his decision to fight British colonialism and its loyalist allies as partly to provide his existence

---

[65] Keen, *Conflict and Collusion*, 56–81; Elisabeth Jean Wood, *Insurgent Collective Action and Civil War in El Salvador* (Cambridge, 2003), 234–7.
[66] Ibid., 18–9.
[67] Lonsdale, 'Wealth, Poverty and Civic Virtue,' 326.

with meaning. If we admit that this is true for insurgents, then we must also acknowledge that loyalists may have fought for the same reasons. The choice between Mau Mau and loyalism was not easy, and the middle ground was precipitous. Besides the obvious hardships of life in the forests, by joining the forest fighters, Mau Mau supporters mortgaged their immediate desire for self-mastery on behalf of successive generations. Criminality, which Mau Mau unquestionably and increasingly relied on for survival, could not beget self-mastery.[68] The gains of violent and criminal acts bequeathed no moral authority to their practitioners. Among loyalists, it was frequently argued that Mau Mau contravened what Iliffe terms 'the householder ethic' by threatening self-mastery's requirement for respect for the apparently natural leaders of society: the landed wealthy, senior elders, and educated.[69] Instead, the rebels demanded power and influence out of turn, and demonstrated little affinity for the discipline required to work towards self-mastery. As we shall see in Chapter 4, loyalist critiques of Mau Mau returned again and again to the issues of indiscipline, disrespect, and impatience. The forest fighters could never shake off the accusations of idleness and delinquency. Ultimately, self-mastery required access to land, but all could see how the land of, first, Mau Mau's leaders and, latterly, its rank and file were confiscated by the government.[70] As the Emergency progressed, increasing numbers of Kikuyu became persuaded of the possibility of achieving self-mastery through loyalism, or at least, Mau Mau's inability to achieve that aim.

Self-mastery was a powerful and enduring code of behaviour before and during the 1950s, not because it spoke to a homogeneous, untainted Kikuyu identity, but because it addressed in widely understood phraseology the diverse concerns of those who, by accident of birth, hailed from the slopes of Mount Kenya and Aberdares. Combatants and non-combatants alike spoke the language of moral ethnicity. They understood and explained their allegiances by assessing which, out of armed rebellion, neutrality, or loyalism, offered the most likely route towards self-mastery. Yet, however sophisticated and complex the intellectual history of loyalism and Mau Mau may have been, it was insufficient to override the logic

---

[68] Lonsdale, 'Mau Maus of the Mind,' 419.
[69] John Iliffe, *Honour in African History* (Cambridge, 2005), 11–180, especially 110–1.
[70] KNA WC/CM/1/4, Minister for African Affairs, 'Village Construction: Meru District,' 6 July 1955; Minister for African Affairs, 'Forfeiture of Terrorists' Land and Property,' 7 July 1955; KNA WC/CM/1/2, Minutes of 120th War Council meeting, 8 July 1955; KNA AHC/9/52, 'More Terrorists to Lose Their Land,' *Mwanamke*, 14 July 1954.

of violence that drove communities apart along the lines of victimisation with scant regard to the past.

Loyalism, Decolonisation, and Counterinsurgency

In Central Kenya, as in Algeria, 'colonialism drove a logic of extremes, obliterating the possibility of meaningful, moderate nationalism.'[71] But this did not mean that African responses to colonialism were uniformly those of resistance or nationalism. As any history of colonial Kenya prior to 1952 will reiterate, politics there were scarcely characterised by consensus. Alliances between individual Kikuyu and the various arms of the colonial state, as Chapter 1 makes clear, were incorporated into the strategies of various actors engaged in political competition from the very beginning of British rule. For five decades, the people of the Central Highlands debated political action, leadership, land tenure, and the rights and responsibilities of group membership. The resources of the colonial state were too valuable to ignore in such a context. To expect to find any substantive difference in the 1950s seems odd, particularly because Mau Mau represented the most fervent rejection of so many of the ideas that had dictated the terms of social and political relations prior to the insurgency's genesis. Denied access to arenas of political influence and penalised by the colonial state's support for settler agriculture, discontents attempted to exploit one of the few available methods of mobilising support allowed under colonial rule, ethnicity. In Central Province, Kenyans attempted to use ethnicity to mobilise support for an attempt to reform and, latterly, to overthrow the colonial framework. Yet, the appeal to ethnicity did not produce unity. Instead, it opened up political activities to the scrutiny of the moral economy, a powerful but contested code of behaviour.

Dissenters to Mau Mau's project were not in the main, as Chapter 1 demonstrates, mobilised by the clumsy attempts of the colonial government to encourage a backward-looking conservative reaction to Mau Mau's presumed transgressions of norms and values. Instead, it was the violence of Mau Mau that alienated so many Kikuyu in the earliest stages of the insurgency. The two main institutions entrusted with countering that violence, the chieftaincy and the Home Guard, are the subjects of Chapter 2. But these forces were inadequate to guarantee the safety of

---

[71] James McDougall, 'The *Shabiba Islamiyya* of Algiers: Education, Authority, and Colonial Control, 1921–57,' *Comparative Studies of South Asia, Africa and the Middle East* 24 (2004), 153.

other loyalists and themselves polarised Kikuyu society through their own reliance on violence. Trapped between two sides, allegiances were initially a good deal more fluid than generally assumed. Indeed, the vast majority of Kikuyu were at one time or another during the conflict both loyalist and Mau Mau, sometimes simultaneously.

It was only when the levels of violence peaked by the end of 1953 and early 1954 that individuals were forced to choose one side or the other, a decision informed as much by the lived experience of previous violence as by any pre-war sympathies. As Chapter 3 describes, the violence of the conflict was thus privatised by individuals. The violence of the civil war thereby produced the cleavage between Mau Mau supporters and loyalists rather than being driven by it. The decision, however, was sustained by the notion of moral ethnicity, as explored in Chapter 4. Loyalists and Mau Mau originated from the same families, neighbourhoods, and villages as one another. Moreover, the intellectual justification for loyalism was rooted in the same local political debates that had spawned the radicalism of Mau Mau. Both sought honour, respect, and dignity.

The viability of loyalism from mid-1954 onwards as a vehicle for self-mastery acted as the chief sustaining mechanism, among others, for loyalism, not least because, as we see in Chapter 5, counterinsurgency and preparations for decolonisation intertwined. The divisions within Kikuyu society became institutionalised within the structures of the outgoing colonial state and its post-colonial successor. To be labelled a loyalist by the late 1950s was to be qualified to participate in formal politics, to have hope of future wealth, and to have access to the decolonising institutions of the state. The post-colonial legacies of these overlapping processes are explored in the final chapter.

I

Vomiting the Oath

The Origins of Loyalism in the Growth of Mau Mau

The Greedy Eaters

By the middle of 1950, the colonial regime had set itself on the path towards the tragedy of the Mau Mau war. With a series of arson attacks on
settler infrastructure earlier that year, the militancy within Kikuyu communities began to directly affect the political economy of the colony. The
government felt compelled to take action to quell the growing unrest.[1]
Unmoved by African demands for reform, the government identified oathing by militants as the root cause of the violence and banned the practice.
In this first attempt to neuter the seeds of the coming insurgency, the
colonial government created the conditions under which civil war eventually took hold of the Central Highlands. The attempt to criminalise
oathing was certainly motivated by the notion, albeit misplaced, that in
so doing the state was countering a threat to its continued existence. The
unintended outcome of the banning of oathing was to give Kikuyu names
and faces to the tyranny of colonialism.

Officers within the ranks of the Kenya Police and the Provincial Administration's Tribal Police were charged to disrupt oathing ceremonies and
arrest ringleaders. Chiefs were expected to lead patrols through their
home locations to disrupt oathing ceremonies. Elders sat in court advising
judges on whom to convict for oathing, and witnesses from Kikuyu communities provided the evidence on which those decisions were based. It
was these individuals who attracted the ire of the militants, distracting the
latter away from their original intended targets: the settlers. The wider

---

[1] Furedi, *Mau Mau War*, 110–1.

goal of militancy, the defeat of colonialism itself, was put to one side, and more immediate concerns exercised the minds of the radical Kikuyu politicians. Anxious to protect their flows of recruits, finances, and intelligence and to avoid imprisonment, the militants had to intimidate potential witnesses, silence dissenters, and sabotage judicial proceedings in one way or another. The value of insurgent violence directed against other Kikuyu appreciated rapidly, setting in motion the cycle of violence that culminated in the outbreak of civil war by March 1953.

These initial roots of loyalism were demonstrated in the first week of June 1950, when Parmenas Kiritu took the witness stand during one of the earliest trials of oath organisers in Naivasha. The town of Naivasha and the European farms of the surrounding area in the eastern Rift Valley Province had become something of a haven for Kikuyu labour evicted from other parts of the province in the post-1945 period. Discontent was rife, and the radicalisation of the largely Kikuyu workforce of the area well under way. Although militant oathers were then operating in favourable conditions, not all of Naivasha's population were won over to the militant cause. Kiritu, a shopkeeper in the town, later became one of most prominent loyalists in the area, and during his testimony, he made a significant contribution to the later conflict by being the first to use the term 'Mau Mau' to label the militant radical faction within Kikuyu politics. Kiritu began his statement to the court by describing the oathing that had been prevalent in and around Naivasha for the previous two years. He blamed what he called the Mau Mau Association. Kiritu then proceeded to tell the court that Mau Mau 'is a Kikuyu word which means that you want to do something very quickly.'[2] To Kiritu, Mau Mau appeared impatient, undisciplined, and dangerous.

Kiritu's fears of Mau Mau were provoked by the militant's oathing practices, which were used to mobilise support from among the Kikuyu community of the Central Highlands. The oaths were, it is generally accepted, an attempt to instil ethnic unity among an otherwise divided community. However, the focus of scholars on the symbolic aspects of oathing has blinded many to the functional uses of the custom. Even those who acknowledge oathing was an important method of mobilisation have overlooked the fact that, first and foremost, oathing allowed Mau Mau to cultivate lines of intelligence and silence potential opponents. Second, the

---

[2] Quoted in Rosberg and Nottingham, *Myth of Mau Mau*, 332. See also Josiah Mwangi Kariuki, *'Mau Mau' Detainee: The Account of a Kenya African of His Experiences in Detention Camps 1953–1960* (Nairobi, 1975), 24.

assumption that an appeal to a unified Kikuyu community underpinned by the threat of violence would have met with a homogeneous positive response is mistaken. To assume that support for Mau Mau was near universal among Kikuyu, simply because the insurgents appealed to the ethnic community is a misreading of the nature of ethnicity. Kikuyu ethnicity was a site of contestation and debate, not a determinant of action during the coming conflict. Kiritu and other loyalists turned Mau Mau's attempts to monopolise Kikuyu political action against the insurgents by calling into question the ethnic authenticity of the words and actions of the oathers.

By labelling the militants as Mau Mau, Kiritu was speaking pejoratively. To Kiritu and others, the term Mau Mau implied youthful indiscipline on the part of the oathers and their supporters. 'Its only meaning was "greedy eating,"' an informant later told Barnett when discussing the etymology of Mau Mau, 'sometimes used by mothers to rebuke children who were eating too fast or too much.'[3] The eating referred explicitly to the consumption of goat meat, either to the manner in which raw meat was consumed during the oathing ceremonies or to the corruption of established methods of oathing.[4] The apparent impatience, gluttony, and hedonism of Mau Mau promised, at least to Kiritu, instability and uncertainty. These were not characteristics, he and others thought, becoming of political leaders or likely to instil the unity among Kikuyu and other Kenyans necessary to usurp British rule.

Kiritu's testimony indicates the origins of loyalism and the terms in which the debate between Kikuyu insurgents and counterinsurgents would be conducted. Kiritu and other loyalists drew on earlier precedents of alliances between Kenya's colonised subjects and the colonial state. I do not mean to suggest, however, that an ally of the colonial government in the 1930s was inevitably a loyalist in the 1950s. We need only look at the life histories of two prominent individuals to recognise the myopia of such a linear approach to Kenya's history. Harry Thuku, a young radical and protest leader in the 1920s, was one of the colonial

---

[3] Donald Barnett, '"Mau Mau": The Structural Integration and Disintegration of Abderdare Guerrilla Forces' (PhD dissertation, University of California, Los Angeles, 1963), 46.

[4] Ibid., 46–7; Renison Muchiri Githige, 'The Religious Factor in Mau Mau With Particular Reference to Mau Mau Oaths' (MA dissertation, University of Nairobi, 1978), 43 & footnote 12, 72. Peterson has uncovered evidence suggesting the term was an onomatopoeia of the noise made by animals when eating, but also conveying the meaning of 'greedy eating.' See Peterson, 'Home Guard,' 11.

government's fiercest allies in the 1950s.[5] Chief Koinange wa Mbiyu, discussed further in the Conclusion, was an appointed government servant of the earlier colonial period and a prominent patron of the radical activists by the 1950s.[6] Although not establishing a genealogy of loyalism, earlier examples of such alliances demonstrate that the loyalists of the 1950s were not thinking the unthinkable. They were instead, as their parents and grandparents had done, attempting to make use of powerful resources to mediate and resolve a whole range of disputes and situations of which but a few had anything to do with colonialism.

Oathing provided the first stage of a trail of causation that meant that by 1953, the disputes between Kikuyu would be resolved within a context of civil war. In other words, the earliest roots of loyalism lay within the oathing practices developed by Mau Mau. Although the colonial government identified oathing as an issue around which alliances with Kikuyu opponents of Mau Mau could be constructed, it misunderstood the nature of that opposition. The colonial government developed what was known as counteroathing as its first line of defence against Mau Mau. Inspired by ethnography, counteroathing ceremonies were designed to counter the supernatural compulsion to support Mau Mau thought by the colonial government to be at the heart of the oaths. Counteroathing was a significant failure and but one of a number of policies introduced between 1950 and 1954 designed to reduce the threat posed by Mau Mau that in reality acted only to stymie counterinsurgency and foment rebellion. Counteroathing was, in the first instance, intellectually misguided. Moreover, by merely providing a forum for Kikuyu opponents of the insurgency to express their discontent with Mau Mau, the policy failed to provide the substantive resources necessary to underpin permanent alliances between loyalists and the colonial state. Of the resources desired by potential Kikuyu allies but provided by the state, the most important in the first months and years of the insurgency was security. For this reason, the colonial government was unable to exploit Mau Mau's shortcomings and build alliances with Kikuyu opponents of the insurgency until later in the conflict.

Contest and Accommodation in Colonial Kenya

The bonds of ethnicity can be easily overestimated. Kiritu's words to the Naivasha court in 1950 implied a very different understanding of

---

[5] Harry Thuku, *Harry Thuku: An Autobiography* (Nairobi, 1970).
[6] Jeff Koinange, *Koinange-wa-Mbiyu: Mau Mau's Misunderstood Leader* (Lewes, 2000).

what it meant to be Kikuyu than that often ascribed to the group by the mid-twentieth century. For Kiritu, Kikuyuness was defined by conflict rather than the unity described within the well-known and politically charged ethnographies of Louis Leakey[7] and Jomo Kenyatta.[8] Earlier in the century, both Leakey and Kenyatta had set out to re-create Kikuyu identity in their own image and for reasons of personal political interest. Rather than seeing a community struggling to come to terms with its internal contradictions, both Leakey and Kenyatta saw Kikuyu society as inherently ordered. The two writers significantly differed on the source of that coherence, with Leakey believing it to have emerged from a vertical power structure based on clans, in which elders, with whom Leakey identified closely, dominated their juniors. Kenyatta located order in the horizontal age-sets that each adult male joined at the time of circumcision. Kenyatta was attempting to consolidate age-sets as his own power base during his challenge for political power. The frailties of the arguments of both Leakey and Kenyatta were amply demonstrated during the civil war of the 1950s.

When he took the witness stand in Naivasha, Kiritu gave a more accurate depiction of Kikuyu ethnicity on the eve of Mau Mau than is commonly assumed. Instead of speaking of age-sets or hierarchies of power, Kiritu's interpretation of Mau Mau instead detailed a house divided. Kikuyu society was by 1950 split along the fault lines of class, gender, generation, religious affiliation, literacy, and varying degrees of exposure to the colonial political economy. Kiritu was one of the first Kikuyu to recognise that an alliance with the British regime represented one way to resolve the disputes within Kikuyu society in favour of the interests that he himself supported. Kiritu was fortunate that his willingness to cooperate with the court case in Naivasha provided him access to the protection of the state security forces, which was initially offered to but a few Kikuyu opponents of Mau Mau. Although such alliances – based on the proffering of information in return for security – became commonplace from 1954 onwards, in 1950, Kiritu was one member of an exclusive club.

---

[7] Louis Leakey, *The Southern Kikuyu Before 1903*, 3 vols. (New York, 1977). See also Bruce Berman and John Lonsdale, 'Louis Leakey's Mau Mau: A Study in the Politics of Knowledge,' *History and Anthropology* 5 (1991) 170–3; Carolyn Clark, 'Louis Leakey as Ethnographer: On *The Southern Kikuyu Before 1903*,' *Canadian Journal of African Studies* 23 (1989), 380–98.

[8] Jomo Kenyatta, *Facing Mount Kenya: The Tribal Life of the Gikuyu* (New York, 1965). See for a similar discussion to that surrounding Leakey's work, Bruce Berman, 'Ethnography as Politics, Politics as Ethnography: Kenyatta, Malinowski, and the Making of *Facing Mount Kenya*,' *Canadian Journal of African Studies* 30 (1996).

Lacking both the resources to extend protection to most Kikuyu and a sufficiently nuanced understanding of the nature of the insurgency to identify potential allies, the British at first failed to construct the alliances with subjects that defined imperial rule in other settings.

The construction of alliances with colonised peoples was a particular skill of British imperialists. Indeed, such alliances can be seen as a defining feature of modern European imperialism. This process of alliance-building is inadequately labelled within the literature as collaboration, but those identified as collaborators by historians 'made colonial rule possible';[9] they were the 'non-European foundations of European imperialism.'[10] This was by no means a phenomenon unique to perfidious Albion. Girard has characterised the first wave of French imperial expansion to incorporate territories in the Americas, West Africa, and the Indian Ocean as resulting in an 'empire of collaboration.'[11] Finding themselves alone among 200,000 or so colonial subjects in West Africa, French colonial officers had little choice but to rely on indigenous allies.[12] Kamen has made a similar argument for the Spanish empire.[13] Such allies were a particularly strong feature of British imperialism, more so than in the other European empires.[14] Locally recruited allies were the keystone of British imperialism and, through indirect rule, were absorbed into its institutional structures.[15] Those recruits allowed for 'colonialism on the cheap'[16] and, at least in the imagination of colonial rulers, aided the translation of the raw aggression of colonial conquest into local 'idioms of power.'[17] Alliances with prominent leaders from among the subject

[9] Heather Sharkey, *Living With Colonialism: Nationalism and Culture in the Anglo-Egyptian Sudan* (Berkeley, 2003), 119.

[10] Ronald Robinson, 'Non-European Foundations of European Imperialism: Sketch for a Theory of Collaboration,' in *Studies in the Theory of Imperialism*, eds. Roger Owen and Bob Sutcliffe (London, 1972).

[11] Philippe Girard, 'Empire by Collaboration: The First French Empire's Rise and Demise,' *French History* 19 (2005).

[12] Patrick Manning, *Francophone Sub-Saharan Africa, 1880–1995* (Cambridge, 1999), 57.

[13] Henry Kamen, *Empire: How Spain Became a World Power* (New York, 2003).

[14] Manning, *Francophone Africa*, 58.

[15] John Cell, 'Colonial Rule,' in *The Oxford History of the British Empire*, eds. Judith Brown and Wm. Roger Louis (Oxford, 1999).

[16] Timothy Parsons, *The African Rank-and-File: Social Implications of Colonial Military Service in the King's African Rifles, 1902–1964* (Oxford, 1999), 21; Sharkey, *Living With Colonialism*, 68.

[17] Sean Redding, 'Government Witchcraft: Taxation, the Supernatural, and the Mpondo Revolt in the Transkei, South Africa, 1955–1963,' *African Affairs* 95 (1996), 555–6. See also John Lonsdale, 'The Conquest State of Kenya: 1895–1905,' in *Unhappy Valley: Conflict in Kenya and Africa*, eds. Bruce Berman and John Lonsdale (Oxford, 1992), 18.

populations of British possessions would give, it was hoped, a semblance of legitimacy to colonial governance.

Although required by British colonial rulers, such alliances could not be imposed on resistant colonised societies. Instead, the British typically exploited preexisting social and political cleavages by empowering particular factions contesting power and authority within newly colonised societies. This point is amply proved by Steinhart. Writing about Western Uganda during the colonial occupation of the late nineteenth and early twentieth centuries, Steinhart describes how the catalysts for the construction of alliances between newly colonised subjects and the incoming British originated in competition between indigenous elites.[18] Alliances were therefore used in Western Uganda to settle internal disputes within local society that had little to do with colonialism per se.[19] In this way, the imperial project became a 'convergence of interests' between the colonial state and sections of colonised societies, albeit under unequal terms of exchange.[20] Alliances with the incoming colonial power, as Anil Seal first argued, became a resource to be appropriated by political entrepreneurs and put to use in political, economic, or social competition internal to colonised peoples.[21] Robinson argues that such alliance-building 'was as much and often more a function of Afro-Asian politics than of European politics and economics.'[22] Although much of the writing on this subject has examined the period of the colonial conquest, the issue of alliance-building remained at the heart of the colonial project right up to the end of empire.

The violence of the colonial conquest of Central Kenya is a potent example of the symmetry observed by Louis between the establishment of European rule and its eventual demise.[23] During the conquest, the destructive power of the colonial armies was readily apparent, particularly in Embu and northern areas of Kikuyu settlement.[24] The trauma was

---

[18] Edward Steinhart, *Conflict and Collaboration: The Kingdoms of Western Uganda, 1890–1907* (Princeton NJ, 1977), 35.

[19] Ibid., 154 & 257–60.

[20] Jurgen Osterhammel, *Colonialism: A Theoretical Overview*, Shelley Frisch trans. (Princeton NJ, 1997), 64.

[21] Anil Seal, *The Emergence of Indian Nationalism: Competition and Collaboration in the Later Nineteenth Century* (Cambridge, 1968).

[22] Robinson, 'Non-European Foundations,' 138–9.

[23] Wm. Roger Louis, 'Suez and Decolonization: Scrambling out of Africa and Asia,' in *Ends of British Imperialism: The Scramble for Empire, Suez and Decolonization*, ed. Wm. Roger Louis (London, 2006), 10.

[24] Lonsdale, 'Conquest State'; A. Fiona D. MacKenzie, *Land, Ecology and Resistance in Kenya, 1880–1952* (Edinburgh, 1998) 61–2; Godfrey Muriuki, *A History of the Kikuyu, 1500–1900* (Nairobi, 1974), 160–6.

compounded by the famine, locusts, smallpox, rinderpest, and jiggers, which acted as advance parties for the colonial armies of conquest. Up to 40 percent of the population of some Kikuyu settlements died, mostly the young, elderly, and poor.[25] The suffering that resulted from the conquest and the attendant humanitarian crisis exacerbated existing internal conflicts among the peoples of the Mount Kenya region. Nineteenth-century Kikuyuland was no outpost of 'Merrie Africa.' Long before the arrival of British rule, the Kikuyu poor were silenced by their clan elders in political debates. With land tenure controlled by clans, the poor were tenants-at-will (*ahoi*). They accepted the hegemony of their clan's elders in return for access to the clan's land, which would allow them opportunities to build up their own wealth and, eventually, to become elders themselves.[26] The potential for political power in the short term was mortgaged for future prosperity. This acquiescence by the poorer and more junior sections of society to the hegemony of the elders was conditional on the elders guaranteeing the poor's security and access to land. This already frayed social fabric was torn to shreds by the conquest and famine of the 1890s, as groups of young men, showing scant regard for their reciprocal obligations to their clan and household, resorted to pillaging to survive.[27] These were the original greedy eaters to whom Kiritu alluded in 1950, consuming as they did the fruits of the labour of others.

The connection made by opponents of the insurgents in the 1950s to this earlier period of intense upheaval is deserving of far greater attention than has hitherto been granted, at the very, least as a precedent for the loyalism of the later period. From the very first interactions between Europeans and the peoples of Mount Kenya, entrepreneurial political figures sought to make the best use of the resources the former could provide. For example, the population of the area between today's Tigania, Imenti, and Tharaka in Meru sought to build an alliance with the American trader, William Astor Chanler, in 1892. Chanler's armed escorts provided the community with protection against raiding parties from neighbouring groups in return for livestock and grain.[28] Once these external forces developed into a formal empire, both the destructive power of the outsiders and their potential worth as allies increased exponentially.

---

[25] Lonsdale, 'Conquest State', 23–5; MacKenzie, *Land, Ecology*, 58–60; Muriuki, *History of the Kikuyu*, 155–6.
[26] Kershaw, *Mau Mau From Below*, 213 & 216.
[27] Lonsdale, 'Conquest State,' 30.
[28] Jeffrey A. Fadiman, *When We Began There Were Witchmen: An Oral History From Mount Kenya* (Berkeley, 1994), 124.

During the ostensible colonial conquest of Embu during July 1906, the invaders were primarily made up of Mbeere of the lowlands to the east of Mount Kenya and Kikuyu seeking resolution of long-standing conflicts with the Embu people.[29] Alliances with the incoming colonial power served various purposes. Many Kikuyu found the antidote to suffering in the venom of the colonial conquest itself. Alliances spared their Kikuyu stakeholders the most destructive aspects of military subjugation and humanitarian amelioration by providing access to sources of paid labour and the resources necessary to secure food supplies.[30] In return, Kikuyu leaders provided the auxiliary manpower necessary to support the military expeditions through the Central Highlands and the establishment of administrative centres. Men such as Karuri wa Gakure, Mbuthia Kaguongo, and Wang'ang'a played a critical role in the military conquest of the region by mobilising labourers to meet the needs of the British.[31] Drawing on precolonial prophecies, moderate elders urged Kikuyu and Meru to learn the secrets of colonial power from within and later use the newly acquired information against their conquerors.[32] In hindsight, those same elders may have been attempting to justify their failure to organise resistance to the conquering armies,[33] but seeking accommodations with the British was more than just an attempt to save face. Alliances with the new colonial government provided Kikuyu leaders with the means to establish new networks of patronage to replace those disrupted by the trauma of the previous decade. At a time of famine, there was no shortage of clients looking for wealthy and influential patrons.[34]

The first generation of Kikuyu allies of the colonial state were appointed to be chiefs and headmen, leaving them in the best position to exploit the agricultural production boom in the first years of the twentieth century. They and their clans disproportionately reaped the benefits of the establishment of new markets and the recovery of Kikuyu society from

---

[29] Ibid., 128–9.
[30] Lonsdale, 'Conquest State,' 25–6.
[31] MacKenzie, *Land, Ecology*, 23; Muriuki, *History of the Kikuyu*, 160–1.
[32] Alfred M'Imanyara, *The Restatement of Bantu Origin and Meru History* (Nairobi, 1992), 71; Kenyatta, *Facing Mount Kenya*, 43; Kershaw, *Mau Mau From Below*, 324; John Lonsdale, 'The Prayers of Waiyaki: Political Uses of the Kikuyu Past,' in *Revealing Prophets: Prophecy in Eastern African History*, eds. David Anderson and Douglas Johnson (London, 1995), 240–1; Muriuki, *History of the Kikuyu*, 137.
[33] Lonsdale, 'Prayers of Waiyaki,' 253.
[34] Bruce Berman and John Lonsdale, 'Coping With the Contradictions: The Development of the Colonial State 1895–1914,' in *Unhappy Valley: Conflict in Kenya and Africa*, eds. Bruce Berman and John Lonsdale (Oxford, 1992), 86.

the crisis of the 1890s. This economic revival was in part instigated by the infant state in the first years of the new century to make the new colony pay.[35] For the same reason, European settlers arrived and the attendant land alienations took place to facilitate commercial farming. The settlers required a labour force and found it with their promises of access to land in exchange for work. By 1906–7, individual clan members from southern areas of Kikuyuland became the first squatters on the newly established European farms of the Rift Valley, attracted by the promises of land that could not be matched by their elders. Having abandoned their reciprocal labour responsibilities, the new squatters left Central Province with the curses of the clan elders ringing in their ears.[36] By the beginning of World War I, therefore, thousands of individual Kikuyu had sought alliances with different branches of the colonial state. Colonialism in Kenya was always in part an exercise in alliance-building.

In the areas the squatters left behind, Kikuyu allies of colonialism busily set about constructing a new political order. The local figureheads were the new chiefs.[37] Although Kikuyu chieftaincy was an invention of British minds, the appointees were not powerless sycophants.[38] They instead added the powers of state patronage to those they gleaned from their position among the wealthy, as elders, heads of household, clan, and age-sets.[39] Chiefs and their headmen were expected to act as gatekeepers. Their function, as seen from a Kikuyu perspective, was twofold. They had to both protect their people from the excesses of the state, particularly in the form of land alienation. At the same time, the chiefs were to aid the local community's access to state resources, such as trading licences. If a chief or headman was able to exert sufficient influence to protect the

[35] Ibid., 78.
[36] Kershaw, _Mau Mau From Below_, 90–2.
[37] Marshall Clough, 'Koinange wa Mbiyu: Mediator and Patriot,' in _Biographical Essays on Imperialism and Collaboration in Colonial Kenya_, ed. Benjamin Kipkorir (Nairobi, 1980) Marshall Clough, _Fighting Two Sides: Kenyan Chiefs and Politicians, 1918–1940_ (Niwot CO, 1990); Koinange, _Koinange_; Godfrey Muriuki, 'Background to Politics and Nationalism in Central Kenya: The Traditional Social and Political Systems of Kenya Peoples,' in _Hadith 4: Politics and Nationalism in Colonial Kenya_, ed. Bethwell A. Ogot (Nairobi, 1972); William Ochieng, 'Colonial African Chiefs – Were They Primarily Self-Seeking Scoundrals?' in _Hadith 4: Politics and Nationalism in Colonial Kenya_, ed. Bethwell A. Ogot (Nairobi, 1972); Margaret Ndabiri, 'A Biographical Essay on Ex-Senior Chief Njiri wa Karanja' (BEd dissertation, University of Nairobi, 1977).
[38] See for more details, Robert Tignor, 'Colonial Chiefs in Chiefless Societies,' _Journal of Modern African Studies_ 9 (1971).
[39] Lonsdale, 'Wealth, Poverty and Civic Virtue,' 326, 343, 362, 403 & Throup, _Economic and Social Origins_ 144.

population and provide the means for betterment, he could rely on the support of the community.[40] But such a position was open to abuse.

During the inter-war period, the chiefs steadily became more unpopular. The overzealous punishment of infractions of colonial law and the behaviour of certain chiefs and their minions resulted in the emergence of grievances that lingered long after independence.[41] Moreover, instead of acting as gatekeepers and mediators between the colonial state and subjects, the chiefs became a conservative faction within local politics. Having failed to reverse land seizures or moderated other contentious colonial policies related to tax and low wages, the chiefs' claims to authority were greatly undermined. The Kiambu chiefs, under the guise of their Kikuyu Association, found themselves to be in direct opposition to the East African Association (EAA) led by Harry Thuku during the early 1920s.[42] The EAA's anger at low wages and the hated passes all Africans had to carry garnered the group's widespread support. Its protests culminated in mass demonstrations following the arrest of Thuku in March 1922. But with opposition to colonial rule placed in disarray by Thuku's imprisonment and the heavy-handed tactics of the colonial government, the chiefs were able to ride out that first storm. Leading figures within the EAA regrouped and in 1924 founded the Kikuyu Central Association (KCA).

The KCA was a political organisation for the farmers and traders who benefited from a transformation of the rural economy under colonial rule. They had built up their wealth independently outside the patron–client networks established by the chiefs and resented the chiefs' monopolisation of local positions of influence and access to state resources. The ranks of the KCA were bolstered by two further moments of crisis in Kikuyuland. First, the KCA exploited the political fallout from attempts by missionaries in 1929 to ban the practice of clitoridectomy. With many chiefs supporting the unprecedented intervention into the everyday lives of Kikuyu, KCA leaders became closely associated with the outraged response that ultimately manifested itself in the establishment of independent churches and schools free from missionary meddling.[43] The political weakness of the chiefs, by then operating under the banner of the Loyal Kikuyu Patriots, was consolidated by the Kenya Land Commission, which reported its

[40] Kershaw, *Mau Mau From Below*, 118.
[41] Muriuki, *History of the Kikuyu*, 15.
[42] Clough, *Fighting Two Sides*, 91–136.
[43] Ibid., 137–51.

findings in 1934. The Commission recommended only negligible altera-
tions to the boundaries between African- and European-owned land, thus
dismissing for good any hope of a rollback of the land alienations that
had accompanied the establishment of colonial rule. Unable to claim that
they were able to further the critical question of land access or protect the
Kikuyu community from the pernicious attention of the colonial state, by
the late-1930s, the political authority of the chiefs had evaporated.[44]

Although the KCA were able to capitalise to a certain extent on this
vacuum, political competition remained the arena for inter-elite squab-
bling until the 1940s.[45] The chiefs jealously guarded the economic priv-
ileges garnered from working with the colonial regime, which their rivals
coveted. Neither the KCA nor the chiefs were greatly concerned with the
land claims and fear of alienation of women and tenants.[46] Beneath the
surface, however, local politics in the Central Highlands slowly moved
towards radicalisation.[47] Militant action required a long gestation period,
though. Although by the mid-1930s the chiefs were no longer a credible
political force, leading Kikuyu political figures still envisaged the necessary political and economic reforms being elite driven and taking place
within an imperial framework. British rule in itself, it was thought, did
not entail dispossession and disenfranchisement. It was the particular
relationship between the colonial regime in Nairobi and the colony's
European settlers that posed the immediate threat to the prosperity of
Kikuyu, or so Jomo Kenyatta and other leading politicians believed.[48]
The rhetoric of imperialism, embedded with notions of patronage and
reciprocity, appeared to offer the opportunity for full citizenship for those
prepared to be disciplined and hard-working subjects of the Crown.[49]

Those hopes were dashed in the period after the end of World War
II. The colonial state repeatedly demonstrated its unwillingness to seek
accommodation with the moderate Kikuyu political leaders. Wartime
legislation was used to ban the KCA, although it reformed as the Kenya
African Union (KAU). In the years up to 1950, a number of measures
designed to reduce the political temperature were introduced. However, these were too little, too late and served only to benefit the elite.

---

[44] Ibid., 166–7.
[45] Ibid., 134–6.
[46] MacKenzie, *Land, Ecology*, 65.
[47] Kershaw, *Mau Mau From Below*, 104.
[48] John Lonsdale, 'Ornamental Constitutionalism in Kenya: Kenyatta and the Two
Queens,' *Journal of Imperial and Commonwealth History* 34 (2006), 88.
[49] Ibid., 90.

Production of high-value cash crops previously open only to European farmers, such as coffee, was opened up but only to those with large landholdings.[50] Eliud Mathu was appointed to the Legislative Council in 1947 as the first African representative, but majority rule seemed as distant as ever before. Although the Beecher Report of 1950 recommended an increase in state aid for African education, the report's insistence on strict enforcement of the age of entry for pupils (seven years) and that school attendance should remain constant for at least four years, was inflammatory. Poor families were unable to know if there would be sufficient money to pay for entry of a child at the age of seven, nor if they would be able to maintain payment of fees to allow the child to remain in school continuously for four years. The independent schools, with their acceptance of pupils of almost any age and flexibility that allowed pupils to postpone their studies and return at a later date, were to find such policies impossible to sustain after Beecher.[51] Both landless and land-poor or their children could no longer hope to work or read their way out of poverty.

But in the Central Highlands, the moderate constitutionalist effort was further hampered. Adherents of that political path, the elite, were seen to be exacerbating the material hardships of life for many of Kikuyu society's poorest members. With a rise in land values and soil productivity declining due to a large population increase over the preceding decades, clan elders sought to expel their needy tenants in an effort to increase the returns from the land.[52] Again, the elites had jeopardised their claim to dominate Kikuyu politics by abjectly failing to guarantee security of tenure for their juniors. Similarly, the elite failed in their other legitimising function: to protect the population from the most intrusive aspects of colonial rule.

In the aftermath of World War II, and despite the first stuttering steps towards economic and political reform, the colonial state became ever more invasive. As part of the empire-wide effort to increase production of export commodities so as to aid the ailing metropolitan economy, a number of unpopular development schemes were introduced across Kenya. In the Highlands, these primarily took the form of soil conservation and included prohibitive restrictions on livestock grazing and labour-intensive compulsory terracing of the hillside farms. Other measures included compulsory cattle-dipping so as to prevent disease crossing

[50] Kershaw, *Mau Mau From Below*, 226–7.
[51] Ibid., 230; Lonsdale, 'Wealth, Poverty and Civic Virtue,' 424.
[52] Kershaw, *Mau Mau From Below*, 109–10, 135, 155, 177 & 226.

from African-owned herds to the settler-owned dairy and beef farms. All were underwritten by an intolerant and inflexible regime of enforcement, which was entrusted to the chiefs, their retinues of Tribal Police, and their local courts. Despite these powers, the chiefs struggled to impose the new regulations and bylaws on their communities.[53] Resistance was widespread and politicised by the chiefs using their influence over soil conservation implementation to further hound their opponents within the structures of the KAU.[54] Leaders of the KAU thus needed little persuading to begin to champion the cause of the peasants forced to terrace their clan's land.

Those same peasants were hardly content in any case. They had seen landholdings dramatically shrink by up to half in Central Province during the 1930s and 1940s.[55] Forty percent of households in Kiambu were thought to be below the poverty line by 1950.[56] Feeling abandoned by the elites, the poor found a voice through an emerging militant Kikuyu political leadership that had little faith in the ability of more established and moderate leaders to deliver real change. Among similarly minded company, these leaders made no secret of their preferred methods of delivering reform. James Beauttah and others in Nyeri and Nanyuki had committed themselves to political violence as early as 1948, and Bildad Kaggia and Fred Kubai's Nairobi-based militants followed soon after.[57]

Just as it had done in the 1890s, Kikuyu society began to fall apart at the seams after 1945. In April 1949, a meeting of chiefs agreed 'that generally speaking children almost certainly lacked discipline, that young men and women were totally indisciplined [*sic*] and succumbing more and more to crime and immorality.'[58] By 1951, Chief Njiri in Fort Hall, too, was despairing of the young: 'What has so changed the Kikuyu youth? They now say they cannot help themselves because they must have more education. I have a poor opinion of the Kikuyu youth.'[59] But the young did not hold Njiri and his fellow chiefs in high regard either.

---

[53] See, for example, Bill Bravman, *Making Ethnic Ways: Communities and Their Transformations in Taita, Kenya, 1800–1950* (Oxford, 1998), 234.

[54] Throup, *Economic and Social Origins*, 3–4.

[55] Gavin Kitching, *Class and Economic Change in Kenya: The Making of an African Petite-Bourgeoisie* (New Haven, 1980), 118–20.

[56] Kershaw, *Mau Mau From Below*, 165–7; Throup, *Economic and Social Origins*, 144.

[57] Lonsdale, 'Wealth, Poverty and Civic Virtue,' 435–6.

[58] KNA VP/2/12, 'Notes on a Meeting of Chiefs of Nyeri District Held Between 5th and 7th April 1949,' 2.

[59] Quoted in BGC, collection 81, box 13, file 13, V. Blakeslee, 'The Kikuyu People,' 26 October 1951, 5–6.

The reciprocal ties between patrons and clients were eroded. Although the poor were being forced towards Nairobi in an effort to find an income, the elders were more concerned with diversifying their economic interests away from clan land and were distracted by endemic land litigation.[60] The prevalence of land litigation reached a peak immediately before a State of Emergency was declared in October 1952. Squatters on the European-owned farms of the Rift Valley were evicted and forced to return to their places of origin. With few other options open to them and their families, the returned squatters attempted to recover access to the land they or their parents had left in the past.[61] The land cases split senior family members anxious to protect what they held from more junior family members desperate to access a source of potential wealth.[62]

On Her Majesty's Supernatural Service

By 1950, the dye was cast. The refusal of the rich to be virtuous patrons meant the poor repudiated their responsibility to be good clients.[63] Any number of possible escape routes from poverty for the tenants had been closed down by the Kikuyu elite, the settlers, and the colonial state. The KAU's failure to counter these developments demonstrated the shortcomings of legal protest, and so the militant cause spread out across the Central Highlands.[64] The radical message was carried from Nairobi and the squatter labour lines in the Rift Valley in the form of mass oathing of the Kikuyu population, reaching every single Kikuyu settlement by the middle of 1952. Although the grievances of the militants were grounded in the present, their use of oathing to mobilise support deliberately harked back to the past and in a manner that privileged a notion of a unified Kikuyu identity that had never been anything other than a chimera.

Although the political content of Mau Mau's oaths was relatively new, oaths had long been part of everyday life in the Mount Kenya region.[65] During the nineteenth century, oaths were used primarily to cement social and legal contracts between parties that demanded future

[60] Kershaw, *Mau Mau From Below*, 195–6.
[61] Ibid., 198.
[62] Peterson, 'Writing in Revolution,' 83–4.
[63] Lonsdale, 'Wealth, Poverty and Civic Virtue,' 407.
[64] Ibid., 409; Tamarkin, 'Nakuru,' 120; Tamarkin, 'Loyalists in Nakuru,' 249; Throup, *Economic and Social Origins*, 10.
[65] Kershaw, *Mau Mau From Below*, 311–20; Harold Lambert, *Kikuyu Social and Political Institutions* (London, 1956), 122–8.

commitments, for example, in relation to land or marriage. The oaths were sworn exclusively by elders and strictly controlled by custom. If either party failed to honour the commitments agreed to in the oath, the transgressor would be inflicted with *thahu*, a state of spiritual uncleanliness that would manifest itself in misfortunes visited on the transgressors, their families, and their clans. Oaths were also used to break relationships through the infliction of spiritual uncleanliness by a curse declared by wronged parties on transgressors who had failed to keep their side of a particular bargain.[66] Restricted to elders, women and junior members of Kikuyu society were explicitly banned from participation. Transgression of such customary regulations during oathing again invoked spiritual uncleanliness.[67] If incurred, that spiritual uncleanliness could be corrected by the unclean person undergoing a purification ceremony.[68]

By the second decade of the twentieth century, Kikuyu oathing had moved away from being solely a legal practice. The KCA, the rivals to the monopoly of chiefs over state patronage, adapted oathing to become a method of political mobilisation.[69] Constrained to the arena of intra-elite competition, the restrictions of oathing to elders and the explicit exclusion of less elevated members of society from the practice remained intact. In other words, although the purpose of oathing had changed a great deal as a result of its introduction to the political sphere, the practice itself remained largely unchanged. Two decades later, however, oathing underwent a far more significant transformation once oaths of unity were being taken by the restless Kikuyu labour force of the European-owned farms in the Highlands.[70] The previous restrictions of the practice to elders were ridden roughshod over as non-elites, women, and youths were oathed and administered oaths to others. As the colony entered the maelstrom of the 1950s, the unifying oath championed by the militant faction within Kikuyu politics was dispersed into Central Province. Used to mobilise support for the radicals, oathing quickly became synonymous with the resulting insurgency.[71]

[66] Kershaw, *Mau Mau From Below*, 311.
[67] Githige, 'Religious Factor,' 79; Louis Leakey, *The Southern Kikuyu Before 1903*, 3 vols., vol. 3 (New York, 1977), 1232–9.
[68] Ibid., 1232–3.
[69] Clough, *Fighting Two Sides*, 123.
[70] Throup, *Economic and Social Origins*, 120.
[71] Robert Buijtenhuijs, *Essays on Mau Mau: Contributions to Mau Mau Historiography* (Leiden, 1982); Marshall Clough, *Mau Mau Memoirs: History, Memory and Politics* (Boulder, 1998), 60, 70, 76–7, 98–102, 118–20; Githige, 'Religious Factor'; Maia Green,

Two levels of oathing were eventually used by the militants in their attempts to construct a strong basis of support among Kikuyu in the Rift Valley, Nairobi, and Central Province. The first, the oaths of unity, were administered in an attempt to ensure the support of local populations for the militants and to warn against any attempt to pass on information regarding their activities to the authorities.[72] Following the announcement of a State of Emergency, on 20 October 1952, second oaths were given selectively and voluntarily to 'all those who were likely to be called on to give active service to the movement.' These second, *batuni* oaths were to prepare Mau Mau's fighters for war and, in particular, to kill.[73] Initiates swore to abstain from European beer, pledged to provide food and shelter for Mau Mau units, to fight for land and freedom, to never betray rebels, to destroy European property, to kill the enemy, to hide others who had been oathed, and to never disclose secrets. During the rituals attendant to both the first and second oaths, which shared many elements with circumcision ceremonies, various symbolic paraphernalia, including the thorax and other body parts and meat of a goat, soil, and banana leaves, and acts such as prayers towards Mount Kenya, were employed.[74] All oaths finished with the invocation of *thahu* as a penalty for transgressing its clauses: 'And if I fail to do these things, May this oath kill me.'[75]

The violence and coercion of oathing should not be underestimated. Oathing ceremonies were not sought out by eager participants. As the memoirs of Mau Mau veterans repeatedly make clear, initiates were generally taken to ceremonies under false pretences,[76] and many took their oaths under duress.[77] The armed guards present at the ceremonies were not there for decorative purposes. 'During the course of our initiation,' Karari Njama later wrote, 'one person refused to take the oath and was mercilessly beaten. Two guards were crying [out] seeking permission from their chief leader to kill the man. The man learnt that death had approached him and he quickly changed his mind and took the oath.'[78]

'Mau Mau Oathing Rituals and Political Ideology in Kenya: A Re-Analysis,' *Africa* 60 (1990), 69–87; Kariuki, *Mau Mau Detainee*, 25–33.

[72] Githige, 'Religious Factor,' 198.
[73] Kariuki, *Mau Mau Detainee*, 30.
[74] Buijtenhuijs, *Essays*; Green, 'Mau Mau Oathing,' 69–87.
[75] Kariuki, *Mau Mau Detainee*, 28–30.
[76] Clough, *Memoirs*, 98.
[77] Anderson, *Histories*, 42–3, 99, 231.
[78] Donald Barnett and Karari Njama, *Mau Mau From Within: An Analysis of Kenya's Peasant Revolt* (London, 1966), 119.

But willing initiates were also roughed up as part of the preparation for the oathing ceremony. 'The other three who were in my group were hit about a little,' J. M. Kariuki recalled.[79] Even Karigo Muchai, a member of the KCA and KAU and Mau Mau recruiter, was beaten in early 1953 prior to taking the second oath reserved for those already oathed and expected to take to the forests to actively fight.[80] Having been oathed, particularly in relation to the first oaths, should not therefore be conflated with support for Mau Mau. Moreover, for a community whose prevailing political approach for the previous five decades was characterised by restraint and peaceful reformism, oathing was never likely to produce cohesion and unity behind the militants unless supported by violence.

Oathing spread not as a result of a popular desire to express support for the radical faction of Kikuyu politics, but instead as a means of opening flows of information and supplies from the populace to the militants. Perhaps most important, oathing was an attempt to dissuade any potential informants from approaching the colonial authorities. But these tactical and pragmatic uses of oathing were lost on the colonial government, who could not see beyond the ritual and superstition of the practice. Mau Mau's oathing practices lay at the heart of colonial myth-making. By presenting Mau Mau as the product of witchcraft[81] and as a psychological condition,[82] the state chose to ignore the legitimate socioeconomic origins of the insurrection and the instrumentality of oathing. To the colonial eye, Mau Mau's oaths had become a multilayered structure of ever-increasing and apparently fathomless depravity, including bestiality and cannibalism.[83] Encouraged and exaggerated by a very small number of African opponents of Mau Mau close to the regime, these conclusions were fantastical products of European paranoia intended to deny the legitimate grievances of the insurgents.[84] The principal method of political mobilisation used by an insurgency obsessed with the markers of

---

[79] Kariuki, *Mau Mau Detainee*, 26.
[80] Karigo Muchai, *The Hardcore: The Story of Karigo Muchai* (Richmond BC, 1973), 18.
[81] Kenya, *Origins and Growth*, 167.
[82] John Carothers, 'The Psychology of Mau Mau' (Nairobi, 1954). See also Sloan Mahone, 'The Psychology of Rebellion: Colonial Medical Responses to Dissent in British East Africa,' *Journal of African History* 47 (2006).
[83] KNA MSS/129/9, attachment to Scott Dickson to all heads of missions, 24 March 1953, 4.
[84] Buijtenhuijs, *Essays*, 90–115; Green, 'Mau Mau Oathing,' 69–87; Kariuki, *Mau Mau Detainee*, 33.

modernity[85] was dismissed as the ultimate expression of a people unable to come to terms with modernisation.[86] This misdiagnosis resulted in the formulation of the wholly inadequate initial response of counteroathing.

Senior figures within the colonial government were convinced of the supernatural potency of the oaths and thought it essential to address the ceremonies as a matter of urgency. The intellectual inspiration for counteroathing emerged from the ethnographic writings of Louis Leakey, the celebrated archaeologist and palaeoanthropologist. The child of missionary parents, Leakey grew up in Kiambu and considered himself a white Kikuyu. As early as 1929, Louis Leakey was officially recognised as an expert in Kikuyu customs and history. In 1932, both Louis and his father, Canon Henry Leakey, supported Kikuyu submissions to the Kenya Land Commission that called for the reversal of land alienation.[87] As a result of Louis Leakey's high public profile and close connections to the colonial regime, he was commissioned by the Rhodes Trust to write an ethnographic study of the Kikuyu in 1936. The resulting *The Southern Kikuyu Before 1903* was not published until 1977, three years after Leakey's death, but the manuscript had been widely circulated among colonial administrators following its completion in the late 1930s.[88]

Throughout that work, Leakey portrayed Kikuyu society as a highly codified moral world. Its arbiters of right and wrong were, according to Leakey, to be drawn solely from the ranks of elders.[89] Leakey willingly acquiesced to the exploitation of his research as elders attempted to use it to reassert their political authority in the face of their declining influence over Kikuyu society.[90] During the struggles between the elders and the KCA discussed earlier in this chapter, Leakey was far from neutral. Besides the codification of elders' authority through his ethnography, as an intelligence officer during World War II Leakey formulated and enforced anti-KCA measures that culminated in the outlawing of the organisation.[91] Built on his reputation as an expert of Kikuyu politics

---

[85] Peterson, 'Writing in Revolution'; James Smith, 'Njama's Supper: The Consumption and Use of Literary Potency by Mau Mau Insurgents in Colonial Kenya,' *Comparative Studies in Society and History* 40 (1998).

[86] Carothers, 'Psychology.'

[87] Lonsdale, 'Ornamental Constitutionalism,' 87.

[88] Berman and Lonsdale, 'Leakey's Mau Mau,' 180.

[89] Clark, 'Leakey as Ethnographer,' 394–5.

[90] Ibid., 381.

[91] Berman and Lonsdale, 'Leakey's Mau Mau,' 174–8.

and culture, by mid-1952, Leakey had carved out an undefined role for himself at the heart of colonial government, from where he attempted to influence the war against Mau Mau.[92] Through his writings, most notably *Mau Mau and the Kikuyu* published in 1952, and as an advisor to the government, Leakey was able to shape both public opinion and state policy towards Mau Mau.

Although Leakey was the most forthright European critic of Mau Mau's oathing, he did not subscribe to the apocalyptic imagery of colonial accounts. Instead, Leakey condemned what he saw as violations of cultural values and norms. According to Leakey, an oath was to be considered proper if it were 'one which could not be entered into lightly,' was 'taken voluntarily and with approval of the rest of the family,' and was 'administered in public and in front of many witnesses.'[93] The administering of Mau Mau's oaths in secret, often without the consent of the oath-taker, and to women and children, meant, for Leakey, that these were oaths 'utterly and completely contrary to native law and custom.'[94] He further argued that the contraventions of the conventions governing oaths meant those who had taken the Mau Mau oath would be considered to be in 'a state of spiritual uncleaness.' However, they 'could be "cleansed" from the effects of the oath by an act of ceremonial purification.'[95] Leakey thus set about the formulation of ceremonial acts of purification, which became official policy in mid-1952.

Leakey's politically biased ethnographic knowledge was thus thrust into battle against his long-standing opponents within the ranks of Mau Mau. Applied anthropology in times of war has a long and inglorious history. There is little new in the recent call to arms for academics willing 'to get out of their ivory tower of theory and to get stuck into the practical application of their skills.'[96] Nor is the current scepticism of the efficacy of such projects unprecedented.[97] As early as 1919, Franz Boas denounced four anthropologists working in Central America who 'have prostituted

---

[92] Ibid., 143–5.
[93] Louis Leakey, *Mau Mau and the Kikuyu* (London, 1952), 54.
[94] Ibid., 99.
[95] Ibid., 45–6.
[96] Beatrice Hauser, 'The Cultural Revolution in Counter-Insurgency,' *Journal of Strategic Studies* 30 (2007).
[97] Roberto Gonzalez, 'Towards Mercenary Anthropology? The New US Army Counterinsurgency Manual FM-24 and the Military-Anthropology Complex,' *Anthropology Today* 23 (2007).

science by using it as a cover for their activities as spies.'[98] Although the Vietnam War–era Project Camelot[99] and the Thailand Controversy[100] have received the greatest attention, the military enactment of anthropological knowledge was a feature of twentieth-century colonial warfare. The tendency of the British and French to stress the cultural origins of anti-colonial resistance rather the unpalatably real grievances of colonised peoples only increased the attraction of anthropologists to colonial regimes. In Algeria, for example, anthropology was used with disastrous results by the French forces to shape the formation of collaborationist groups.[101] During the Malayan Emergency, the British attempted to use anthropological work and the appointment of anthropologists to key positions to garner the support of the indigenous population.[102] The influence of Leakey over the earliest stages of the counterinsurgency campaign in Kenya then had clear precedents.

The counteroathing ceremonies based on Leakey's work began concurrently in Kiambu and Nyeri in mid-1952 and by November were held across Central Province and the White Highlands.[103] The first recorded counteroathing ceremonies were poorly attended.[104] Attendance fluctuated greatly, from the 107 reported at a ceremony at Ngong Forest to more than 1,000.[105] The average attendance at the six ceremonies held in Kiambu prior to the Emergency was 600.[106] Performed by medicine men nicknamed 'Her Majesty's witch doctors,' the ceremonies took several

[98] Gerald Berreman, 'Is Anthropology Alive? Social Responsibility in Social Anthropology,' *Current Anthropology* 9 (1968), 392.
[99] Mark Solovey, 'Project Camelot and the 1960s Epistemological Revolution: Rethinking the Politics-Patronage-Social Science Nexus,' *Social Studies of Science* 31 (2001).
[100] Eric Wakin, *Anthropology Goes to War: Professional Ethics and Counterinsurgency in Thailand* (Madison WI, 1992).
[101] Camille Lacoste-Dujardin, *Opération Oiseau Bleu: Des Kabyles, des ethnologues et la guerre en Algérie* (Paris, 1997).
[102] Tim Harper, 'The Politics of the Forest in Colonial Malaya,' *Modern Asian Studies* 31 (1997), 20–4; John Leary, *Violence and the Dream People: The Orang Asli in the Malayan Emergency, 1948–1960* (Columbus OH, 1995).
[103] KNA BG/2/8, minutes of Embu African District Council meeting, 11 November 1952; Maloba, *Mau Mau and Kenya*. For an account of counteroathing in the peripheral district of Machakos, see Katherine Luongo, 'If You Can't Beat Them, Join Them: Government Cleanings of Witches and Mau Mau in 1950s Kenya,' *History in Africa* 33 (2006).
[104] Kershaw, *Mau Mau From Below*, 238.
[105] *East African Standard (EAS)*, 1 August 1952, 1.
[106] Kershaw, *Mau Mau From Below*, 238.

forms.[107] The most basic was the _gũtahĩkia_ ceremony, literally meaning 'to cause to vomit.' Those to be cleansed squatted in a line, along which the medicine man, carrying a male goat's foot, proceeded to cleanse each individual in turn by saying, 'Emit the oath you took,' while 'touching the lips of the suspect with the goat's foot.' The recipient would reply, spitting as they did, 'I emit it.' The same reply would be repeated, again while spitting, following the command by the medicine man to 'Emit the vows you made.'[108] Leakey described the purpose of the spitting and the goat's foot as 'the symbolic "vomiting" of the evil and uncleanness by placing some object repeatedly to the lips of the patient.'[109]

Some counteroathing ceremonies took the form of a trial by ordeal. One variety adapted a form of oathing known as _kũringa thenge_, translated literally as 'striking the he-goat.'[110] The use of a male goat's body parts was thought, as in Mau Mau's own oaths, to increase the potency of the oath and to increase the level of spiritual uncleanliness invoked if the clauses were not broken by the oath-taker.[111] The oath-taker 'broke the legs of a he-goat, at the same time declaring that their limbs, and those of their family, be broken likewise if they were telling lies.'[112] During the counteroathing ceremonies, participants swore 'that I will be loyal to this government and, if I fail, may this _thenge_ kill me. Also I truly swear that I will never take the Mau Mau oath and if I see Mau Mau hiding, taking an oath or carrying weapons, I will inform the government, and, if I fail, may this _thenge_ kill me.'[113] Other similar counteroaths were sworn on sacred stones. The sacred stone, in reality often the atlas bone of an elephant, was rested on a support of hibiscus branches. The oath-taker passed pieces of grass through each of the symbolically significant seven holes while repeating a counteroath renouncing Mau Mau.[114]

Other counteroaths took the form of cursing ceremonies, again inspired by Leakey. In _The Southern Kikuyu Before 1903_, Leakey described at length the process of cursing by a _Mwĩthaga_, a member of the _Aĩthaga_ clan believed to have 'inherited powers' of potency in cursing. A

[107] Peter Evans, _Law and Disorder: Scenes of Life in Kenya_ (London, 1956), 24; Ngugi Kabiro, _Man in the Middle_ (Richmond BC, 1973), 44.
[108] E. N. Wanyoike, _An African Pastor_ (Nairobi, 1974), 192.
[109] Leakey, _Southern Kikuyu_, 1242.
[110] Ibid., 1012–3.
[111] Githige, 'Religious Factor,' 88–91, 107–8.
[112] Kershaw, _Mau Mau From Below_, 313; Muriuki, _History of the Kikuyu_, 130.
[113] Waruhiu Itote, _Mau Mau in Action_ (Nairobi, 1979), 73.
[114] Kenyatta, _Facing Mount Kenya_, 215–6; Kershaw, _Mau Mau From Below_, 313; Leakey, _Southern Kikuyu_, 1009–12; Muriuki, _History of the Kikuyu_, 130.

Mwĩthaga 'reinforced their curses with a publicly performed ceremony.' During the ceremony, an empty gourd would be burst in a heated pot. The pot would then be cooled by water poured from a banana-leaf container, which would then be burned, together with blackjack plants. Each act would be carried out while the *Mwĩthaga* announced a curse on whomever the target was. For example, while the plant material was burnt, the *Mwĩthaga* would exclaim, 'May that person burn up thus, may his children burn up thus, may his stock burn up thus, may his homestead burn up thus, may his wives burn up thus.'[115] In the week prior to the beginning of the Emergency, two such ceremonies took place at Lamuria, 40 miles from Nanyuki, and Naro Moru. Besides 400 Kikuyu farm labourers, reporters, the Nanyuki district commissioner, chiefs, and white farmers were in attendance. A *Mwĩthaga*, wearing colobus monkey skins and an airman's greatcoat, performed the ceremony. He cursed 'all who used violence, all who hurt and killed cattle, all who burned houses and property, all those who used witch-doctors' magic for Mau Mau – and all those who tried to settle personal grievances by saying innocent people belonged to Mau Mau.'[116]

For obvious reasons, alternative arrangements were made for Christians who had taken a Mau Mau oath. Before returning to the church, oathed Catholics had to publicly declare 'before God and Gospel, having not realised what I was doing in the past days, swear I will never follow Mau Mau, or anything forbidden of it, now and forever.'[117] After similar declarations, Presbyterians were issued with a card stating:

I wholeheartedly say that I shall never have any connection with the Mau Mau or any other association which may be against Her Majesty's Government and the good order of this country, or which may stand against Christianity.

The card was signed by a clergyman, with the pronouncement that the bearer of the card 'is loyal to the Christian Church and Government.'[118] The frequency of counteroathing ceremonies increased in the wake of the declaration of a State of Emergency. Recruits into the newly formed loyalist militia in Nyeri and Fort Hall all underwent counteroathing.[119]

---

[115] Leakey, *Southern Kikuyu*, 1218–20.
[116] *EAS*, 19 October 1952, B.
[117] Lawrence Njoroge, *A Century of Catholic Endeavour: Holy Ghost and Consolata Missions in Kenya* (Nairobi, 1999), 167–8.
[118] Wanyoike, *African Pastor*, 195.
[119] KNA VQ/1/30, District Commissioner (DC) Fort Hall to District Officers (Dos), 9 February 1953, 1–2.

So, too, did all Kikuyu government and local council employees in Fort Hall.[120] However, claims made by one official that counteroathing 'had been quite effective' were incorrect.[121] Other colonial officials quickly became unconvinced of the value of the exercise. As one remarked, 'the Cleansing Ceremony itself is of little use and is taken by many with their tongues in their cheeks.'[122] Ngugi Kabiro recalled 'the light-hearted manner in which the medicine man conducted the ceremony.'[123] Even among those Kikuyu who took the concept of counteroathing seriously, mainly 'old men and those in the 40–50 Age Group,' there was outrage at the sacrilegious use of sacred stones during counteroathing.[124] Others simply felt that Leakey overemphasised the extent to which Mau Mau's oaths contravened accepted custom.[125] 'For my part,' Ngugi writes, 'as I didn't believe in either the magic of the oath or the curses used in the cleansing ceremony, it wouldn't have mattered whether the witch doctor performed the ceremony correctly or not.'[126] As the rising incidence of Mau Mau activity through 1953 clearly demonstrated, counteroathing failed to turn those supposedly cleansed of Mau Mau's nefarious influence away from the insurgency. The much vaunted counteroathing became an embarrassing failure for the colonial regime.

Despite the failings of counteroathing, the episode does reveal much of the nature of the counterinsurgency campaign against Mau Mau in the first years of the war. First, counteroathing demonstrated a profound mis-diagnosis of the causes of the insurgency. Most Kikuyu did not view the rebellion as an outpouring of magical impropriety requiring a response like that of counteroathing. The ceremonies served only to antagonise Mau Mau fighters, who desecrated and cursed designated locations for counteroathing in an attempt to sabotage the process.[127] Second, the ceremonies made little acknowledgement of the need for the security of opponents of Mau Mau. Those who willingly underwent counteroathing were targeted by the insurgents and were easily identifiable due to

[120] KNA VQ/1/30, DC Fort Hall to Provincial Commissioner Central, 23 February 1953, 1.
[121] KNA DC/VQ/1/30, DC Fort Hall to PC Central, 23 February 1953.
[122] KNA VQ/1/30, DC Nyeri, 'Home Guards', 11 February 1953, 2.
[123] Kabiro, *Man in the Middle*, 44.
[124] KNA VQ/1/30, DC Fort Hall to PC Central, 23 February 1953, 1; Kershaw, *Mau Mau From Below*, 237–8; 246ff.
[125] Ibid., 237–8.
[126] Kabiro, *Man in the Middle*, 45.
[127] Itote, *Mau Mau in Action*, 73–4. See also Githige, 'Religious Factor,' 204–5.

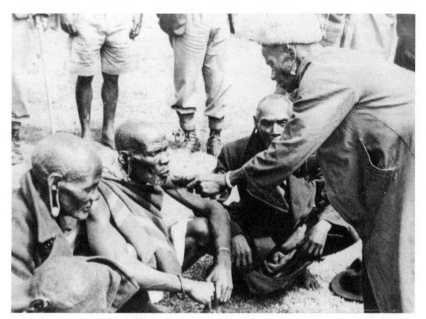

FIGURE 2. Counteroathing ceremony, Kiambu, 1952. Reproduced with permission of Kenya National Archives.

the very public nature of the ceremonies.[128] Third, corruption during counteroathing was rife and undermined any lingering legitimacy of the practice. Medicine men, elders, and chiefs demanded payment from those cleansed in return for their services.[129] Fourth, and most significantly, counteroathing depended on force and compulsion, turning the ceremonies into degrading events that counterproductively propagated Mau Mau support among the population.

Of these failings, it was the violence of counteroathing that was most damaging to the effort. Ironically, considering counteroathing was thought necessary as a result of Mau Mau's contravention of oathing customs, counteroathing was accompanied by significant coercion on the part of its champions. As Leakey himself wrote in an indictment on Mau Mau oathing, use of force in such settings 'was utterly and completely contrary to native law and custom, which has always laid down that an oath must be taken voluntarily and with the consent of members of the family of the person concerned.'[130] Such warnings were not

[128] Leakey, *Mau Mau and the Kikuyu*, 99. See also Githige, 'Religious Factor,' 205.
[129] Evans, *Law and Disorder*, 24.
[130] Leakey, *Mau Mau and the Kikuyu*, 99.

heeded by those officers within local government responsible for organising counteroathing ceremonies. In Kiambu, those suspected of taking
Mau Mau oaths were escorted to counteroathing ceremonies by headmen and Home Guards. During the ceremonies themselves, the Home
Guards 'used their batons and rifle butts to make sure that a suspect
squatted properly and uncomplainingly and made response distinctly as
the medicine-man cleansed him.'[131] During counteroathing ceremonies
held on the white-owned farms, European employers kept attendance
registers of their labour force. The Nanyuki district commissioner recommended the immediate dismissal of absentees.[132] The implications of
compelled counteroathing ceremonies were devastatingly demonstrated
by the Marige massacre in Kiambu during April 1953 when five people
were killed by a Mau Mau, in part as a reaction to the introduction of
forced counteroathing.[133]

Counteroathing ultimately represented an attempt by the colonial government to open the mouths of Kikuyu by enabling them to provide
information about Mau Mau. However, the colonial authorities failed
to recognise that it was not elaborate ritual, or indeed compulsion, that
would lead to the ready provision from the populace of intelligence about
the embryonic insurgency. That could only come about with the guarantee of safety for informers. Moreover, by insisting that Mau Mau oathing
was the most likely aspect of the insurgency to mobilise Kikuyu opposition, the colonial state misunderstood the significance of Mau Mau, the
purpose of oathing, and the nature of potential collaboration. Counteroathing did not address the unease of Mau Mau's opponents with
the insurgency. Their concerns were with the youthful indiscipline, law-
lessness, and violence of Mau Mau.[134] Yet, most Kikuyu were willing
to tolerate Mau Mau's transgressions of custom, for example, oathing
by non-elders, if its promises were to be achieved and if the colonial
government could not protect dissenters.

The Breaking Storm

For those reasons, the Kikuyu elite found their opposition of the militants not to be shared by the great majority of the populace. Murders of

---

[131] Wanyoike, *African Pastor*, 192.
[132] *EAS*, 19 October 1952, B.
[133] Kershaw, *Mau Mau From Below*, 248–63.
[134] Ibid., 237.

loyalists and arson attacks on their properties became more frequent over the course of 1952.[135] Appeals for calm were made across the Central Highlands by various leading Kikuyu political figures. In an address to the Embu African District Council in late July, the African representative on the Legislative Council, Eliud Mathu, spoke out against 'those responsible for the recent increase in crimes of violence in the Colony,' and argued that 'they should receive no lenience from the Courts.'[136] But such denunciations appeared to fall on deaf ears; between 1 August and the onset of the Emergency on 20 October, 34 Africans were murdered by Mau Mau. The victims were mainly chiefs, headmen, informers, and Christians who refused to take an oath.[137] Opponents of Mau Mau found they had been left to fend for themselves by a regime more concerned with protecting the European settlers.

'On 24th Sept 1952,' Wainaina Gitondu, of Githumu in Fort Hall, later wrote, 'I [was] forced to take Mau-Mau oath as I was last one in my village.' The following Sunday, Wainaina stood up during a church service, confessed his oathing, and 'said to the crowd that those people are anti-Christ.' From that day, 'all Mau-Mau followers blamed me through the location.' Wainaina subsequently became an informer and was rewarded with permission to plant coffee in 1954.[138] Others were not so fortunate. Ngugi Mrefu, believed to have been a police informer, was reported missing in late September. A month later, his body was found at the foot of a waterfall in Kiambu.[139] Informers and denouncers were treated alike. A few days before his death on 29 September, Gichuki Gichumu, of Kerugoya in Embu, had condemned Mau Mau at a public rally.[140] The need for greater protection for Mau Mau's opponents was readily apparent.

Just five days after his arrival in Kenya at the end of September 1952, the new governor, Evelyn Baring, toured Central Province. During his meetings with a variety of Kikuyu leaders, Baring later recalled, 'They said that there had been a complete breakdown of law and order, there

---

[135] TNA: PRO CO 822/449, Anon, 'Mau Mau Attacks on Chiefs, Headmen, etc.,' October 1952; Throup, *Economic and Social Origins*, 11.
[136] KNA BG/3/8, minutes of meeting of Embu ADC, 29 July – 1 August 1952, 12.
[137] Colony & Protectorate of Kenya, *History of the Loyalists* (Nairobi, 1961), 6–9. See also RHL Mss Afr s 424, ff.166–187, J. A. Rutherford, 'History of the Kikuyu Guard,' 1957, 3.
[138] KNA DC/MUR/3/1/18, Wainaina Gitondu to DC Fort Hall, 27 October 1956.
[139] KNA MLA/1/469, CC 43/1953, 'Muchugu Kago & 2 Others.'
[140] KNA MLA/1/536, CC 56/1953, 'Gacharia Gikunja & 2 Others.'

FIGURE 3. A woman named Wanjiku assisting in the search for Mau Mau insurgents, Muguga Forest, Kiambu, 1952. Reproduced with permission of Kenya National Archives.

was a murder every night and unless you [Baring] proceed on the people who are doing this our position in future is perfectly impossible.'[141] A few days later, the reality of such fears was vividly demonstrated by the murder of the most prominent Kikuyu ally of the colonial government, Chief Waruhiu wa Kungu.[142] Waruhiu was a strong Christian, who opposed oathing on the grounds of faith. He had been heavily involved in organising counteroathing ceremonies in Kiambu.[143] His death was greeted 'with three days of beer drinking' by Mau Mau supporters.[144] The response of the colonial government was severe.

[141] RHL Mss Afr s 1574, 'Transcript of Recording of a Discussion Between Lord Howick & Margery Perham,' 19 November 1969, 9–10.
[142] Anderson, *Histories*, 55.
[143] Kershaw, *Mau Mau From Below*, 241.
[144] Mohamed Mathu, *The Urban Guerrilla: The Story of Mohamed Mathu* (Richmond BC, 1974) 15.

FIGURE 4. Mau Mau suspects after arrest, 1952. Reproduced with permission of Kenya National Archives.

At midnight on 20 October 1952 a state of Emergency was declared. Leading political figures associated with the militants, most controversially Kenyatta and other senior KAU office holders, were arrested. British troops arrived to bolster five battalions of the King's African Rifles.[145] The insurgents were not easily cowed, though. Just two days later, Chief Nderi and two police escorts were murdered in Nyeri after they had attempted to disrupt an oathing ceremony.[146] Despite such high-profile incidents, a state of phoney war took hold of the Central Highlands for the next few months. The Provincial Administration in Embu believed only three murders in the district could be attributed to Mau Mau throughout the whole of 1952.[147] In early January 1953, one missionary in Meru even wrote 'that the progress of this subversive movement appears to have been arrested in Meru.'[148] Rumours of Mau Mau's demise were though greatly exaggerated, as the attack on the homesteads of five loyalists in Aguthi,

---

[145] Anderson, *Histories*, 62–3.
[146] Kenya, *Origins and Growth*, 107.
[147] KNA DC/EBU/1/1/1, Embu District Annual Report 1952, 2.
[148] KNA MSS/124/4, W. H. Laughton to Rev. T. A. Beetham, 4 January 1953.

Nyeri on Christmas Eve demonstrated.[149] Despite such violent attacks remaining relatively rare, compared to what soon followed from March 1953 onwards, Mau Mau oathing had escalated in the period after the Emergency began in October 1952. To counter this development, screening teams were formed across Central Province from trusted government servants in order to interrogate those suspected of taking oaths. These were men such as Bendanson Kamau Mwaniki, an employee of the Agricultural Department in Fort Hall.[150] The size of the task was immense. By the close of 1952, it was estimated that up to 90 percent of the population of Nyeri and Fort Hall had been oathed.[151] In the Ndia division of Embu at the turn of 1953, it was thought 'that the population was 100% behind Mau Mau.'[152] Half the population of Kiambu were thought to have been oathed by April.[153] Behind this wall of silence created by oathing, the insurgents were planning to escalate the conflict.

Until that escalation took hold from the second quarter of 1953, insurgent violence tended to be discriminately targeted at local figures known for their opposition to the insurgency.[154] Victims also included agricultural assistants like Samueli Maina Kagume, the local representatives of the hated soil conservation and husbandry programmes.[155] The killing of unpopular loyalists served the dual purpose of unifying the insurgents and increasing the ability of Mau Mau units to move around localities without harassment.[156] But it would be wrong to represent all Mau Mau's early victims as carefully selected and deserving targets. Those that jeopardised the security of the underground movement inadvertently found themselves targeted by the militants.

The most obvious examples of this were Christians, particularly members of the East African Revival movement, who thought the oath to be an affront to their faith. Jeremiah Nyagah, a devout Christian, wrote he 'would rather die than take the oath.'[157] Some mission converts shared

[149] Anderson, *Histories*, 72–3.
[150] KNA DC/MUR/3/1/18, Bendanson Kamau Mwaniki to DC Fort Hall, 2 November 1956, 1.
[151] KNA DC/MUR/3/4/21, N. Langford-Smith, 'Judgement Must Begin: An Interim Report on the African Anglican Church in the Northern Highlands,' January 1953, 1.
[152] KNA DC/EBU/1/1/2, Embu District Annual Report 1953, 1.
[153] Kershaw, *Mau Mau From Below*, 248–9.
[154] Maloba, *Mau Mau and Kenya*, 116.
[155] KNA VP/6/2, Wangai Kagiuri to the Treasury, 24 April 1959. See also Kershaw, *Mau Mau From Below*, 260–1.
[156] Barnett, 'Mau Mau,' 82.
[157] RHL Mss Afr s 1727, J. J. Nyagah to M. Foote, 16 October 1954.

the belief of their leaders that 'this society of Mau Mau is not African, it comes from Satan.' The Anglican hierarchy, both European and African, argued that 'any Christian who takes this oath is denying his Lord and denying his faith.'[158] Bishop Cavellera, of the Consolata Catholic mission, declared unequivocally that 'Mau Mau is evil,' and promised it would 'be countered by every possible means within our power.'[159] Obadiah Kariuki, a leading Anglican clergyman during the Emergency, later wrote that Mau Mau's oaths 'made it impossible for many Christians to join the movement, as such oathing called for a spiritual commitment which Christians could only give to Jesus Christ.'[160] Christians were not targeted because of their faith, rather the peril in which they placed the insurgents. In their determined refusal to take oaths on religious grounds, Christians threatened Mau Mau.[161] Mau Mau's oaths were intended, in part, to quieten oathees so as to restrict the flow of intelligence to the movement's opponents. That silence could not be assumed on the part of those who refused to take the oath. After teaching against Mau Mau oathing in his Sunday school class, Daniel Gathiomi Mbugi was seized by local activists, strung up to be hanged, but escaped.[162] But it should not be assumed that Christians lined up behind the colonial regime; Christianity and loyalty did not necessarily flow into one another.[163]

In this first stage of the conflict, lasting up to March 1953, a number of preexisting cleavages within Kikuyu society were then militarised. These included that between mission church adherents and members of independent churches, that between government employees and those excluded from positions of such influence, and that between the peasantry and the agents of the agricultural development programmes introduced in the late 1950s. With the exception of the latter – which was in any case significantly less observable than the other two in the first wave of violence – these cleavages were not militarised for ideological reasons but rather because of the strategic imperatives of the insurgents for the

---

[158] KNA DC/MUR/3/4/21, Kariuki, Muraguri & Langford-Smith to all members of Fort Hall African Anglican Church, January 1953.

[159] Quoted in *EAS*, 29 August 1952, 25.

[160] Obidiah Kariuki, *A Bishop Facing Mount Kenya: An Autobiography, 1902–1978*, George Mathu trans. (Nairobi, 1985), 78.

[161] Peterson, 'Writing in Revolution,' 86–7.

[162] Dorothy Smoker, *Ambushed by Love: God's Triumph in Kenya's Terror* (Fort Washington PA, 1994), 80–2.

[163] Peterson, 'Wordy Women,' 488–9; John Lonsdale, 'Jomo Kenyatta, God and the Modern World,' in *African Modernities: Entangled Meanings in Current Debate*, eds. Jan-Georg Deutsch, Peter Probst, and Heike Schmidt (Oxford, 2002), 58.

protection of channels of intelligence. However, it is also true that these cleavages can be telescoped and the initial stage of the war described in broad terms as a conflict between elites and non-elites. It would be entirely wrong though to extrapolate from this first phase of bloodshed a broader pattern applicable to the entire war. This neat alignment between preexisting cleavages and the warring parties was temporary. Once the violence perpetrated by insurgents and counterinsurgents alike escalated from the second quarter of 1953, a cycle of violence took hold that dictated new allegiances that made little or no reference to pre-1952 cleavages.

Violence, Control, and Information

The Kikuyu ethnic community was in 1952 as it had always been; divided among itself. In the competition for political power, social influence, and economic survival, individuals sought to make use of the full range of options open to them. For some, militant politics and, a little later, armed resistance to colonial rule appeared the best route towards acquiring and securing access to those all-too-scarce resources. For others, accommodation with the colonial state appeared to offer the same opportunity. '"Colonialism" in Kenya,' Kanogo reminds us, 'was anything but monolithic.'[164] Africans took a wide variety of positions in their everyday lives in relation to the colonial state, far beyond those allowed by the narrow field of vision of any simplistic resistance paradigm. When Henry Muoria Mwaniki, the Kikuyu journalist, pamphleteer, editor, newspaper publisher, and later committed supporter of Mau Mau, came to consider Kenya's political prospects in 1944, he later admitted, 'I found it rather daunting to think of the future.' Kenyans, Muoria believed, were affected by colonial rule 'in a way that made them feel as though they were living in an enormous cage out of which they could never escape.'[165] Muoria was hardly alone in holding such thoughts. We should not, therefore, expect to find within the historical record a singular African response to colonial rule. The tension and symbiosis between conflict and accommodation defined relations between colonial states and their colonised subjects, but also provided different tools and resources to those contesting power and authority within colonised societies.

Because the experience of colonialism had produced such a divergent range of opinions among Kikuyu, neither the insurgents nor the colonial state could assume the support of the populace once the Mau Mau war

---

[164] Tabitha Kanogo, *African Womanhood in Colonial Kenya 1900–50* (Oxford, 2005), 4.
[165] Henry Muoria, *I, the Gikuyu and the White Fury* (Nairobi, 1994), 91.

began. That support had to be cultivated and coerced. More significantly, dissent had to be discouraged. The war between Mau Mau and
the colonial state was, in this first stage, less about hearts and minds
and rather more concerned with the eyes, ears, and mouths of potential
informants. Information dictates the narrative of war by determining the
targets, timing, and nature of violence. Inadequate intelligence is capable
of rendering even the most technologically advanced military force as
barbarous as its earlier, more primitive versions.[166] Operating with an
enormous shortfall in arms and resources relative to the state security
forces, Mau Mau had to exploit all other advantages in its favour. Ready
access to information from a broadly sympathetic or coerced population
was just such an advantage. With the nature of insurgency demanding
secrecy, information became a critical resource in a condition of irregular
civil war. The value of creating networks of information gathering and
the disruption of an opponent's network cannot be underestimated.[167]

For that reason, all combatants attached great importance to the collection of information, the protection of sources, and the punishment
of defectors and denouncers. This is not surprising. Indeed, one study of
demobilised fighters on both sides of the ongoing Colombian conflict suggests that single largest cause for killing civilians was as punishment for
passing information to the perpetrators' enemy.[168] The means by which
the combatants in Kenya gathered information and disrupted each other's
intelligence networks were not, therefore, incidental to the path of civil
war violence. Instead, the battle for intelligence became a critical determinant of the nature of the conflict. Through its ritual and the attendant
threat of violence, oathing was a means by which Mau Mau successfully
attempted to create a monopoly over information amongst the Kikuyu
population.

Through oaths, Mau Mau coerced the population into a situation in
which Kikuyu would provide reliable information to the insurgents and
be silent when confronted by police and other colonial agents. The success
of this project was seen repeatedly through the coming war, when investigations into the deaths even of ostensible loyalists known locally to be
aiding Mau Mau were met with silence.[169] Those, such as Christians, who
refused to be oathed thus placed the movement in jeopardy and had to

[166] Marilyn Young, 'The American Empire at War,' in *The Barbarisation of Warfare*, ed.
George Kassimeris (London, 2006), 175.
[167] Kalyvas, *Logic of Violence.*
[168] Arjona and Kalyvas, 'Demobilized Combatants,' 42–3.
[169] Anderson, 'Surrogates,' 165.

be eliminated, even if their opposition to oathing was not a manifestation of any connection or sympathy with the colonial regime. Counteroathing was a misguided but deliberate part of attempts to break this silence, but in the absence of protection willing informants were uncommon. The incapacity of the state to protect its supporters undermined its efforts to counter Mau Mau in the earliest stages. In contrast, the insurgents were operating without substantial impediment until early 1953 and able to guarantee the safety of its informants. This asymmetry between the protective and punitive capabilities, or lack thereof, of the two sides meant that fear of being declared a loyalist drove many Kikuyu to take oaths in order to protect themselves.[170]

[170] Luise White, 'Separating the Men From the Boys: Constructions of Gender, Sexuality, and Terrorism in Central Kenya, 1939–1959,' *International Journal of African Historical Studies* 23 (1990), 10.

2

Terror and Counter-Terror

March 1953–April 1954

The Lari Massacres

Mau Mau's control over local communities was at its peak during the first quarter of 1953. In March, the Kenya Police acknowledged the 'impossibility of providing personal police protection to all informers.'[1] The situation in Embu, where the district commissioner admitted that 'the Mau Mau gangs were able to move about without much hindrance,'[2] was similar in much of Central Province. Returning home from his boarding school to Fort Hall for the Easter vacation in 1953, Benson Paul found himself forced to join the insurgency. 'We were forced by the terrorists to go into the forest,' the schoolboy later wrote, 'and as there were no homeguards at that time we had no way of saving ourselves.'[3] With the security forces stretched thinly, opponents of the militants faced an uncertain fate. Any effort to protect most loyalists had to be initiated by loyalists themselves. The embryonic loyalist militia units that later became known as the Home Guard were, in the words of a senior British military officer, a 'confused rabble' and easily outflanked by their opponents.[4] Once the course of events made it imperative for the government to wrest that control from the insurgents, the counterinsurgency campaign lacked

[1] TNA: PRO WO 276/381, Commissioner of Police to Assistant Commissioners of Police Nairobi & Nyeri, & Senior Superintendents of Police Rift Valley, Coast, Nyanza & Northern Provinces, 11 March 1953, 1.
[2] KNA DC/EBU/1/1/12, Embu District Annual Report 1953, 1.
[3] KNA AHC/9/24, Benson G. Paul to Editor, *Kayu ka Embu*, 31 January 1955, 1.
[4] KNA ARC(MAA) 2/5/307 I, Major R.S. Mayers, 'Memorandum on the Re-Organisation of the Kikuyu Resistance Groups,' 26 March 1953, 1.

the will and information to discriminately target coercion against active supporters of Mau Mau. The use of terror by Mau Mau was met in kind.

That change in the course of events was driven by incidents in the village of Lari in the Kiambu district during the final week of March 1953.[5] With both a substantive loyalist faction and a 100-strong Home Guard force to protect it, Lari was in many ways atypical of the broader situation that prevailed across the Central Highlands. Local Mau Mau activists did not enjoy the strategic advantages that their fellow insurgents benefited from elsewhere. Isolated opponents could not be identified and clinically disposed of in the same manner as was the norm at this stage of the war. Instead, a more concerted and less discriminate approach had to be adopted by any insurgents feeling compelled to attack their loyalist opponents. Besides their local Home Guard unit, the loyalists of Lari were initially granted the additional protection of a platoon of the King's African Rifles. The withdrawal of that unit on 25 March triggered perhaps the most significant single event in the entire war.

The following evening, Gitau Ndundu was in his home in Lari with his family. Although a member of the Home Guard, he was off-duty that night. Had he been out on patrol with his fellow Home Guards, he, too, would have been called away from Lari to investigate the murder of a loyalist a few miles away. This deliberate diversion distracted the entire on-duty Home Guard force and left Lari undefended on the evening of 26 March. In their absence, approximately 600 Mau Mau fighters attacked. Between 74 and 100 loyalists and their families died from machete wounds or in huts set on fire. Two-thirds of the victims were women. Gitau's house was one of those targeted, and his 13-year-old daughter, Njambi, was slashed on the shoulder. However, both she and her father were able to escape their assailants and flee from Lari.

The main targets of the attack were clearly ex-Chief Luka Waka-hangare, Chief Makimei Kuria, their families, and their clients. Although Makimei himself survived, he, Luka, and Lari's other loyalists paid a high price for a series of divisive decisions over the previous decade or so. Luka had acquiesced in 1940 to the seizure of land at Tigoni, also in Kiambu, for white settlement. The subsequent resettlement programme at Lari was corrupted in favour of Luka's clients, who in turn with their

---

[5] The material contained in the following passage is taken from the accounts of Anderson, *Histories*, 139–51; Clough, *Memoirs*, 156–7; Furedi, *Mau Mau War*, 122; Rosberg and Nottingham, *Myth of Mau Mau*, 156–7; M. Keith Sorrenson, *Land Reform in the Kikuyu Country: A Study in Government Policy* (Nairobi, 1967), 100.

patron, dominated the local political economy as traders, farmers, councillors, and, as the Emergency began, Home Guards. Lari's dispossessed had reluctantly followed Luka from Tigoni to a life of economic uncertainty and subjugation. Luka's successor as chief, Makimei, contributed to further discontent. Makimei disdainfully refused to welcome the repatriates streaming back to the Native Reserve from the Rift Valley, expelled by frightened European settlers and rejected by clan elders unwilling to assume responsibility for a new wave of landless clients. Gitau was targeted by Mau Mau because he was a tenant of Makimei and a member of the local Home Guard.

Despite surviving that assault by Mau Mau, Gitau soon found his life threatened by the colonial state. The insurgents' attack on Lari was met with a fierce response on two fronts. The first was unleashed by local loyalists seeking vengeance against anyone suspected of involvement in the initial massacre. Perhaps up to 400 members of the local population lost their lives in retributive killings.[6] A second form of revenge was pursued through the courts. Besides the scores killed in the retributive killing over the days following the events of 26 March, hundreds more were rounded up for questioning. Once their cases reached court in a series of mass trials beginning later that same year, Gitau was among those who faced prosecution for his alleged role in the attack on Lari. Gitau was specifically tried for the murder of the two infant children of Makimei's senior headman, Machune Kiranga. The evidence against Gitau was largely provided by his patron, Chief Makimei, who was intent on enacting revenge for the attack on his family. From the witness box, Makimei not only alleged that Gitau had participated in the massacre but also denied that Gitau was a member of his Home Guard unit and that Giatu's home had been attacked. On the basis of Makimei's evidence, Gitau was convicted with 47 co-defendants of murder and sentenced to hang. In a final twist of fate, however, Gitau and his fellow appellants had their convictions quashed on 1 December 1953 after the judges of the Appeal Court scorned Makimei's evidence.[7]

---

[6] See also TNA: PRO CO 822/489, F. Brockway to Secretary of State for the Colonies, 30 April 1953 in which Brockway alleges the killing of 44 people in revenge for the Lari killings.

[7] TNA: PRO CO 822/702, Court of Appeal for Eastern Africa at Nairobi, Criminal Appeals Nos. 339–386 of 1953, 1 December 1953, 24–5 & 28; Anderson, *Histories*, 164–9. For Njambi's evidence, see KNA RR/11/35, Regina v. Chege Mwaura & 51 Others, 29 June 1953, Vol. 8, 859. For Makimei's evidence see KNA RR/11/34, Regina v Chege Mwaura & 51 Others, 29 June 1953, Vol. 7, 765–7.

Although the specifics of Gitau's experience were both unique and extreme, it appears to be representative of a much larger cross-section of Kikuyu society in the first stage of the war. Kikuyu were trapped between the colonial state and the insurgents, both of which presented imminent and potent threats to personal livelihoods and survival. Expressions of agency could quickly be rendered irrelevant if either side doubted the sincerity of an individual's allegiances. The suspicion of loyalists held by the colonial government, encouraged in Gitau's case by the rabid desire for revenge on the part of Makimei, translated into a failure to distinguish friend from foe. Not being a chief, headman, or government servant, Gitau did not belong to the loyalist elite as understood by the colonial government. Instead, Gitau and other loyalists were also left exposed to a colonial government and some elite loyalists who, because of the prevailing sense of fear, suspected all Kikuyu of harbouring Mau Mau sympathies.

Lari remains the conflict's signature event. The initial massacre of loyalists has been repeatedly dissected by historians rightly intent on demonstrating the logic of the initial massacre of loyalists. The long prehistory of the attack on Luka and Makimei's families has been excavated to demonstrate that the first wave of killings were not the senseless acts as represented by the colonial government but instead readily explainable. However, in so doing, the significance of Lari to Kikuyu at large has been somewhat overlooked. As later chapters of this book argue, loyalism progressively became a safer and more attractive position to adopt for Kikuyu. As this process unfolded from mid-1954 on, the massacre of loyalists at Lari was revealed to have played a critical role in the consolidation of an opposition to Mau Mau that in 1953 dared not speak its name.

The enormous propaganda campaign mounted by the colonial government in the aftermath of the massacre saw to it that few, if any, of the population of Kenya remained ignorant of the killings of loyalists.[8] This, of course, also ensured that the retributive killings of hundreds of alleged suspects in the initial massacre were quickly forgotten. The images that lingered in the minds of eventual loyalists were those of the charred bodies of the wives and children of loyalists lying among the embers of their homesteads. On posters, in the newspapers, and on newsreels, pictures of the loyalist victims of Lari assumed a totemic position within the colonial

---

[8] See, for example, 'Watanyongwa kwa Mauaji (Sentenced to Death),' *Mwanamke*, 6 January 1954.

propaganda campaign inside Kenya and elsewhere.[9] To many loyalist eyes, Lari was the defining event of the war. Harry Thuku, for example, wrote that 'my reasons for hating Mau Mau were first, that they killed innocent women and children – sometimes pregnant women.'[10] Mau Mau could never shake off the legacy of Lari. The murder of women and children was hard to equate with a fight for land and freedom. Mau Mau's General Kimbo recognised as much. In a letter sent from the forests to the district commissioner's office in Nyeri, Kimbo threatened an all-out assault on the district over Christmas 1953. The attack would, the general promised, dwarf the assault on Lari. But Kimbo acknowledged that although Mau Mau had been 'ready to kill everybody from babies to old ones,' the guerrillas had recognised such an approach 'is not good.' And although the general concluded his festive greetings with the threat that 'we shall do as [at] Lari in the whole of Kenya' if the counterinsurgency continued, that warning remained unrealised for the remainder of the conflict.[11] But the damage to Mau Mau's reputation had been done.

Fighting Both Sides

The Lari massacres triggered an upsurge in violence, during which both Mau Mau and the colonial government demanded unequivocal support. After Lari and a series of attacks on settler farms, the political costs of inaction on the part of the colonial state were too high for it not to escalate its counterinsurgency campaign. Mau Mau insurgents had little choice but to respond. Between late March 1953 and the middle of 1954, the combatants engaged one another in a series of frequently bloody but brief skirmishes centred on Home Guard posts constructed throughout Central Province. Guerrillas attacked posts under the cover of darkness to eliminate informers and committed loyalist opponents, and to seize scarce supplies. The insurgents then stealthily disappeared back into the nearby forests or concealed themselves among the local population. At the same time, individual Kikuyu sought recourse in violence as they set about conducting their affairs in conditions of civil war. Many Kikuyu refused to align with one side or the other until ultimately necessary, but nevertheless murder and denunciation became a commonplace component of everyday life in the Central Highlands.

[9] Lonsdale, 'Mau Maus of the Mind,' 405.
[10] Thuku, *Thuku*, 69.
[11] TNA: PRO WO 276/399, General Kimbo to DC Nyeri, November/December 1953.

Throughout this period of the war, colonial officials were unable to divine where the sympathies of communities lay. 'It is,' one conceded, 'very hard to say who is a loyal Kikuyu.'[12] Rather than give impetus to efforts towards a more subtle analysis of the conflict within local communities, such confusion on the part of colonial officials instead encouraged the suspicion of all Kikuyu. Settlers insisted, 'Nobody can be declared "loyal" unless and until he has been tested.'[13] No loyalist was, in the early stage of the war at least, considered above suspicion of harbouring sympathies for Mau Mau. Harry Thuku became the subject of groundless attempts by the European political body, the Electors' Union, to have him jailed for being 'one of the co-founders of this menace.'[14] Demonstrations of the divided loyalists of Kikuyu society, however, simply reflected the uncertainty and multiplicity of allegiances in society at large. The division between Mau Mau and their loyalist adversaries in this first phase of the civil war was rarely as stark as generally assumed. The fatal blow, albeit one with a lengthy incubation period, was not struck by the colonial security forces until April 1954. Until then, control of local areas changed with the setting and rising of the sun – government by day and insurgent by night.[15]

Many Kikuyu on both sides identified violence as a way, indeed perhaps the only way, to pursue social, economic, and political interests under the conditions of civil war. The war's violence was not a form of miasma inevitably descending on blameless communities and without warning or agency. Instead, individuals recognised that they had little option but to work with new or adapted institutions that privileged those skilled in the use of violence. Two of those institutions, the chieftaincy and the loyalist militia, the Home Guard, are the subject of the remainder of this chapter. The personnel of neither were uniformly vociferous in their opposition to the insurgency. Like the population from which they were drawn, many chiefs and members of the Home Guard avoided public expressions of allegiance. Moreover, this loyalist faction diversified and widened significantly as the war developed, at first restraining their concerns with Mau Mau until it was safe to give voice to their disquiet.

---

[12] KNA MAA/7/546, Deputy Chief Secretary to Chief Native Commissioner (CNC), 27 October 1953.
[13] RHL Mss Afr s 424, ff.336, O.H. Night to the Editor, *Trans-Nzoia Post*, 25 February 1954, 1.
[14] RHL Mss Afr s 596, box 38 A(1), Canon W.J. Rampley to Lt. General N.M.S. Irwin, 2 August 1954, 1. See also other correspondence in this file relating to Thuku.
[15] Anderson, *Histories*, 255; Sorrenson, *Land Reform*, 109.

Any such attempt to steer a path through the violence became less and less viable as the violence intensified.

As a continuation of their long-standing position at the bottom of hierarchical power structure of the Provincial Administration, chiefs maintained their status as the local representatives of state power throughout the war. Supported by their assistants, the headmen, and the retinues of Tribal Police, a parallel force that answered to their superiors among the Provincial Administration rather than the Kenya Police, the chiefs had an effective presence in all locations of every division of the colony. The chiefs thus made an ideal platform on which to construct a counterinsurgency strategy. Through the war, the chiefs acted as advisors to district commissioners and officers, gathered intelligence, and enforced punitive sanctions imposed on suspected Mau Mau sympathisers. Although this portfolio of duties was consistent across Central Province, the proclivity of individual chiefs towards the military campaign against Mau Mau varied greatly. Few took to their role in the front line of the war against Mau Mau with as much enthusiasm as Samuel Githu of Fort Hall. Appointed during the Emergency, Githu was personally responsible for the deaths of 17 of a 25-strong Mau Mau unit that attacked his Home Guard post. Over the course of the conflict, Githu lost over £1,000 worth of property as a result of his opposition to Mau Mau, but in the process, won a Queen's Recommendation for Brave Conduct.[16] Githu was far from alone in his determined stand against Mau Mau, but some chiefs went beyond the law and vigorously pursued primitive accumulation under the cover provided by the counterinsurgency campaign.

Recalled as the 'Hitler of Kinyona' and as a man who 'could force babes to walk on their feet,'[17] Chief Njiri wa Karanja of Kinyona of Fort Hall was perhaps the most infamous loyalist of all. Njiri was responsible for the massacre at Mununga, the war's worst atrocity, during which approximately 400 civilians were killed over two days in June 1953. In her memoirs, Virginia Blakeslee, a missionary based at the nearby Githumu hospital, recalled that 'billows of smoke rolled heavenward early one morning.' Blakeslee wrote of 'awe-stricken men' coming to the hospital 'speaking in low tones and holding their hands over their mouths.' They told Blakeslee that 'the men of Icamuguthi and Gathukiini, hundreds of them, are lying all about the villages and in the bushes dead. Their villages

---

[16] KNA ARC(MAA) 2/5/311, DC Fort Hall to Director of Information, 11 March 1954, 2.

[17] Ndabiri, 'Chief Njiri,' 35.

have been burned. Their cattle and sheep have been taken. Their gardens
have been destroyed. The women and children have fled to caves and
thickets to hide.' The killing began after Chief Njiri had sent his son,
Thigiru, to supervise the communal forced labour. Led by General Kago,
a group of Mau Mau fighters attacked and decapitated Thigiru. His head
was then delivered to his father. Njiri sent 'all the Home Guards and the
King's African Riflemen stationed at his village to Mununga to kill every
man on the ridge.'[18] But even such an example of brutality concealed a
more complex reality than might at first appear. Although the son of a
senior chief, a headman, and the leader of the local Home Guard unit,
Thigiru was known to be sympathetic to local Mau Mau activists and
may have even given supplies to the insurgents from the local area hiding
out in the forest close to Mununga. Thigiru was not killed by these local
insurgents but by a renegade Mau Mau unit, led by General Kago, passing
through Mununga.[19]

Njiri, Githu, and other similar zealots were, however, representative
merely of one extreme of a spectrum of chiefly loyalty. Not all, indeed not
even most, chiefs gave such unambiguous support to the colonial regime.
Several of the other most senior chiefs attempted to steer a course through
the turmoil for themselves and their communities. Some, such as Muhoya
of Ihururu in the North Tetu division of Nyeri, were notably successful
in treading the middle path between Mau Mau and the government.
Muhoya was apparently the ideal loyalist. Having been a strong supporter
of the government from the 1920s, Muhoya was a proponent of the ban
on clitoridectomy in the 1930s. Moreover, as a large landowner and what
the colonial government liked to call a progressive farmer, Muhoya was
an advocate of agricultural development in the late 1940s. In the years
following World War II, Muhoya was a patron of co-operatives, had
attempted to enact an ad hoc land consolidation programme, and began
dairy farming with his own herd of grade cattle.[20] It is not surprising,
then, that Muhoya's Home Guards were among the first to be formed
and subsequently armed in April 1953.[21] However, Muhoya's loyalty
during the Emergency was far from unequivocal. He later enigmatically
described himself as having been 'among many who constantly strived
to change people's mind to respect law and order and rehabilitate them

[18] Virginia Blakeslee, *Beyond the Kikuyu Curtain* (Chicago, 1956), 254–5.
[19] Anderson, 'Surrogates,' 163–8.
[20] Sorrenson, *Land Reform*, 136.
[21] 'Rifles Issued to Loyal Kikuyus – and System of Home Guard Strongpoints Being Built,'
      East African Standard, 21 April 1953, 1.

FIGURE 5. Chiefs Wambugu (l) and Njiri wa Karanja (r), undated. Reproduced with permission of Kenya National Archives.

to normal life.'[22] That reference to persuasion was no euphemism for coercion and instead an accurate description of the nature of the conflict in Muhoya's home location.

[22] KNA VP/1/104, Senior Chief Muhoya Kagumba to PC Central, 28 May 1963.

As with Thigiru and local Mau Mau units at Mununga, ties between
Home Guards and insurgents restrained the conflict in and around Ihururu. The Home Guards in North Tetu were, in the words of one local
police officer, 'in sympathy with Mau Mau and, actively, one way or
another, assist them.'[23] The leaders of the two factions, Muhoya and
Dedan Kimathi, further consolidated this trend. Kimathi had worked
with Muhoya in the Ihururu Dairyman Cooperative Society in 1949, and
the Senior Chief's sons were Kimathi's age-mates.[24] Kimathi and members of Muhoya's Home Guard had gone to school with one another at
Tumutumu.[25] During communications between Kimathi and the Provincial Administration regarding possible negotiations in 1954, the guerrilla
leader identified Muhoya as a go-between.[26] 'If you want to live try and
behave like Chief Muhoya,' Kimathi wrote to a headman in 1954. 'I
mean you should be neutral in this war.'[27] Although suspicious of the
exact nature of the relationship between the chief and the Mau Mau general, the government was unable to find evidence to remove Muhoya. The
closest the elderly chief came to dismissal was when he was placed on
leave by the government in a scheme intended to allow leading loyalists a
few days of relaxation and non-taxing propaganda work at the Coast or
in Nyanza.[28] Muhoya, however, was sent to Mombasa as a warning.[29]
This was as far as the local administration could afford to antagonise him,
however. The elder statesman of Nyeri politics remained in his post until
independence. Not all chiefs, however, had sufficient poise and influence
to pursue this middle path with any great success. Most who displayed
similar tendencies were swiftly replaced.

Even chiefs struggled to exercise agency in any meaningful way through
the war. Those chiefs, lacking either the necessary skills or the inspiration to implement the counterinsurgency strategies and tactics decreed
from Nairobi, were expected to quickly adhere. In particular, chiefs were
expected to arrest significant numbers of alleged Mau Mau supporters.

---

[23] KNA VQ/1/51, Assistant Superintendent of Police, Provincial Special Branch, Nyeri Area
to PC Central, 16 June 1954, 1.
[24] Duncan Ngatia Muhoya, unrecorded interview with author, Ihururu, Nyeri, 7 February
2004.
[25] Duncan Ngatia Muhoya, Sihar Gitahi Ribai & Kariuki Kiruma, interviews with author,
Ihururu, Nyeri, 7 February 2004.
[26] Dedan Kimathi to DC Nyeri, 21 May 1954 in Maina wa Kinyatti, *Kenya's Freedom
Struggle: The Dedan Kimathi Papers* (London, 1987), 58–9.
[27] Dedan Kimathi to Headman, 1954 in Ibid., 62.
[28] KNA VP/1/86, DC Nyeri to PC Coast, 23 August 1954.
[29] I am grateful to John Nottingham for this information.

Low arrest rates were interpreted by the colonial government as indicative of a chief's sympathy towards the insurgency. Those who either refused to increase arrests or were unable to do so because of a lack of intelligence or insurgent activity in their home areas faced significant sanctions. Punishment most commonly took the form of removal from office, but in cases of suspected collusion, chiefs were sometimes detained. Of the Kiambu chiefs in office at the start of the Emergency, half had been replaced by the close of 1954 because of their reluctance to prosecute the counter-insurgency with the required enthusiasm.[30] Chiefs in Embu proved to be exceptionally unreliable,[31] a problem most acute in the Ndia division of the district, where one chief was thought to be the principal local Mau Mau recruiter.[32] No member of the chiefly community epitomised this stance more than ex-Senior Chief Koinange, discussed further in the Conclusion, detained at the outset of the Emergency for his support of the militants.[33] Koinange, though, was far from alone.

The best illustration of the pressures placed on chiefs took place among a family Koinange knew well, the Njonjos of Kiambu. The Njonjos are still remembered in Kenya as having been among the most prominent loyalists despite the patriarch, Chief Josiah Njonjo, having been suspected of having taken two Mau Mau oaths.[34] Such suspicions did not, however, preclude Josiah from joining a number of chiefs from across the colony in a visit to Britain in June 1953 to attend the coronation of Queen Elizabeth II. While Josiah was away, his third son, Lewis Mungai, was appointed to act as chief during his father's absence. Mungai was at the time a headman in his father's division of Kiambu. While in that post, Mungai had come under pressure from British officials because of his low rate of arrests. The presence of his father and the high regard in which Josiah was held by the colonial government allowed Mungai to deflect this attention to a certain degree. However, the coercion increased immediately after his father's departure for Britain in mid-May. Yet, despite lacking the protection of his father, Mungai continued to refuse to

[30] KNA DC/KBU/1/43, Kiambu District Annual Report 1952, 6; KNA DC/KBU/1/44, Kiambu District Annual Report 1953, 5; KNA DC/KBU/1/45, Kiambu District Annual Report 1954, 7.
[31] KNA DC/EBU/1/1/11, Embu District Annual Report 1952, 4–5 & KNA DC/EBU/1/1/12, draft of Embu District Annual Report, 1953, 5–7.
[32] KNA DC/EBU/1/2/4, DO Ndia, 'Handing Over Notes,' June 1956, 31.
[33] Clough, 'Koinange,' 57–86; Koinange, *Koinange*.
[34] TNA: PRO WO 276/388, Kiambu District Intelligence Committee Summary for the week ending 13 June 1953, 3.

approve indiscriminate detentions of the young adult men of his division. Instead, without hesitation, he requested to be relieved of his duties, but this was rejected by the Provincial Administration. After just seven days as acting chief, on the morning of 21 March, Mungai took a shotgun into a lavatory at his home and shot himself.[35]

Mungai, Koinange, Njiri, and Muhoya represented different points on the spectrum of allegiances during the conflict. The civil war forced individuals to adopt positions and roles from which they may have ordinarily recoiled. Survival necessitated such behaviour. The more senior the chief was, the more likely he was to at least attempt to temper the storm directed at Mau Mau sympathisers. These more senior chiefs were also likely to be more successful in such actions because of their influence within the structures of colonial rule and ties to local communities. Younger chiefs had no such power and were easily replaced at no great cost to the regime. Without the bargaining chip of local influence built up over the preceding years and decades, those appointed during the Emergency proved to be the most enthusiastic and unequivocal supporters of the government.

The Home Guard

The desire for survival was no less a significant motivation for action among loyalists operating beneath the chiefs. Until mid-1954, most of these individuals expressed their opposition to Mau Mau through membership of the Home Guard. The militia group started life in July 1952, when the Provincial Administration in Fort Hall attempted to organise self-protection groups of likely targets of Mau Mau's violence.[36] By September, the groups had spread to neighbouring Nyeri. There, Chief Muhoya and Catholic missionaries, again encouraged by the local officers of the Provincial Administration, took the lead in establishing the first Home Guard units.[37] In the settled districts of the White Highlands, settlers quickly formed paid Home Guard-style units from their labour force as part of their efforts to protect themselves and their property

[35] KNA MAC/KEN/34/2, 'Diary of the Kenya Crisis – Appendix 10,' 3; TNA: PRO WO 276/388, Kiambu District Intelligence Committee Summary for week ending 22 June 1953, 2.

[36] RHL Mss Afr s 424, ff.166–187, J. A. Rutherford, 'History of the Kikuyu Guard,' 1957, 3.

[37] KNA VQ/1/30, DC Nyeri to Senior Supt of Police Nyeri, 1 December 1952.

from insurgent attack.[38] To anoint the militia with a veil of autochthony, in Nyeri, the Home Guard units were initially intended to replicate nineteenth-century methods of Kikuyu military organisation that had, the Nyeri District commissioner believed, patrolled home areas against Maasai raiding parties.[39] In truth, the Home Guard introduced in Central Province during 1952 had a more immediate template. The militia bore most resemblance to the Home Guard units operating in Turkana and elsewhere along Kenya's troubled northern border from the 1940s. There, under the guidance of chiefs and headmen, Home Guards defended Turkana settlements from Merille cattle raiders.[40] The Central Province Home Guards, however, quickly abandoned this purely defensive function and instead became significant actors in the development of the conflict.

The first event that instigated a change in the character of the Home Guard was the declaration of a State of Emergency in October 1952. With the Kenya Police and army concentrating on the destruction of the growing guerrilla army in the forests, the Home Guard was expected to act as the government's eyes and ears in the Native Reserve of Central Province. Yet, despite this clear linkage between the colonial state in its various guises and the militia, the Provincial Administration was reluctant to play any other role than cheerleader in the first months of the Emergency. As had been the case in Nyeri from September 1952, district commissioners and their junior officers were happy to allow chiefs and missions to take the leading role in formation of local units.[41] Such attitudes were a reflection of official policy. Although senior government figures urged the Provincial Administration in the Central and Rift Valley Provinces to push loyalists to form Home Guard units,[42] the governor and his district commissioners in Central Provinces agreed at a meeting held in late November that 'these groups must not be treated as a

---

[38] RHL Mss Afr s 746, J. Beffinger to M. Gotha, 25 December 1952.
[39] KNA ARC(MAA) 2/5/307 I, DC Nyeri to General Hinde, 11 February 1953; RHL Mss s 746, box 12, file 5, minutes of meeting of Standing Committee on Law & Order, 12 February 1953, 1–2.
[40] KNA DC/LDW/2/18/17, DO Lokitaung to DC Turkana, 6 December 1942; DO Lokitaung, 'Lokitaung Sub-District –.303 Rifle Holders in Addition to Kenya Police, Tribal Police and E.T. Police,' 2 March 1943; DC Turkana to Chief Secretary, 24 February 1944; DO Lokitaung to DC Turkana, 24 December 1947.
[41] RHL Mss Afr s 424, ff.166–187, J. A. Rutherford, 'History of the Kikuyu Guard,' 1957, 5; Kenya, *Loyalists* 13.
[42] KNA VQ/1/30, CNC to PCs Central & Rift Valley, 24 November 1952.

Government-engineered organisation.'[43] The unclear limit of state influence over Home Guards was a defining characteristic of the force throughout its existence.

By the New Year, the loyalty and size of Home Guard units differed greatly from place to place. Geographical variations, coupled with the unproven loyalties of militia members, meant that the Home Guard 'cannot yet be regarded as a practical force to be reckoned with.'[44] The patchy development of the Home Guard reflected the importance of local entrepreneurs in the formation of the local militia groups and the immediacy of the insurgent threat. In Kiambu, the slow development of units was a product of both an absence of such entrepreneurs – evidence of 'spineless' loyalists in the eyes of the government – and the low level of incidents involving Mau Mau in the district.[45] Over the first months of the war, Home Guard units were also slow to develop in both Embu and Meru for similar reasons. Yet, in Fort Hall, Chief Njiri had a unit of 500 men under his control alone.[46] The embryonic units were best organised in Nyeri, where by late March, certain units were acting independently and effectively against groups of Mau Mau fighters.[47] Unlike Kiambu, Embu, and Meru, the Nyeri Home Guards had enthusiastic patrons who sensed an imminent threat from Mau Mau. The Nyeri Home Guard was made up of men like Arphaxad Migwi Wamahiu, a former pupil at the Tumutumu Presbyterian mission school with 20 years of clerical experience. Migwi joined the Home Guard in Kirimukuyu in Nyeri during October 1952, before joining an interrogation team in Nanyuki in January 1953.[48] Migwi's fellow Home Guards in the first months of the Emergency in Nyeri were 'generally progressive farmers, school-teachers, traders, etc., whose farms and businesses are suffering seriously by the absence on Home Guard duty.'[49] In addition to the Home Guard, several

43 KNA VQ/1/30, DC Nyeri to Senior Supt. of Police Nyeri, 1 December 1952.
44 KNA ARC(MAA) 2/5/307 I, Capt. O. H. Waring, 'Details of the Home Guards Operating in the Four Main Districts,' January 1953. See also KNA VQ/1/30, PC Central to CNC, 27 December 1952.
45 KNA DC/KBU/1/43, Kiambu District Annual Report 1952, 1–2.
46 KNA ARC(MAA) 2/5/307 I, Capt. O. H. Waring, 'Details of the Home Guards Operating in the Four Main Districts,' January 1953. See also KNA VQ/1/30, PC Central to CNC, 27 December 1952.
47 See, for example, RHL Mss Afr s 746, box 12, file 6, 'Incident Report as at 11 a.m. on Tuesday, 24th March 1953'; ibid., 26.
48 KNA DC/NYK/3/16/36, Arphaxad Migwi Wamahiu to DC Nanyuki, 3 May 1955.
49 KNA ARC(MAA) 2/5/307 I, DC Nyeri to General Hinde, 11 February 1953.

thousand joined informal and entirely unregulated so-called 'resistance groups' in Nyeri and Fort Hall,[50] which later became absorbed into the expanding official militia.[51]

The Home Guard became more formalised over the course of the first three months of 1953.[52] By February, Fort Hall had more than 1,700 Home Guards.[53] A system of rewards, mainly food but sometimes money, was introduced. Communal labour was put to work building huts for Home Guard members close to police stations, chiefs' camps, and mission buildings.[54] Exemption from the 20 shillings Emergency tax, introduced in the final weeks of 1952 to contribute to the cost of anti-Mau Mau operations, was an additional benefit.[55] In February, the first signs of future rewards could be found in the promise of the Nyeri district commissioner to a rally of Home Guards that 'after all this, you will continue to work together as local committees, to assist the Government and to advise yourselves how best law and order can be maintained in your areas, and farming and other progress restored and furthered.'[56] But these benefits were unrealised for another three years. The district commissioner was envisioning what loyalism would become, not what the Kikuyu opponents of Mau Mau actually were in early 1953 – a disorganised grouping lacking incentives, fearful of insurgent attack, and suspected by the state of secretly harbouring pro-Mau Mau sentiments.

The failure of the Home Guard at Lari to prevent the initial attack and the subsequent upsurge in violence threw into stark relief the shortcomings of the local militias. State-instigated reforms of the militias increased. Just a week after the massacre at Lari, the decision to arm the Home Guard and to appoint European officers to oversee the units was made. The intention was to enable the force to defend loyalists more effectively

---

[50] The irony of terming a colonial collaborative movement a resistance group has been noted in David Maughan-Brown, *Land, Freedom and Fiction: History and Ideology in Kenya* (London, 1985), 97.

[51] For brief details of these groups, see KNA VQ/1/30, Capt. G.W. Anderson, 'Suggestions for the Organisation of Resistance Groups,' 4 February 1953; DC Fort Hall to PC Central, 23 February 1953, 2; DC Nyeri, 'Home Guards,' 11 February 1953, 1; DC Nyeri, 'Resistance Groups – Nyeri District,' 11 February 1953.

[52] See, for example, RHL Mss Perham 467, file 3, minutes of meeting of Home Guard leaders, Nyeri district, 21 February 1953.

[53] KNA VQ/1/30, DC Fort Hall to PC Central, 23 February 1953.

[54] KNA VQ/1/30, DC Fort Hall to DOs Fort Hall, 9 February 1953.

[55] Kenya, *Loyalists*, 29.

[56] RHL Mss Perham 467, DC Nyeri, 'Address to Home-Guards, Nyeri District,' 21 February 1953, 2.

and play a more proactive role in the war.[57] Shortly afterwards, the Home Guard in the reserves of Central Province was formally brought under the control of the Provincial Administration. The force came to be known at that point as the Kikuyu Guard in the Kikuyu districts of Kiambu, Fort Hall, and Nyeri. Their peers in Embu district were known as the Embu Guard and in Meru district as the Meru Guard. Similar units were established in the Rift Valley and Southern Provinces, along with other groups, such as Farm Guards, to provide additional protection for European-owned farms in the White Highlands.[58] To avoid confusion, all militia groups professing (although not necessarily practicing) opposition to Mau Mau, formed from the civilian population and armed by the state, are referred to here collectively as Home Guard.

The newly organised Home Guard in Central Province was supervised by new district officers who were in turn answerable to the district commissioners.[59] The militia was entrusted with a more systematic role within the overall colonial counterinsurgency campaign. Chief among its duties were the protection of prominent loyalists, the gathering of intelligence on Mau Mau activities, and the denial of food and other supplies to the insurgents. As the war developed, the Home Guard steadily assumed responsibility for policing the reserves, thereby allowing the army and police to concentrate on military operations in the forests and Nairobi. Because of concerns among the military regarding Home Guard discipline and fears of its development into a private army, Home Guards did not see active combat in the forest areas reserved for military and police operations.[60] The Home Guard was given the legal status of Special Tribal Police, however, which gave its members enhanced powers of

---

57 KNA VQ/1/30, minutes of 'Organising and Strengthening of Home Guard and Resistance Groups in the Reserve' meeting, 3 April 1953.

58 See correspondence in KNA ARC(MAA) 2/5/309 for details of the genesis of these various organisations. See for details of the formation of the Rift Valley Home Guard, KNA ARC(MAA) 2/5/309, Provincial Director Kikuyu Home Guard, 'A Guide to Officers Commanding Guards in the Rift Valley Province,' appendix to Provincial Director Kikuyu Home Guard Rift Valley Province, 'Rift Valley Province, Kikuyu Home Guards Progress Report No.3,' 6 August 1953. See also Tamarkin, 'Loyalists in Nakuru,' 247–61.

59 RHL Mss Afr s 1580, File XI, Office of the Director of Operations, 'Emergency Directive No. 3: Kikuyu Guard,' April 1953, 2.

60 TNA: PRO CO 822/497, Commander in Chief East Africa, 'Emergency Directive No.8: Role of and Cooperation with the Kikuyu, Embu and Meru Guards,' 15 July 1953, 4; TNA: PRO CO 822/692, Governor to Secretary of State for the Colonies, 30 June 1953; Brigadier J Orr, Commander 70 Brigade quoted in RHL Mss Afr s 1580, file II, minutes of meeting held in Nyeri, 29 May 1954.

arrest and the right to shoot in particular defined areas. However, when on regular duty, Home Guards did not have any greater legal jurisdiction to arrest, detain, or shoot suspects than any other citizen.[61]

Although the government remained reluctant to assume full responsibility for overseeing the militia's daily activities, over the weeks following the Lari massacre, the force was given an overhaul, to compensate for its haphazard origins. By early May 1953, the militia had expanded from local self-protection groups into a force whose organisational structure resembled that of the Home Guard developed in Malaya. Although much smaller – the Kenyan force only numbered a tenth of the 240,000 Malayans recruited into the Home Guard there[62] – a clear hierarchy connecting local units to central government through the Provincial Administration was delineated in accordance with the model established during the fight against Communist insurgents in Southeast Asia. Colonel Philip Morcombe was recruited as the force's director, a role similar to that he had performed in Malaya.[63] This process of formalisation of the Home Guard not only replicated the Malayan model but institutionalised colonial Kenya's distinctive marker, the settlers, within the East African campaign. In Kenya, the presumed need for European officers to oversee local units of Home Guards was frequently met by the recruitment of younger members of the settler community to serve as district officers (Home Guard) in every division of every district in Central Province. The Home Guard thus provided the settler community and the Provincial Administration with substantial influence over the nature of the counterinsurgency effort in the localities. The Administration was fiercely protective of this hard-won stake in the military campaign. The district commissioner of Nyeri wrote that 'nothing should be said or done to take the authority of the Administration over the [Home Guard] away from us and the Chiefs.'[64] These ties between loyalists, the officials of the Provincial Administration, and the settler community had a profound influence on the conduct of the Home Guards.

---

[61] KNA ARC(MAA) 2/5/309, Lieutenant Colonel GSO I to DD. Ops. (Deputy Director of Operations), 12 March 1954.

[62] James Corum, *Training Indigenous Forces in Counter-Insurgency: A Tale of Two Insurgencies* (Carlisle PA, 2006), 22–3. See also Tim Harper, *The End of Empire and the Making of Malaya* (Cambridge, 1999), 94–194.

[63] Kenya, *Loyalists*, 17–8. The head of the Home Guard in Rift Valley province, Colonel Henfrey, had similar experiences in Malaya and Burma. See KNA ARC(MAA) 2/5/309, PC Rift Valley to Director of Operations, 24 June 1953.

[64] KNA VQ/1/30, DC Nyeri to PC Central, 4 July 1953.

War of the Home Guard Posts

Recruitment to the Home Guard steadily increased from April 1953. At its height in March 1954, 25,600 were serving in the force in Central Province,[65] a figure slightly higher than the peak number Mau Mau's forest fighters reached at the end of 1953.[66] Although overwhelmingly a male force, women were recruited in Fort Hall during 1954 to interrogate other women suspected of Mau Mau involvement.[67] Besides the regular force, large numbers of irregulars, often teachers and government employees, participated in Home Guard activities with varying degrees of enthusiasm. In some cases, the entire adult population of localities, male and female, were compelled to join patrols of the locales during the night.[68] To protect and house the Home Guard, a network of heavily fortified guard posts that, tracking the spread of the war north and east, spread out from Kiambu during 1953.[69] Overlooked by a watchtower and two corner bastions, the posts each housed a unit of Home Guards 25 to 60 men strong,[70] with up to 200 civilians. Loyalists flocked to their local post for protection from insurgent attacks.[71] Mass arrests by the Home Guards further meant that the posts housed dozens of suspected Mau Mau sympathisers awaiting interrogation or onward transportation to detention camps or courts.[72]

---

[65] KNA MAA/7/761, minute from 'F' to CNC & Secretary for African Affairs, 3 March 1954, 1.

[66] Anderson estimates the number of Mau Mau fighters in the forests at the end of 1953 to be in the region of 18,000–24,000 (Anderson, *Histories*, 244).

[67] KNA AHC/9/52, "Home Guard' Wakikuyu Wanawake (Kikuyu Women's Home Guard),' *Mwanamke*, 11 August 1954, 1.

[68] Stephen Murocha & James Mutgi, interviews with the author, Chogoria, South Meru, 15 September 2003; Celestino Kirengeni, interview with the author, Chogoria, South Meru, 18 September 2003.

[69] The following details of the guard posts are taken from KNA ARC(MAA) 2/5/307 I, Director of Kikuyu Guard to PC Central & DCs Kiambu, Fort Hall, Nyeri, Embu and Meru, 11 August 1953 & Kenya, *Loyalists*, 40.

[70] KNA ARC(MAA) 2/5/307 I, PC Central to DC Kiambu, 16 May 1953; Director of Kikuyu Guard to PC Central & DCs Kiambu, Fort Hall, Nyeri, Embu and Meru, 11 August 1953.

[71] KNA ARC(MAA) 2/5/307 II, DC Nyeri to PC Central, 7 October 1953; Duncan Ngatia Muhoya, Sihar Githahi Ribai & Kariuki Kiruma, interviews with the author, Ihururu, Nyeri, 7 February 2004.

[72] TNA: PRO CO 822/480, Governor's Deputy to the Secretary of State for the Colonies, 22 May 1953; TNA: PRO WO 276/388, Kiambu District Intelligence Summary for week ending 4 July 1953, 1.

From late March 1953 until the middle of 1954, the combatants engaged one another in a series of frequently bloody but brief skirmishes centred around these Home Guard posts. An official history of loyalists represented this period in terms of a noble Home Guard living in constant fear of attack, bravely repelling the invading Mau Mau hordes that periodically descended from the forests.[73] Pro-colonial propaganda describing one attack on the loyalist stronghold of Ichichi, Fort Hall, declared that 'a mob of screaming terrorists spent an entire night throwing themselves at the barbed wire while the heavily outnumbered garrison beat off one charge after another.'[74] Rarely does close examination of the evidence support such an interpretation,[75] not least because, in the words of one district officer, many Home Guard 'were so frightened under fire that they invariably ran away.'[76] Successful insurgent raids against the Home Guard posts were often assisted by those inside, who would usher in Mau Mau attackers. Once within the compounds, the attacking guerrillas then targeted particular individuals, often chiefs or headmen, within the post. The attack on the Kinanjogo guard post in Mathira on 4 October 1953 was a typical example. The post was under the leadership of Mesharam, a teacher at the local Presbyterian mission school. On the night of the attack, 27 Home Guards and 35 other loyalists were inside the post. At about 9 o'clock, Mau Mau fighters were heard outside the perimeter calling 'Come out! Come out!' Some of the post's inhabitants let the insurgents in, and most of their fellow militia members simply walked away. Just two Home Guards were killed in the incident.[77] Home Guard posts were not in many cases strongholds of loyalty.

As this increasingly bitter conflict developed, the makeup of the Home Guard changed profoundly. The onset of the war initially triggered a series of explosions along the preexisting fault lines of Kikuyu society. Whether the most salient fault line was one of class, political allegiances, generation, religion, or any other form of historic grievance was contingent

---

[73] Colony and Protectorate of Kenya, *History of the Loyalists*, 29–50.
[74] A. Lavers, *Kikuyu Who Fight Mau Mau*, 26.
[75] One notable exception to the argument set out here would be the attack on the Othaya Home Guard and police posts described in D. M. Anderson, *Histories of the Hanged*, 151; M. S. Clough, *Mau Mau Memoirs*, 153; H. K. Wachanga, *The Swords of Kirinyaga*, 60–2.
[76] KNA MAA/7/233, 'Tour Notes No.11: Colonel A. Morcombe – 15th-16th December 1953,' 2.
[77] TNA: PRO ARC(MAA) 2/5/307 III, DC Nyeri to PC Central, 7 October 1953.

FIGURE 6. Home Guard post, Kiajogu, Nyeri, 1953. Reproduced with permission of Kenya National Archives.

on the specific local setting in which violence broke out. Events at Lari make a good, albeit extreme, example of this process. However, once violence took hold within local communities and armed factions established a local presence, entirely new processes were set in motion. The perpetration of violence and, more importantly, shared experiences of victimisation created new factions within the politics of Central Province that paid little heed to prior cleavages. Individual Kikuyu sought allies to enact revenge, to access the resources necessary for personal security, and to pursue personal advancement in the conditions of war. These new groupings cut across the political, economic, and social boundaries that had divided the population of the region before the onset of the conflict.

For just these reasons, the profile of Home Guards changed rapidly as the violence grew through 1953. Initially, the Home Guard resembled that described by Sorrenson in his *Land Reform in the Kikuyu Country*. Sorrenson cites a study of one Home Guard unit at Githunguri, Kiambu, conducted by its district officer, J. D. Campbell, in August 1953. Campbell stated that the unit was overwhelmingly drawn from the elder sections of society and wealthy, in stark contrast to the rebels of Mau Mau.[78] Sorrenson assumes that this group was representative of loyalists more generally throughout Central Province during the whole of the war. However, other data contradicts such extrapolation. Informants were less willing to distinguish the members of Home Guard units on the basis of age, status, or wealth.[79] Similarly, a unit of Home Guards examined by Kershaw shows that unit, also from Kiambu, to be generally between 26 and 40 years of age, poorly educated, and subsistence or peasant farmers.[80] The ranks of loyalism came to contain thousands of such landless and land poor, but largely silent, loyalists once the cycle of violence took hold of Kikuyu society. The elitist Home Guard quickly became more representative of the population at large. By July 1953, with the war at its height, the declining average age of guardsmen was readily apparent.[81] Campbell's unit at Githunguri was an exception, a remnant of an earlier period of the war.

Although individuals' lived, personal experience of violence pushed Kikuyu towards either loyalism or insurgency, it is important not to exaggerate the agency actors possessed. Recruitment into the Home Guard was a decentralised process informed by local pressures and actors, during

---

[78] Sorrenson, *Land Reform*, 107–8. The original document is to be found in KNA ARC(MAA) 2/5/307 II, DO Kiambu, 'Survey of K.G. Position, Githunguri Division, Kiambu Division as on 14th August, 1953.'

[79] Richard Kanampiu Githae & Stephen Murocha, interviews with author, Chogoria, South Meru, 15 September 2003; Celestino Kirengeni, interview with the author, Chogoria, South Meru, 18 September 2003; Duncan Ngatia Muhoya, Sihar Gitahi Ribai & Kariuki Kiruma, interviews with author, Ihururu, Nyeri, 7 February 2004.

[80] Kershaw, *Mau Mau From Below*, 327–8.

[81] TNA: PRO CO 822/692, Governor to Secretary of State for the Colonies, 7 July 1953, 3.

which the recruits themselves had varying levels of agency. Ostensibly, recruitment to the formalised Home Guard was to follow the precedents set in July 1952. The first units were formed around a core committee of known local loyalists who conducted the necessary screening of applicants.[82] In truth, practice varied greatly from place to place. There were some areas where recruitment was in line with recommended guidelines, for example, in Ndia in Embu, where the units were intended to form a 'corps d'elite.'[83] Very different recruitment methods were employed elsewhere. Chief Heman M'Mbui, of Miiriga Mieru in Meru, recruited into his Home Guards 'one or two known "bad young men" on the principle that they might as well do their thuggery on the side of law and order and in any case he knows what they are up to!'[84] In Kangema, Fort Hall, up to 30 percent of the Home Guards were compulsorily enlisted. The district officer wrote, 'Most [Home Guards], do not in fact join the [Home Guard] voluntarily but are persuaded into it by a variety of methods. Originally the method had to be pure press gang techniques or we should never have got started.' Through their participation in the war in one of the most violent divisions of the entire province, the conscripts became 'so thoroughly implicated' with the Government that leaving the Home Guard was not a practicable option. Interestingly, Kagamoini guard post was considered to be manned by the most able Home Guard in Kangema. The recruits there were recruited 'by heavy handed methods' from a pool of 'ex Mau Mau thugs.'[85] Bearing in mind these origins, the violent and frequently criminal actions of Home Guards in the war are not, therefore, particularly surprising.

Although, as argued later, entrusted with counter-terror, most Home Guards did not embrace that role at first. The reliance on tools of coercion on the part of loyalists entrusted with combating Mau Mau became the norm only later in the war. In the conflict's first months, many Home Guards instead attempted to prevent violence for as long as possible. In late 1952 and through much of 1953, Home Guards repeatedly assisted Mau Mau units. Such behaviour, Kiambu's district commissioner admitted, was 'all too frequent.'[86] Mathira in Nyeri and Ndia in Embu were

[82] RHL Mss s 1915, 'Interview/Discussion on the Mau Mau Emergency in Kenya with Sir Frank Loyd, Robin Wainwright and Dick Wilson,' 12 January 1984, 20.
[83] TNA: PRO WO 276/394, Embu District Intelligence Summary for week ending 3 December 1953, 4.
[84] KNA VQ/1/30, telegram, DC Meru to PC Central, 8 January 1953.
[85] KNA ARC(MAA) 2/5/307 II, DO Kangema to DC Fort Hall, 23 August 1953.
[86] KNA ARC(MAA) 2/5/307 II, DC Kiambu to PC Central, 24 August 1953.

identified as the two divisions in Central Province where the Home Guards were most likely to sympathise with Mau Mau.[87] This was no localised phenomenon; across Central Province, Home Guards were suspected of providing Mau Mau units with ammunition.[88] During April 1953, in Chura division, Kiambu, one particular group of Mau Mau activists were known to have pledged particular 'antagonism to the Home Guard, and to report loyalists for execution.' The same group made a concerted but futile attempt to attack the Tiekunu guard post, which was under the command of Chief Hinga. However, it was also known that, when the insurgents were moving around the division, they were accommodated by Head-man Nyoro's Home Guard.[89] During November 1953, Home Guards in Embu participated in an attack on a lorry carrying Mau Mau suspects rounded up during mass interrogations, freed its cargo, and abducted and killed a Tribal Policeman escorting the detainees.[90] In Gatundu, again in Kiambu, in December 1953, a Home Guard patrol stumbled across a group of six Mau Mau fighters. After discussions between the two groups, which established that the Mau Mau unit was far better armed, the Home Guards 'took to their holes, remaining concealed until the gang had gone its merry way.'[91] While under interrogation following his surrender to the security forces, a former Mau Mau oath administrator stated that the Home Guard in Embu was generally cooperative and sold supplies to the insurgents.[92] At Gituaru in Kiambu, members of the Home Guard took the profits of a beer-brewing enterprise to imprisoned Mau Mau activists.[93] In essence, such practices were critical parts of locally negoti-ated attempts to prevent the occurrence of violence within communities.

Allegiances crystallised only after the onset of violent conflict within each community at various points through 1953. Neutrality and ambi-guity were impossible to sustain in the long term. The arrival of the war

---

[87] KNA ARC(MAA) 2/5/307 II, Assistant Superintendent of Police, Provincial Special Branch to PC Central, 17 August 1953.
[88] KNA ARC(MAA) 2/5/307 III, Director of Kikuyu Guard to PC Central & DCs Kiambu, Fort Hall, Nyeri, Embu & Meru, 4 December 1953.
[89] TNA: PRO WO 276/388, Kiambu District Intelligence Summary for week ending 25 April 1953, 2–3.
[90] TNA: PRO WO 276/394, Embu District Intelligence Summary for the week ending 19 November 1953, 4.
[91] TNA: PRO WO 276/388, Kiambu District Intelligence Summary for the week ending 19 December 1953, 2.
[92] TNA: PRO WO 276/400, Captain [surname illegible], Special Branch, Embu to Military Intelligence Officer, Central Province, 17 November 1953.
[93] TNA: PRO WO 276/388, Kiambu District Intelligence Summary for the week ending 15 August 1953, 2.

in each locality triggered a collapse in the range of available strategies for the settlement of disputes between neighbours and family members. The authority of institutions available to facilitate peaceful arbitration was usurped entirely by that of individuals skilled in the use of violence and institutions attuned to the prevailing climate of conflict and dispute. Violence and denunciation became the most readily available methods of settling disagreements among individuals, families, and clans. In other words, to borrow Kalyvas' term, the violence of the conflict became privatised as individuals assumed the labels of Mau Mau or loyalist to pursue rivals who had declared for the other group.[94]

Once reinforced by perpetration and victimisation of violence, these labels assumed a degree of permanence not apparent at the beginning of the war. One senior police officer explained much of the violence committed by the Home Guard as the result of 'the desire to settle personal scores.'[95] This leant a high degree of intimacy to the violence, as with many other civil wars in which the same mechanisms are observable. With two accomplices, Kiara Wanjiri killed his brother, Ngugi, in the latter's hut in Gatundu, Kiambu, on 21 February 1954 after a family dispute. Ngugi's body was dismembered and buried in a shallow grave half a mile from his home.[96] One of the earliest independent successful ambushes carried out by a Home Guard unit on its own initiative was described by the authorities as 'the climax of a family vendetta' in Kairuthi, Nyeri.[97] Whereas land disputes, in particular, would have been referred to the courts prior to the Emergency, during the conflict, alternative methods of resolution were used. Simeon Kimani Kairu was an elder of the Presbyterian Church and a well-known opponent of Mau Mau in Makungu, Embu. On the night of 11 October 1953, Simeon and his half-brother Mburungu were inside their hut when it was set on fire. Mburungu escaped, but Simeon was cut down by machetes wielded by his assailants as he attempted to flee the blaze. One of those convicted, Kahoni Gachenga, was a fellow member of the local Presbyterian mission. Simeon had emerged victorious from a land dispute with his other killer, Maina Kanyugi, just three months prior to his death.[98] Over half

---

[94] Kalyvas, *Logic of Violence*, 362–3.
[95] RHL Mss Afr s 1694, K. Hadingham to Provincial Commissioner, Central Province, 14 December 1954, 2.
[96] KNA MLA/1/846, CC 170/1954, 'Kariuki Chege, Mugo Kariuki & Kiara Wanjiri.'
[97] RHL Mss Afr s 746, Box 12, File 6, 'Incident Report as at 11 a.m. on Tuesday, 24th March 1953,' 2.
[98] KNA MLA/1/718, CC 7/1954, 'Maina Kanyugi & Kahoni Gachenga.'

the murders in Kiambu throughout 1953 were thought to have occurred in similar circumstances.[99]

Once this process of privatised violence was triggered, revenge became another critical catalyst for the violence. Munene Muimbo shot Philip Makumi, a Home Guard and teacher from Starehe, Kiambu, in Makumi's home on a Sunday afternoon in May 1953. Munene mistakenly believed his victim had testified against him in a trial the previous year, when Munene was acquitted of being a Mau Mau oath administrator.[100] In Central Kenya during 1953, we find that 'intimate violence signals less a process of politicisation of individual life and more a process of pervasive privatisation of politics; less a transgression of social ties and more their full, though perverse, expression.'[101] Whereas the very first outbreaks of violence in each community tended to be a manifestation of the tension between preexisting conflicting social groups or competing ideologies, once the conflict took hold in localities, the alignment between wartime allegiances and peacetime political and social groupings became confused.

Any account of the war within Kikuyu communities must recognise that a large proportion of that violence was perpetrated by members of the Home Guard. The importance of institutions and the organisational structures of insurgent groups have long been recognised as one of the chief determinants of the extent and nature of violence inflicted by those actors during civil wars.[102] The same is true of counterinsurgents. The very existence of irregular collaborative vigilante or militia groups reveals much about the nature of a counterinsurgency campaign. The presence of militias indicates the weakness of regular armed forces and their inability to curb rebel activity. Moreover, irregulars are deployed when internal and external constraints on states prevent the more extensive use of regular forces.[103] Irregular forces such as the Home Guard profoundly impact on the nature and extent of violence during civil war. Because of the devolution of the tools of coercion, counterinsurgencies reliant on locally recruited non-state actors may be prone to be

---

[99] Sorrenson, *Land Reform*, 101.

[100] KNA MLA/1/504, CC 44/1953, 'Munene Muimbo.'

[101] Kalyvas, *Logic of Violence*, 362–3.

[102] Lucien Pye, *Guerrilla Communism in Malaya: Its Social and Political Meaning* (Princeton NJ, 1956); Weinstein, *Inside Rebellion*.

[103] Achilles Batalas, 'Send a Thief to Catch a Thief: State-Building and the Employment of Irregular Military Formations in Mid-Nineteenth Century Greece,' in *Irregular Armed Forces and Their Role in Politics and State Formation*, eds. Diane Davis and Anthony Periera (Cambridge, 2003), 149–77.

'perverse and destructive.'[104] The devolution of military and police power to incorporate armed citizens in militias, albeit with temporarily granted legal status and titles such as Home Guards, Special Police, or Auxiliary Police, is likely to result in an increase of violence, declining levels of discipline, and a heightened prevalence of corruption. Accounts of militia activities in twentieth-century Greece, Kashmir, Guatemala, and Kurdistan, and nineteenth-century Missouri amply prove this point.[105]

Despite such easily recognisable dangers inherent in the use of militias, we find precisely those same groups being armed and deployed in British colonial counterinsurgency campaigns with depressing regularity and consistency in results. First demonstrated by the Native American forces deployed against Washington's Continental Army in the 1770s,[106] the capacity of irregular forces to wreak havoc was shown in the twentieth century by the Black and Tans and Auxiliary Police in Ireland[107]; the Home Guards and Special Police in the Kenya, Cyprus, and Malaya campaigns of the 1950s; and subsequently, the Ulster Special Constabulary.[108] The extent to which militias have been institutionalised within British counterinsurgency strategies was again revealed by the recent disclosure of collusion between the Royal Ulster Constabulary and loyalist paramilitary groups in Northern Ireland during the late 1990s.[109] With three centuries of experience to call on, the potential costs and benefits of placing a gun in the hand of an untrained, loosely disciplined Kikuyu peasant farmer were then well known to the British.

The utility of militias to counterinsurgency campaigns lies in an attempt to replicate the inherent strength of an insurgent group, namely that, in Townshend's words, '"the people" can be the most destructive of all military forces.'[110] Militias like the Home Guard can be entrusted with counter-terror. 'Nothing breaks them up like turning their own people against them,' wrote General George Crook on the use of Apache

---

[104] Keen, *Conflict and Collusion*, 2.
[105] Kalyvas, *Logic of Violence*, 108.
[106] Armstrong Sharkey, *European and Native American Warfare, 1675–1815* (London, 1998), 111–36.
[107] William Lowe, 'The War Against the R.I.C, 1919–21,' *Eire-Ireland* 27 (2002), 79–117.
[108] Jean Marie McGloin, 'Shifting Paradigms: Policing in Northern Ireland,' *Policing*, 26, 2003, 118–43.
[109] Nuala O'Loan, 'Statement by the Police Ombudsman for Northern Ireland on Her Investigation Into the Circumstances Surrounding the Death of Raymond McCord Junior and Related Matters,' 22 January 2007.
[110] Charles Townshend, 'People's War,' in *The Oxford History of Modern War*, ed. Charles Townshend (Oxford, 2005), 197.

scouts during the Apache wars of the early 1870s. 'It is not merely a question of catching them better with Indians, but of a broader and more enduring aim – their disintegration.'[111] It was with good reason that the South Africans named their counterinsurgency police force recruited from among the Ovimbundu population of Namibia as *koevoet*, which in Afrikaans means crowbar. Once the ambiguity of 1952 and early 1953 was forcibly cast aside, the Kenyan Home Guard assisted in the prising apart of Kikuyu society.

The Home Guard were deliberately intended to be a grouping of local forces 'based on local customs and conditions and under local leadership. It should not, therefore, be subjected to too great a degree of centralised regimentation.'[112] As a consequence, the localised experience of the Home Guard during the Emergency was dependent on local actors. This led to what was termed 'inadequate leadership and control'[113] in certain areas, creating conditions in which indiscipline and abuse of power could flourish. That lack of control was no accident. Nor was the relationship between the Home Guard and the Provincial Administration incidental. The Provincial Administration used the Home Guard to sate a widely held European desire for revenge for Mau Mau atrocities. In his account of mass interrogations in Kiambu during May 1953, David Martin, a teacher and part-time member of the Kenya Police Reserve, noted that European officers justified the beating of suspects by Home Guards by saying, 'It was men just like this who did Uplands [Lari].'[114] Moreover, the murders of settlers, particularly the Ruck family, had a galvanising effect on European opinion.[115] Furthermore, control of the militia acted as a strong counterbalance on the influence of the military and the Kenya Police, controlled ultimately by Nairobi. By encouraging the Home Guard to play a highly active and forceful role in the Reserves during the Emergency, the Provincial Administration was able to remain in control of the direction of the war. Thus, the Provincial Administration was able to reverse a loss of influence within colonial governance.[116]

[111] Douglas Porch, 'Imperial Wars: From the Seven Years War to the First World War,' in *The Oxford History of Modern War*, ed. Charles Townshend (Oxford, 2005), 108.

[112] RHL Mss Afr s 1580, File XI, Office of the Director of Operations, 'Emergency Directive No. 3: Kikuyu Guard,' 2.

[113] RHL Mss Afr s 1694, K. Hadingham to Provincial Commissioner, 14 December 1954, 2.

[114] RHL Mss Perham 467, File 1, 'Statement by Mr D. Martin, Alliance High School, Kikuyu,' 17 May 1953, 1–2.

[115] Anderson, *Histories*, 93–8.

[116] Berman, *Control and Crisis*, 347–70.

FIGURE 7. Inspection of Home Guards, undated. Reproduced with permission of
Kenya National Archives.

With the encouragement of local colonial officials, the infliction of
violence during interrogations, known as screening, became an everyday
function of the Home Guard's members. During screening, Home Guard
units would go to a village, urban neighbourhood, or labour line and
gather together the inhabitants. The people would then be taken to a
cordoned off area by Home Guards for interrogation, often by informers wearing hoods to protect their identities. Mau Mau suspects would
then be taken away for further questioning or sent to detention.[117] Principally drawn from the ranks of the Home Guard[118] and paid for their
work,[119] screeners were deeply unpopular with Mau Mau supporters and
the population at large. A large number were killed, whereas others had

[117] Kariuki Kiruma, interview with the author, Ihururu, Muhoya's location, Nyeri, 7 February 2004.
[118] For background of screeners see DC/KBU/2/1, DO Gatundu, 'Handing Over Report –
Gatundu Division, C.A. Holmes to G.H. Knaggs,' June 1955, appendix C; correspondence in KNA DC/NYK/3/16/36 in which screeners requesting Government employment
describe their record of service; Kershaw, *Mau Mau From Below*, 326–7.
[119] For details of salaries see KNA MAA/7/205, Anon, 'Payment of Screening Teams,' 29
September 1953. Salaries varied greatly from Shs.3.53 per day in Nairobi to Shs.250
per month for screeners on the settler farms of Central Province.

family members targeted[120] and property destroyed by the insurgents.[121] Violence typified screening.[122]

One particular screening operation gained much public attention. After being sent to Tanganyika in October 1953 to screen the labour force of European farms surrounding the town of Arusha, 10 Home Guards and their 19-year-old European district officer, Brian Hayward, were arrested after of a series of assaults on suspects.[123] The team was accused of using violence in its interrogations in no less than 40 cases, 20 of which were successfully prosecuted, spread out over five days.[124] Suspected Mau Mau supporters among the labour force were subjected to death threats, whipped on the buttocks and soles of feet, hit with rifle butts, and drenched in water. This continued until confessions of Mau Mau involvement were extracted.[125] One 60-year-old victim was beaten so much that 'he asked to be killed in order to put him out of his agony,' before being 'made to stand holding above his head a heavy brick for two hours.' Another was burnt with a lit cigarette on his ear. Two victims, one of which committed suicide shortly afterwards, were made to lie under bricks while being beaten.[126]

At the subsequent trial, all the accused pleaded guilty. Hayward was fined £100, paid for by contributions from the European community in Kenya, and sent to prison for three months. The Kikuyu members of the

---

[120] KNA DC/NYK/3/16/36, Karanja Kahui to DC Nanyuki, 2 December 1954, 2; Arphaxad Migwi Wamahiu to DC Nanyuki, 3 May 1955; Peter Wanjohi Rurigi to DC Nanyuki, 9 October 1956.

[121] KNA DC/NYK/3/16/36, Peter Wanjohi Rurigi to DC Nanyuki, 9 October 1956.

[122] See for fuller descriptions of such practices, KNA MAA/8/169, Deputy City African Affairs Officer to City African Affairs Officer, 22 March 1953; RHL Mss Perham 567, file 1, 'Statement by D. Martin, Alliance High School, Kikuyu,' 17 May 1953; KNA ARC(MAA) 2/5/323, Peter Gachati, 'An Account of How I Was Beaten Up by a Party of Home Guard Led by Kingarua Maina on Monday 15th March 1954'; Elkins, *Imperial*, 62–90.

[123] The complete list of accused was as follows: Pino Kiromboro Silas, Poro Kirigu, Kaigai Kamau, Njuguna s/o Njeroge, Frederick Mungai, Kinosie Katore, James Kagombe, Edward Kamoya, Nganga Karanja, and William Ruminju.

[124] PRO CO 822/499, Anon. 'Report on the Case of the Queen versus Brian Hayward,' 5 December 1953, 1.

[125] PRO CO 822/499, 'In the District Court of Arusha District, Criminal Case No. 1463 of 1953, Regina Versus Brian Walter Hayward and Ten Others,' 10–12 November 1953, 17–9.

[126] PRO CO 822/499, 'In the District Court of Arusha District, Criminal Case No. 1463 of 1953, Regina Versus Brian Walter Hayward and Ten Others,' 10–12 November 1953, 19–21.

screening team were fined £5 each.[127] What was perhaps most startling about this case was the extent to which it revealed violence had become normalised during such operations. Indeed, this formed a major part of the defence case. One defendant, while admitting his role in the beating of one of the victims, stated 'I know that it was wrong but we did so in Kenya when they refused to answer.'[128] That Hayward and his unit were brought to justice, albeit without severe punishment, in Tanganyika is not incidental, not least because it was a member of the local settler community who reported the abuses to the police. Such an act would have been unthinkable in Kenya. More significantly, in Kenya, the local officers of the Provincial Administration were generally able to prevent prosecution for the gross abuses of human rights perpetrated by Home Guards on a daily basis in Central Province.[129] The protection offered by the Provincial Administration meant that the militia's members could quite literally get away with murder.

The case of the attempted prosecution of Chief Mundia, one of Mundia's headmen, a Tribal Policeman, and two Home Guards stands out above all others. Early in September 1954, Mundia's Home Guard unit in Mathira, Nyeri, shot an innocent civilian. To cover their tracks, a falsified report of a skirmish with a Mau Mau unit was made to the colonial authorities. However, when police investigations began, three eyewitnesses came forward with a very different version of events. The witnesses instead accused Chief Mundia and the four other suspects of murder.[130] In response, Mundia exploited his powers of arrest and had two of the witnesses detained on trumped up charges of 'illegal possession of drugs' and for being 'a considerable Mau Mau supporters [*sic*].'[131]

---

[127] PRO CO 822/499, Anon. 'Report on the Case of the Queen versus Brian Hayward,' 5 December 1953, 2.

[128] PRO CO 822/499, 'In the District Court of Arusha District, Criminal Case No. 1463 of 1953, Regina Versus Brian Walter Hayward and Ten Others,' 10–12 November 1953, 8.

[129] Not all Home Guards escaped justice. On 27 February 1954, two Home Guards from Gathiga, Kiambu, Ihugu Njuhiga and Kumonyo Njau, were hanged at Nairobi prison for murdering an old man in front of his wife and children after he refused to give them money (KNA MLA/1/626, CC 263/1953, 'Ihugu Njuhiga & Kumonyo Njau'; Judge Holmes to Governor, 28 January 1954). Other Home Guards were found guilty of murder by the courts, but escaped the hangman (KNA MLA/1/709, CC 290/1953, 'Njoroge Mahioya'; KNA MLA/1/900, CC 310/1954, 'Njuguna Kibe.')

[130] RHL Mss Afr s 1694, D. MacPherson to Commissioner of Police, 23 December 1954, 4.

[131] RHL Mss Brit Emp s 486, Box 5, File 5, O.E.B. Hughes to Provincial Commissioner, Central Province, 11 September 1954.

At this stage, the Provincial Administration became involved in the affair.

Despite knowing a police investigation into the murder was under way and that criminal proceedings against Mundia were likely, the Nyeri district commissioner, Hughes, authorised the detention of the witnesses.[132] The district commissioner justified his actions in a letter to the provincial commissioner for Central Province, Johnston, by warning of 'serious political results' if the prosecution of a prominent loyalist such as Mundia was allowed to proceed.[133] Hughes feared the publicity generated by any prosecution would lead to the ebbing of support away from the government from both loyalists and the general population. Johnston concurred and took up the affair with the police in Nyeri. The provincial commissioner wrote to the police officer overseeing the investigation and enquired if 'you would consider dropping the case.'[134] But Johnston reckoned without the resolve of the police in both Nyeri and Nairobi. Deeply concerned by the apparent impunity with which the security forces were committing atrocities across Central Kenya, the police commissioner, Arthur Young, and attorney general, John Whyatt, were both determined to eradicate such practices. Young had allies in this process in the head of the police's Criminal Investigation Department (CID) at headquarters, Donald MacPherson, and the senior CID officer in Nyeri, K. Hadingham.

Hadingham and the Nyeri police refused to let the bureaucracy interfere with the course of justice. Instead, following procedure, they sent the case notes to police headquarters in Nairobi for a decision on whether or not to charge Mundia and the other suspects.[135] A furious Johnston reminded the Nyeri police that 'it would be politically inexpedient to bring any charge of this nature against Chief Mundia who is one of the leading loyalists in the Mathira Division.'[136] Frustrated at his own inability to persuade the police to drop the case, the provincial commissioner passed the affair up to the highest office in the colony.

---

[132] RHL Mss Afr s 1694, D. MacPherson to Commissioner of Police, 23 December 1954, 4.
[133] RHL Mss Brit Emp s 486, Box 5, File 5, O.E.B. Hughes to Provincial Commissioner, Central Province, 11 September 1954.
[134] RHL Mss Brit Emp s 486, Box 5, File 5, C. M. Johnston to Assistant Superintendent of Police, Criminal Investigation Department (CID), Nyeri, 16 September 1954.
[135] RHL Mss Brit Emp s 486, Box 5, File 5, C. M. Johnston to Assistant Commissioner of Police, Nyeri, 7 October 1954.
[136] RHL Mss Brit Emp s 486, Box 5, File 5, C. M. Johnston to Assistant Commissioner of Police, Nyeri, 16 October 1954.

Evelyn Baring, the governor, agreed with the Nyeri district commissioner and the Central Province provincial commissioner that the case against Mundia needed to be shelved for reasons of political expediency. The governor, in an 'off the record' conversation, also attempted to persuade the local police in Nyeri 'that it would be politically most inexpedient to prosecute a loyal Chief who had taken a leading part in the fight against Mau Mau.'[137] But with the police unwavering in their pursuit of a prosecution, orders came from Nairobi to arrest the suspects.

Having found their best efforts to persuade the police to drop the case thwarted, the Provincial Administration attempted to sabotage the prosecution case. Two district officers, Elworthy and Richmond, gave false statements about the original murder and provided Mundia with a fabricated alibi.[138] With his junior officers obstructing the investigation, the provincial commissioner continued to press for the release of the suspects.[139] The obstinate Johnston refused to assist the police in their enquiries. During an interview about the affair, the provincial commissioner told the interviewer that he was 'too junior a Police Officer to record a statement from him.'[140] But such obduracy was unsustainable in the face of the police's resolve. Belatedly recognising that the actions of the Provincial Administration were at best legally dubious, on 4 December the governor ordered that all obstructions to the police investigation be removed.[141] Yet, in a final twist, Mundia and his co-accused still escaped justice. As part of attempts to persuade Mau Mau fighters to surrender to the security forces, an amnesty for crimes committed during the war was announced early in 1955. Crucially for Mundia, the amnesty included loyalists as well. Mundia, his headman, the Tribal Policeman, and the Home Guards were able to walk away as free men without facing trial.

The Mundia case was but one of many in which the Provincial Administration, supported by senior figures within the government, hindered

[137] RHL Mss Brit Emp s 486, Box 5, File 5, K. Hadingham to Commissioner of Police, 22 November 1954.
[138] RHL Mss Afr s 1694, D. MacPherson to Commissioner of Police, 23 December 1954, 4–5.
[139] RHL Mss Brit Emp s 486, Box 5, File 5, 'Record of Interview Which Took Place Between C.M. Johnston, Esq, Provincial Commissioner, Nyeri, and Mr. H. R. Walker,' 27 November 1954, 2.
[140] RHL Mss Afr s 1694, D. MacPherson to Commissioner of Police, 23 December 1954, 5.
[141] RHL Mss Afr s 1694, D. MacPherson to Commissioner of Police, 23 December 1954, 5.

criminal investigations into the actions of loyalists.[142] The resulting frustration led in large part to the resignation of Police Commissioner Young.[143] The Provincial Administration was not simply trying to protect friends and hold up loyalist morale, but was rather more concerned with clearing the path for a campaign of counter-terror. Studies of state-perpetrated violence elsewhere urge scholars to avoid seeing such actions as aberrations or the behaviour of those individual operating outside the law, commonly termed "bad apples." Instead, when such behaviour recurs with great frequency, it should be understood as part of a state's 'operating logic.'[144] So it was in Kenya during the Emergency. The headmaster of Alliance High School, E. Carey Francis, wrote that abuses were 'so widespread as to be regarded as the normal policy of the Security Forces.'[145] By December 1953, the provincial commissioner for Central Province wrote of the 'people fearing the security forces more than Mau Mau.'[146] Presented with an enemy that it saw as pursuing the tactics of terrorism, the colonial authorities felt they had little choice but to institute counter-terrorism. The Home Guard thus represented state-sanctioned and sponsored terror intended to bring the population of Central Kenya under the control of the incumbent regime.

Even while stressing the complicity of loyalists in some of the very worst atrocities of the civil war, it should not be forgotten or denied that Mau Mau insurgents also committed significant abuses. To ignore the latter is to overlook a significant dynamic in the conflict and renders useless any attempt to explain loyalism. In many cases, loyalist targets of Mau Mau's violence remained understandable in the context of the war and its historic hinterland. Moses Kamunyapo's brother was killed in early March 1953 while an agricultural instructor.[147] Thairu Mukua was supervising the deeply unpopular communal labour at Kiamacimti when he was fatally attacked in July 1953.[148] Wanderi Thirami lost two brothers. The first, Ndirangu, had been a police informer in Nyeri township, and the second, Githira, a Home Guard at Murugutu.[149] But as

---

[142] Anderson, *Histories*, 289–327.
[143] Ibid., 305.
[144] Martha Huggins, Mika Haritos-Fatouros, and Philip Zimbardo, *Violence Workers: Police Torturers and Murderers Reconstruct Brazilian Atrocities* (Berkeley, 2002), 79.
[145] RHL Mss Perham 467, E. Carey Francis, 'Government Statement on Brutality,' 29 April 1953.
[146] RHL Mss Afr s 1580, File 1, Johnston to Hinde, 3 December 1953.
[147] KNA VP/6/2, Moses Kamunyaupo to DC Nyeri, 26 March 1960.
[148] KNA VP/6/2, Munyoka Thairu to DC Nyeri, 24 February 1960.
[149] KNA VP/6/2, Wanderi Thirami to DC Nyeri, 10 November 1959.

the violence increased, so the social backgrounds of the insurgent's targets widened. Among the hundreds of Mau Mau's victims were elders, Christians, minor government employees, nuns, schoolchildren, preachers, teachers, and tax clerks.[150] And as it became more and more difficult to discriminately target loyalists, attacks on their vulnerable family members became more frequent. Agala Masai was killed in Nyeri in December 1952 as a result of her husband's opposition to Mau Mau.[151] Tira Waweru worked as a sub-locational Home Guard leader in Muhito location, South Tetu, a screening elder in Nairobi, and finally a chief in Nanyuki, but it was his son and brother who were both murdered in Nairobi.[152]

The Shifting Tides of the War

To describe loyalist violence in terms of surrogacy is to tell only half the story.[153] Although such an approach may explain the attraction of the Home Guard to the colonial regime, it does not help us understand Kikuyu perpetration of violence nor the enthusiasm for atrocity. The Home Guard represented a significant decentralisation of force and an alliance between loyalists and the colonial government, who had very different reasons for wishing to defeat Mau Mau. Chief among these was revenge for Mau Mau's attacks and a desire for security. Fear of violence severely constrained the daily lives of loyalists and their family members. Kenneth Matiba, then a pupil at Alliance High School, had to remain at the school for two years without returning to his loyalist family home in Fort Hall, as it was unsafe to do so. When he did leave Alliance in December 1954, Matiba joined his grandparents living within the compound of the Kahuhia mission.[154] Even Boy Scouts required an armed escort when travelling to meetings.[155] The tactical use of terror by both sides that occurred in 1953 and 1954 was in large part the consequence of the trajectory of the war. Locally negotiated settlements that postponed the onset of large-scale violence steadily broke down as

---

[150] Correspondence in KNA DC/MRU/2/1/2 gives very brief details of each victim in Meru (see Appendix I).
[151] KNA VP/6/2, Masai Gacheche to DC Nyeri, 14 February 1960.
[152] KNA VP/6/2, Tira Waweru to DC Nyeri, 25 October 1959.
[153] Anderson, 'Surrogates.'
[154] Kenneth Matiba, *Aiming High: The Story of My Life* (Nairobi, 2000), 32–3 & 35–7.
[155] Timothy Parsons, *Race, Resistance, and the Boy Scout Movement in British Colonial Africa* (Athens OH, 2004), 167.

a result of three developments: repatriation to Central Province of large numbers of disaffected labour from Nairobi and the White Highlands, a growth in the strength of the security forces, and the course of events in the war in the forest.

Fearful of a spread of Mau Mau across the colony, the colonial government forcibly returned up to 100,000 Kikuyu to Central Province from the Rift Valley.[156] Embittered by their experiences during repatriation, the repatriates were widely suspected of Mau Mau sympathies. Certainly, the repatriates contained few loyalists.[157] The loyalist reaction to the squatters' return was hostile. In the immediate aftermath of the Lari massacre, Kiambu's chiefs urged Baring to halt the returns.[158] A month later, 'there was almost a riot amongst the Home Guard at Lari when they saw repatriates returning to their reserve.'[159] Their return had been untimely and unwelcome. So too was that of large numbers of Nairobi's labour force routinely expelled from the city and sent back to their home districts. The dramatic increase in support for the insurgency that emerged in Meru and Embu from June 1953 was a product of the return of large numbers of urban migrants rounded up during screening in Nairobi.[160]

The forced displacement back to Central Province of society's most disenfranchised and radicalised elements provided a groundswell of recruits for the insurgency. Their militancy shocked even long-standing opponents of colonialism. Elisha Munene Mweya, a leading figure in the KAU in the years prior to the war, bemoaned 'the nasty words and leadership which were performed by the group which came from Nairobi and reached Kyeni Location.'[161] Equally significantly, the returned migrants disturbed local patterns of control by introducing unknown and therefore

[156] Elkins, *Imperial*, 57–8; Furedi, *Mau Mau War*, 122.
[157] Furedi, 'Social Composition,' 499.
[158] 'Governor Hints at New Measures. And Gets Some Advice From Loyal Chiefs,' *East African Standard*, 31 March 1953, 1.
[159] TNA: PRO WO 276/388, Kiambu District Intelligence Summary for week ending 25 April 1953, 1.
[160] KNA DC/EBU/1/1/12, DC Embu, Embu District Annual Report 1953, 2–3; KNA MSS/124/4, W. H. Laughton to D. A. Beetham, Methodist Missionary Society, 17 May 1953; W. H. Laughton to B. Owen, 2 July 1953; W. H. Laughton to D. A. Beetham, Methodist Missionary Society, 14 September 1953; David Throup, 'Crime, Politics and the Police in Colonial Kenya, 1939–63,' in *Policing and Decolonisation: Politics, Nationalism and the Police, 1917–65*, eds. David Anderson and David Killingray (Manchester, 1992), 145.
[161] KNA AHC/9/24, Elisha Munene Mweya to Editor, *Kayu ka Embu*, 30 January 1954, 1.

untrustworthy individuals into local communities. Within three days of Mwinza Ngorori's arrival at his brother's home in Ngariama location in Embu, local Mau Mau activists attempted to oath him. Mwinza did not acquiesce and instead threatened to go to the police. The newcomer was then killed and his brother, Shadrack Kisou, forced to participate in the murder.[162] When the insurgent Kahendo Wariu returned from the forest to his village in Ribai, Kiambu, in December 1953, he heard of the presence of Ndungu Njonge, a new arrival. Ndungu was forcibly escorted to an oathing ceremony, but apparently he too refused to be oathed and was strangled.[163] The resettlement of migrant workers back in their districts of origin boosted the constituency of the aggrieved, but threatened the insurgents' control.

The repatriations occurred concurrently with a significant increase in the numbers of security forces operating in the reserves. Besides the growth of the regular army and the Home Guard, a massive expansion in the police force had taken place. In October 1952, only four police stations had been operational in the Native Reserves of Central Province. At the close of the following year, every location had at least one permanent police station.[164] There were no Kenya Police in Meru district at all until early June 1953.[165] A month later, Meru town had a new police station, European police officers, and 'hordes of African inspectors, NCOs [Non-Commissioned Officers] and constables.'[166] With the government adopting the position of 'He that is not with us is against us.' opportunities to avoid declaring an allegiance reduced accordingly.[167] And so did the ability of Mau Mau units to remain unvexed in the reserves and forests.

For threatening the supply of recruits, funds, and provisions to Mau Mau at the source, loyalists became the main target of the rebels.[168] Benson Njora Kagori, for example, became a victim of Mau Mau on the Fairfield farm, where he worked, in Nakuru district after he agitated for the formation of a Home Guard unit. On 8 May 1953, he was taken to a

---

[162] KNA MLA/1/735, CC 218/1953, 'Mutahi Kigombo & Six Others.'
[163] KNA MLA/1/1354. CC 7/1956, 'Kahendo Wariu.'
[164] Ibid., 141.
[165] KNA VQ/1/31, DC Meru to Colonel A. Morcombe, Director of Kikuyu Guard, 7 August 1953, 2.
[166] KNA Mss/124/4, W. H. Laughton to J. Grigor, 2 August 1953.
[167] The legend adorned an information poster for the Nairobi Home Guard to be found in RHL Mss Afr s 721.
[168] Barnett, 'Mau Mau,' 82; Kershaw, *Mau Mau From Below*, 260, footnote 2.

riverbank, shot, and strangled, and his body was thrown into the water.[169] Between April and August 1953, particularly in Fort Hall, the insurgents made a concerted effort to destroy the embryonic Home Guard. Sixty-eight guardsmen were killed in the Kangema division of Fort Hall alone in this period.[170] The war spread quickly from its point of origin in Kiambu and Nairobi to Fort Hall and Nyeri, where it remained at its most fierce for the next three years. By August 1953, the conflict had reached Embu and Meru districts as well as the districts in the Rift Valley adjacent to Central Province.[171] However, the security forces steadily regained the initiative, not least because of an ever-strengthening Home Guard. The force was built up to allow for the withdrawal of army and police units to Nairobi ahead of Operation Anvil in April 1954. Moreover, Kikuyu Guard Combat Units, heavily armed groups intended to replicate the capabilities of departing regular army battalions, were formed.[172]

The forest fighters felt the pressure from mid-1953 onward. The arrival of a new military commander, General Erskine, in June of that year marked the beginning of a much more effective military campaign by the British.[173] Mau Mau's forest fighters were slowly forced from its preferred bases close to their home areas, with plentiful access to food, intelligence, and reinforcements.[174] The first signs of dissipating cohesion, which eventually led to the great schism between the followers of the two Mau Mau generals, Kimathi and Mathenge, could be first detected in July 1953.[175] The establishment of the government's War Council in March 1954 further increased the coordination of the counterinsurgency campaign and provided much-needed centralised direction from the very top

---

[169] KNA MLA/1/572, CC 199/1953, 'Mungai Kihika & Seven Others.'
[170] KNA VQ/1/31, DC Fort Hall, 'The Future of Kikuyu Guards,' 2, attached to DC Fort Hall to PC Central, 31 October 1953.
[171] Anderson, *Histories*, 251, 253 & 263–4; Kenya, *Loyalists*, 34; Rosberg and Nottingham, *Myth of Mau Mau*, 298.
[172] KNA ARC(MAA) 2/5/310, DC Fort Hall to Major-General Heyman, 28 January 1954; KNA ARC(MAA) 2/5/313, Major-General, Chief of Staff to Commanders 39 Infantry Brigade, 49 Independent Infantry Brigade, 70 (EA) Infantry Brigade & OC Kenya Regiment, 5 February 1954; KNA MAA/7/239, Colonel A. Morcombe, Director of Kikuyu Guard, 'Kikuyu Guard Instruction No. 4: Kikuyu Guard Combat Units (K.G.C.U.s),' 12 February 1954; KNA MAA/7/239, extract from minutes of 9th meeting of the War Council, 23 April 1954; KNA MAA/7/239, DC Nyeri, 'The Kikuyu Guard Combat Unit,' 30 April 1954.
[173] Anderson, *Histories*, 257–8.
[174] Ibid., 266–7.
[175] Lonsdale, 'Authority,' 63.

of government.[176] Sustained attempts began to induce mass surrenders by the forest fighters between February and March 1954.[177] The guerrillas began to find themselves fighting high in the mountain forests and on the fringes of the reserves, often far from home. By April 1954, the conflict had spread to the Maasai districts of Ngong and Narok in Southern Province.[178] Mau Mau had to operate on its ideological and geographical periphery to survive.

On Becoming and Not Becoming a Terrorist

In a study of the responses of communities to the Sri Lankan conflict of the 1980s and 1990s, Spencer demonstrated the value of analyses 'On not becoming a "terrorist."'[179] 'What, he asks, 'are the circumstances which allow a space for the nonparticipant?'[180] In Kenya in the 1950s, those circumstances were simply the absence of violence from daily lives. As violence increased, so the agency of actors involved in the conflict and the space for neutrality reduced. In late 1952 and early 1953, communities attempted to avoid entering the cycle of violence that led inexorably towards civil war. Such a position was difficult to sustain, however. Communities were flooded by outsiders as 1953 progressed. Repatriates, Mau Mau insurgents with no prior connection to the localities in which they now operated, soldiers, and policemen all destabilised locally negotiated settlements designed to avoid violence. Without the previous social ties necessary to enable trust between the newcomers and local communities, allegiances had to be proven by deeds. Neither side could tolerate the presence of strangers who could denounce their new neighbours at any moment. Nor could newly arrived combatants afford to take locals at their word when they vowed support.

As the security forces and Mau Mau became more rapacious in response to the course of events, communities were increasingly unable to remain neutral. But in a climate of fear and conflict, the warring parties presented new opportunities for local populations to resolve older

[176] Anderson, *Histories*, 269.
[177] Ibid., 273.
[178] KNA ARC(MAA) 2/5/505 I, CNC to PC Central, 13 April 1954; PC Southern to CNC, 21 April 1954; KNA MAA/7/250, PC Southern to CNC, 10 April 1954.
[179] Jonathon Spencer, 'On Not Becoming a 'Terrorist': Problems of Memory, Agency, and Community in the Sri Lankan Conflict,' in *Violence and Subjectivity*, eds. Veena Das, et al. (Berkeley, 2000), 120–40.
[180] Ibid., 120.

disputes. In response to the prevailing climate of civil war, individuals privatised the violence to exploit the resources available to them to settle disputes that had little or nothing to do with any ideological issue or socioeconomic grievance. The power to inflict violence on or at least denounce rivals to one of the warring parties became a powerful bargaining chip in social relations. Violence stitched together a new social fabric.

3

From Mau Mau to Home Guard

The Defeat of the Insurgency

Triggering Mechanisms

Between April 1954 and the close of 1956, a broader loyalist constituency emerged and dealt a fatal blow to the insurgency. In October 1954, Chief Joshua Gacingiri of Kirimukuyu, Nyeri, wrote to his district commissioner with his reflections on his first year in office. At the time of his appointment in October 1953,

> I could not get any assistance from anybody because the majority of the population was far more intimidated by the large number of terrorists which was roaming about all over the location with very little and unsuccessful interference.

A year later, 'the population in my location has begun to grow tired of helping and sheltering the Mau Mau.'[1] Anti-Mau Mau action steadily became more popular among the people of Central Kenya as the course of events in the forests and reserves turned decisively against the rebels.[2] Although the exact timing of this turning point differed from place to place – the war in Ndia was at its height in August 1954, for example[3] – a tangible difference in public attitude towards Mau Mau was identifiable in most areas beginning in late 1954.[4] Mass sweeps of locations involving

---

[1] KNA VP/1/16, Chief Joshua Z. Gacingiri to DC Nyeri, 1 October 1954.
[2] Anthony Clayton, *Counter-Insurgency in Kenya: A Study of Military Operations Against Mau Mau* (London, 1976), 30.
[3] KNA DC/EBU/1/2/4, DO Ndia, 'Handing Over Notes,' June 1956, 1.
[4] KNA MSS/124/5, W. H. Laughton to M. McKeag, 16 January 1955; KNA DC/EBU/1/1/15, Embu District Annual Report 1956, 1. For a similar shift in public opinion in the Rift Valley in 1955, see Furedi, *Mau Mau War*, 124.

thousands of civilians were reported across Central Province in 1955.[5] Although 1,252 loyalists were thought to have lost their lives in the first two years of the Emergency, in the two years following October 1954, just 352 loyalists were believed killed by Mau Mau.[6] Over the next two years, the security forces steadily exerted a strengthening grip over the remaining Mau Mau guerrilla units until the military conflict was declared over on 17 November 1956.[7] The central role of loyalist forces in the defeat of the insurgency was clear.[8] The Central Province Home Guard and Tribal Police accounted for over 4,500 of the 11,503 Mau Mau fatalities recorded by the end of 1956.[9]

With harsh penalties imposed for Mau Mau support and generous rewards introduced for loyalists, there was little, by now, to be gained by opponents of the insurgents through playing both sides. As one loyalist wrote in November 1954, the fence sitter was 'useless. He is not on either side and so there is nothing good that we can expect from such.'[10] Condemnations of Mau Mau were fiercer. Perminas Njeru of Embu warned Mau Mau, 'You are corpses in the grave; we hunt you like antelopes.'[11] Duplicity was no longer wise. As elsewhere, violence had vanquished moderation and removed political choice.[12]

In his account of Lithuanian resistance to the German and Soviet occupations, Petersen seeks to explain how individuals move along a spectrum of political action towards active participation in rebellion. Noting the tremendous variety of roles played by individual actors in conflict, Petersen dismisses those binary accounts of violent resistance that portray individuals as having only the choice between resistor and

[5] 'Women Rise up Against Terrorists: 8.000 act as 'Beaters' in South Nyeri Operations,' *East African Standard*, 8 August 1955; KNA AB/8/31, minutes of Meru ADC meeting, 6–7 December 1955, 1; KNA ARA/6/1, G. Irvine, 'Chogoria Hospital,' attachment to Dr. C. Irvine, 'Chogoria Hospital Report: 1955,' 4; KNA VP/1/47, Lt. Col. Watson Gandy, Commanding Officer (CO) 7th King's African Rifles (KAR), 'Operation Schemozzle,' 5 December 1955; Gerald Lathbury, 'The Security Forces in the Kenya Emergency,' in *Rhodesia and East Africa*, ed. Ferdinand Joelson (London, 1958), 41.

[6] KNA WC/CM/1/5, Department of Information, 'Notes for the Press on the Kenya Emergency,' 18 October 1955, 3.

[7] TNA: PRO WO 236/20, Lieutenant-General G. W. Lathbury, 'The Kenya Emergency: May 1955 – November 1956,' 27.

[8] Clayton, *Counter-Insurgency*, 29.

[9] KNA MAA/7/236 II, Director of Tribal Police to PC Central, 11 March 1957; Kenya, *Origins and Growth*, 316.

[10] KNA AHC/9/23, Deshon Waweru to Editor, *Uhoro wa Nyeri*, 3 November 1954.

[11] KNA AHC/9/24, Perminas Njeru to Editor, *Kayu ka Embu*, 30 June 1954.

[12] See for comparison, Hart, *I.R.A.*, 24.

non-resistor. Petersen therefore stresses that we should concentrate on the events and processes that initiate movement along the spectrum that encompasses all actions, from active collaboration, to neutrality, to active resistance. But Petersen also argues that the reasons that cause an individual to move along that spectrum need not be the same as those that fix their position at any given point. He therefore differentiates between triggering mechanisms, which induce the movement on the spectrum, and sustaining mechanisms, which fix an individual's position for a period of time.[13] The remainder of this chapter discusses the triggering mechanisms for loyalism that were activated in mid-1954. The sustaining mechanisms are examined in the next two chapters.

Two clear triggering mechanisms for a general swing towards loyalism from mid-1954 on can be identified. The first was the violence of Mau Mau. The militants had always shrouded their actions with the threat of violence, but that threat was more frequently realised up to the middle of 1954, albeit as a response to the actions of the colonial government. The second triggering mechanism was a shift in the control of local areas across Central Province that took place from May 1954 on. Loyalism became more commonplace as the security forces usurped Mau Mau from their positions of local domination. The processes underlying this trend were far more complicated than simply a desire to back the winning side.

What took place between mid-1954 and the end of 1956 was not a growth in sympathy for the colonial regime or any realignment in the goals of political action, which remained, as in the past, increased access to land and greater security of tenure. Instead, the shift towards loyalism is best understood as a change in the preferred partner for the privatisation of violence and a steady convergence of the rewards of loyalism with those longer-standing political goals. Mau Mau units were usurped from their positions of local control and thus their ability to protect their own lines of intelligence, and supplies decreased rapidly. The value of Mau Mau guerrillas to individuals looking to forge alliances to make the best use of violence in the conduct of their social relations thus depreciated. In their place, loyalists emerged as strong and viable alternatives. With Mau Mau's fortunes on the decline, Home Guards were able to provide protection for informers wishing to denounce neighbours and had the means to act on that information. By the end of 1956, the Home Guard was victorious.

[13] Petersen, *Resistance*.

The Crystallisation of Identity

In 1953, that victory had seemed a long way in the distance. At that time, Richard Kanampiu Githae was Mau Mau's oath administrator in the area around the Presbyterian mission station of Chogoria, high on the eastern slopes of Mount Kenya. Kanampiu had much experience of political action, but had not always been so adversarial to the colonial government. Living just across the district boundary in Embu in the late 1940s, Kanampiu was a leading figure within the structures of the KAU in that district. Indeed, his nickname then had been the 'Voice of KAU'[14] Despite his political allegiance, Kanampiu was supportive of the government's attempts to enforce controversial soil conservation measures in 1947.[15] Indeed, under Kanampiu's leadership, the Embu district commissioner held 'no fears that [the] K.A.U. will degenerate into an anti-authority political Association as started to happen in other districts.'[16] Yet, five years later, Kanampiu was one of the insurgency's leading lights in his home area of Chogoria.[17] Chogoria remained comparatively peaceful for the whole war. Mau Mau suspects there were recruited into the Home Guard or employed by the local Presbyterian minister, Jediel Micheu, to work in his quarry. Informants recalled that in mid-1954, under orders from Nairobi, police rounded up these suspects in one sweep, including many of the local Home Guards.[18] Memories of the war in Chogoria are today far less ridden with bitterness than elsewhere.[19]

Chogoria was lucky. The absence of violence there allowed for the survival of ambiguity of identity. In most other locations, loyalist and Mau Mau identities were fired in a kiln of violence many had striven to avoid. Exposure to the widespread violence was ultimately the most important predictor of allegiance and the principal initial agent in the crystallisation of identity. This process could be clearly observed at Chuka, to the south of Chogoria, following the murder of 22 loyalists by members of the

[14] Richard Kanampiu Githae, interview with the author, Chogoria, South Meru, 15 September 2003.
[15] KNA DC/EBU/6, DC Embu, Embu District Annual Report 1947, 1.
[16] KNA DC/EBU/6, DC Embu, Embu District Annual Report 1947, 1–2.
[17] Richard Kanampiu Githae, interview with the author, Chogoria, South Meru, 15 September 2003.
[18] Richard Kanampiu Githae, interview with the author, Chogoria, South Meru, 13 September 2003; Reverend Jediel Micheu, interview with the author, Chogoria, South Meru, 18 September 2003.
[19] For a contrast, from a loyalist survivor of Lari, see Anderson, *Histories*, 343; and from a Mau Mau victim of loyalist abuses, see Elkins, *Imperial*, 367.

King's African Rifles in mid-June 1953. Until early 1954, the question of 'how to distinguish friend from foe' proved uniquely challenging to the British in Kenya.[20] Suspicious of all Kikuyu, British military and civilian officers lacked the will and knowledge to distinguish loyalists from insurgents. Such attitudes meant loyalists could find themselves attacked not only by Mau Mau, but also by the colonial state.[21] Covered up by the authorities, the massacre at Chuka was apparently organised by the army unit's senior European officers in the wake of a dispute between the soldiers and the population of Chuka centred on the rape of local women.[22] The operation was overseen by an officer, Major Griffiths, who, according to one of his junior officers, thought 'all Kikuyu were Mau Mau and there was no way of differentiating between those who had taken the oath voluntarily and those who had taken the oath compulsorily.'[23] But such attitudes were counterproductive and not likely to enforce a change of heart on the part of the population.

Prior to the murder of the 22 loyalists by the King's African Rifles, there was little concern about the support of the local population of Chuka for the government. In the same week as the massacre, local Home Guards were reported to 'have undoubtedly got their tails up' and had proved highly effective during operations against Mau Mau.[24] Just a week later, those same units 'had ceased to exist' in the area.[25] Support for Mau Mau among the general population surged. By mid-November, 40 percent of the Home Guards were thought to be Mau Mau sympathisers.[26] Chuka remained a stubborn stronghold of support for the insurgency until the last days of the military campaign.[27] Despite their initial backing

---

[20] Porch, 'Imperial Wars,' 110.

[21] Lonsdale, 'Mau Maus of the Mind,' 396.

[22] For a more detailed discussion of this event, see David Anderson, Huw Bennett, and Daniel Branch, 'A Very British Massacre,' *History Today* 2006, 20–2 and listen to BBC Radio 4, 'Kenya's Bloody Summer,' broadcast 10 July 2006 [available online at http://www.bbc.co.uk/radio4/history/document/document_20060710.shtml – accessed 10 October 2007].

[23] UKNA: PRO WO 32/16103, evidence of 2nd Lieut. D. Innes-Walker in 'Summary of Evidence in the Case of WOPC Hussein and Nine Others (The Capt. Griffiths Case),' 42. For further details on Griffiths see Anderson, *Histories*, 259.

[24] TNA: PRO WO 276/392, Meru District Intelligence Summary for week ending 18 June 1953, 2; Meru District Intelligence Summary for week ending 25 June 1953, 1.

[25] TNA: PRO WO 276/392, Meru District Intelligence Summary for week ending 25 June 1953, 1–2.

[26] TNA: PRO WO 276/392, Meru District Intelligence Summary for weeks ending 3 December 1953, 2, & 19 November 1953, 2.

[27] KNA DC/MRU/1/3/13/1, DC Meru, 'Handing-Over Notes: Mr. W. B. G. Raynor to Mr. J. A. Cumber,' 11 May 1955, 1.

given to the colonial government, the allegiances of Chuka's population underwent a *volte-face*. With their nominal ally unwilling and unable to distinguish its supporters from its enemy, the population of Chuka quite reasonably decided that if the government were to treat them like Mau Mau, it made sense for them to seek the protection offered by the insurgents. The strength of support for Mau Mau in Chuka was a product of the violence of the Emergency rather than understanding that violence as the result of popular support for the insurgency.

Events such as those at Chuka were repeated across Central Kenya in mostly less extreme forms during 1953 and early 1954. Victimisation took its toll and hardened attitudes between adversaries, as the testimony of one captured Mau Mau guerrilla in March 1954 adequately shows. Despite heavy losses to the twin scourges of Royal Air Force bombing and pneumonia among the forest fighters, the insurgents would not surrender 'for fear of being annihilated by Homeguard.' The prisoner continued to argue that 'the war between the gangsters [Mau Mau] and the Homeguard will never end, as the Homeguards were the main enemies and not the Europeans.'[28] Temporary allegiances crystallised into more permanent identities. The cycle of violence had reached its logical apex, civil war. Whereas the violence of Chuka drove the local population towards Mau Mau, more commonly, the process worked in the opposite direction. Kariuki Kiruma felt compelled to join the Home Guard after his brother, Njugi, had been killed for refusing to be oathed at Ng'arua, near Thomson's Falls.[29] The local narrative of Lari's war was clearly dictated by the memories of the massacre there. One elder told the *East African Standard* that local loyalists 'have no room in their hearts for sorrow: only hate for the Mau Mau.'[30] The Lari Home Guard, Headman Charles Ikenya, and Chief Makimei were heavily implicated in the extrajudicial killings of Mau Mau suspects in October 1953.[31] During the fierce fighting in the Kikuyu Escarpment forest between April and August 1953, the Home Guards from that part of Kiambu 'gave an excellent

---

[28] KNA VP/2/20, Naivasha District Intelligence Summary for the week ending 26 March 1954, 2.

[29] Kariuki Kiruma, interview with the author, Ihururu, Nyeri, 7 February 2004.

[30] 'Uplands – Mothers See Children Die,' *East African Standard*, 28 March 1953, 5.

[31] KNA MAA/8/169, statements of Aristariko Kamau wa Muna & John Cege wa Jakobu, 21 October 1953; K. L. Downing, Africa Inland Mission, Kijabe to Rev. W. Scott Dickson, Christian Council of Kenya, 22 October 1953; K. Downing, African Inland Mission, Kijabe to Rev. W. Scott Dickson, Christian Council of Kenya, 28 October 1953; K. Downing, African Inland Mission, Kijabe to Paul, 30 October 1953.

account of themselves.'[32] Where large-scale killings did not take place at all, allegiances were ambiguous and ill defined for a far longer period.

Few factors solidified support for loyalism more than being the victim, or proximal to a victim, of Mau Mau's violence, regardless of past political allegiance or social standing. Experience of violence thus had the effect of crystallising identity and dramatically reordering identity repertoires, hierarchies of self-identity possessed by each individual.[33] As Hobsbawm observes, identities are never singular.[34] Contradictory, complex, and constantly in flux, hierarchies of identity, whether self-declared or determined by others, are contingent on the setting in which individuals find themselves.[35] But there seem fewer forces capable of encouraging such swift modifications to these identity repertoires than violence.[36] The transformative effect of violence on identity repertoires has been frequently observed, perhaps most notably by Amartya Sen.[37] In such a setting, victimisation and thus the immediate desire for security during conflict are the most obvious incentives for individuals to realign identity repertories to match those of the combatants.[38] But perpetration of violence can also have a similar effect. Loyalist and Republican violence served to tie together the perpetrators with even their most ambivalent supporters in Northern Ireland.[39] 'Violence,' writes Spencer, 'acts as a privileged marker in drawing the boundaries of community.'[40] It is the capacity of violence to define group membership, satisfying the desire for both security and revenge, which empowers bloodshed to scramble identity repertoires and crystallise what was previously fluid into something

---

[32] KNA DC/KBU/1/44, DC Kiambu, Kiambu District Annual Report 1953, 1.

[33] For further discussion of identity repertoires, see Daniel Posner, *Institutions and Ethnic Politics in Africa* (Cambridge, 2005).

[34] Eric Hobsbawm, *Nations and Nationalism Since 1870: Programme, Myth, Reality* (Cambridge, 1990), 123. See also David Laitin, *Identity in Formation: The Russian-Speaking Populations in the Near Abroad* (Ithaca NY, 1998).

[35] Robert Bates, 'Ethnic Competition and Modernization in Contemporary Africa,' *Comparative Political Studies* 6 (1974); Daniel Posner, 'The Political Salience of Cultural Difference: Why Chewas and Tumbukas Are Allies in Zambia and Adversaries in Malawi,' *American Political Science Review* 98 (2004).

[36] Vigdis Broch-Due, 'Violence and Belonging: Analytical Reflections,' in *Violence and Belonging: The Quest for Identity in Post-Colonial Africa*, ed. Vigdis Broch-Due (Abingdon, 2005), 2.

[37] Amartya Sen, *Identity and Violence: The Illusion of Destiny* (London, 2006).

[38] Noah Feldman, *What We Owe Iraq: War and the Ethics of Nation Building* (Princeton NJ, 2004), 79.

[39] William Kelleher, *The Troubles in Ballybogoin: Memory and Identity in Northern Ireland* (Ann Arbor MI, 2003), 35.

[40] Spencer, 'Not Becoming a Terrorist,' 120.

worth killing and dying for. And that in Kenya in mid-1954 was increasingly loyalism.

In the Meru and Embu districts, the violence of the war had a very distinctive effect on identity repertoires. It is clear that the events of the 1950s profoundly amplified the salience of ethnicity, which in both Meru and Embu was defined primarily as being non-Kikuyu. Previously, and without much dispute from the respective populations of the districts of Central Province, Kikuyu, Embu, and Meru were considered by the colonial government to be if not one and the same group then at least extremely closely related. With the three groups sharing much common linguistic ground, the boundaries among each were hazy. Indeed, it was for that very reason that all were joined together in one administrative bloc. Yet, during the 1950s, the distinctive identities of Embu and Meru became ever more significant. Even within Embu, the Mbeere people steadily made increasing claims to be treated as distinct from their fellow inhabitants of the district. In each case, these newly salient, although far from new, ethnic identities intertwined with loyalism.[41] Mbeere, the occupiers of lowlands to the east of the Embu district, were particularly keen loyalists. In December 1953, for example, 600 Mbeere 'armed with bows, arrows and shields' and including 'old warriors well over 70 years of age' volunteered for a mass sweep under the supervision of the police and army.[42] Mbeere support for the government was eagerly reciprocated. As one Mbeere loyalist recognised, Mbeere 'have progressed quite well during the Emergency due to their loyalty,' principally in the form of improved educational facilities.[43]

Disputes between Mbeere and the other inhabitants of Embu, and between Embu and Meru on one hand and the Kikuyu districts on the other, were not new. Mbeere, for example, had long been engaged in disputes over cultivation rights and shared boundaries with their neighbours in Embu.[44] But these generally peaceful conflicts had not previously been expressed in terms of ethnicity. This was certainly the case, however, by the end of the war. Perhaps the most objectionable manifestation of this heightened salience of ethnicity within Central Province during the war

---

[41] For a discussion of the contingency of ethnic salience, see Posner, 'Cultural Difference.'
[42] KNA AHC/9/22, 'Loyal People of Mbere,' *Muembu*, 26 December 1953.
[43] KNA AHC/9/25, Leonard M. Njoka, 'Wambere People During the Emergency,' *Kaya ka Embu*, 30 June 1955; KNA DC/EBU/1/1/14, Embu District Annual Report 1955, 17.
[44] KNA DC/EBU/3/3, DC Embu, file note, 15 August 1938; DC Embu, 'Report on Wambere in Embu Division,' 31 August 1946; KNA DC/EBU/1/2/5, Embu District Annual Report 1946, 2.

was the removal of Kikuyu from the Embu district and the support for such measures by loyalist members of the district council. The Kikuyu in question inhabited the locations of the district closest to the boundaries with the Nyeri and Fort Hall district boundaries. They had moved to Embu at various stages between 1933 and 1947, quite possibly because of the lower population density in the district and thus a lesser pressure on land than in the Kikuyu districts. For that very reason, their original arrival had caused disquiet in Embu, whose inhabitants were anxious to avoid the upheaval so evident at that time in the neighbouring districts.[45] This earlier opposition was aired for a new audience in 1955. In the words of the district council members, those Kikuyu in Embu 'have been guilty of tribal segregation, and do not want to mix with Embu people except in very rare cases.' The legitimacy of such claims is questionable, but what is clear is that the council members saw the Kikuyu residents of Embu as a convenient scapegoat for the spread of the insurgency to the district, thus allowing Embu to escape the most repressive counterinsurgency measures.[46]

In so doing, the council played on the dominant colonial interpretation of the insurgency as a Kikuyu tribal conspiracy. From Meru in the north to Narok in the south, administrators of districts and locations along the periphery of Kikuyu settlement were caught unaware by outbreaks of violence in 1952 and 1953. Such events called into question the claims to authority made by those same administrators, who professed to be experts of 'their' districts. The opportunity to blame the outbreaks of violence on a tribal conspiracy spread in secret and by supernatural methods within Kikuyu communities was too convenient to ignore. Thus, existing Kikuyu communities outside of the main Kikuyu districts came to be held responsible for the rise of Mau Mau in those outlying areas. Yet, all the evidence points to labour migration as the conduit for the spread of Mau Mau to such places. Nevertheless, in Meru, Embu, and in the Massai districts of Narok and Kajiado, long-term Kikuyu residents became the scapegoat for insurgent activity.[47] In Embu, this meant that all Kikuyu

[45] KNA DC/EBU/1/2/5, Embu District Annual Report 1946, 2.
[46] KNA ARC(MAA) 2/5/218 V, minutes of Special meeting of Embu African District Council, 2 December 1955, 2.
[47] DC/EBU/1/1/11, Embu District Annual Report 1952, 1; KNA DC/EBU/1/2/3, DC Embu, 'Handing Over Report: Mr. R. A. Wilkinson to Mr. F. R. Wilson,' 19 July 1954, 1 of 'Emergency in Embu District' section; KNA ARC(MAA) 2/5/218 V, minutes of Special meeting of Embu ADC, 2 December 1955, 1; minutes of Embu ADC meeting, 16–17 February 1956, 1. For similar accusations in Meru, see DC/MRU/1/3/13/1, DC

in the district, including loyalists, were forcibly relocated in 1955 to two punitive villages, Kithimu and Kihumbu, until it was decided what to do with them. Eventually, land at Mulinduko was allocated by the government to the Kikuyu loyalists in Embu. The remainder were expelled to the Kikuyu districts.[48]

Attitudes towards Kikuyu had, for a time, become fixed. Embu and Meru delegations to the Regional Boundaries Commission, which toured Kenya in 1962 prior to independence, were vociferous in their insistence that they be separated from the Kikuyu districts in the redrawing of provincial boundaries prior to independence.[49] Their wish was granted. With the exception of the Ndia, Mwea, Gichugu, and Kerugoya divisions, which make up the Kirinyaga district of Central Province, the remainder of Embu and the whole of Meru, both of which have since been subdivided into smaller districts, were put into the Eastern Province at independence. As the example of Embu suggests, the experience of the violence played a profound role in shaping allegiances by creating new bonds between perceived victims on one hand and perpetrators on the other. The violence of the conflict itself can similarly be identified as one trigger mechanism for the move towards loyalism undertaken by many Kikuyu during the course of the war. The second key trigger was a change in the overall shape of the war and the balance of power in local communities.

The Swing in Control

The polarisation of the population, the swing towards loyalism, and the crystallisation of a loyalist identity reflected a steady improvement in the security of loyalists. Government control of Central Kenya was reconstructed following the successful execution of a series of military operations and provided loyalists with the security to openly enunciate

Meru, 'Handing Over Notes: Mr. W. B. G. Raynor to Mr. J. A. Cumber,' 11 May 1955, 1. In Southern Province, those of mixed Kikuyu and Maasai parentage were held responsible for the growth in support for the insurgency in Narok and Kajiado: see KNA MAA/7/250, PC Southern to Chief Native Commissioner, 10 April 1954. For discussions in the War Council of encouraging such views in Embu and Meru, see KNA WC/CM/1/3, minutes of 121st meeting of the War Council, 12 July 1955 & minutes of 146th meeting of the War Council, 6 December 1955.

[48] KNA AHC/9/25, 'The Words Which the D.C. Told Ahoi During the Meeting on 29.12.55,' *Kaya ka Embu*, 15 January 1956; KNA ARC(MAA) 2/5/218 V, minutes of Embu ADC meeting, 16–17 February 1956, 1–2.

[49] Regional Boundaries Commission Kenya, *Kenya: The Report of the Regional Boundaries Commission* (London, 1962).

opposition to Mau Mau. Most significant of these military operations
was Operation Anvil, a mass screening and detention exercise carried
out in Nairobi in April 1954. The city was an integral part of the wider
struggle. Nairobi acted as an important supply centre for the forest fighters in terms of money, weapons, and new recruits.[50] Organising committees in Nairobi provided an essential element of central direction over a
movement that had been decapitated by Operation Jock Scott. Repatriates brought back with them a heightened sense of grievance exacerbated
by sustained exposure to the radicalised politics of the city. Outbreaks
of public expressions of support for Mau Mau in the outlying districts
of Central Province correlated with arrivals of repatriates expelled from
Nairobi under suspicion of involvement in the insurgency.[51]

In 1952 and 1953, 'Mau Mau in Nairobi,' Kabiro recalled, 'seemed
to have the support of almost all the Africans.'[52] An influx of thousands
of Kikuyu families escaping the repressive counterinsurgency campaign
in the reserves added to the city's marginalised communities.[53] Titus
Murong'a, who served as a police officer, recalled the city to be chaotic.
Crime soared throughout the eastern areas of the city populated by the
African community.[54] As the urban discontents sought supplies of food,
money, and weapons, attacks on Asian-owned shops occurred frequently.[55] The insurgents strictly enforced boycotts of European buses, ciga-
rettes, and beer, punishing transgressors with floggings or even execution.[56] The urban authorities attempted to wrest control of the streets
from Mau Mau. Kikuyu families were shuffled around the city, both to

---

[50] Frank Furedi, 'The African Crowd in Nairobi: Popular Movements and Elite Politics,'
    Journal of African History 14 (1973), 285.
[51] KNA MSS/124/4, W. H. Laughton to B. Owen, 2 July 1953; KNA MSS/124/4, W. H.
    Laughton to Rev. T. A. Beetham, 14 September 1953; KNA DC/EBU/1/1/12, Embu
    District Annual Report 1953, 1, 3 & 6; KNA DC/EBU/1/2/3, DC Embu, 'Handing Over
    Report: Mr. R. A. Wilkinson to Mr. F. R. Wilson,' 19 July 1954, 1 of Emergency
    chapter; KNA MSS/124/5, W. H. Laughton to M. McKeag, 16 January 1955, 1; KNA
    DC/MRU/1/3/13/1, DC Meru, 'Handing-Over Notes: Mr. W. B. G. Raynor to Mr. J. A.
    Cumber,' 11 May 1955, 1; J. T. Samuel Kamunchula, 'The Meru Participation in Mau
    Mau,' *Kenya Historical Review* 3 (1975), 201–2.
[52] Kabiro, *Man in the Middle*, 50.
[53] Kenya National Archive Migrated Archive from Tel Aviv held at Rhodes House Library,
    Oxford (TA) Kenya 016, DC Nairobi to Officer-in-Charge Nairobi Extra-Provincial
    District (EPD), 3 December 1953; ibid., 50.
[54] Titus M'Imanene Murong'a, interview with the author, Chogoria, South Meru, 16
    September 2004.
[55] Richard McCormack, *Asians in Kenya: Conflicts and Politics* (Brooklyn NY, 1971),
    119.
[56] Kabiro, *Man in the Middle*, 60–61.

be more easily policed and as punishment.[57] Mass clearances of areas suspected of general Mau Mau support were enacted.[58] Trading licences were restricted to those with appropriate security clearances.[59] But these punitive actions were insufficient to check Mau Mau's domination of the city.

For loyalists like John Gitonga, an employee of the Department of Information, life in Nairobi before Anvil was 'intolerable.'[60] Although the Administration attempted to provide secure accommodation for loyalists, particularly in Bahati, their lives were at great risk.[61] Attacks on loyalists from late 1952 to early 1954 were commonplace.[62] Attempts to establish the African Home Guard were repeatedly thwarted by widespread fear of Mau Mau reprisals.[63] Tribal Police appointed before October 1953 had to be transferred from other districts.[64] Kikuyu inhabitants of Nairobi were reluctant to act as court assessors, leaving the courts reliant principally on those from Kiambu.[65] Loyalists, such as the self-styled 'Muslim Home-Guards of Pumwani,'[66] who did publicly demonstrate their opposition to Mau Mau in Nairobi before Anvil were drawn from the Kikuyu Islamic landlord class anxious to defend their property.[67] As outside the city, the Nairobi Home Guard frequently demonstrated its propensity for misbehaviour. Even fellow loyalists accused the Pumwani Home Guard of extortion and theft.[68]

---

[57] TA Kenya 101, DC Nairobi & City African Affairs Officer, 'Report on the Removal of Kikuyu/Embu/Meru from Kaloleni,' 20 October 1953.

[58] '12,345 Held After Pumwani Swee Police and Military in Biggest Clean-Up,' *East African Standard*, 23 March 1953, 1; 'Bulldozers Raize Mathari Shanties,' *East African Standard*, 20 April 1953, 1; Furedi, 'African Crowd,' 285.

[59] TA Kenya 091, Anon., 'Issue of Hawkers and Traders Licences to African Traders, December 1953? 1; KNA AHC/9/52, 'Njoo Sokoni (Come to the Market),' *Mwanamke*, 21 April 1954, 2.

[60] TA Kenya 059, John Gitonga to Director of Establishment, 12 June 1956, 2.

[61] TA Kenya 092, DC Nairobi, 'Housing in Bahati Location,' November 1953, 1.

[62] Anderson, *Histories*, 190–200.

[63] TNA: PRO WO 276/398, Nairobi District Intelligence Committtee Summary for week ending 28 August 1953, 3.

[64] KNA OP/1/195, DC Nairobi to Officer-in-Charge Nairobi EPD, 16 November 1954.

[65] KNA DC/KSM/1/15/34, Deputy Registrar Supreme Court to DC Nairobi, 29 April 1954; Deputy Registrar Supreme Court to DC Nairobi, 28 April 1954; Labour Officer Nairobi to Registrar Supreme Court, 31 August 1953; Labour Officer Nairobi to Registrar Supreme Court, 29 August 1953.

[66] TA Kenya 040, Muslim Home-Guards of Pumwani to DC Nairobi, 25 November 1953.

[67] Lonsdale, 'Wealth, Poverty and Civic Virtue,' 357.

[68] TA Kenya 042, Anon. to DC Nairobi, 27 March 1954; TA Kenya 099, Government Servants c/o Starehe Government Quarters to Mr Payel, 5 March 1954.

Mau Mau's strength in Nairobi demanded a proportionately powerful response by the colonial authorities. Earlier urban counterinsurgency
tactics had been ineffective and too localised in focus to have any great
impact on the larger narrative of the war. However, for a month from 24
April 1954, a security cordon was thrown around the city and its Kikuyu
population, approximately 50,000 strong, were systematically screened.
A total of 24,100 were detained and a further 6,150 repatriated to Central Province.[69] More than half of the city's largest ethnic group was thus
removed in the space of four weeks, with profound effects for Nairobi's
social fabric, its economy, and the course of the war. Inevitably, bearing
in mind the size of the operation, the prevailing ambiguity of allegiances
among the population, and the inability of the colonial authorities to
successfully differentiate between friend and foe, many loyalists found
themselves caught in Anvil's net.[70] One such individual, David Muriithi,
found himself in the police cells on Kingsway before being repatriated
to Kiambu. His fellow suspects sang Mau Mau songs and promised that
'it would be a bad day for the Home Guard when freedom came.'[71] Yet
even as Mau Mau supporters sang of victory, a loyalist triumph drew
ever closer. Anvil was, General Erskine remarked at the end of his tour
of duty, 'the turning point in the Emergency.'[72]

John Gitonga later wrote how 'We cleaned the city.' The security forces
'arrested many Mau Mau treasurers, gunmen, hardcores, we disrupted
all their methods arresting many members of Mau Mau District Council,
Mau Mau Parliament members; we recovered many guns and ammunition of various kinds etc.' 'All that we did is still recorded,' Gitonga
proudly declared. 'People boarded buses, they drank beer, they smoked
without fear.'[73] In the months following Anvil, the number of city dwell-
ers originating from Central Province was restricted to 25 percent of
the total African population.[74] Although Mau Mau activity, in particular, attacks on loyalists, did not cease entirely,[75] the improving security situation allowed middle-class Kikuyu loyalists to emerge as court

---

[69] For accounts of Anvil, see Anderson, *Histories*, 200–12; Elkins, *Imperial*, 121–5.
[70] Anderson, *Histories*, 206–9.
[71] KNA MAA/8/169, statement by David Muriithi attached to E. Carey Francis to CNC,
     3 May 1954.
[72] TNA: PRO WO 236/18, General Erskine, 'The Kenya Emergency: June 1953 – May
     1955,' 25 April 1955, 27. See also ibid., 268.
[73] TA Kenya 059, John Gitonga to Director of Establishment, 12 June 1956, 2.
[74] KNA RN/4/113, minutes of Nairobi EPD Emergency Committee meeting, 8 February
     1956, 1.
[75] Ibid., 212–4; Mathu, *Urban Guerrilla*, 56.

assessors[76] and as members of the Home Guard.[77] In January 1955, Isack Karanja Kagiro, an informer writing for the first time under his real name, described in a letter to the Nairobi district commissioner how 'owing to increased enrolling of the Home Guards' and the large numbers of willing informers, 'Mau Mau gangsters are finding difficulties in penetrating into African locations.' Karanja described how Nairobi was beginning to resemble a 'city of Homeguards.'[78]

The urban war was lost for Mau Mau. Assistance for the rebellion evaporated, and Mau Mau units came to rely on ever-younger recruits, apparently forcibly conscripted into the ranks of the guerrillas.[79] The Home Guard enthusiastically translated their newfound power into ill-gotten material gains.[80] As the Nairobi district commissioner reluctantly recognised, 'the prestige of Her Majesty's Government is likely to be brought into disrepute.'[81] But tolerance of such excesses was part of the terms of the alliance between the colonial state and loyalists.

Developments in the countryside mirrored those in the city. Completed at various stages throughout 1954, the Provincial Administration in Central Province initiated a radical programme of social revolution. The focus of this process was the construction of villages as part of the counterinsurgency programme, a process known as villagisation.[82] Practically the entire rural population of Central Province was forcibly relocated from their dispersed dwellings set among their smallholdings into the newly built villages. Villages were intended to each house up to 500 people and were located within 500 yards of a Home Guard post, each of which was responsible for two or three villages.[83] Each village

---

[76] KNA DC/KSM/1/15/34, DC Nairobi to Registrar Supreme Court, 15 September 1954.
[77] KNA MAA/7/251, minutes of Nairobi Emergency Committee meeting, 14 July 1954.
[78] TA Kenya 046, Isack Karanja Kagiro to DC Nairobi, 15 February 1955.
[79] David Anderson, 'The Battle of Dandora Swamp: Reconstructing the Mau Mau Land Freedom Army October 1954,' in *Mau Mau and Nationhood: Arms, Authority and Narration*, eds. Elisha Stephen Atieno Odhiambo and John Lonsdale (Oxford, 2003), 171–2.
[80] TA Kenya 053, the Tenants of City Council Houses, Shauri la Moyo to City Council African Affairs Officer, 26 August 1954; TA Kenya 050, Surinder K. Kochhar to DC Nairobi, 31 August 1954; TA Kenya 051, Security Officer, Block Hotels to DO Pumwani, 2 September 1954; TA Kenya 054, Major F. R. Corner to N. F. Harris Member of Legislative Council (MLC), 20 September 1954; TA Kenya 052, Traffic Superintendent, Kenya Bus Services to DC Nairobi, 23 October 1954.
[81] TA Kenya 043, DC Nairobi to Secretary for African Affairs, 9 August 1954.
[82] For a fuller discussion of villagisation, see Elkins, *Imperial*, 233–74.
[83] KNA DC/MRU/2/1/4, DC Nyeri, 'Paper on Village Settlement for District Team,' 22 April 1954, 2.

belonged to one of two forms. The first was punitive villages for Mau Mau suspects and their families, characterised by high degrees of surveillance and extremely coercive. The second form was protective villages constructed for Home Guards and their dependents.[84]

The villages loomed large in the lives of the population of Central Province even before each community was forced to relocate to them. Work began on each village three months before it was habitable. The designated occupants were required to construct the village during forced labour duties. When sufficient buildings were erected, the new inhabitants were forcibly rehoused. At the same time, and as a result of the limits on space within the villages, all livestock was confiscated.[85] The village into which the community moved was, however, far from complete. Instead, the entire population was crammed into a small number of huts while they continued construction of the rest of the dwellings, until there was one for each family. The forced labour was deployed to dig protective moats surrounding each village and Home Guard post.[86] Once completed, the punitive villages were 'extremely crowded and often badly planned.'[87] In the rush to construct the punitive villages, schools, medical services, and shops were not relocated.[88] 'Such a type of village,' the Emergency Joint Staff reported, 'is invariably unpopular with the inhabitants as it is crowded, dirty and unhygienic.'[89] Communal labour was an integral part of life in the Emergency villages, and one district officer even insisted on using children as part of the work gangs, contrary to official policy.[90]

The power of chiefs and the Home Guard permeated throughout daily life in the villages, with their approval required for nearly every conceivable aspect of public life. During the day, the chiefs determined the timetable of the day, for example, by dictating at what times cattle

[84] KNA DC/MRU/2/1/4, DC Nyeri, 'Memorandum: Kikuyu Village Settlement,' 11 February 1954, 1.
[85] KNA DC/KBU/2/1, DO Gatundu, 'Gatundu Division Handing Over Report,' 6 September 1954, 10.
[86] KNA DC/EBU/1/2/4, DO Ndia, 'Handing Over Notes,' June 1956, 2.
[87] KNA DC/EBU/1/2/7, DO Ndia, 'Ndia Division Handing Over Notes: Gordon – Johnson,' April 1957, 8.
[88] Sorrenson, *Land Reform*, 149.
[89] KNA WC/CM/1/1, Emergency Joint Staff, 'Control of Villages,' 29 January 1955, 1.
[90] KNA VP/13/6, Supervisor of Schools, Church of Scotland Mission Tumutumu to DO Mathira, 15 November 1955; DC Nyeri to DO Mathira, 18 November 1955. See also C. Elkins, *Imperial Reckoning*, 117.

should be taken to the guarded enclosures for the night.[91] After darkness fell, each village was subject to a dusk-to-dawn curfew monitored by the local Home Guard unit.[92] Loyalist elites were also in control of local policy formation and the implementation of directives imposed from Nairobi on a newly centralised and pliant population. Dominating local councils, from which Mau Mau supporters were barred, and other committees set up to discuss post-conflict reconstruction, loyalists were able to profoundly influence the nature of village life and the future trajectory of local communities.[93] But the biggest gain for loyalists from villagisation was the improved security. With the population under constant surveillance and substantial fortifications put in place, it was extremely difficult for guerrilla units to liaise with their supporters among the population at large. Through the denial of valuable supplies, intelligence, and reinforcements, the insurgency was substantially weakened by villagisation.[94] Moreover, the brutal nature of life in the villages made continuation of support for the forest fighters impossible for all but the most committed.

Once in the villages, attendance at large public propaganda meetings was compulsory.[95] The population of each was subjected to sustained efforts to encourage confessions by Mau Mau activities and the passing of information regarding the loyalties of others.[96] Although attacks on loyalists did not cease entirely, deaths of Mau Mau suspects at the hands of the security forces were many times more common in this period, as has been extensively documented.[97] Abuses committed by the Home Guards were widespread in the villages. 'Some of the [Home Guards],' one district officer wrote, 'are genuine out and out thugs and are probably guilty of far

---

[91] KNA MA/1/2, Acting African Courts Officer to DC Kiambu, 19 July 1956, 1.
[92] KNA DC/KBU/2/1, DO Gatundu, 'Gatundu Division Handing Over Report,' 6 September 1954, 10.
[93] All chiefs, African Assistant DOs, and senior churchmen sat on the provincial committee established to discuss Emergency policies, including surrender terms and post-conflict reconstruction (KNA VP/1/38, minutes of the 3rd & 4th 'Meeting to Consider Policy and Reconstruction in the Kikuyu Native Land Unit,' 4–5 March 1954 & 11–13 May 1954).
[94] KNA VP/14/13, DC Nyeri, 'Review of Situation – Nyeri District,' 27 July 1955, 1.
[95] KNA VP/2/3, DC Nyeri to DO Othaya, 13 November 1954.
[96] KNA VP/1/47, DO North Tetu to DC Nyeri, 26 May 1955.
[97] This issue is extensively discussed throughout the secondary literature on Mau Mau, but most fully in Anderson, *Histories*, 289–327; Elkins, *Imperial*, 117 & 233–274. The most damning primary material is in RHL Mss Afr s 1964 & RHL Mss Brit Emp s 486, box 5.

more than is reported.'[98] Their misdemeanours included murder,[99] cattle
rustling,[100] the theft and destruction of livestock[101] and property of those
suspected of Mau Mau sympathies,[102] and the abduction of women.[103]
The guard posts were frequently cited as the location for atrocities during
interrogations.[104] Such atrocities were in fact much more frequent in the
period after the military conflict had ended. The beatings and corruption
commonly associated with the Home Guard and the chiefs and headmen
were both acts of vengeance on a newly compliant population and a
response to the economic crisis that subsumed Central Province during
the war.

Loyalists were far from immune from the effects of this downturn in the
local economy. Prior to the land reforms discussed in the next chapter,
access to existing landholdings was hampered by a number of factors.
Firstly, the demands of employment in the Home Guard or other loyalist institutions monopolised the time of loyalists, diverting them away
from their land. Moreover, the Emergency movement restrictions made
it exceptionally difficult to move produce to market, which thus acted as
a disincentive to productivity. Finally, fear of attack by Mau Mau fighters while working on remote landholdings further discouraged loyalists
from maintaining their agricultural production. Although better than for

[98] KNA DC/KBU/2/1, DO Gatundu, 'Gatundu Division Handing Over Report,' 6 September 1954, 11.
[99] See correspondence in KNA AM/1/21 'Murders Nyeri Area' relating to alleged murders
of Mau Mau suspects committed by Home Guards under the supervision of European
officials and half-hearted attempts at investigation of such cases.
[100] KNA ARC(MAA) 2/5/323, G. Adamson to DO Mukugodo, 1 August 1954; George
Adamson, *Bwana Game: The Life Story of George Adamson* (London, 1968), 201–2.
[101] KNA DC/FH/3/16/39, Mucuru Muturi to DC Fort Hall, 29 May 1955. Jackson has
argued that the consumption of meat played a central role in Mau Mau discourses due
to its limited availability. The recurrence of consumption of livestock in accusations
against loyalists may be a reflection of this (Kennell Jackson, "Impossible to Ignore
Their Greatness': Survival Craft in the Mau Mau Forest Movement," in *Mau Mau and
Nationhood: Arms, Authority and Narration*, eds. Elisha Stephen Atieno Odhiambo
and John Lonsdale (London, 2003), 182).
[102] KNA ARC(MAA) 2/5/198 I, Bernard Njoroge Kamau to CNC, 16 August 1956. In
the same file, see also Kirumba Waharwigi to Secretary for African Affairs, 10 August
1956; G. Wabuga Kibuku to Chief Secretary, 7 October 1956; Njau Kimau to Ministry
of African Affairs, 24 November 1956; Justo Karanja Ngure to CNC, 29 November
1956; Njoroge Mwaniki to Minister of African Affairs, 6 December 1956; Waiyaki
Makanga Gichuhi to Minister of African Affairs, 6 December 1956.
[103] KNA DC/FH/3/16/39, Station Master Fort Hall to DC Fort Hall, 6 December 1955. The
Ndakaini Home Guard unit reported their headman as carrying out similar activities
in KNA DC/FH/3/16/39, Ndakaini Home Guards to DC Fort Hall, 13 February 1955.
[104] See for an account of 'Kenya's Belsen,' Anderson, *Histories*, 297–307.

the rest of the population, opportunities for loyalists to earn a legitimate income were extremely limited during the first two years of the war. It is not surprising, then, that many loyalists exploited their service within the supposedly unwaged Home Guard 'to receive immediate material gain.'[105] Extortion and corruption were commonplace, ultimately leading to the disbandment of the formal Home Guard force at the beginning of 1955.[106]

At the time of the dissolution of the Home Guard, some of the force's members were absorbed into the Tribal Police and its Reserve, both of which were controlled by the Provincial Administration. Most were appointed to unarmed "Watch and Ward" groups responsible for security in the immediate vicinity of their homes.[107] Other Home Guards in Central Province were recruited into the expanded Home Guard in operation in the settler districts.[108] By mid-1955, 15,000 Watch and Ward Home Guards were still operating in Central Province, together with 1,894 Tribal Police and 6,833 Tribal Police reservists.[109] These bureaucratic manoeuvrings had little effect on the nature of the war on the ground. Whatever their new titles, the Home Guards remained responsible for securing a radically changed Central Province, primarily through exerting an iron grip over the villages.

The most comprehensive account of life in a loyalist village, Kabare to the south of Mount Kenya in the Kerugoya location of Embu district, was compiled in 1956 by Greet Kershaw, née Sluiter. The report was commissioned by the Christian Council of Kenya and details everyday life and matters of faith, and considers the relationship between church and society in the context of the war, with particular reference to the issue of community and political leadership. Kabare was chosen as the site for the study, as since 1910 it had been the site of a substantial

---

[105] KNA VQ/1/51, DC Kiambu to PC Central, 26 June 1954.
[106] The announcement was made in KNA WC/CM/1/1, 'H.E. the Governor's Directive No. 4 of 1954,' 31 December 1954. For explicit acknowledgement of the significance of accusations of abuses to the disbandment of the Home Guard see KNA ARC(MAA) 2/5/327, PC Central to Minister for African Affairs, 16 December 1954; KNA DC/NYK/3/1/30, 'Record of a Meeting Held at Government House on Thursday, December 23rd 1954,' 24 December 1954, 1.
[107] KNA DC/NUK/3/1/30, Anon, 'The Role and Tasks of the Tribal Police, Tribal Police Reserve and Ward Units of the K.E.M. Guard,' attached to Secretary for African Affairs to PC Central, 10 February 1955.
[108] KNA DC/NYK/3/1/30, DC Nanyuki, 'Kikuyu Guard – Numbers Employed in Nanyuki District,' 21 April 1956; KNA DC/NYK/3/9/18, DC Fort Hall to DC Nanyuki, 31 December 1954.
[109] KNA OP/1/998, G.N.C, 'Memo,' 15 June 1955, 2–3.

Anglican mission station. In common with other similar locations across Central Province, Kabare became home to 'a strong loyalist-population' during the Emergency. By no means was the entire population loyalist, however. A substantial proportion was either neutral, again a possible stance considering the guerrillas were effectively defeated by this stage, or broadly sympathetic to the insurgency but insufficiently active to cause the authorities any great concern. Kabare's residents in 1956 numbered approximately 1,360 men, women, and children. However, of this number, just 176 were men.[110] That gender imbalance hints at the sense of moral and social crisis that pervades throughout Kershaw's report from Kabare. With fathers separated from their families by either labour migration or as a consequence of the war, breakdowns in household discipline characterised life in the villages. Kabare was far from atypical. By 1955, in some Nyeri villages, where the rate of detentions and participation in the guerrilla army was highest, women outnumbered men by seven to one.[111] In contrast, comparatively peaceful Kiambu, where the war had burned hard but fast in 1952 and 1953, another of Kershaw's reports demonstrated that social life was far closer to the peacetime norm.[112]

In Kabare, the disruption to daily life caused by the Emergency was significant despite its strongly loyalist population. The surviving custom of men living in separate huts from women and children conflicted with the issue of just one hut per family. The men had, therefore, moved en masse with almost no exceptions to the Home Guard post.[113] The burden of labour thus fell heavily on the women of Kabare.[114] Communal labour was a source of great contention among all residents of the village because of the use of compulsion on the part of the Provincial Administration's local officers. Communal labour was thus understood as punishment, but for what offence was unclear, as loyalists too had to join the communal labour gangs. This was a source of great amusement to the non-loyalist sections of the community, who ridiculed their loyalist neighbours by asking them 'if this was the reward of the government they had served so

[110] KNA DC/EBU/9/1, G. Sluiter, 'A Study of Kabare-Village in the Embu-District,' May 1956, 2–3.
[111] Leonard Beecher, 'Christian Counter-Revolution to Mau Mau,' in *Rhodesia and East Africa*, ed. Ferdinand Joelson (London, 1958), 90.
[112] RHL Mss Afr s 633, box 18, file 4, G. Sluiter, 'Confidential Report on Migrant Labour and Connected Matters in Four Villages in the Kiambu Reserve of Kenya,' 1957, 8.
[113] KNA DC/EBU/9/1, G. Sluiter, 'A Study of Kabare-Village in the Embu-District,' May 1956, 17.
[114] KNA DC/EBU/9/1, G. Sluiter, 'A Study of Kabare-Village in the Embu-District,' May 1956, 29.

faithfully?'[115] Although Kabare and other such loyalist settlements were very far from the punitive villages described so vividly by Elkins, it is clear that loyalists received little relief from some of the most intrusive elements of village life.

Restrictive curfews were imposed on Kabare's residents without distinction. So too were the regulations that demanded livestock be housed in enclosures overnight. The denial of opportunities for the remaining guerrillas to gather food had been one of the primary objectives of the villagisation programme. Along the southern edge of the forest reserve that enclosed Mount Kenya, villagisation had proceeded simultaneously with the construction of a vast ditch that was designed to keep the guerrillas inside the forest and away from their sympathisers among the population. That trawling of the fish from the swamp was consolidated by the construction of the villages. Under guard day and night and supervised while working in the fields, the provision of food to the insurgents by villagers was extremely difficult. Food supplies to the villagised population were also carefully controlled to prevent hoarding and the passing of surplus to the guerrillas. With trading restricted to loyalist shopkeepers and famine relief channelled through those shops, revenge and intra-community tensions could be manifested on the shop floor.[116] As a result of such policies, by June 1956, famine among the wives of detainees was reported in Kiambu.[117] High infant mortality was a further significant worry in Kiambu.[118] Blacker estimates 26,000 deaths among children under the age of 10 as a result of the war, and attributes most of those casualties to malnutrition and diseases encountered in the villages.[119] But such concerns were only a distant worry for the loyalists of Kabare. Their anxieties with the food denial aspects of villagisation were rather more economic in nature than having to do with simply staying alive.

To prevent guerrillas seizing livestock for food, cattle were stabled overnight in guarded enclosures after villagisation. But there was insufficient space for all cows, so many were forced to sell their livestock when they moved to the villages. Ownership of goats was a further problem.

[115] KNA DC/EBU/9/1, G. Sluiter, 'A Study of Kabare-Village in the Embu-District,' May 1956, 37.

[116] KNA VP/1/16, DC Nyeri to PC Central, 25 June 1954; KNA VP/14/13, DC Nyeri, 'Review of the Situation,' 27 July 1954, 2.

[117] KNA PC/NKU/2/17/8, DC Kiambu to PC Central, 20 June 1956, 2.

[118] RHL Mss Afr s 633, box 18, file 4, G. Sluiter, 'Confidential Report on Migrant Labour and Connected Matters in Four Villages in the Kiambu Reserve of Kenya,' 1957, 9.

[119] Blacker, 'Demography of Mau Mau,' 225–6.

Although no doubt primarily concerned with food denial, the authorities banned the keeping of goats within village homes on the grounds of public health.[120] With a glut of livestock reaching the market at the same time, prices must have fallen, and the value of investment in cattle and goats tumbled. In Nyeri, loyalist farmers in North Tetu were particularly aggrieved. With the war there kept under control by the negotiated settlement between Muhoya and Kimathi, loyalists felt under little threat. But the insistence of the Provincial Administration that their livestock be placed every night in guarded enclosures provoked considerable resistance among members of the local dairy farmers' cooperative. Such policies threatened the livelihoods of the farmers, as it severely disrupted the production and delivery of dairy products to Nyeri.[121]

Villagisation had other economic effects as a consequence of the severe restrictions placed on the movement of goods and people. The population was essentially restricted to its designated village and immediate surrounds. Permits from the Provincial Administration were needed for travel outside of the location, but these were not easily acquired from an institution determined to strangle any remaining opportunities for the survival of the insurgency. The demand for public transport was then correspondingly low. But the schools continued to graduate pupils, meaning Kabare's ever-growing number of school-leavers found it difficult to find work in the village.[122] Moreover, the demands placed on the time of tradesmen as a result of their membership of the Home Guard, restrictions placed on the opening and operation of shops, and the difficulty in shipping in goods from outside meant that the population of Kabare had to travel outside of the village to purchase almost any item. Yet, the difficulty in getting movement permits, even for loyalists, and finding available transport meant that 'there was a greater wish for spending money than opportunities for spending.' Therefore, many of those earning a monetary income deposited savings at the local post office, which accumulated over the span of the war.[123] By 1960, when the last of the Emergency restrictions were lifted, some loyalists had built up not inconsequential savings. This suggests some of the wealth that is commonly

[120] KNA DC/EBU/9/1, G. Sluiter, 'A Study of Kabare-Village in the Embu-District,' May 1956, 5.
[121] KNA ARC(MAA) 2/3/307 III, DC Nyeri to PC Central, 5 October 1953.
[122] KNA DC/EBU/9/1, G. Sluiter, 'A Study of Kabare-Village in the Embu-District,' May 1956, 6 & 21.
[123] KNA DC/EBU/9/1, G. Sluiter, 'A Study of Kabare-Village in the Embu-District,' May 1956, 4–5.

attributed to the misappropriation of land or possessions of Mau Mau fighters during the war was instead the result of the investment of capital legally accumulated during the war.

Violence and Control in the Rise of Loyalism

Through 1954, allegiances became more firmly set as the conflict continued and the public sought the protection of one side or the other. With the government regaining control of Central Province after the war's most decisive military act, Operation Anvil in Nairobi, more and more of the population declared itself loyalist. In making themselves visible, this second wave of loyalists allowed the government to identify, protect, and reward loyalists far beyond the first group of chiefs and Christians. A near-universal suspicion of Kikuyu on the part of European officials and settlers gave way to a more discriminating analysis of the war. Security for loyalists greatly improved through 1954, and unprecedented social, political, and economic reforms were instituted for the benefit of the regime's African allies. All of this could only be implemented because of the changing balance of power in localities, during which the pendulum swung towards loyalists and the colonial government.

Control of an area by one warring party or the other is likely to engender support for that party from the local population during civil war. Most obviously, control allows dominant actors to extract support from local populations through the implementation of coercive penalties and induce loyalty through the provision of rewards. However, control also lowers the risk of being killed by the opposing group for those wishing to work with the incumbent group. The greater the level of control an incumbent has, the more difficult it is for rivals to operate in that area. Control, over time, socialises the local population so as to encourage greater voluntary support and demonstrates the credibility of the incumbent group, thus boosting their claims to authority.[124] Such arguments certainly hold true for Kenya. The colonial government established control over local communities through the enactment of military operations, such as Anvil, and the villagisation of the rural population of Central Province.

The villages in particular wreaked a terrible toll on the insurgency's support base. Mau Mau were encouraged to surrender by those unable

---

[124] Kalyvas, *Logic of Violence*, 113–31.

to continue making sacrifices.[125] The swing in control had not just made it safer to be a loyalist, but had also meant the colonial government had replaced the insurgents as the preferred partner for individuals seeking to privatise the violence of the war. In June 1954, a captured Mau Mau guerrilla in Nyeri described to his police interrogators the changing nature of the war and loyalism:

> The majority [of the Home Guard] have taken the Mau Mau oath and they look upon the Home Guard as a better way of achieving the objects of Mau Mau. They think that, after the Emergency, they will be able to persuade the Government to give them land in return for their services.[126]

Loyalism emerged as a viable alternative to Mau Mau after Operation Anvil. The insurgency was moving towards defeat, and continued support for it was costly and unlikely to result in any meaningful reward. The loss of insurgent control triggered a move towards loyalism. But the sustenance of the loyalist position, as opposed to mere dissent with the insurgency, was dependent on a major change in the attitudes of the colonial government towards their loyalist allies.

[125] Lonsdale, 'Authority,' 62.
[126] KNA VQ/1/51, Assitant Superintendent of Police, Special Branch (ASP SB) Nyeri to PC Central, 19 June 1954.

4

Loyalism, Land, and Labour

The Path to Self-Mastery

The Second Prong

Exactly four years after the British colonial regime had declared war on Mau Mau's insurgents, the rebellion was finally defeated. In the early morning of 21 October 1956, the movement's last remaining leader and symbolic figurehead, Dedan Kimathi, was captured. The military struggle against the colonial state had been in terminal decline since mid-1954. Aerial bombardment, military patrols, sanctions against civilian supporters, and the sheer unpleasantness of life in the damp, cold, high-altitude forests took their toll.[1] In the forests of Mount Kenya and the Aberdares, British and African soldiers squeezed the guerrillas to the breaking point. The Kenya Police patrolled the streets of Nairobi. In Central Province, the Home Guard mopped up those who had fled the offensive and crushed any signs of lingering support for the rebellion. After the military leader of the forces on Mount Kenya, General China (the *nom de guerre* of Waruhiu Itote), was captured in January 1954, and Kimathi's fellow leader in the Aberdares, Stanley Mathenge, had disappeared, Kimathi became the focus of British attempts to finish the rebellion. When he was finally captured, Kimathi was all alone. His last followers had scattered over the previous days as the net tightened around him.[2]

Driven from the relative safety of the forest because of hunger, Kimathi spent his last night at large in a village in the Nyeri district close to the treeline. There, the trap was sprung. Cornered by the security forces,

---

[1] Anderson, *Histories*, 230–88; & Clough, *Memoirs*, 127–77.
[2] The policeman in charge of the operation subsequently recorded the pursuit in Ian Henderson and Philip Goodhart, *The Hunt for Kimathi* (London, 1958).

Kimathi attempted to flee back to the forest. Forced into the open, a group of Tribal Police[3] opened fire and shot the Mau Mau general. He was arrested shortly afterwards and, lying on a stretcher, he was displayed to the international media. Four months later, Kimathi was executed, and his body was buried in an anonymous mass grave. His death signalled the end of Mau Mau's military struggle. Kimathi was the war's most significant historical figure. By contrast, Sihar Gitahi Ribai, a member of the Tribal Police unit that captured Kimathi, was one of the war's many anonymous characters. Gitahi, a Presbyterian convert, was a poor man. He was a peasant farmer and butcher in Ihururu, in Nyeri district, and, like many of his adversaries in the 1950s, had served with the British army in Asia during World War II. During his military service, he learned the first aid skills that allowed him to tend to Kimathi's wounds after his capture. His patient that day was no stranger. Both Kimathi and Gitahi had attended school and grown up together, and they recognised one another in October 1956.[4]

Neither Kimathi's isolation on that fateful day or Gitahi's opposition can be fully understood by only the course of events in the military struggle. The manner of the insurgency's denouement, the strength of loyalism, and the lasting significance of Mau Mau's defeat requires a close examination of the non-military aspects of counterinsurgency. Termed the 'second prong' by the governor, Evelyn Baring, non-military counterinsurgency in Kenya took the shape of social, economic, and political reform.[5] The most significant and best-known aspect of this programme was agrarian reform. Less commonly discussed by historians were the labour opportunities provided to loyalists. Both are explored in this chapter. The rewards for elite loyalists, a temporary monopoly over the political process and recruitment into the Provincial Administration, are examined in the next chapter.

Collectively, the second prong was a sustaining mechanism for loyalism, but not its trigger. Promises of future bounty, it is true, were made to loyalists by colonial officials from the very beginning of the conflict.

---

3 The Tribal Police is now known as the Administration Police. It is a force distinct from the Kenya Police and is now, as it was in the colonial period, controlled by the Provincial Administration.

4 Sihar Gitahi Ribai, interview with the author, Ihururu, Muhoya's Location, Nyeri, 7 February 2004. Gitahi gave an account of his role in Kimathi's capture in the television programme 'The Hunt for Kimathi,' *Empire Warriors*, BBC2, 10 December 2004.

5 RHL Mss Afr s 1574, 'Transcript of Recording of a Discussion Between Lord Howick and Dame Margery Perham,' 19 November 1969, 24.

In 1952, 1953, and 1954, the government promised loyalists that they would 'form the foundation' on which the government would 'seek to build during the reconstruction period.'[6] Loyalists 'will get our prior support in time to come in the fields of reconstruction – agricultural and social – and it is he who will gain the ear of Government through village, Locational and other Councils,' promised the Nyeri district commissioner in August 1954.[7] But these pledges remained vague, and formal rewards were minimal during the initial stages of the war. The combined benefits of membership of the Home Guard, as discussed in Chapter 2, totalled just Sh.15 per month per full-time member of the force.[8] Even the repatriates from the Rift Valley suspected of Mau Mau sympathies could, if only in theory, earn Sh.30 per month in Fort Hall through their employment in labour gangs.[9] 'You work for nothing,' Mau Mau supporters in Nyeri contemptuously told the Home Guards.[10] The fruits of loyalism were then harvested retrospectively.

Non-military forms of counterinsurgency have long formed central components of such campaigns. In theory, the efficacy of non-military counterinsurgency derives from not just bolstering the morale of supporters, but also from allowing states to restore legitimacy by demonstrating their responsiveness to the needs of their subjects.[11] In practice, however, the effectiveness of this measure has differed from place to place. In the cases of Peru and El Salvador, for example, insurgent violence continued long after the introduction of land reform. Violence perpetrated by the state in both countries undermined the message of social concern that non-military counterinsurgency was intended to convey.[12] In Kenya, by contrast, high levels of state-sponsored violence failed to decrease the

[6] KNA VQ/1/31, 'Extract From the Provincial Commissioner, Nyeri's Memorandum on Future Administration of the Kikuyu Districts,' 31 July 1953.
[7] KNA VP/1/16, DC Nyeri, 'Administrative Directive No. 5,' 12 August 1954.
[8] KNA MAA/7/761, minute from 'F' to Chief Native Commissioner & Secretary for African Affairs, 3 Mar. 1954, 1–2.
[9] KNA VP/14/13, DC Fort Hall, 'Agricultural Policy in the Emergency,' 21 Apr. 1954. Elkins' informants who were once employed in these labour gangs stated that they rarely, if ever, received payment (Elkins, *Imperial*, 128).
[10] KNA VQ/1/51, Assistant Superintendent of Police Special Branch Nyeri to PC Central, 16 June 1954, 1.
[11] Guy Pauker, 'Notes on Non-Military Measures in Control of Insurgency,' (1962). (http://www.rand.org/pubs/papers/2006/2642.pdf – accessed 10 December 2007).
[12] T. David Mason, "Take Two Acres and Call Me in the Morning': Is Land Reform a Prescription for Peasant Unrest?' *Journal of Politics* 60 (1998); Richard Weitz, 'Insurgency and Counterinsurgency in Latin America, 1960–1980,' *Political Science Quarterly* 101 (1986).

potency of non-military counterinsurgency. This was not because of any greater sense of state legitimacy, but partly because of the impending decolonisation that became, in effect, part of the package of reforms. While the war continued in the mid-1950s, however, independence was but a chimera. In that context, non-military counterinsurgency in Kenya resonated powerfully and coincidentally with long-established notions of power and authority within Kikuyu society. By accident rather than design, the second prong provided loyalists with the means to reconstruct networks of patronage and the moral economy of Central Kenya. These same structures consolidated the strength of the loyalist elite long into the post-colonial period. The economic, social, and political rewards were elongated to not only sustain loyalism through the final years of the Emergency, but to become the base for the moderate, modernising, and cautiously reformist platform within the nationalist movement once the outcome of the military conflict became clear. Non-military counterinsurgency was an exercise in state-building.

Land

The social and economic components of the second prong were predominantly concerned with the rural areas of the Central Highlands. Through an overhaul of land use and tenure, the colonial government initiated a social revolution in the countryside. Initially, a neatly delineated class-based Kikuyu society was identified as the means by which any recurrence of Mau Mau could be prevented. Then, toward the end of the 1950s, the process of class formation was encouraged in order to protect British strategic and economic interests after independence. Elite loyalists, one colonial official wrote in 1954, were to 'become the anchor of the tribe, the solid yeoman farmer, the land owner who knows that he has too much to lose if he flirts, however lightly, with the passions of his nationalistic friends.'[13] To this list of responsibilities, employer and landlord were to be added. By providing encouragement to elite loyalists, the colonial government hoped that the new yeoman farmers would be able to provide employment to the landless masses of Central Province. Moreover, those yeomen farmers could then be entrusted with the protection of British interests in Kenya once decolonisation arrived. But without private titles, African farmers lacked sufficient mortgagable assets to capitalise their production. And without access to cash crops and markets restricted to

[13] KNA VQ/1/51 PC Central, 'The Civil Problem of Mau Mau,' 14 January 1954, 5.

European farmers, African farmers lacked the incentives to develop new agricultural methods and sources of income. Agrarian reform delivered as part of the counterinsurgency campaign was intended to correct both impediments to the consolidation of the new Kikuyu gentry.

The first instalment of this process was the Swynnerton Plan. Published in late 1953, the plan removed the structural obstacles to African agricultural production within the political economy of colonial Kenya.[14] The report recommended the encouragement of African cash crop production, establishment of credit facilities, and provision of farm planning services. The plan also called for consolidation of existing fragmented land holdings and subsequently the introduction of private land tenure. One of the critical components of the plan was the creation of a landed elite and an agricultural labouring class. Indeed, Swynnerton believed such class formation to be 'a normal step in the evolution of the country.'[15] Although not without lasting agricultural success and economic significance,[16] implementation of the Swynnerton Plan assumed a 'counter-revolutionary' function to punish Mau Mau supporters, reward loyalists, and hasten the end of the Emergency.[17] The enactment of Swynnerton allowed the colonial authorities to reward supporters and punish recalcitrant backers of the insurgents.

The Provincial Administration made no secret of its determination to exploit the strategic potential of Swynnerton.[18] Through preferential access to credit, farm planning, cash crops, and domination of cooperatives, loyalists were able to build power and wealth while Mau Mau supporters went without.[19] It was through land consolidation, a central prerequisite for full implementation of the Swynnerton Plan, however, that elite loyalists reaped the greatest benefit. Land consolidation was

---

[14] Roger Swynnerton, *A Plan to Intensify the Development of African Agriculture in Kenya* (Nairobi, 1953), 57.

[15] Ibid., 10.

[16] Edward Brett, *Colonialism and Underdevelopment in East Africa: The Politics of Economic Change 1919–1939* (London, 1973), 211–2; Berman, *Control and Crisis*, 369; John Harbeson, *Nationalism and Nation-Building in Kenya: The Role of Land Reform* (Ann Arbor MI, 1970), 71–5. Kitching has disputed the extent to which the benefits of Swynnerton trickled down through society: Kitching, *Class and Economic Change*, 372–4.

[17] Hastings Okoth-Ogendo, 'African Land Tenure Reform,' in *Agricultural Development in Kenya*, eds. Judith Heyer, J. K. Maitha and W. M. Senga (Nairobi, 1976), 163.

[18] KNA VP/1/16, DC Nyeri, 'Administrative Directive No.5,' 12 August 1954; KNA VP/4/1, DC Nyeri to PC Central, 15 August 1954, 1.

[19] Ng'ang'a, 'Loyalists and Politics'; Sorrenson, *Land Reform*, 241.

a three-stage process. First was the measurement of existing, fragmented land holdings that had become dispersed over previous decades of sub-division and litigation. Second was the reallocation of a single consolidated plot. By merging the formerly dispersed plots in one location, consolidation promised to substantially improve the efficiency of farming. Finally, a private land title was issued, which guaranteed the ownership of the consolidated plot and enabled the owner to mortgage the property to access capital to invest in more efficient farming methods.

Experiments with consolidation had taken place in Nyeri prior to the war and had been initiated by African farmers. The pioneer was Chief Muhoya in the North Tetu district, who first consolidated his holdings and those of his family in 1945. With the support of Agricultural Department officials, others followed suit.[20] The programme stagnated, however, until it recommenced in Nyeri at the instigation of the chiefs and headmen in June 1953.[21] Yet, partly because of the requirement for villagisation to take place prior to consolidation, a concerted effort to introduce consolidation across the province began in earnest only at the beginning of 1956.[22] In the final throes of the conflict, the attraction of consolidation to the Provincial Administration were obvious. The surveying of existing land holdings, the allocation of consolidated plots, and the issue of private land titles provided ample opportunity to punish Mau Mau sympathisers and reward loyalists. In Nyeri, the Provincial Administration argued that 'consolidation should be used as a reward while the Emergency continues.'[23] Excessive irregularities were recorded during consolidation, and preferential access to the material benefits of the Swynnerton Plan for loyalists were readily apparent, particularly in Fort Hall.[24] This was principally achieved by allowing loyalist elders procedural control of the entire process.[25] Thus, 'there should be little difficulty in re-allocating land so as to benefit themselves and their fellow

---

[20] KNA MA/7/5, Assistant Agricultural Officer Nyeri to Provincial Agricultural Officer Central, 5 June 1953, 1; ibid., 135–6.
[21] KNA MA/7/5, Assistant Agricultural Officer Nyeri to Provincial Agricultural Officer Central, 5 June 1953, 1–2; ibid., 243.
[22] ibid., 119–20.
[23] KNA VP/1/27, DC Nyeri & Assistant Agricultural Officer Nyeri, 'Directive on Land Consolidation and Farm Planning,' 3 January 1956, 2. See also Maloba, *Mau Mau and Kenya*, 143.
[24] Sorrenson, *Land Reform*, 166–7.
[25] RHL Mss Afr s 633, box 18, file 4, G. Sluiter, 'Confidential Report on Migrant Labour and Connected Matters in Four Villages in the Kiambu Reserve of Kenya,' 1957, 48; Ng'ang'a, 'Loyalists and Politics,' 371; Sorrenson, *Land Reform*, 166.

loyalists.'[26] In such conditions, it is not surprising that leading loyalists were enthusiastic supporters of consolidation.[27]

Although some loyalists were able to manipulate the process of consolidation for their own material benefit, many Mau Mau supporters found themselves disenfranchised. The bureaucratic machinery of consolidation certainly did them no favours. Plots of land were issued at public meetings. Without having knowledge of the meeting or being able to be present to ensure some form of representation, detainees were often unable to make their land claims public. The reissue of plots of land at Ndeiya by the Kiambu African District Council, for example, was carried out in 1957 while many detainees were still behind wire.[28] Those Kikuyu that did attend these meetings had to bring with them screening certificates, which obviously only the most covert and cunning insurgent supporters possessed.[29] Moreover, loyalists dominated the consolidation committees that controlled the implementation of the policy. These committees were able to subvert the process by simply declaring to the surveyors drawing up the new plot boundaries that there were fewer land claimants than there actually were so that unwanted individuals would be overlooked entirely.[30] This loyalist domination was later usurped when detainees returned home, and, from 1957 onwards, were able to seize control of the elected land consolidation committees.[31] But in many areas, the return of detainees occurred too late to effect consolidation. Widespread and popular grievances rapidly emerged from the process.[32]

The extent of the corruption of consolidation is difficult to precisely determine. Levels of manipulation varied from district to district. In Kiambu, for example, almost all landowners received their proper entitlement back after consolidation.[33] Those who complained were given short shrift by the district commissioner, who reflected in letters sent to

[26] KNA VP/1/27, R. G. Wilson, L. Ward & R. Sandford, 'Fort Hall District: Land Reform,' 7 April 1954, 7.
[27] Charles Trench, *Men Who Ruled Kenya: The Kenya Administration 1892–1963* (London, 1993), 269.
[28] KNA DC/KBU/1/45, Kiambu District Annual Report 1957, 4.
[29] KNA MA/7/7, Land Consolidation Officer Kiambu to Chief Kihika, 29 August 1957.
[30] KNA MA/7/7, Anon., 'A Guide to Consolidation in Kiambu District,' 1957, 9.
[31] KNA MA/7/7, file note, 'Kihingo Land Consolidation Committee Members,' 1958; Anon., 'New Members of Ndeiya Land Committee,' 28 August 1957; Land Consolidation Officer Kiambu to DO Limuru, 16 November 1957; Sorrenson, *Land Reform*, 241.
[32] KNA VP/2/70, ASP SB Nyeri to Senior Superintendent of Police Provincial Special Branch, 12 September 1960, 1.
[33] Kershaw, *Mau Mau From Below*, 258–9.

unsuccessful appellants that 'we are all pebbles on the beach of time, you a little black pebble and I a little white one. I wish indeed that your pebble and its resting place could be larger, but locked as we are in the inexorable jaws of fate this cannot be so.'[34] Of course, some black pebbles did find larger resting places than others. The process of consolidation was most obviously manipulated for the benefit of loyalists in the Fort Hall district. Interestingly, the Provincial Administration took a less active role in the implementation of consolidation there than it did elsewhere. This inadequate supervision allowed loyalists responsible for overseeing the process in Fort Hall to seize the initiative and indulge in primitive accumulation. After consolidation was completed in the district in 1960, an aerial survey was carried out. From the photographs, on which the newly delineated plots were marked by shrubs planted on the boundary, the manipulation of consolidation in favour of loyalists was all too apparent. Even the colonial government recognised that the theft of land was indefensible. The entire consolidation process, therefore, had to be started again from scratch, but this time under the supervision of elected committees dominated by ex-detainees.[35] In Nyeri, too, the aerial survey carried out after the completion of consolidation in 1959 revealed significant discrepancies between the planned boundaries and those that existed in reality. Approximately half the plots were too large, and the other half too small. Unlike in Fort Hall, these inconsistencies were not considered substantial enough by the government to warrant restarting the whole process.[36]

Although the land lost by Mau Mau supporters and their families during consolidation was seized covertly under the guise of agricultural development, more overtly, punitive land seizures were carried out during the entire war. Initially, tenure of land owned by local councils was most easily manipulated for the purposes of punishing Mau Mau supporters and rewarding loyalists. With the district commissioner acting as chair of each district council, tenancy agreements could be easily torn up. The Kiambu African District Council controlled 9,000 acres of such land at Ndeiya. There, throughout the Emergency, Mau Mau-supporting tenants were evicted in favour of loyalists, such as James Mworia, a

[34] KNA MA/7/7, DC Kiambu, template letter for rejection of appeals against adjudication during land consolidation, undated.
[35] Sorrenson, *Land Reform*, 165–81.
[36] Ibid., 135–50.

decorated Tribal Policeman who had lost his property in Nyethuna.[37] A
similar process was undertaken in Nyeri in 1954, where plots belonging
to family members of guerrilla fighters were confiscated and reissued to
loyalists.[38]

Land seizures became more common after laws sanctioning the practice were passed in 1955. The threat of confiscation was used to encourage
Mau Mau fighters to surrender in 1955.[39] Indeed, the colonial government considered the seizures to be something of a propaganda coup and
widely publicised confiscations of the land of Mau Mau fighters.[40] Such
actions continued apace, even after the military struggle was over. By mid-
1957, Kiambu's Land Board was 'largely occupied recently considering
vast numbers of confiscations of terrorist land.'[41] The confiscations served
a useful purpose during consolidation and the simultaneous construction
of a range of public services in the villages. Under normal circumstances,
landowners would surrender a small percentage of their entitlement. The
accumulated fractions of holdings would then be used to provide land
for a public purpose, such as the construction of schools, dispensaries, or
churches.[42] Confiscated land, therefore, reduced the claims of these public buildings on the land holdings of the rest of the community. Moreover,
confiscated land could be included in the general pot to be redistributed
during consolidation, thereby increasing the size of allocated plots.[43]
Whether through avoiding punitive land seizures or by their entitlement
to benefit fully from the consolidation programme, loyalists found their
support of the government reciprocated in increased security of tenure.

[37] KNA DC/KBU/1/45, Kiambu District Annual Report 1955 17; Kiambu District Annual
Report 1957, 4; KNA DC/KBU/2/1, DO Kikuyu, 'Handing Over Report Kikuyu Division – Kiambu: J. D. Campbell to E. D. Fox,' 30 May 1955, 3; KNA MA/7/7, Land
Consolidation Officer Kiambu to DC Kiambu, 28 September 1957.
[38] KNA VP/1/27, DC Nyeri to DOs North Tetu & Mathera, 10 May 1954; DO North
Tetu to DC Nyeri, 21 June 1954.
[39] KNA WC/CM/1/1, minutes of 120th meeting of War Council, 8 July 1955, 2; KNA
WC/CM/1/4, Minister for African Affairs, 'Forfeiture of Terrorists' Land and Property,'
7 July 1955.
[40] KNA AHC/9/52, 'Magaidi Wengine Wanapoteza Nchi zao (More Terrorists to Lose
Their Land),' *Mwanamke*, 14 July 1954, 1; 'Trees From Terrorist's Land Used to Build
and Protect Villages,' *East African Standard*, 9 June 1955.
[41] KNA DC/KBU/2/1, DO I Kiambu, 'Handing Over Report, District Officer I, Kiambu,
D. E. Johnston – A. Simmance,' June/July 1957.
[42] KNA VP/2/24, minutes of Kiambu District Land Board meetings, 8 June 1954, 9 September 1954, 8 November 1955, 23 October 1956 & 20 November 1956.
[43] KNA VQ/5/15, minutes of Embu District Land Board meeting, 18 May 1956, 1.

Labour

Land reform did not help those loyalists who had no land in the first place, but rather, it increased the strength of the elite. Poor loyalists sought reward in other forms. They inundated local Provincial Administration offices with requests for assistance of all kinds. Itagu Munyori, who had joined the Home Guard in 1952 and was heavily involved in screening of Mau Mau suspects in Nanyuki, asked the district commissioner for a forestry permit to allow him to begin work in the timber industry.[44] In October 1956, Zakanyo M'Itaru M'Nabeu was working in the Lairagwan screening camp in Meru when he wrote to the Meru district commissioner asking to be issued a license to brew beer, to be appointed as a headman, or to be made a tribunal elder in local courts.[45] Solomon Kamiti Magana, a clerk at the Kandara detention camp, requested a driver's licence to allow him to set up a manure delivery service to support his father and five brothers during their education.[46] Requests for permits for livestock trading were commonplace, as loyalists sought to exploit the steady relaxation of Emergency restrictions that prevented movements of people and goods around the Central Highlands.[47] Johana Mwangi simply wanted the Nanyuki district commissioner to buy him a second-hand bike, although Mwangi did promise to pay the official back later.[48] The most frequent requests, however, were from loyalists for employment in the Tribal Police,[49] which was to remain in existence after the war was over, or for clerical jobs within the government.[50]

That loyalists eagerly pursued reward in the form of employment in the government is not surprising. After all, as the Provincial Administration

44 KNA DC/NYK/3/16/36, Chief Itagu Munyori to DC Nanyuki, 28 November 1956.
45 KNA DC/NYK/3/16/36, Zakanyo M'Itaru M'Nabeu to DC Meru thro' DC Nanyuki, 8 October 1956.
46 KNA DC/NYK/3/16/36, Solomon Kamiti Magana to DO Kandara, 29 April 1956; Solomon Kamiti Magana to Transport Licence Board, 10 October 1956.
47 KNA DC/NYK/3/16/36, Kiragu Kamau to DC Nanyuki, 9 September 1956; Wachiuri Maene to DC Nanyuki, 9 October 1956; Ndiritu Wamutitu to DC Nanyuki, 9 October 1956.
48 KNA DC/NYK/3/16/36, Johana Mwangi Daudi Kiiru to DC Nanyuki, 24 September 1956.
49 KNA DC/NYK/3/16/36, Gattalengo Muchena Kamau to DO Nanyuki, November 1956; Maina Jacob to DC Nanyuki, 9 November 1956; Kimotho Njeru to DC Nanyuki, 12 November 1956; Mulwa Muli to DC Nanyuki, 19 November 1956; Geoffrey Njeru Mburi to DC Nanyuki, 26 November 1956; M'Marete Riumpu to DC Nanyuki, 1 December 1956
50 KNA DC/NYK/3/16/36, Wanjangi Ndebere to DC Nanyuki, 10 December 1956.

had expanded during the war and taken on the responsibility for leading the counterinsurgency campaign in Central Province, it had become a significant employer of loyalist labour. The public purse in each district provided the upkeep for thousands of Home Guards, Tribal Policemen, interrogators, chiefs, headmen, court elders, drivers, and clerical staff.[51] Indeed, the Provincial Administration was, with the local district councils, the largest employer during the war in Central Province.[52] Although elite loyalists received their rewards in the form of land reform, access to the bureaucracy, and the right to vote and stand in elections, their poorer brethren benefited chiefly from being assisted in the search for wage labour.

Several key sectors of the Kenyan economy found the pool of available labour drastically reduced by the war. The government, concerned about the spread of the insurgency, repatriated large numbers of Kikuyu workers from Nairobi and the European farms of the Rift Valley between 1952 and 1954. Even while the conflict was at its height, loyalists, including women, were urged to help reduce the labour shortfall.[53] Local Provincial Administration officials formed partnerships with major employers to provide them with the manpower necessary to continue operations. East African Railways and Harbours (EARH), for example, made such an arrangement with officials in Kiambu and Nyeri to avoid disruption when members of the existing workforce were detained. When employees were arrested, EARH contacted government officials in Kiambu and Nyeri who maintained lists of loyalists seeking employment. On the recommendation of the Provincial Administration officers, these loyalists would then be recruited by EARH.[54] As the war moved towards conclusion, such practices became more common.

During the military phase of the war, Emergency regulations prevented the easy movement of those seeking employment. Those wishing to move outside their home division, the sub-district administrative units, needed approval from their local Provincial Administration officer and,

---

[51] See Nanyuki district employment registers in KNA DC/NYK/3/16/49.

[52] RHL Mss Afr s 633, box 18, file 4, G. Sluiter, 'Confidential Report on Migrant Labour and Connected Matters in Four Villages in the Kiambu Reserve of Kenya,' 1957, 12.

[53] KNA AHC/9/23, 'Working at Nyeri,' *Uhoro wa Nyeri*, 3 December 1954; AHC/9/52, 'Wanawake Waafrika Wengi Wameandikiza Kazi Nairobi (More African Women Employed in Nairobi),' *Mwanamke*, 16 June 1954, 1.

[54] KNA VP/1/103, District Engineer, Nairobi Engineering District, East African Railways and Harbours (EARH) to DCs Fort Hall, Nyeri & Thika, 30 August 1954; DC Nyeri to District Engineer, Nairobi Engineering District, EARH, 14 September 1954; minutes of Nyeri DOs' meeting, 16 September 1954.

until 1957, the equivalent officer in the division to which they wished to relocate.[55] But this permission was not readily forthcoming except in unusual circumstances.[56] Movement outside of Central Province was even more difficult. Until May 1955, Kikuyu not already in residence were banned from entering the Rift Valley Province altogether.[57] But once the insurgency's defeat seemed only a matter of time, that proscription was gradually relaxed to meet the labour demands of European farmers in the province. Initially, allowance was made for 'those who have been most active in their support of the government.'[58] Large-scale resettlements of loyalist labour to the Rift Valley, therefore, took place throughout 1955 and 1956. Five hundred fifty families were sent to Solai, Laikipia, and Subukia, for example.[59] Another 120 loyalist families from Fort Hall were settled in Ol Joro Orok and South Kinangop in November and December 1955.[60] But these movements were carefully controlled. Loyalists identified for resettlement were vouched for by local committees of other loyalists in their home areas of Central Province. Provincial Administration officials in the Rift Valley were also required to approve the individuals being moved.[61] These migrations of loyalist labour from Central Province to the Rift Valley took place alongside the resettlement of former Rift Valley residents who had been detained for suspected support of the insurgency. The detainees steadily returned to their former European employers from 1956 onwards.[62]

Within Central Province, movement restrictions were again relaxed for loyalists significantly earlier than for the rest of the population. This was particularly true for loyalists seeking work in Nairobi.[63] The district officer in the Kikuyu division of Kiambu even went so far as to act as a loyalist recruitment agency by maintaining registers of loyalists for

55 KNA VP/5/1, minutes of Central Province DCs meeting of 28 February to 1 March 1957, 2.
56 KNA DC/EBU/9/1, G. Sluiter, 'A Study of Kabare-Village in the Embu-District,' May 1956, 5.
57 KNA DC/NKU/2/25/48, DC Nakuru to Kirichi Kaguai, 14 June 1955; DC Nakuru to Mburu Njoroge, 14 June 1955; DC Nakuru to Mbugua Kimani, 15 June 1955; DC Nakuru to J.N. Sheffield, 16 June 1955.
58 KNA DC/NKU/2/25/48, DC Nakuru to Njoroge Kirubi, 29 April 1955.
59 KNA WC/CM/1/2, minutes of 104th meeting of the War Council, 10 May 1955, 3-4.
60 KNA WC/CM/1/3, minutes of the 149th meeting of the War Council, 29 December 1955, 7-8.
61 KNA WC/CM/1/3, minutes of the 144th meeting of the War Council, 22 November, 4.
62 Furedi, *Mau Mau War*, 157.
63 KNA VP/5/1, minutes of meeting of DCs Central Province, 28 February - 1 March, 1957, 2.

European employers wanting 'the most trustworthy people you can get.'[64] In contrast, released detainees had restriction orders placed on them by loyalist screening committees at the time of their release. By limiting the former detainees' movement to the immediate surrounds of their home areas, such actions restricted their ability to seek work.[65] Furthermore, the discretionary powers the Provincial Administration exercised over the issue of passbooks and residence permits allowed its officers to influence the process of labour recruitment in the manner they saw fit.[66] As with almost every other aspect of life during the 1950s, that discretion entailed the punishment of Mau Mau supporters and the rewarding of loyalists.

Beginning in 1955, loyalists travelled to the White Highlands and Nairobi in search of work and the anonymity of new lives.[67] This flight of loyalist labour was hugely significant in terms of numbers and in its effects on the memory of loyalism during the war. By 1959, the majority of loyalists in Nyeri had found work outside of the district.[68] For many, there was little reason to remain. Although never realised, fears of retribution by the former detainees were widespread among those involved in the worst excesses of the war. Moreover, the failure of the agrarian reform programme, discussed earlier, to expand wage labour within the African farming sector meant there was little incentive for the landless to remain in the villages of Central Province. Taking advantage of the opportunities for employment provided by the government elsewhere made good sense in terms of personal security, politics, and household economics. The landless loyalists left behind their wartime allies, who had a reason to stay by virtue of their land holdings and jobs. This rump of landowners, chiefs, and recruits in the Provincial Administration, discussed in the next chapter, were the loyalists encountered by the detainees on their release in the late 1950s. As the popular memory of the war solidified in the late 1950s, this group came to represent loyalism in its entirety.[69] Out

[64] KNA MA/1/2, DO Kikuyu to all Residents of Kikuyu and Kabete Settled Areas, 3 February 1955.
[65] KNA VP/1/42, Laragwan Screening Camp Screening Team, 'Application for a Restriction Order Dossier: Gickuki Tama,' 20 February 1956; DC Nyeri to DO Othaya, 23 February 1956; DC Nyeri to DO Othaya, 4 April 1956; DC Nyeri to DO Othaya, 4 June 1956.
[66] KNA DC/NYK/3/16/49, DC Nanyuki to all employers of Kikuyu, Embu, and Meru labour in Nanyuki district, 8 June 1955.
[67] Gakaara wa Wanjau, *Mau Mau Author in Detention*, Paul Ngigi Njoroge trans. (Nairobi, 1988), 207.
[68] KNA DC/NYI/1/1, Nyeri District Annual Report 1959, 8.
[69] For a discussion of changing memories of allegiances during the war formed in the late 1950s and early 1960s, see Kershaw, 'Fieldwork,' 288–9.

of sight and mind, the landless and poor loyalists were quickly forgotten and written out of subsequent histories.

Loyalism and Self-Mastery

The effectiveness of non-military counterinsurgency in Central Kenya cannot be understood using simplistic terms, such as carrot and stick or hearts and minds. Instead, land reform and the provision of labour opportunities neatly, but accidentally, dovetailed with Kikuyu political thought. To explain the success of non-military counterinsurgency, it is essential to explore that intellectual tradition and its relationship with political action during the 1950s. Writing to a local newspaper in November 1954, Francis Gatheru explained his opposition to Mau Mau. He believed that it was the promise of Mau Mau to deliver 'freedom, land and every good thing we wished to have' that won it the popular support of a deeply divided society earlier in the decade. 'By that,' Gatheru wrote, 'and that only, very many people were oathed voluntarily.' But by November 1954, Mau Mau appeared to Gatheru unable to deliver. 'Look at the results of the oath,' he implored. 'Surely it is contrary to what we expected.' Mau Mau's foot soldiers in the mountain forests were on the defensive, the population of much of Central Province was forced into fortified villages, and tens of thousands of the insurgency's real or imagined sympathisers were detained. In contrast, loyalists were able to continue their lives, expand their land holdings, and grow cash crops. For Gatheru, the choice between Mau Mau and loyalism appeared simple. 'If we are getting the opposite of what Mau Mau promised us when we were taking the oath, why then,' he rhetorically enquired, 'shouldn't we do the contrary of what we promised.'[70] By meeting the demands of individuals such as Gatheru, the strategies of non-military counterinsurgency sustained loyalism through the final years of the conflict and into the era of decolonisation.

Mau Mau promised its supporters *ithaka na wiathi*, literally translated as land and freedom, but better understood as self-mastery through land.[71] Loyalists came to condemn the rebellion's supporters for their apparent refusal to labour virtuously and failure to achieve land, freedom, or self-mastery. Baring's second prong of agrarian and labour reform was

---

[70] KNA AHC/9/23, F. Gatheru to Editor, *Uhoro wa Nyeri*, 3 Dec. 1954.
[71] Lonsdale, 'The Problem,' 326. See for more detailed discussion, Lonsdale, 'Wealth, Poverty and Civic Virtue.' Although a Kikuyu term, *wiathi* was common to Embu and Meru peoples. See ibid., 347–8.

effective because it allowed loyalism to become the means by which this self-mastery could be achieved. Loyalism was thus sustained by what is known as moral ethnicity, the 'contested process of defining cultural identity, communal membership and leadership.'[72] During the rise of militancy within Kikuyu politics, those who became insurgents critiqued the actions and words of their self-proclaimed leaders. Prior to the war, the Kikuyu elites abdicated their monopoly on leadership. They failed to protect the poor's access to land and forced their clients off the land. The landless subsequently found allies among the urban radicals and squatters evicted from the European farms, both of whom felt a much older sense of abandonment by those same rural patriarchs. Mau Mau thus represented in part the 'repudiation of clientage' by a society that felt 'betrayed by their patrons, white and black.'[73] By exploiting the opportunities created by the second prong, loyalism allowed those same patrons to reclaim their authority to lead by reconstructing networks of patronage.

In so doing, loyalism drew on long-established themes within Kikuyu political thought. As the clamour for reform grew through the late 1940s, Kikuyu vigorously debated the nature of leadership, the value of particular forms of protests, and the relationship between the elite and their clients. The *Mumenyereri* (*The Guardian*) newspaper was launched in May 1945 by Henry Muoria Mwaniki. Described as 'the most influential Kikuyu newspaper at the time,' by 1950, the newspaper was published twice weekly.[74] Its circulation reached 11,000 households. The newspaper was intended to be a platform for Kenyatta and the KAU, and was thus banned under Emergency regulations.[75] Between 1944 and 1949, when not editing *Mumenyereri*, Muoria was also one of several pamphleteers writing in Kikuyu and stimulating debate across the Central Highlands.[76] Although commonly viewed as representing one intellectual strand of the various origins of the insurgency,[77] within Muoria's work

---

[72] Bruce Berman, Dickson Eyoh, and Will Kymlicka, 'Ethnicity and the Politics of Democratic Nation-Building in Africa,' in *Ethnicity and Democracy in Africa*, eds. Bruce Berman, Dickson Eyoh, and Will Kymlicka (Oxford, 2004), 4–5.

[73] John Lonsdale, 'Moral and Political Argument in Kenya,' in *Ethnicity and Democracy in Africa*, eds. Bruce Berman, Dickson Eyoh, and Will Kymlicka (Oxford, 2004), 82.

[74] Lonsdale, 'Wealth, Poverty and Civic Virtue,' 318.

[75] Cristiana Pugliese, 'Complementary or Contending Nationhoods? Kikuyu Pamphlets and Songs, 1945–52,' in *Mau Mau and Nationhood: Arms, Authority and Narration*, eds. Elisha Stephen Atieno Odhiambo and John Lonsdale (Oxford, 2003), 99.

[76] Cristiana Pugliese, 'Gikuyu Political Pamphlets and Hymn Books 1945–1952' (Nairobi, 1993); Pugliese, 'Complementary or Contending.'

[77] Ibid., 116–7.

and *Mumenyereri*, parallels with loyalist thought in the 1950s can be clearly identified.

Muoria, Pugliese writes, 'had a decisive role in shaping a Kikuyu conscience.' Through his pamphlets and *Mumenyereri*, 'we can perceive the effort made by a section of the Kikuyu to comprehend and master Western culture and to create what can be called Kikuyuism, a common background to unite people who were far from being a single entity.'[78] Although *Mumenyereri* and the pamphlets dealt with a wide range of cultural and social issues, it was politics and the relationship between Kikuyu and the colonial state that mostly exercised the minds of their contributors. These questions coalesced on the land issue, which almost all Kikuyu agreed was the foremost issue of the day. If a Kikuyu were not to agitate for the return of land, *Mumenyereri* stated, 'we would look upon him as a spy.'[79] But who should lead that agitation and what form it should take were open to debate. Driven by notions of dignity and respectability, writers such as Muoria returned repeatedly to the themes of political leadership, the nature of protest, and the significance of education to the future development of Kikuyu politics.

Muoria firmly believed that Kikuyu were to be guided by established and respected political leaders.[80] Contributors to *Mumenyereri* preserved the notion that political leadership was the monopoly of the wealthy. It was they alone who could demonstrate their right to lead through their household's wealth and their respect of the reciprocal ties to their poorer clients. For contravening that latter clause in the unwritten contract between the leaders and the led, the chiefs were thought to have abandoned their claim to political preeminence. 'Chiefs should know,' an article from January 1948 argued, 'that to be respected through fear is not as good as respect through love.'[81] Other existing political leaders, most notably Kenyatta and the first African member of the colony's legislature, Eliud Mathu, were thought to be more deserving of authority and more likely to deliver a reversal of colonial land policy. George Njoroge Kinyoro asked 'my people to obey our leaders like Jomo Kenyatta and E. M. Mathu and Editors for they know that the time will come when

---

[78] Ibid., 116–7.
[79] KNA MAA/8/106, Director of Intelligence and Security (DIS) to Member for Law & Order (MLO) and CNC, 15 September 1948.
[80] Henry Muoria, *I, the Gikuyu and the White Fury* (Nairobi, 1994), 184.
[81] KNA MAA/8/106, DIS to CNC, 6 February 1948.

we shall have self Government.'[82] The form of protest was, though, considered to be more important than the choice of leader.

A high value was attached to the educated elites by *Mumenyereri* and *Muoria* because of the nature of political protest believed most likely to deliver change. Although later a supporter of Mau Mau from exile in Britain, Muoria was adamant that freedom could not be achieved through 'using the force of arms.'[83] Persuasion and negotiation required intelligence, eloquence, and education. 'Because Africans have no weapons, but their weapon is to speak the truth and to be honest,' protests were to be peaceful and dignified.[84] Another article argued, 'The Kikuyu really believe that conversation is loveliness and therefore the object of their main societies is to talk over with Government their troubles without disturbance.'[85] Here was the voice of the middle ground of Kikuyu society that would be so alarmed by both the imminent emergence of Mau Mau and the state's disproportionate use of force to crush it.

The commitment to non-violent protest derived from two strands of thought. The first was pragmatic. Muoria's support for peaceful means of political action was partly informed by the collective memory of the violent suppression of resistance to the colonial conquest and the protests after Harry Thuku's arrest in 1922.[86] Such events demonstrated to Muoria and others the strength of the colonial state and its willingness to use force. Violent resistance thus seemed futile. Muoria felt 'we [K]ikuyu people have still no power in the form of the force of arms which can enable us to think in terms of having a fight with the white people.'[87] A negotiated, peaceful resolution of Kikuyu grievances was, Muoria believed, more likely to meet with success. However, the preference for non-violent protest was also derived from a distinctive Kikuyu history of political and social thought.

Even as (or perhaps because) the militant faction gathered strength, violence was considered by the middle ground of Kikuyu society to be the actions of a criminal. Rather than conveying authority on those who grew wealthy through theft, criminality brought shame on them. 'I think we cannot progress in Education, Trade, Farming and Politics,' one of

---

[82] KNA MAA/8/106, DIS to CNC, 17 February 1948.
[83] Muoria, *White Fury*, 147.
[84] KNA MAA//8/106, DIS to MLO & CNC, 15 September 1948.
[85] KNA MAA/8/106, DIS to CNC, 9 August 1948.
[86] Muoria, *White Fury*, 142.
[87] Ibid., 140.

Mumenyereri's correspondents wrote, 'if we are stealing.'[88] Anticipating the rise of militancy, Kenyatta warned attendees of a KAU meeting in May 1948 that 'we cannot progress if we are criminals and unwilling to work hard.'[89] Muoria agreed, claiming, 'There is nothing which can be gained through hatred except poverty, suffering and pain.'[90] Entitling his third pamphlet 'Our Victory Does Not Depend on the Use of Force of Arms, but on the Use of the Word of Truth,' Muoria argued that

> ...restoring to fighting does not prove the presence of intelligence on the part of such a group of people. If anything, it proves that they are primitive since fighting involves using instinctive feelings which are also used by lower animals who know no other way of settling their disagreements.[91]

Violent agitation was thus thought a waste of time and its propagation the work of idle minds. Hard work was then, unsurprisingly, repeatedly prescribed as the panacea for youthful, political indiscipline.

In writing the pamphlets and editing *Mumenyereri*, Muoria hoped to reach the 'crowds of lazy people all over our country,' so that 'they could start using their minds and hands to produce something of value.'[92] 'Lazy people do no good,' he wrote in his first pamphlet.[93] The connection between work, virtue, and attainment of political goals remained undimmed throughout Muoria's writing. 'For work is actions which are said to speak louder than words,' he wrote. 'It follows, hard work, knowledge and dissemination of knowledge, unity, love for one another are all the ways which point towards victory for our people.'[94] Hard work allowed every man to 'avoid poverty from overwhelming him.' That poverty in turn, according to Muoria, could only lead to misery. 'Poor people are more likely to murder each other through sheer desperation than those people who are well-to-do,' he argued.[95] 'Being rich and being poor are two different aspects of life, one valuable and the other useless.'[96] Kikuyu society's deviants were a hindrance to political and economic development. The ignorant, jealous, criminal, and untrustworthy

[88] KNA MAA/8/106, DIS to CNC & Labour Commissioner, 13 July 1948.
[89] KNA MAA/8/106, DIS to CNC, 8 June 1948.
[90] Muoria, *White Fury*, 93.
[91] Ibid., 137–8.
[92] Ibid., 81.
[93] Ibid., 85.
[94] Ibid., 170.
[95] Ibid., 86.
[96] Ibid., 96.

were not 'capable of doing anything useful for themselves.'[97] Those who turned to criminal behaviour were to be shunned by society.[98]

For Muoria and many other Kikuyu, the most socially and politically valuable form of hard work was to be undertaken through education. Education was valued as an engine of development and as a means of achieving citizenship. 'Education shows people how to do things and how to do them better,' Muoria wrote. 'Knowledge is a kind of sharpness and a sharp knife is capable of cutting many hard things.'[99] These 'hard things' included poverty, land alienation, and colonial subjugation, which was commonly likened to slavery in the pages of *Mumenyereri*. One of the paper's writers argued, 'There is no other way of progress except education in order that slavery may be abolished.'[100] One article from January 1948 stated, 'Education removes ignorance,' and another, also from January 1948, stated, 'Trade removes poverty, and Political affairs removes slavery.'[101] This was hardly the manifesto of radical anti-colonial militancy.

Given the value it attached to education and its advocacy of non-violent methods of political protest, it is not surprising that *Mumenyereri* thought of Kikuyu society as being engaged in a 'Brain Battle' with the colonial state. In an open letter to the Governor, printed in November 1947, the paper asserted, 'You will be surprised to see what we shall be in 50 years to come, if you do not oppress [K]ikuyu by hindering them in Education; stopping their Trade and by depriving them of their pieces of land.' *Mumenyereri* was not advocating the forced removal of European settlers or bloody rebellion, but the opportunity to eat from the same table as Kenya's immigrant communities. The paper wanted Kikuyu to:

... be ambitious to know what there is to know that they may be wise like British people. They do not want to feel they are below the white man or Indians, we want to be like them and we know that the only way to get to this stage is to have wisdom and money and to work hard with our hands. Give us the chance to make an effort because most of the Africans we see with motorcars and stone buildings, have not achieved their gains by the money earned from Europeans, but from their trading business and from their shambas.[102]

[97] Ibid., 90.
[98] Ibid., 178.
[99] Ibid., 86.
[100] KNA MAA/8/106, DIS to CNC, 10 August 1948.
[101] KNA MAA/8/106, DIS to CNC, 6 February 1948.
[102] KNA MAA/8/106, DIS to MLO & CNC, 28 November 1947.

Although this rare glimpse of the future imagined by Kikuyu intellectuals is demonstrably moderate in tone and aim, Muoria's conviction that 'all Africans ought to know that their aim is get their freedom' grew stronger as time progressed.[103] One of many tragedies of late colonial rule in Kenya is how these conciliatory and authoritative individuals were rebuffed by the state.

The decision taken by many Kikuyu to support the insurgency was not one taken lightly. Even after Mau Mau's fighters had taken to the forests, they sang, 'We don't want war we want justice.'[104] Nevertheless, many of those same guerrillas initially thought they had chosen the only path that would lead to wealth, political authority, and, ultimately, freedom. In the early stages of the war, loyalists were derided for their opposition to the insurgency as much for their myopia as for their support of the colonial government. From the forests, it seemed that the pursuit of a negotiated settlement with the colonial government had run its course.

Those advocating moderation in 1952 and 1953 were, Mau Mau supporters sang, unable to see that 'They will remain slaves for ever.' In contrast, the insurgents believed that through their actions, 'We shall get freedom and our property.'[105] The two groups used the language of Kikuyu ethnicity to critique one another. Loyalists thought the demographic profile of the insurgents and their violent actions made them deserving of the label of 'uncircumcised boys.' This was an attempt to dispute the authority of Mau Mau's rebels to lead political action, which was meant to be the preserve of elders. But the guerrillas brushed off these taunts and playfully adopted the label.[106] They could afford to do so and made the same pointed accusation of loyalists with far greater potency.[107] In the first 18 months of the war, loyalists could hardly claim that their support of the government was advancing Kikuyu claims to land and freedom. Poorly rewarded for their loyalism and inadequately protected by the state security forces, the adoption by Home Guards of the nomenclature of junior elderhood, *kamatimu*, appeared ridiculous. Loyalists stood accused of tearing families apart for no reason. One Mau Mau song told loyalists, 'When a Kikuyu baby cries you tell it to stop

[103] Muoria, *White Fury*, 147.
[104] Quoted in Bethwell A. Ogot, 'Politics, Culture and Music in Central Kenya: A Study of Mau Mau Hymns, 1951–1956,' in *Reintroducing Man into the African World: Selected Essays 1961–1980*, ed. Bethwell A. Ogot (Kisumu, 1999), 241.
[105] Quoted in ibid., 242.
[106] Githige, 'Religious Factor,' 47.
[107] KNA DC/LKA/1/4, Laikipia District Annual Report 1953, 7.

because it's [sic] father's in Manyani (detention camp) and the mother's in Kamiti (prison).'[108] However, once the nature and direction of the conflict changed, so too did the balance of power within the war of words.

From the very first signs of the emergence of the militant faction within Kikuyu politics, opponents had used the very same idioms and metaphors as Muoria and the contributors to *Mumenyereri* to justify opposition to the radicals. Parmenas Kiritu's definition of Mau Mau, 'greedy eating,' discussed in the opening of Chapter 1, was part of the same intellectual tradition as Muoria's writing. Although *Mumenyereri* has long been identified as representing one of several intellectual inspirations for the insurgency, we can also see the same values and notions of work, freedom, and wealth expressed in loyalism. From Kiritu's perspective, Mau Mau's use of criminality and its threat to the land tenure of Kikuyu elites meant that it was consuming what it had not worked for without regard for the needs of others.

Even though relatively isolated until mid-1954, other loyalists agreed and used language Muoria would recognise from his writings to condemn Mau Mau. 'There is plenty of work to be done but the workers are few,' James Nyaga wrote in January 1954. 'Are you one of those who have reduced the number of the workers? Let me repeat again that if you have no work the devil has plenty of work to give you – Terrorism!'[109] James Komu, a market supervisor in the Embu district, believed Mau Mau to be 'an enemy of the country and its progress.'[110] Of course, although loyalism was unrewarded and exposed its adherents to a high risk of insurgent attacks, such a stance was never popular. But the population of the Central Highlands could see only too well the insurgency's changing fortunes. From the heady days of early 1953, when Mau Mau activities were unchecked by the weak security forces, its position of strength had steadily been eroded. Furthermore, Mau Mau's own tactics partly explain the growing strength and changing nature of loyalism.

As the war became more bitterly contested and the insurgents more desperate, the growing number of non-combatant casualties and increasing prevalence of theft undermined Mau Mau's claim to hold the moral high ground. Particularly significant, bearing in mind the importance attached to education by Kikuyu noted earlier, were insurgent arson attacks

---

[108] Githige, 'Religious Factor,' 311.
[109] KNA AHC/9/24, James Nyaga, 'Devil Finds Work to the Lazy,' *Kayu ka Embu*, 15 January 1954, 2.
[110] KNA AHC/9/24, James Komu to Editor, *Kayu ka Embu*, 30 January 1954.

carried out on schools. These actions were particularly common in Embu and Nyeri.[111] Sixty-seven schools were torched from June 1953 to June 1954 in the Embu district alone.[112] Although explainable by the loyalist activities of teachers or parents affiliated with the school, such behaviour was unlikely to engender much sympathy for the rebellion among local populations.

At the same time the insurgents began to contradict the aims and motivations of their supporters, loyalism emerged as a viable alternative path to land and freedom. The implementation of the second prong coincided with the downturn in the insurgency's fortunes after mid-1954. As the security of loyalists and potential benefits of collaboration improved, condemnations of Mau Mau became more commonplace. Many of those who publicly denounced the rebellion from 1954 onwards had been previously sympathetic to the cause of the insurgents, whom they now accused of failing to deliver on their promises. The loyalist critique of Mau Mau certainly touched on the themes of the propaganda campaign conducted by the colonial regime. However, the criticisms of the guerrillas and their supporters were constructed in a far more complex manner than the state's depiction of the division between the two warring sides as being a simplistic dichotomy between progress and backwardness.[113] Instead, loyalism was rooted in the same intellectual debates about authority and wealth that had accompanied the advent of the rebellion.

Reflecting the dramatic growth of influence of the churches in the Emergency villages, the most notable difference between the loyalists of the 1950s and the intellectuals of the late 1940s was the extent to which Christianity influenced the rhetoric of the condemnations of the rebellion. Loyalists, thought Maina Kinaichu, 'are the light of your future country. They are the people who could give light to the people who are in the Mau Mau darkness.'[114] 'As a result of refusing to obey God's commandments,' James Mbogo Mwangi wrote of Mau Mau, 'these people could have no good in themselves and nothing good could be produced by them.'[115]

[111] Anderson, *Histories*, 232; Kenya, *Loyalists*, 80.
[112] KNA DC/EBU/1/2/3, DC Embu, 'Handing Over Report: Mr. R. A. Wilkinson to Mr. F. R. Wilson,' 19 July 1954, 1–2 of chapter V; KNA AHC/9/52, 'Macukuru Meru Bururi wa Embu (New Schools in Embu),' *Mundu-wa-Nja*, 10 March 1954. See also DO Kandara to DC Fort Hall, 19 March 1954 for details of cess imposed after destruction of school in Gatundu.
[113] Susan Carruthers, *Winning Hearts and Minds: British Governments, the Media and Colonial Counter-Insurgency 1944–1960* (Leicester, 1995), 156–7, 165.
[114] KNA AHC/9/23, M. Kinaichu to Editor, *Uhoro wa Nyeri*, 3 November 1954.
[115] KNA AHC/9/25, J. M. Mwangi to Editor, *Kayu ka Embu*, 31 August 1955.

Lessons absorbed from the pews of mission churches were put to use to explain the often-unchristian response to Mau Mau. Samuel Mugo wrote in June 1954, 'We read in [the] Holy Bible that what you put in seed the same you will harvest. Now, Mau Mau have planted death in the country and now the time has come for them to harvest what they have planted and that is death.'[116] Few Christian loyalists were pacifists. Even many of those who refused to carry weapons or to join the Home Guard saw no problem in the use of extreme force to crush the insurgency. The future politician, Jeremiah Nyagah, wrote in October 1954, 'The terrorists have to and must be defeated with their own weapon – force.'[117] Beneath the new language of Christianity, however, lay older, more powerful critiques of Mau Mau.

Justus Njoroge Wanyaga, a veteran of the Burma campaign during World War II, was one of very few opponents of the rebels who explained his stance with reference to a sense of imperial loyalty. Njoroge joined the Home Guard in the Rift Valley, as he was 'determined to help again with Her Majesty's Government in Kenya.'[118] More commonly expressed were fears of the futility of Mau Mau's struggle in the face of the armed forces of a mighty empire. Many loyalists understood their opposition to Mau Mau in strictly pragmatic terms. Senior elders could easily recall the violent suppression of earlier Kikuyu mass protest movements, such as that led by Harry Thuku, and the colonial conquest.[119] Their juniors, who had served overseas during World War II, had more recent memories of the might of the British Empire. The destructive power of the British armed forces left an indelible impression on many of those who had witnessed it first-hand. 'How can they [Mau Mau] win this war?' asked Maina Kinaichu. 'Did you not see the war of the British and the Japanese, Italians, and the Germans? What are you compared to all that?'[120] Other loyalists saw Mau Mau violence not just as futile, but as evidence of the indolence of the insurgents, who were accused of attempting to take by force what they did not have the energy or patience to acquire through hard work.

Loyalist criticisms of Mau Mau returned again and again to the question of labour. With the war raging across the Central Province, the

---

[116] KNA AHC/9/24, S. Mugo to Editor, *Kayu ka Embu*, 20 June 1954.
[117] RHL Mss Afr s 1727, J. J. Nyagah to M. Foote, 16 Oct. 1954.
[118] KNA DC/NKU/2/24/73, J. N. Wanyaga to DC Kiambu, 29 September 1953.
[119] Lonsdale, 'Authority,' 59.
[120] KNA AHC/9/23, M. Kinaichu to Editor, *Uhoro wa Nyeri*, 3 September 1954.

congregation of the Chogoria Presbyterian church sang, 'Work, for the night is coming.'[121] Mau Mau supporters 'left the other people working for the progress of their country and took the Mau Mau oath because of their laziness and selfishness and went to live in the forests like wild animals.'[122] Mau Mau, a Home Guard from Riakiania observed, caused 'other people to be punished and do hard work without gain.'[123] The insurgents, Deshon Waweru argued, 'use force as they please and at the same time eat and spend what they have not worked for. What sort of goodness can we expect from such?'[124] As Leonard Njeru, of the Keboria Intermediate School in Embu, wrote, 'the outcome of laziness is theft.'[125] According to Benjamin Njue M'Chandi, young 'Cowboys' were held responsible for the growth of Mau Mau. They had, he claimed,

... ignored working to earn their own living and who later when they became poor and with nothing whatsoever, cunningly and cleverly found this Mau Mau movement through which they could get everything they required for their own living, by deceiving other people that if they help them with money, food etc. they will expel all Europeans out of this country, and thereby acquire for them the nicest thing – self-government.[126]

Mau Mau's refusal to work and their criminality marked the insurgents as delinquents, unqualified and ill-equipped to lead Kikuyu.

Mau Mau's youthful ill discipline was then a common complaint of loyalists, who attempted to impose generational discipline on the insurgents. Chief Muhoya bid Mau Mau to 'Go back to your ordinary life of obedience to your parents.'[127] Muhoya's fellow chief, Stanley Kiama, bemoaned that with Mau Mau, 'young people started to ignore their parents' advice' and 'got into the filthy things.'[128] It was the 'children and boys wandering about in the markets and Towns in this district without doing any work' who, according to Bernard Ngari Harrison of the Kegonge School in Embu, formed 'terrorist gangs' and 'deceived

[121] KNA ARA/8/4, 'Original Kikuyu Hymn Book (Presbyterian).'
[122] KNA AHC/9/24, M. M. Nyambura, 'A House-Fly and Tsetse-Fly,' *Kayu ka Embu*, 28 February 1955.
[123] KNA AHC/9/24, G. K. N. Njirata to Editor, *Kayu ka Embu*, 15 February 1955, 2.
[124] KNA AHC/9/23, D. Waweru to Editor, *Uhoro wa Nyeri*, 3 November 1954.
[125] KNA AHC/9/25, L. Njiru, 'What Could Develop our Country,' *Kaya ka Embu*, 15 January 1956.
[126] KNA AHC/9/25, B. N. M'Chandi to Editor, *Kayu ka Embu*, May 1955.
[127] KNA AHC/9/23, Senior Chief Muhoya, 'The Disobedience of the Kikuyu Children,' *Uhoro wa Nyeri*, 3 November 1954.
[128] KNA AHC/9/23, Chief S. Kiama, 'A Conspiracy,' *Uhoro wa Nyeri*, 18 August 1954.

others to enter the forest.'[129] The resulting bloodshed and absence of any sign of victory demonstrated, according to loyalists, the paucity of the insurgents' claims on leadership of the Kikuyu peoples.

The claim by the insurgents to have usurped a morally bankrupt and political impotent generation of leaders was disputed by loyalists. Pointing to the killing of chiefs, elders, and other prominent figures within society, Maina Kinaichu asked Mau Mau activists, 'How do you think people can live harmoniously without a leader? Your policy is to kill all the leaders; how then shall we manage the life?'[130] Loyalists disputed that Mau Mau's leaders could step into the breach. 'When you kill your fellow men because of foolishness,' a loyalist from Embu claimed, 'I tell you that you are far from becoming a leader of any sort.'[131] Without wealth, the guerrillas lacked the substance necessary to authenticate their designs on leadership. And loyalists warned their fellow Kikuyu that 'if you follow deceitful leadership, you will fall into the pit of destruction.'[132] That poverty of Mau Mau supporters was repeatedly used as evidence of the inability of the insurgency to deliver land and freedom. 'My friends, Mau Mau terrorists are after no good, they are poor people and as you can see so far from their actions, they will in no way defeat the Government,' one headman wrote.[133] Loyalists suggested that a man unable to produce wealth from his own household was incapable of delivering wealth to an entire country.

Belittled by loyalists as impoverished, criminal delinquents, Mau Mau supporters were believed to be morally ill-equipped to lead political action or participate in debate. Mau Mau stood accused of destroying the political unity and social cohesion that many considered essential for economic and social development. Despite the troubles of the 1950s, Nancy Njarua believed 'one thing we must not drop is the progress. This we must carry on in spite [of] the emergency.'[134] Mau Mau's forest fighters were frequently derided by loyalists as 'wild animals,' in particular, as 'hyenas.'[135] Allegories were used to condemn those who shirked the

---

[129] KNA AHC/9/25, B. N. Harrison to Editor, *Kaya ka Embu*, 15 November 1955.

[130] KNA AHC/9/23, M. Kinaichu to Editor, *Uhoro wa Nyeri*, 3 September 1954.

[131] KNA AHC/9/24, E. Munene to Editor, *Kayu ka Embu*, 30 January 1954.

[132] KNA AHC/9/24, S. Njeru, 'What Should I Do?' *Kayu ka Embu*, 28 February 1955, 2.

[133] KNA AHC/9/24, Headman N. Mabui to Editor, *Kayu ka Embu*, 31 January 1955.

[134] KNA AHC/9/23, N. Njarua, 'Care of the Children – The African Women Advised,' *Uhoro wa Nyeri*, 3 November 1954.

[135] See, for example, KNA AHC/9/23, K. Waiganjo to DC Nyeri, 8 June 1954, *Uhoro wa Nyeri*, 18 August 1954; KNA AHC/9/24 H. Mwaniki to Editor, *Kayu ka Embu*,

labour required to gain wealth and virtue, apparently preferring instead
to steal and scavenge.[136] The term 'hyena' was a pejorative word that
denoted sexual indiscipline, another trait of youthful delinquency.[137] In
contrast, loyalism was identified as the only way 'to help in the growth
of our country and our tribe.'[138] Loyalists complained that Mau Mau
was hindering progress. One loyalist wrote that Mau Mau 'made our
country go back into darkness.'[139] Another urged people to think only of
'ways which would raise our standard of living abandoning what would
keep us behind.'[140] The modernity of this loyalist critique of Mau Mau
retrospectively demonstrated the profoundly mistaken initial response of
the colonial government to the insurgency. It was not the guardians of
customs and tradition that were most offended by Mau Mau.

    Many Kikuyu women grasped the modernising opportunities presen-
ted by loyalism. They enunciated their opposition to Mau Mau through
the domestic modernity preached by the government-run *Maendeleo
ya Wanawake* (Women's Progress).[141] First established in 1952, the
Maendeleo ya Wanawake established local clubs across Kenya. By 1954,
there were 508 clubs, more than half in Central Province and Nairobi,
in which African women were taught domestic science. Building on pre-
Emergency notions of social welfare, the clubs were deliberately adapted
to become a counter to Mau Mau.[142] In Central Province, 'no woman
shall be a member of a Maendeleo Club unless she has foresworn Mau
Mau.'[143] Mary Muthanji, an employee of the Community Development
department, established a branch at Kirigi village in Embu with the support of the local district officer and loyalist elite. 'In this club,' Muthanji
wrote, 'I teach women general cleanliness, children welfare and laundry.

30 June 1954; KNA AHC/9/24, C. N. M. Kaguyu, 'A Story of an Oldman and His
   Three Sons,' *Kayu ka Embu*, 22 November 1954.
[136] See for widespread use of animals in morality tales, Ciarunji Chesaina, *Oral Literature
   of the Embu and Mbeere* (Nairobi, 1997), 59–122; Rose Mwangi, *Kikuyu Folktales:
   Their Nature and Value* (Nairobi, 1983), 57–130.
[137] White, 'Men From the Boys,' 23.
[138] KNA AHC/9/24, O. Kunguru, 'Advice to all Teachers,' *Kayu ka Embu*, January 1955.
[139] KNA AHC/9/24 B.M. Njeru to the Editor, *Kayu ka Embu*, 30 June 1954.
[140] KNA AHC/9/57, W. Kireru to Editor, *Utheri wa Nyeri*, August 1957, 5.
[141] See also Elkins, *Imperial*; White, 'Men From the Boys' Audrey Wipper, 'The Maendeleo
   ya Wanawake Organization: The Co-Optation of Leadership,' *African Studies Review*
   18 (1975), 99–120.
[142] Joanna Lewis, *Empire State-Building: War and Welfare in Kenya 1925–52* (Oxford,
   2000), 298–359; Presley, *Kikuyu Women*, 165–7.
[143] KNA AHC/9/25, 'Maendeleo ya Wanawake Clubs,' *Kaya ka Embu*, 30 June 1955.
   Also cited in Elkins, *Imperial*.

I also teach them some gardening work, because as you know Kenya is a farming country.' However, 'all work and no play make Jack a dull boy,' and sport played a prominent role in the group's activities.[144] Hygiene, an issue of critical importance in the Emergency villages, formed a major part of the message of the *Maendeleo ya Wanawake*. On 7 June 1955, the Gitumbi club 'went round the whole village and collected all youths and bathed them, cut their hair, took their jiggers off and washed their clothes.'[145] Juliana Muthoni compared her membership in the *Maendeleo ya Wanawake*, where 'I have benefited much,' with Mau Mau, 'which will bring you no good rather than to destroy anything which could help your children in future.'[146] Through the *Maendeleo ya Wanawake*, women opposed to Mau Mau also criticised the insurgents' presumed anti-progressive agenda.

The loyalism of Kikuyu women also should be understood as an expression of their gendered experience of the conflict. As discussed in the previous chapter, with many men fighting or detained, villages were dominated by women and children. Increasingly, since 1954, women impelled Mau Mau fighters to surrender. They were no longer able to make the sacrifices necessary to support themselves, their families, and a losing guerrilla army.[147] Nancy Njarua pleaded with her fellow Kikuyu women, 'To save your life and save your children's lives you should try in whichever way possible to see that the few remaining gangsters have surrendered.'[148] Although self-mastery was an expression of male dominance of the household, its meaning was debated by women too.

In the 1940s, landlessness 'compelled husbands and wives to argue about masculinity and marriage in a context where men could not be good husbands.'[149] In the midst of war, the conditions for this argument were multiplied many times over.[150] With land confiscations commonplace, detention widespread, and the level of bride-price rising significantly, women's loyalism was in part a condemnation of the failure of men

---

[144] KNA AHC/9/24, M. Muthanji to Editor, *Kayu ka Embu*, 31 January 1955.
[145] KNA AHC/9/25, S. M. Ngai to Editor, *Kaya ka Embu*, 30 June 1955.
[146] KNA AHC/9/25, J. Muthoni to Editor, *Kaya ka Embu*, 15 December 1955.
[147] Lonsdale, 'Authority,' 62.
[148] KNA AHC/9/23, Nancy Njarua, 'African Women,' *Uhoro was Nyeri*, 3 November 1954.
[149] Peterson, 'Wordy Women,' 471.
[150] See for a similar case, Mike Kesby, 'Arenas for Control, Terrains of Gender Contestation: Guerrilla Struggle and Counter-Insurgency Warfare in Zimbabwe 1972–1980,' *Journal of Southern African Studies* 22 (1996).

to be husbands.[151] Those who turned to the *Maendeleo ya Wanawake*
used its brand of modernity to consolidate control of households and
their budgets. Whether the product of pride derived from their role in
the war or a sense of abandonment resulting from widowhood, orphan-
hood, or the absence of men fighting and in detention, Kikuyu women
developed what Heyer terms 'an independence and self-sufficiency' during the Emergency.[152] Loyalism became a means towards advancement
for women as well as men.

Echoing the words of Muoria and his fellow writers in the previous
decade, loyalists, men and women alike, seized on education as a totem
for progress and modernity. In the words of one Nyeri loyalist, 'in the
true education lies the chief hope of [the] African race and it is the key to
the welfare and happiness of the people.'[153] 'In order that a country may
acquire self-government,' another wrote, 'it must first have many educated people.'[154] Education for girls was a recurrent topic of discussion.
'The only way to step towards modern civilization is to have educated
men and women,' Samuel King'ori believed.[155] Grace Wambura claimed
'the happiest people are those married to educated girls.'[156] In contrast
to the insurgents' arson campaign discussed earlier, the government paid
school fees for up to three children per family[157] and issued grants to
schools in loyalist areas.[158] Loyalists were not slow to realise that the
Emergency increased the educational opportunities for themselves and
their children. One wrote that 'owing to the loyalty of the people in this
country, there has been great improvement in Education. Many people
now who two years ago could neither read nor write are quite happy to
see themselves able to read as well as to write.'[159] But loyalism was not
just concerned with social advancement. Opposition to the insurgency
also became tied to political development.

---

[151] KNA DC/EBU/9/1, Greet Sluiter, 'A Study of Kabare-Village in the Embu-District,'
May 1956, 6.
[152] Heyer, 'Nowadays,' 264.
[153] KNA AHC/9/57, D. Ndujiu to Editor, *Utheri wa Nyeri*, June 1957, 5.
[154] KNA AHC/9/24, N. Jacob to Editor, *Kayu ka Embu*, 15 September 1954.
[155] KNA AHC/9/57, S. King'ori to Editor, *Utheri wa Nyeri*, July 1957, 5.
[156] KNA AHC/9/24, G. Wambura to Editor, *Kaya ka Embu*, 30 July 1955.
[157] This was agreed in KNA VQ/1/51, 'Record of a Meeting Held at Nyeri on 22nd
December, 1953,' 24 December 1953.
[158] See, for example, KNA DC/MUR/3/4/21, Education Officer, Fort Hall to Supervisor,
A. A. C. Weithaga & President, African Christian Churches and Schools (ACC&S),
Gituru, 8 September 1953.
[159] KNA AHC/9/25, L. M. Njoka, 'Wambere People During the Emergency,' *Kaya ka
Embu*, 30 June 1955.

In the early 1950s, many Kikuyu 'thought that in the very near future Mau Mau would do much for the development and welfare of our country and so we help it with all our strength.'[160] By late 1954, loyalists accused Mau Mau of hampering that quest and impoverishing its supporters. Muthoni Karanga, a schoolgirl from Embu who lived at the Githure guard post, wrote in November 1954: 'Why are you giving help to Mau Mau terrorists in the bush as if they are growing food for you in the bush? Why are you foolish to go naked and hungry and still give Mau Mau your money and food, what good will they do to you?'[161] Loyalists blamed the excesses of the civil war on their adversaries. Mau Mau, according to Eusebio Ngari, 'have brought, poverty, famine, and murdering in the country.'[162] The vicious cycle of killings that accompanied the breakdown of ambiguity through 1953 left a strong but one-sided impression on the insurgents' opponents. 'Freedom,' Headman Stephen Mututo Kibubu wrote, 'does not come from hatred and such things like murdering.'[163] Instead of violence, criminality, and detention, loyalists could see their collaboration offering a path towards self-mastery, land, and freedom.

At the heart of Kikuyu politics and notions of leadership and action lay the need to protect access to land. In the 1930s, Kikuyu elders abdicated responsibility for organising political activity by failing to find recompense for the land alienations that accompanied the first years of colonial rule.[164] Mau Mau initially emerged as a vehicle for redress of those grievances. Ironically, by inducing consolidation, confiscations, and the introduction of private tenure, Mau Mau stood accused of exacerbating those same injustices in the mid-1950s. Through preferential treatment during the non-military phase of the counterinsurgency campaign, loyalism had become a path towards land, self-mastery, and, as we will see in the next chapter, freedom. The success of non-military counterinsurgency in Kenya can be attributed to the fortuitous alignment between Kikuyu notions of land, political leadership, and moral virtue on one hand and a colonial determination to encourage class formation to prevent any recurrence on the other. However, the introduction of land reform and the granting of jobs came too late to explain the initial swing in allegiances away from the insurgents. Non-military counterinsurgency

---

[160] KNA AHC/9/25, S. M. Ngai to Editor, *Kaya ka Embu*, 30 June 1955.
[161] KNA AHC/9/24, M. Karanga to Editor, *Kayu ka Embu*, 22 November 1954.
[162] KNA AHC/9/24, E. N. Ngari to Editor, *Kayu ka Embu*, 31 July 1954.
[163] KNA AHC/9/23, Headman S. M. Kibubu to Editor, *Uhoro wa Nyeri*, 18 October 1954.
[164] Kershaw, *Mau Mau From Below*, 186.

sustained loyalism and persuaded Kikuyu to pursue a moderate line in the years leading up to independence. The rewards for loyalism were not, though, its trigger.

Rule Yourselves

Mau Mau's insurgents took up arms 'to regain stolen lands and to become an adult.'[165] But by the end of 1956, they could not hope to achieve either aim. Throughout its existence, Mau Mau was subject to a theory of labour that asserted 'everyone who cultivates the soil is a Kikuyu.'[166] The insurgency's answers to that rigorous and ongoing examination became progressively less and less satisfactory. Land reform and the terror of the counterinsurgency war had dispossessed and disenfranchised many of the movement's supporters. Once economic rewards, most notably land, for collaboration were formalised, loyalism travelled in the opposite direction along the continuum of labour, wealth, and virtue. From being told, 'You work for nothing,'[167] landless and landed loyalists were able to toil towards wealth. Loyalism was sustained beyond the initial trigger provided by insurgent violence precisely because of the intersection of the terms of the alliance between loyalists and the state with Kikuyu political thought. Non-military counterinsurgency, a frequently used strategy by states seeking to combat rural revolts, thus carried particular weight in the Kenyan context.

Non-military counterinsurgency sustained loyalism by providing the incentives for the Kikuyu peasantry to remain within or rejoin patronage networks. Between 1950 and 1954, local insurgent leaders promising greater equity in land distribution threatened to supplant incumbent elite patrons and create new networks of clients across Central Province. However, once the security forces began to reverse the insurgents' influence, older patrons were able to regain their position at the head of new patronage networks. There, they were joined by younger loyalists, whose access to various state institutions produced significant resources that could be redistributed to clients. In the context of economic collapse, moral crisis, and proximal threats to personal security, tens of thousands of Kikuyu sought to make the best of an appalling situation. They once again begrudgingly accepted a system of patronage underpinned by the

---

[165] Quoted in Lonsdale, 'Wealth, Poverty and Civic Virtue,' 326.
[166] Quoted in Peterson, *Creative Writing*, 10.
[167] KNA VQ/1/51, ASP SB Nyeri to PC Central, 16 June 1954, 1.

profoundly elitist, heavily gendered notions of moral ethnicity. The pay-back for the clients took the form of access to the rewards provided to loyalists, most notably the security of person, family, and land. The terms of the transaction had changed, though. It was no longer enough to provide just manual labour, but also intelligence and service in the war against Mau Mau.

In February 1957, Maina Wambugu, an employee of the Community Development department in Othaya, described a tea party held at Gatugi village in Nyeri. 'One could hardly see any gloomy or dirty person at the occasion,' Maina wrote. 'All were singing, laughing and making themselves cheerful.' He continued, 'I heard one person remark that the country was experiencing social revolution. During days of trouble many of them could not imagine that such a happy day would again be enjoyed. But now people are nearing to a complete normal life.'[168] Loyalists had gained control of their households. No longer threatened by Mau Mau and free to enjoy the fruits of their labour, loyalists had satisfied Kenyatta's prequalification for political dominance: 'You must rule yourselves in your own lives if you want to rule this country.'[169]

---

[168] KNA AHC/9/57, M. Wambugu to Editor, *Utheri wa Nyeri*, February 1957.
[169] Quoted in Lonsdale, 'Wealth, Poverty and Civic Virtue,' 327.

5

Loyalism in the Age of Decolonisation

The Triumph of the System

Not all members of Kenya's African population were celebrating independence on 12 December 1963. At the Kiganjo police training centre in Nyeri, Ephantus N'Dobi and other long-serving instructors cowered in fear. Two or three times a month during the counterinsurgency campaign, N'Dobi had participated in operations in the Mount Kenya and Aberdare forests. He later claimed to have killed more Mau Mau fighters than he could precisely recall. N'Dobi expected the local population of Nyeri to execute revenge when freed from colonial rule.[1] Despite their military defeat by both loyalists and the colonial state, Mau Mau sympathisers understood Kenya's impending independence as their ultimate victory over both the British and loyalists.[2] In the three years prior to independence, non-violent dissent aimed at loyalists became more common. Those targeted were tainted by their involvement in either the theft of the land of Mau Mau sympathisers or the physical abuse of suspects under interrogation. N'Dobi feared he, too, would be a victim of more violent reprisals once independence arrived, but he and many of his fellow loyalists did not merely survive colonialism's demise. Instead, they thrived.

During the final decade of colonial rule, counterinsurgency and decolonisation intertwined to both defeat Mau Mau and prepare loyalists for new roles after the British departure. Although their poorer brethren were

---

[1] Ephantus N'Dobi, interview with the author, Chogoria, South Meru, 18 September 2003.
[2] wa Wanjau, *Mau Mau Author*, 207.

148

overlooked once the war was over, elite loyalists monopolised the benefits of the recruitment of Africans into the Provincial Administration and civil service, a process labelled 'Africanisation,' and the partial political liberalisation that accompanied preparations for decolonisation. In part, N'Dobi could therefore attribute his survival of independence to his ability to vote in the 1957 legislative council election and to the significant presence of loyalists within the Provincial Administration in the years before and after independence.

Political reforms constituted the second arm of loyalism's sustaining mechanisms. Of course, influence over the key institutions of the state allowed for consolidation of the social and economic gains loyalists had made in the second half of the decade. However, the political reforms delivered as part of Baring's second prong also, to a certain extent, enabled loyalists to bridge the divisions caused by the civil war, if only temporarily. Recruitment into the upper levels of the Provincial Administration and more equitable representation within the legislature had long been aims of African political action. Unlike earlier moments during colonial rule, an alliance between Kenya's subjects in the late 1950s promised substantial returns for Kikuyu that went far beyond simply the opportunity to blunt the jagged edges of British governance. Loyalists could thus point to meaningful political gains as justification for their stance against Mau Mau. Moreover, the access to positions of political power granted to loyalists during the process of decolonisation allowed these individuals to recapture a degree of legitimacy in the eyes of even their most determined opponents. Loyalist politicians elected to represent Central Province in the legislature in the 1950s were among the delegations sent to London to negotiate independence. This process of legitimisation was further consolidated by the loyalist appointment to positions such as district commissioners and members of the legislature, which positioned them between the state and local communities as the conduits of patronage. Loyalists became indispensable to the late colonial and post-colonial state. For that very reason, the divisions created by the civil war of the 1950s remained salient within Kenyan politics into the 1960s and beyond.

The conflict between loyalists and insurgents was modified to become one of radically different conceptualisations of independence. For loyalists, decolonisation became a process of transfer of power from a British elite to a Kenyan elite. For many former insurgents, independence was to herald only the beginning of a sustained programme of social and economic reform. The resolution of those contested understandings of Kenyan independence in favour of incumbent elites set a precedent for the reproduction of state authority during periods of transition, most notably after the death of Jomo Kenyatta in 1978, the re-introduction of multi-party elections in 1992, and the toppling of the Kenya African National Union (KANU) at the polls in 2002.

Independence was an early example of what has been termed 'the triumph of the system.' In their survey of the first elections of the latest multi-party era in 1992, Throup and Hornsby describe Moi's defeat of a splintered opposition movement as a further demonstration of this victory of authority over the aspirations of the people. The blueprint for this victory, drawn up by the governments of both Kenyatta and Moi, deployed the formal and informal powers of the state to secure their own position and the interests of particular alignments of domestic and international capital. When used alongside other measures, manipulation of the electoral process and the Provincial Administration proved integral to the repeated post-colonial triumph of the system.[3] This is not surprising, bearing in mind that the Africanisation of the civil service and the elections of 1957 and 1958 brought to the fore a generation of politicians and administrators who dominated the post-colonial landscape. Among others, Ronald Ngala, Julius Kiano, Oginga Odinga, Jeremiah Nyagah, Masinde Muliro, Tom Mboya, and Daniel arap Moi won their respective seats in either of the first two rounds of elections. Simeon Nyachae, John Michuki, Charles Koinange, Kenneth Matiba, and Charles Njonjo were all recruited into the civil service or Provincial Administration. As political leaders, civil servants, and businessmen, this cohort shaped the post-colonial history of Kenya.

Even as the political arena for Africans was apparently expanded prior to the British departure, the limits of effective change were strictly defined. The colonial motivations for this were not difficult to ascertain: the protection of strategic and economic interests during decolonisation.[4] The colonial government and London were fearful of losing access to military bases, the nationalisation of private metropolitan investments, and the seizure of European-owned land after granting independence. Elite loyalists were therefore absorbed into the structures of economic and

---

[3] David Throup and Charles Hornsby, *Multi-Party Politics in Kenya: The Kenyatta and Moi States and the Triumph of the System in the 1992 Election* (Oxford, 1998).

[4] David Percox, 'Internal Security and Decolonization in Kenya, 1956–63,' *Journal of Imperial and Commonwealth History* 29 (2001); Percox, 'Arming of the State'; Gary Wasserman, *The Politics of Decolonization: Kenya Europeans and the Land Issue, 1960–1965* (Cambridge, 1976).

political power as a counterbalance to the presumed destructive influence of Kenyatta and others often mistakenly assumed to be radical nationalists. As the colonial state advanced this new African elite, it did so by encouraging economic reform, recruitment into the civil service, and political liberalisation. The disparate components of this African elite first fused together and then fused with the Asian and European elite and interests. The product was what Bayart terms a 'dominant national class,' which created post-colonial Kenya in its own image and adapted the state for a new era.[5] Initially, as partners of settler and Asian representatives under the multi-racial constitutional arrangements of the late 1950s, elite loyalists later became gatekeepers of the post-colonial state.

Defining Loyalty

From its founding in 1907 until 1944, Kenya's Legislative Council was restricted to European and Asian members. Eliud Mathu, the first African member, was joined by five additional members between 1947 and 1952.[6] Each was selected by the Governor from lists produced by regional electoral colleges made up of members of local councils.[7] Although the rise of Mau Mau temporarily froze the already slow pace of political reform, discussions began in earnest during early 1954 regarding direct methods of selecting African representatives. Provision was made for African legislative elections in the Lyttelton constitution later that year. In October, it was announced that W. F. Coutts would tour the colony the following year to solicit opinions on methods of selection of African political representatives.[8]

Coutts was not a neutral figure in the local politics of Central Province. Between 1947 and 1949, he was district commissioner in Fort Hall during the peasants' revolt against soil conservation measures, which

[5] Jean-Francois Bayart, *The State in Africa: The Politics of the Belly*, Mary Harper, Christopher Harrison, and Elizabeth Harrison trans. (London, 1993), 152–3.

[6] By 1957, the African members of the Legislative Council were W. W. W. Awori (North Nyanza); M. Gikonyo (Nairobi); J. Jeremiah (Coast); E. W. Mathu, (Central); B. A. Ohanga (South Nyanza), and the future president, D. T. arap Moi (Rift Valley and Masai). Ohanga had replaced F. W. Odede in April 1953 following Odede's suspected involvement in the insurgency.

[7] Geoffrey Engholm, 'African Elections in Kenya, March 1957,' in *Five Elections in Africa: A Group of Electoral Studies*, eds. William MacKenzie and Kenneth Robinson (Oxford, 1960), 394–5, 398–9.

[8] Ibid., 402.

foreshadowed the Mau Mau war. Coutts ultimately sided with a cadre of newly recruited, educated chiefs to suppress the unrest.[9] The advancement of the state's Kikuyu educated and modernising allies was a prominent feature of Coutts' report, compiled after his trip to Kenya in 1955. During his visit, Coutts met with numerous deputations drawn from local councils, churches, chiefs, headmen, and other forums. In Central Province, only loyalists were allowed to meet Coutts, who was escorted throughout by Wanyutu Waweru and Chief Ignatio Morai, both known to Coutts from his time in Fort Hall. The delegations from Central Province were uniform in their agreement that the franchise be extended to Africans, but restricted to proven loyalists.[10] Coutts agreed, but how loyalty was to be proved was another question.

After Coutts' report was published[11] and the government announced its revisions,[12] the legal framework for African elections was established in late March 1956. Campaigning was to be constrained by Emergency regulations, which included a ban on colony-wide political organisations. District-based political groupings were permitted outside Central Province, but non-aligned individuals were expected to run their own campaigns. Participation in all formal political activities by Kikuyu, Embu, and Meru was to be restricted to loyalists. The Provincial Administration was entrusted with the supervision of registration, campaigning, and voting. Each voter was allowed up to three votes depending on how many of the qualification criteria they met. These included: an intermediate school education, income of £120 per year or £500 worth of property, five or more years of service in government employment, or outstanding service to the country. In addition, voters in Central Province had to prove their loyalty to the government during the Mau Mau insurgency. District commissioners were the arbiters of loyalty and issued certificates to those who passed this prequalification test.[13] Voting was not for the

[9] Throup, *Economic and Social Origins*, 139–70.
[10] KNA VP/1/86, Coutts, 'Tour of Central Province,' 5 July 1955; PC Central to Coutts, 20 July 1955.
[11] Colony & Protectorate of Kenya, *Report of the Commissioner Appointed to Enquire Into Methods for the Selection of African Representatives to the Legislative Council* (Nairobi, 1955).
[12] Colony & Protectorate of Kenya, *Report of the Commissioner Appointed to Enquire Into Methods for the Selection of African Representatives to the Legislative Council* (Nairobi, 1956).
[13] Colony & Protectorate of Kenya, *An Ordinance to Provide for the Nomination and Election of African Members to the Legislative Council of the Colony and Protectorate of Kenya; and for Matters Connected Therewith and Incidental Thereto* (Nairobi, 1956).

poor, and the many loyalists who did not meet the qualification standard were as disenfranchised as Mau Mau supporters.

Registration commenced in August 1956 in the eight new constituencies.[14] Within Central Province and Nairobi, disputes soon emerged out of the challenge of defining loyalty. No right of appeal against the rejection of applications for loyalty certificates was instituted.[15] All officials understood 'continuous active and positive loyalty' to represent the necessary level of support for the government's counterinsurgency for the purposes of voter registration.[16] What form that loyalty took and from what date it was to be measured was for individual officers to decide. Although ultimate authority rested with district commissioners, they relied on the guidance of non-binding recommendations of local committees formed for the purpose. These committees included chiefs and headmen. Some were particularly reluctant to recommend to district commissioners the awarding of certificates to all but those they considered to be the most aggressive loyalists.[17] Njuguna Wanjai had been an active member and then a leader of the Fort Hall Home Guard between 1953 and 1955, but was refused a loyalty certificate.[18] In most cases, mere membership of the Home Guard was insufficient proof of loyalty.

The date from which loyalty was to be measured varied from location to location. Advice from Nairobi recommended that loyalty should be proved by applicants from mid-1953, when the growth of the Home Guard provided a forum for demonstrations of opposition to Mau Mau.[19] At Kigumo in Fort Hall, June 1954 was used as the date. This was the period when the tide turned against the rebels and thus the date from which support for Mau Mau could not be excused as a consequence of compulsion.[20] Elsewhere, earlier cut-off dates were employed.[21] Such variations were partly a reflection of the peculiar local trajectories of the war, but also a result of the discretionary powers given to district commissioners. Typical of the enthusiasm with which many had prosecuted

---

[14] The constituencies were: Nairobi; Central Province; Akamba; Coast Province; Rift Valley Province and Masai districts of Narok and Kajiado; Nyanza North; Nyanza Central; and Nyanza South.

[15] KNA DC/MUR/3/1/18, minutes of meeting to discuss procedure for African elections, 14 July 1956, 4

[16] KNA VP/1/86, extract of Central Provinces DCs' meeting, 21–23 May 1956.

[17] KNA DC/MUR/3/1/24, DC Fort Hall to DC Thika, 23 January 1957.

[18] KNA DC/MUR/3/1/24, DO Makuyu to DC Fort Hall, 10 January 1957.

[19] KNA OP/1/552, Special Commissioner to Secretary for African Affairs, 18 July 1956.

[20] KNA DC/MUR/3/1/24, DC Fort Hall to DO Subukia, 13 February 1957.

[21] KNA DC/NYI/1/1, Nyeri District Annual Report 1956, 4.

their responsibilities during the war against Mau Mau, district commissioners were severe in their judgment of loyalty. This led to pressure from London for greater flexibility because of concern over the low numbers of registered voters.[22]

With very few opportunities for women to demonstrate their loyalty during the Emergency, they were particularly unlikely to pass a loyalty test. District commissioners were so uncertain of the ability of women to meet the qualification standards that their applications were forwarded to the provincial commissioner for approval. As one case suggests, the women over whom the provincial commissioner stood in judgment were significant figures in the war in their localities. Millicent Wangui was the wife of Senior Chief Muhoya of North Tetu, Nyeri. Beatrice Wairimu was a divisional leader of the government's women's movement, the *Maendeleo ya Wanawake*. Damaris Wangeci had been employed by the Department for Community Development between 1953 and 1955, and then joined the *Maendeleo ya Wanawake* as an instructor. Wachera Njauini worked in a variety of locations as part of the propaganda effort. Molly Wanjuku had worked for two years as a screener in North Tetu. Rahab Wanjeri, Wanja Kirugami, Alice Nyiah, and Murugui Murage were valuable informers, with Murage providing intelligence leading to the capture of a Mau Mau general.[23] Their experience suggests the very limited extent to which the 1957 elections were a democratic exercise.

Across Kenya, perhaps only one third of eligible members of the population registered to vote.[24] The extensive application of the loyalty test was particularly significant in Central Province, where only 35,644 voters were listed on the electoral roll.[25] Although by far the largest constituency, this figure represented just 7.4 percent of the adult population of the province.[26] As a further punishment for the Mau Mau insurgency, Kikuyu, Embu, and Meru political representation was to be further restricted by the creation of just one seat for the whole of Central Province. In contrast, Nyanza was to have three representatives, despite a total electorate of 57,796.[27] Within Central Province, an imbalance in the

---

[22] KNA OP/1/552, DC Mombasa to anon, 23 November 1956.

[23] KNA VQ/1/6, DC Nyeri to PC Central, 13 November 1956.

[24] KNA VP/1/86, Special Branch Headquarters, 'The African Elections and Their Aftermath,' 18 April 1957, 1.

[25] KNA DC/MUR/3/1/24, Secretary for African Affairs to all PCs, Officer-in-Charge Nairobi & Press Officer, 17 January 1957.

[26] Engholm, 'Elections,' 421.

[27] Like Central Province, the Rift Valley, with an electorate of just over 5,000, the Coast, which had less than 8,000 voters, and Nairobi, which had only 2,348 registered on the

geographical distribution of votes existed. Meru district had more than 26,018 votes out of a total of just over 50,363, followed by Kiambu, with 8,486; Embu with 6,414; Fort Hall with 5,644; and Nyeri with 3,627. Fewer than 200 votes were shared between the labour force of the European settler districts of Thika and Nanyuki.[28] Rewarded by the government for its loyalty during the counterinsurgency campaign, Meru district therefore held the key to electoral success.

Using any benchmark of loyalty, there were unquestionably more loyalists in Meru district than elsewhere in Central Province. The loyalty test, therefore, proved to be significantly less of a barrier to voter registration in Meru than elsewhere in Central Province. Moreover, the Provincial Administration was determined to inflate the numbers of Meru voters to improve the chances of success for a local candidate. It therefore relaxed its definition of loyalty to register as many voters as possible.[29] The Meru domination was somewhat diluted by the qualitative multiple vote system, which favoured the wealthier districts elsewhere in Central Province. However, votes cast in Meru district ultimately added up to just over a half of the papers placed inside the ballot boxes on Election Day.[30]

Campaigning and Polling

The privileging of Meru voters was based on the presumption that voters would, if given the opportunity, vote for local candidates. This outcome was predicted once registration began, meaning a Meru candidate was almost certain to win.[31] Elsewhere in the province, untoward colonial manipulation of the entire procedure was rightly suspected.[32] On nomination day, 22 January 1957, the candidature of Bernard Mate from Meru was confirmed. Mate's rivals were announced as Eliud Mathu,

electoral roll, all had one representative (KNA DC/MUR/3/1/24, Secretary for African Affairs to PCs, Officer-in-Charge Nairobi & Press Officer, 17 January 1957).

[28] These figures include multiple votes, with each voter holding up to three votes (KNA DC/MUR/3/1/24, Assistant Supervisor of African Elections, Central Province to all District Commissioners, Central Province, 16 January 1957).

[29] Stephen Murocha, interview with the author, Chogoria, South Meru, 15 September 2003; Jack Roelker, *Mathu of Kenya: A Political Study* (Stanford CA, 1976), 138.

[30] KNA DC/MUR/3/1/18, Asst. Supervisor of African Elections Central to Supervisor of African Elections, 6 November 1956.

[31] KNA DC/MUR/3/1/18, Asst. Supervisor of African Elections Central Province to Supervisor of African Elections, 15 October 1956.

[32] KNA VP/1/86, Asst. Supt. of Police to DC Nyeri, 7 November 1956, 1.

Jeremiah Nyagah, David Waruhiu, and Stephen Kioni. Aged 33, Mate had
been both an education officer and teacher. This experience in education
was complemented by a distinguished academic career at Makerere,
North Wales, and Edinburgh. His modernist, moderate objectives of
'Happiness, United and progress together, in Education, Trades, Good
Farms, [and] Prosperity' potentially appealed to a broad moderate faction
across the province. Although nicknamed 'Cumber's Mate' by colonial
officials as a result of Mate's close relationship with Meru's district commissioner, John Cumber, Mate should not be dismissed as a mere colonial
quisling. His campaign literature demonstrated a strong commitment to
increasing African political representation. Furthermore, he argued for
Kenyan self-rule, although he felt this would be best achieved by 'complete loyalty to Kenya and the Crown on the part of all her citizens.'[33]

However, Mate unashamedly exploited his Meru roots to ensure electoral success. His campaign material promised that he would 'represent
his tribe with all his heart and power.' Mate reminded voters, 'The man
who is far away will never help you.' During his few campaign meetings
held outside of his home district, Mate could not escape his status as
the Meru candidate. At one meeting in Nyeri, he was asked, 'Why will
you represent Kikuyu, Embu, and Meru when you know that the Meru
are antagonistic towards the Kikuyu on account of their having started
the Mau Mau movement, and the Meru had Kikuyu in Meru District
repatriated to the Reserve?'[34] Within Meru, he could rely on the support of the loyalist council of elders, the *Njuri Ncheke*, local colonial
officials, and missionaries, in particular, his Methodist patron, W. H.
Laughton.[35]

Mate's main rival was Mathu, himself a former teacher. As the main
Kikuyu candidate, Mathu's campaign was the hardest hit by the restriction of political activity to loyalists. Despite his membership of the Legislative Council during the Emergency and support for various counterinsurgency measures, Mathu's relationship with the colonial authorities
was troubled.[36] In October 1952, he had publicly disowned Mau Mau,
but at the same time aired his concerns over restrictions of personal

[33] KNA VP/1/86, untitled election pamphlet for Bernard Mate, 1957; 'Policy of Bernard
    Mate,' 1957.
[34] KNA VP/1/86, Ins of Police to Supt. of Police, 18 February 1957.
[35] KNA MSS/124/5, Laughton to Irvine, 4 January 1956, 2; KNA MSS/124/6, Laughton
    to Calderwood, 14 April 1957.
[36] Ibid., 119–33.

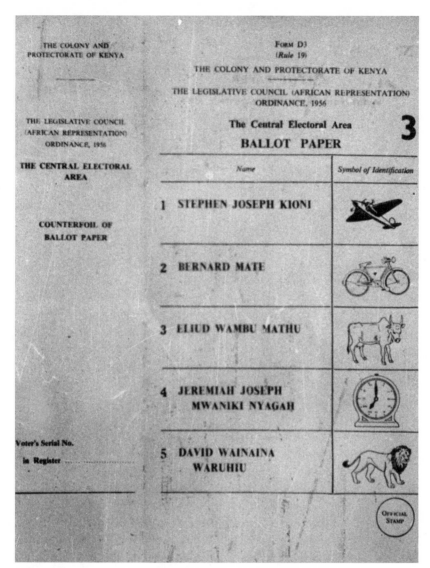

FIGURE 8. Ballot paper for Central Area, Legislative Council elections, 1957. Reproduced with permission of Kenya National Archives.

freedoms and the government's unwillingness to examine the underlying causes of unrest.[37] Mathu appears to have been respected by several

37 KNA MAC/KEN/33/4, Mathu & Koinange, 'The Situation in Kenya,' 12 September 1952, 1; Mathu et al., 'A Statement by the African Members of the Legislative Council,' 15 October 1952.

leading figures within the Mau Mau movement.[38] His candidature initially attracted the derision of leading loyalists outside of Kiambu, who
suspected Mathu of harbouring Mau Mau sympathies.[39] Although the
fractures among the loyalist elites of the Kikuyu districts healed prior to
polling day, Mathu's effort was doomed from the beginning by the size
of the Meru vote. Moreover, he shared his manifesto with the other existing members of the Legislative Council, who campaigned together as the
United Front. Their platform was characterised by excessive moderation
in the arena of political liberalisation, advocating only a slow pace of
reform and non-confrontational action.[40] Even among the elitist voters
of 1957, this proved to be a misreading of the political temperature.
Notably, only Daniel arap Moi retained his seat.

Of all the candidates in Central Province in 1957, Jeremiah Nyagah
went on to have the most prominent career as cabinet minister, vice
president, and founder of an influential political dynasty. Originating
from the loyalist stronghold of Mbeere in Embu, Nyagah had also carved
out a career in education as a schoolmaster and assistant educational
officer. During the worst years of the rebellion, he had been at Oxford,
but he showed himself to be a committed loyalist on his return. Nyagah
was a self-styled '[Chris]tian Liberal politician.'[41] In public meetings held
during his campaign, Nyagah called for a new multi-racial education
system, restrictions on European and Asian immigration, equal pay for
Africans, and the dissembling of perceived Asian dominance over trade.[42]
In common with his principal rivals, Nyagah relied on his home district for
his support, but Embu's electorate was insufficient to sustain a challenge
to Mate or even Mathu. Nyagah would have to wait until the following
year to claim a seat in the legislature.

There were two other candidates, Stephen Kioni and David Waruhiu.
Kioni had been a schoolmaster at the Gatitu Catholic mission in Nyeri.[43]
He made a deliberate appeal to Catholic voters, but this proved in vain, as
the electorate showed no inclination to cast their ballot papers according

---

[38] Jack Roelker, 'The Contribution of Eliud Wambu Mathu to Political Independence in
Kenya' (PhD, Syracuse University, 1974), 204–5.
[39] KNA VP/1/86, Asst. Supt. of Police, 'Chief Stephen Chorio Views,' 7 November 1956.
[40] KNA OP/1/536, African Unofficial Members, 'Statement of Policy by the United Front
of the African Unofficial Members of the Kenya Legislative Council, December 1956;
Roelker, *Mathu*, 141.
[41] RHL Mss Afr s 1727, Nyagah to Foote, 6 January 1957.
[42] KNA VP/1/86; Insp. of Police to Supt. of Police, 22 February 1957.
[43] KNA DC/MUR/3/1/24, 'Minutes of Proceedings at Nyeri on Nomination Day, 22nd
January 1957,' 1.

to religious affiliation.[44] Waruhiu had the most impeccable loyalist credentials of all the candidates. His father was the late Senior Chief, whose murder in October 1952 had led to the onset of the Emergency. David Waruhiu had held a number of positions within government during the conflict, principally due to his firm anti-Mau Mau stance, Christian beliefs, and familial connections. By the time of the election, Waruhiu was an assistant district officer in Kiambu. However, rumours regarding his work in detention camps housing Mau Mau suspects, the single most controversial aspect of the counterinsurgency, doomed Waruhiu's campaign to ignominious failure.[45] That this was the case with a franchise restricted to loyalists again demonstrates the limitations of the crude caricatures of loyalists as unquestioning colonial collaborators. Mathu was widely suspected of having taken at least one Mau Mau oath and of having sympathies with the forest fighters. Mate and Nyagah had managed to avoid having to make forceful public demonstrations of loyalty by concentrating on their teaching careers. Through their delaying of unequivocal declarations of allegiance and possible temporary flirtations with Mau Mau, Mate, Nyagah, and Mathu had much in common with the majority of loyalist voters. Few, in contrast, shared Waruhiu's unambiguous brand of loyalty.

Almost all those registered to vote in Central Province did so. However, outside of Meru, polling on 10 and 11 March 1957 was notable only for the relative levels of disinterest. By contrast, in Meru, large numbers of people had queued overnight in the cold, pouring rain to be among the first to cast their vote, in almost all cases for Mate.[46] At 95 percent, voter turnout in Central Province was considerably higher than elsewhere.[47] Mate won comfortably with 51 percent of the vote, followed by Mathu with 30 percent and Nyagah on 12 percent.[48] Mathu, it should be noted, won the majority of the votes cast in the Kikuyu districts. [49]

1958 By-Elections

A new generation of younger and better-educated leaders, who demanded an acceleration of political reform, had begun to emerge in the 1957 polls.

[44] KNA VP/1/86, Supt. of Police to Asst. Comm. of Police, 21 February 1957, 2.
[45] Ibid.
[46] KNA DC/MUR/4/5, Meru District Annual Report 1957, 2.
[47] KNA VP/1/86, Special Branch, 'The African Elections and Their Aftermath,' 18 April 1957, 3.
[48] KNA OP/1/555, Assistant Supervisor of African Elections, Central Province to Supervisor of African Elections, 15 March 1957, 5.
[49] KNA DC/NYI/1/1, Nyeri District Annual Report 1957, 4.

FIGURE 9. Voters arriving at the polling station in the district officer's camp, Koimbe, Fort Hall, 1957. Reproduced with permission of Kenya National Archives.

Although far from democratic, it would be wrong to dismiss the entire exercise as fruitless. As the Kenya Police's Special Branch recognised, the 1957 election, however flawed, had radically amplified the political awareness and expectations of large numbers of the African population.[50] Recognising this appetite for further and immediate reform, the new African members of the legislature, led by Tom Mboya, successfully pressured the colonial government to agree to the expansion of African legislative representation as part of new constitutional arrangements known as the Lennox-Boyd plan.[51] Central Province was divided into three constituencies, and by-elections were to be held in two of them. Meru was given its own seat, and as the victor in the 1957 election, Mate was not required to stand again. The Nyeri and Embu districts were joined to form one constituency, Nyeri-Embu. Kiambu, Fort Hall, and Thika formed the other, known as the Central Province (South) Constituency. In Central Province (South), there was little evidence of manipulation of the vote by

---

[50] KNA VP/1/86, Special Branch, 'The African Elections and Their Aftermath,' 18 April 1957, 8.
[51] KNA MAC/KEN/33/4, Mboya & Ngala, 'Press Statement,' 19 July 1957; Keith Kyle, *The Politics of the Independence of Kenya* (Basingstoke, 1999), 79–82.

the state. Both candidates, Julius Kiano and Mathu, were acceptable to the government. The same could not be said for Central Province's other contested seat, Nyeri-Embu.

Knowledge of two factors critical to Mate's success the previous year allowed the government to once again determine the outcome of the 1958 election in Nyeri-Embu, even before the candidates were announced. First, the 1958, by-elections relied on the same electoral roll and qualification criteria as the polls of the previous year. Voting and attendance at campaign rallies remained restricted to loyalists.[52] With only a small number of additions of newly qualified voters, the government could predict to a reasonable degree of accuracy the number of votes that would be cast. Second, the colonial government had observed in 1957 that votes would be cast within each district of Central Province for a local candidate. For a regime intent on manipulating the outcome of elections to consolidate loyalist strength and minimise the public influence of former Mau Mau sympathisers, it had the necessary information do so. This was achieved by pairing Nyeri and Embu districts together to form one constituency. Nyeri was the district that had supported Mau Mau most consistently, contained the lowest number of registered voters, and lacked an obvious candidate. Embu contained a much greater number of voters, had proved more supportive of the counterinsurgency, and possessed in Nyagah a candidate whose campaign had attracted much praise the previous year. Nyagah's origins in Mbeere, a loyalist stronghold, further increased his attractiveness to the regime.

Unlike Mate, Nyagah refused to rely on ethnicity in his campaign and instead attempted to appeal to voters in both districts. Although his manifesto changed little from the previous year, Nyagah now finished his campaign meetings by reminding voters of his ballot paper symbol, a clock, 'showing that this is the right time to go forward.' Nyagah claimed that the choice of a chair by his rival, Timothy Kagondu, represented 'sitting down in idleness.' Kagondu's campaign rhetoric did not differ greatly from that of his opponent. However, Kagondu suffered from widespread rumours that he had failed to pass the Language Board test designed to ensure candidates were sufficiently proficient in English to follow proceedings in the Legislative Council.[53] During campaigning, both candidates criticised the remaining anti-Mau Mau measures and both called for the lifting of movement restrictions imposed on Kikuyu,

---

[52] KNA DC/EBU/1/1/17, Permanent Secretary Ministry of African Affairs to PCs & Officer-in-Charge Nairobi, 8 February 1958, 2.
[53] KNA VP/1/86, Asst. Supt. of Police to Sen. Asst. Comm. of Police, 5 March 1958.

Embu, and Meru.[54] They demanded the termination of the loyalist certificate system, which Nyagah felt was dividing Central Province 'into
two factions: loyalist and non-loyalist.'[55] Nyagah also insisted that the
Emergency should be declared over.[56] Nyagah's impressive candidature
allowed him to win support from much of northern Nyeri, as well as
Embu.[57] When the polling stations closed on 23 March 1958 after two
days of voting, Nyagah won, with over 78 percent of the vote, including
a sizeable share from Nyeri.[58] However, his path to electoral success had
been cleared by the decision to join Embu with Nyeri, which had no
prominent or likely candidates to challenge the government's preferred
candidate.

The contest in Central Province (South) was between past and future
political heavyweights. Like Nyagah, Julius Kiano had been out of the
country during the worst years of the Emergency. Having been educated
at Alliance High School in Kiambu and Makerere College in Uganda,
Kiano enrolled at Antioch College in Ohio in 1948. After he graduated
from Stanford, he attended Berkeley, where he became the first Kenyan
African to receive a doctorate degree in 1956. Kiano then returned to
Kenya to take up a lectureship at the Royal Technical College before
his electoral success in 1958. Kiano owed much to his initial close ties
and warm personal relationship with Tom Mboya, the leading African
politician while Kenyatta remained in detention. This campaign has been
thoroughly discussed elsewhere, and there is little need to reiterate the
details.[59] However, the final results confirmed the trend that was evident the previous year, the usurpation of the older generation of African
politicians by a younger cohort. Kiano won convincingly with 63 percent
of the vote.[60] Even among loyalists, Mathu's frequently repeated man-
tra, 'Half a loaf is better than nothing' was unsatisfactory.[61] Mathu's
campaign, based on an argument for multi-racial power sharing, was

---

[54] KNA VP/1/86, Asst. Supt. of Police to Sen. Asst. Comm. of Police, 5 March 1958, 2; 9
March 1958, 1.
[55] KNA VP/1/86, Asst. Supt. of Police to Sen. Asst. Comm. of Police, 9 March 1958, 1; 12
March 1958, 1.
[56] KNA VP/1/86, Asst. Supt. of Police to Sen. Asst. Comm. of Police, 19 March 1958.
[57] KNA VP/1/86, Asst. Supt. of Police to Sen. Asst. Comm. of Police, 10 March 1958, 2;
12 March 1958, 2.
[58] KNA VQ/1/6, Returning Officer Nyeri/Embu to Supervisor of African Elections, 26
March 1958.
[59] Roelker, *Mathu*, 143–6.
[60] KNA VQ/1/6, DC Kiambu to Supervisor of African Elections, 27 March 1958.
[61] Ibid., 77.

not progressive enough to compete with Kiano's platform of African self-rule.[62]

Although an advocate of rapid political change, Kiano was no radical in the arena of socioeconomic reform. Although he later pursued reconciliation between ex-detainees and loyalists,[63] Kiano's efforts were intended to persuade former Mau Mau to accept the elevated status of loyalists in the name of Kikuyu unity.[64] Integral to this position was a refusal to countenance redistribution of land from rich to poor. In 1958, Kiano publicly declared his support for the controversial land consolidation program,[65] which was manipulated to punish Mau Mau sympathisers and reward loyalists.[66] Although he later led attempts to investigate the corruption of consolidation, Kiano remained committed to the principles of private land tenure that were a critical component of consolidation and of the Kenyan economy as a whole.[67] Through the 1960s, Kiano successfully spearheaded the state's attack on the Kenya People's Union (KPU) and dissidents within KANU in Murang'a, as Fort Hall became known after independence. The battle within the district between Kiano and the radicals' leader and militant ex-detainee, Bildad Kaggia, personified the divide between elite loyalists and dispossessed ex-detainees in post-colonial Kenya. Kiano denounced Kaggia's demands for land redistribution as the complaints of the idle poor.[68] After an election defeat in 1979, Kiano was finally toppled from his position of dominance in Murang'a politics; his usurper was not a representative of former Mau Mau activists but Kenneth Matiba, a fellow member of the loyalist elite.

Africanisation

Before turning his attention to electoral politics, Matiba first came to prominence during the recruitment of Africans into the civil service prior to independence. A graduate of Makerere, Matiba began working as

---

[62] Roelker, 'Mathu,' 143–6.
[63] George Bennett and Carl Rosberg, *The Kenyatta Election: Kenya 1960–1961* (London, 1961), 149–50.
[64] Clough, *Memoirs*, 50.
[65] Nick Wanjohi, 'The Politics of Ideology and Personality Rivalry in Murang'a District, Kenya: A Study of Electoral Competition' (Nairobi, 1984), 3.
[66] Sorrenson, *Land Reform*.
[67] Ibid., 249.
[68] Geoff Lamb, *Peasant Politics: Conflict and Development in Murang'a* (Lewes, 1974), 36–7.

a clerk in the Ministry of Education during the university's vacations. Following graduation, Matiba began working full time at the Ministry as an Education Officer in 1960. Following secondments and further studies in Britain, he was appointed as the Permanent Secretary of the Ministry in May 1963.[69] The rapid promotion of individuals such as Matiba has been largely overlooked within studies of decolonisation, with the exception of the work of David Leonard, Peter Marris, and Anthony Somerset.[70] In the case of Kenya, that oversight has come as a price of the interest in constitutional and land reforms.[71] Yet, despite this apparent disinterest, few scholars of the post-colonial nation-state, however, would need convincing of the importance of the Provincial Administration, in particular, the governance of Kenya throughout the past century.

During the first decades of colonial rule, the provincial and district commissioners generally governed their spheres of influence as personal fiefdoms in a manner notable for a 'preoccupation with order and control.'[72] After 1945, the position of the Provincial Administration eroded throughout Britain's African possessions. Increased interest in development demanded the replacement of the 'man on the spot' with trained specialists answerable to colonial capitals and London. In Kenya, however, the decline of the Provincial Administration was arrested by the Emergency. At no other time in the past had district or provincial commissioners' effective control over law and order within their territorial boundaries been so important, nor had they controlled as large and well-armed a force as the Home Guard and expanded Tribal Police. In Nyeri, the number of Tribal Police before the Emergency was 35. By mid-1962, that figure rose to 298. In 1952, the district had 1 district commissioner, 2 district officers, 13 chiefs, and 76 headmen. A decade later, besides the district commissioner, there were 10 district officers, 16 chiefs, and

[69] Matiba, *Aiming*, 45–58.
[70] David Leonard, *African Successes: Four Public Managers of Kenyan Rural Development* (Berkeley, 1991); Peter Marris and Anthony Somerset, *African Businessmen: A Study of Entrepreneurship and Development in Kenya* (London, 1971).
[71] See, as examples of this dominant narrative, Benjamin Kipkorir, 'Mau Mau and the Politics of the Transfer of Power in Kenya, 1957–1960,' *Kenya Historical Review* 5 (1977); Kyle, *Independence of Kenya*; Bethwell A. Ogot, 'The Decisive Years, 1956–63,' in *Decolonization and Independence in Kenya 1940–93*, eds. Bethwell A. Ogot and William Ochieng (London, 1995); Wasserman, *Politics of Decolonization*.
[72] Bruce Berman, 'Bureaucracy and Incumbent Violence: Colonial Administration and the Origins of Mau Mau,' in *Unhappy Valley: Conflict in Kenya and Africa*, eds. Bruce Berman and John Lonsdale (Oxford, 1992), 237.

133 headmen.[73] Across Kenya, the number of district officers, district commissioners, and provincial commissioners grew from 184 in 1951 to 370 by 1962.[74] At the time of independence, Kenya's civil service department was a third larger than Tanganyika's, despite a smaller population.[75]

Following the suppression of Mau Mau, the Provincial Administration fiercely protected its rediscovered importance, successfully fending off any suggestion of significant reform or devolution of powers prior to decolonisation.[76] Raynor, the district commissioner in Kiambu, noted that in 1963, as during the Emergency, 'it is the District Officers, Chiefs, Headmen and Tribal Police who basically collect the intelligence and maintain law and order in the reserves, and not the Kenya Police.'[77] Seeing his KANU party as too weak and parliament as potentially unstable, Kenyatta chose to rule through the Provincial Administration after independence in 1963. Kenya's first president thus maintained the status of the institution as the 'main instrument of social control,'[78] ranking it among the most significant legacies of British rule.[79] This continuity in function and manner demands explanation. In terms of personnel, the Provincial Administration, like other government institutions, underwent a significant transformation during the course of the 1950s and early 1960s. With the support of Mathu in the Legislative Council, the subaltern ranks of the Provincial Administration had been opened to Africans for the first time in 1947.[80] However, Africans were unable to progress further than the junior rank of African assistant administrative officer, leading to considerable frustration.[81] Increased African recruitment and promotion only began once the course of the counterinsurgency campaign entailed a significant change in the size and makeup of the Provincial Administration.

[73] KNA VP/1/111, DO Nyeri, 'The Tribal Police in Nyeri,' 6 June 1962, 1.
[74] Cherry Gertzel, *The Politics of Independent Kenya 1963–8* (Evanston IL, 1970), 25.
[75] Henry Bienen, *Kenya: The Politics of Participation and Control* (Princeton, 1974), 30.
[76] R .O. Hennings, F. A. Loyd, and R. Tatton-Brown, 'Report of the Working Party on the Future of the Provincial Administration,' 1 December 1961 (unpublished report to be found in library of Kenya National Archives).
[77] KNA VP/1/111, DC Kiambu to PC Central, 25 February 1963, 1.
[78] Ibid., 39.
[79] Percox, 'Internal Security,' 110.
[80] Roelker, *Mathu*, 97.
[81] Elisha Stephen Atieno Odhiambo, 'The Formative Years 1945–55,' in *Decolonization and Independence in Kenya 1940–93*, eds. Bethwell A. Ogot and William Ochieng (London, 1995), 33.

The expansion of African representation within the Provincial Administration began in earnest in 1954. As the district commissioners and
officers took on overseeing the radical upheaval of Kikuyu society, the
demands placed on staff increased week after week. The existing establishment of personnel was insufficient to juggle their many roles, much to the
chagrin of Swann, the district commissioner in Kiambu. He believed that
'we are right on the edge of an Administrative Breakdown – particularly
at the Divisional Level.'[82] New recruitment sources had to be tapped. The
government turned to a cadre of young, educated loyalists. In October
1952, the monthly Nyeri district team meeting, attended by the district
commissioner, district officers, and various other figures within the Provincial Administration in that district, included just two Africans. Isaac
Ndiritu attended in his role as secretary to the African District Council, and Ephraim Mithamo was an acting assistant district officer.[83] Ten
years later, the attendance at the same meeting was different. It was
chaired by E. O. Josiah, among the first African district commissioners,
and attended by 10 other senior African officials. Ndiritu was still the
secretary of the African District Council.[84] Four processes were at work.
First, the decision to use the Provincial Administration to lead the counterinsurgency effort in the Native Reserves demanded an expansion of
recruitment. Second, the use of non-military counterinsurgency discussed
in the previous chapter dramatically increased the responsibilities of the
Provincial Administration. Third, recruitment into the institution was
used to reward loyalists. Finally, impending independence demanded the
rapid promotion of this loyalist intake to make adequate preparations for
the British departure.

Once barriers to African recruitment and promotion were dismantled,
the new officers rose through the ranks at great speed. Geoffrey Karekia
Kariithi, for example, was a community development assistant in 1952
and deputy civil secretary (equivalent of deputy provincial commissioner) of Central Kenya by 1963.[85] Indeed, by early 1965 the entire
Provincial Administration had been Africanised.[86] The background of
many of the new cohort of administrative officials is often surmised but
rarely analysed. Other historians have noted that recruits from Central

---

[82] KNA VP/14/13, DC Kiambu to PC Central, 15 April 1954, 1.
[83] KNA VP/2/2, Minutes of Nyeri district team meeting, 3 October 1952.
[84] KNA VP/2/2, Minutes of the Nyeri district meetings, 23 May 1962 & 14 September
1962.
[85] Marco Surveys, *Who's Who in East Africa 1963–1964* (Nairobi, 1963), 24.
[86] Gertzel, *Independent Kenya*, 36.

Province were loyalists.[87] However, like voting, loyalism was merely a pre-qualification to an appointment within the Provincial Administration.

Hughes, the district commissioner in Nyeri, was at the forefront of moves in early 1954 to increase the numbers of Africans working within the Provincial Administration. The first available positions were as assistant district officers.[88] All the potential candidates first suggested by Hughes had some connection to chiefs or depended on their recommendation for consideration. However, from their backgrounds, it is clear that the loyalism of the suggested individuals was based on a more complicated understanding of Mau Mau and collaboration than mere self-interest. Hughes' first suggestion was Silas Gitonga, Chief Muhoya's son. Gitonga's family ties served only as a qualification for consideration as a potential recruit to the Provincial Administration and to reinforce his progressive credentials. A former student at Makerere, where he completed his teaching diploma in 1939, Gitonga spent two years working as a teacher in the Tumutumu Presbyterian mission school. He then spent seven years in higher education in South Africa, including four years at Fort Hare University. After failing his final examination at Fort Hare, Gitonga returned to Kenya and was, at the beginning of the Emergency, working at the Teachers' Training College in Embu.[89] Wilson Kanyi was another ex-pupil of Alliance. After working as an instructor in the army for three years during World War II, he completed a course in social welfare at the Jeanne's School. He then progressed to teaching in North Tetu for three years. Hughes wrote in support of Kanyi's application that 'prior to and during the Emergency he has shown considerable constructive loyalty' in his roles as a community development assistant and as an employee in the Information Department in Nyeri.[90] But mere loyalty was insufficient for recruitment.

Eliud Muchoki's application in 1956 for the post of assistant district officer in Nyeri was supported by Cumber, the district commissioner in Meru, where Muchoki was employed in the works camps. Cumber described Muchoki as 'an outstanding loyalist,' sentiments shared by the provincial information officer and C. Prideaux, staff officer in the

---

[87] Robert Buijtenhuijs, *Mau Mau Twenty Years After: The Myth and the Survivors* (The Hague, 1973), 115–6; Benjamin Kipkorir, 'The Educated Elite and Local Society: The Basis for Mass Representation,' in *Hadith 4: Politics and Nationalism in Colonial Kenya*, ed. Bethwell A. Ogot (Nairobi, 1972), 258; Maloba, *Mau Mau and Kenya*, 150.

[88] KNA VP/1/102, DC Nyeri to PC Central, 18 January 1954.

[89] KNA VP/1/102, DC Nyeri to PC Central, 18 January 1954 & 12 February 1954, 1.

[90] KNA VP/1/102, DC Nyeri to PC Central, 12 February 1954, 2.

Meru works camps.[91] Besides such testimonials, all Muchoki could use in support of his application was his Emergency record, of which he was very proud. Between 1953 and 1955, while working in screening operations at Karatina, Muchoki claimed to have provided information leading to the killing of 81 Mau Mau and the capture of 13, along with 54 guns and 189 rounds of ammunition, as well as the discovery of 1 loyalist corpse. As Pedraza, the district commissioner in Nyeri wrote in 1956, if employment in the Provincial Administration was merely of 'political value,' Muchoki would have been recruited 'as he is loyal and is unlikely to play both sides.' However, and more important, it was doubted that Muchoki had 'the real mental capacity to come up to the standards which we aim at.' 'The real question,' his district commissioner believed, 'is whether he would measure up to the standards which A.D.O.s [Assistant District Officers] should reach.' The colonial official thought not.[92] The loyalty of Muchoki and others meant they met only the pre-qualification criteria for consideration for employment.

For all Muchoki's presumed shortcomings, it is perhaps questionable whether he could have been a worse appointment than George Mugambi, a veteran of 15 years in the Public Works Department as a clerk.[93] The son of Chief Hezekiah Mundia, Mugambi, too, apparently had impec-cable loyalist credentials. Prior to his appointment as a district officer responsible for screening, he acted as an informant for Special Branch. Consequently, Mau Mau activists had destroyed his home in 1953.[94] His former manager in the Public Works Department described Mugambi as 'loyal, efficient and conscientious in his work,' a testimony that helped to secure his new job.[95] Initially, Mugambi's performance was exemplary. Successive district commissioners in Nyeri praised his application.[96] How-ever, in the course of the two years following his appointment, Mugambi accrued an impressive array of misdemeanours. He was suspected of cor-ruption when involved in screening, 'indulged too freely in drink and women and offended local opinion,' and had carried out land consolida-tion 'in a somewhat dictatorial manner.'[97]

[91] KNA VP/1/102, DC Meru to PC Central, 9 February 1956.
[92] KNA VP/1/102, DC Nyeri to PC Central, 23 February 1956.
[93] KNA VP/1/102, DC Nyeri to PC Central, 7 June 1954.
[94] KNA VP/1/102, G. H. Mugambi to Minister for African Affairs, 27 August 1956.
[95] KNA VP/1/102, R. Wilson, Senior Inspector of Works, Nyeri to whom it may concern, 5 June 1954.
[96] KNA VP/1/102; DC Nyeri to G. Mugambi, 3 December 1954; DC Nyeri to G. Mugambi, 6 January 1955.
[97] KNA VP/1/102, DC Nyeri to PC Central, 9 July 1956.

A subsequent police report was damning. Mugambi, according to the police, had been a member of the KAU 'up to the time of its proscription' and was thought to have been oathed twice. He was alleged to have coordinated supplies of food, clothing, and spare parts for firearms to the forest fighters under General Rui. The police believed Mugambi had even acquired the *nom de guerre* of Major Muhia among local Mau Mau activists. While in charge of screening in South Tetu in September and October 1954, Mugambi was thought to have been in regular contact with General Kimbo. In the same year, Mugambi was believed to have acted as a Mau Mau treasurer, using his beer shop at Ruringu as a supply centre for the forest fighters. Mugambi's apparent political activism had not died with the revolt. He had made public his criticisms of 'young European District Officers with no experience playing about with Emergency Regulations.' While drinking in the multi-racial United Social Club in Nyeri, Mugambi was reported to have 'accused the European of colour discrimination and confessed to a desire to see the White Man and the Asian leave Kenya.'[98] Again, the nationalist caricature of loyalists finds little support here.

As these examples suggest, applicants to the new vacancies in the Provincial Administration were well connected to the loyalist elites and highly educated, and many had prior experience in junior positions within the institution. C. G. Maina, a Makerere graduate, was the son of ex-Chief Gideon Gatere.[99] Stephen Mathenge, offered the position of district assistant in Fort Hall in July 1961, had previously served as a land consolidation officer in Nyeri.[100] In 1961, a provincial shortlist of 24 interviewees for the position of district assistant included 21 public servants, of whom 16 were already working within the Provincial Administration or local authority.[101] The younger, well-educated chiefs were increasingly attracted to the positions in the Provincial Administration. Charles Ikamba had been chief in South Tetu and member of the Nyeri African District Council since 1953. He was self-educated, but attended Fort Hare in 1949 and 1950, before returning to work as a teacher. He had joined the Home Guard at the outbreak of the Emergency prior to his promotion to chief. By 1961, he was seeking the role of district assistant or officer.[102] Such

98 KNA VP/1/102, South Nyeri Reserve Special Branch, 'Dossier: George Mugambi s/o Hezekiah Mundia,' 9 June 1956.
99 KNA VP/1/102, DC Nyeri to PC Central, 23 January 1958.
100 KNA VP/1/102, DC Nyeri to DO Mathira, 24 July 1961.
101 KNA VP/1/102, PC Central to DCs Central, 27 July 1961.
102 KNA VP/1/102, Chief Wilson Ikamba to PC Central, 28 July 1961.

attributes were likely to meet with the approval of the loyalist representatives on pre-selection committees charged with drawing up short lists
and on interview panels.[103]

The high level of literacy demanded by work in the Provincial Administration favoured the applications of current and former teachers. Timothy
Muraguri had been schooled at Alliance and trained as a teacher at
Kagumo. Between 1948 and 1951, he had been a teacher before becoming
the assistant supervisor of Presbyterian and Anglican schools in Nyeri. In
1954, he joined the Provincial Administration, first as an assistant education officer and then as a land officer supervising land consolidation in
North Tetu.[104] For the two years prior to his recruitment into the Tribal
Police in 1954, David Ndiritu Nguyo had worked as a teacher. He subsequently became a corporal in the Tribal Police and a renowned pros-
ecutor in the African Courts.[105] Peter Munene, who was a land officer in
South Tetu for seven years beginning in 1954, had been a headmaster for
eight years prior to that position.[106] Job security, prestige, and competi-
tive salaries attracted such individuals to the Provincial Administration.

However, the institution also became viewed as a citadel in which
loyalists sought protection from the returning detainees. Matthew Kimani
had worked as a clerk for East African Railways and Harbours in the first
three years of the Emergency. After a short spell as a school supervisor,
he began work as a rehabilitation assistant in the detention camps. Over
the course of five years, he was based at camps in Athi River, South
Yatta, Fort Hall, Galole, Githiga, and Aguthi, before leaving the job in
February, as the camps were decommissioned. In a plea for employment
in the Provincial Administration, made to the district commissioner in
Nyeri during May 1961, Kimani made no secret of his motivations for
writing:

I will therefore Sir, be most grateful if you could assist me to obtain one [a job
in the Provincial Administration], as you are aware of the fact that having been
working for more than 10,000 hardcores who are now very high officials of
KANU my life in the reserve without a job in the Government Service would be
just like a fish out of water.[107]

---

[103] For nomination of Chief Muhoya & Samuel Githu to the Provincial Pre-selection
Committee, see KNA VP/1/102, DC Nyeri to PC Central, 19 August 1958. For loyalist
representatives on interview panels, see PC Central to DCs Central, 27 July 1961.
[104] KNA VP/1/102, DO North Tetu to DC Nyeri, 20 December 1961.
[105] KNA VP/1/102, DO North Tetu to DC Nyeri, 20 December 1961.
[106] KNA VP/1/102, DC Nyeri to PC Central, 29 December 1961.
[107] KNA VP/1/102, M. A. Kimani to DC Nyeri, 26 May 1961.

Kimani need not have worried. As independence approached, elite loyalists across Central Province were finding their way into various institutions and organisations that offered both protection against any threats from ex-detainees and made the loyalist recruits essential to the everyday functioning of the state.

Elite loyalists, such as Charles Karuga Koinange, of Kiambu (discussed further in the Conclusion) and John Michuki, son and son-in-law of Fort Hall chiefs, were embedded into the upper echelons of the Provincial Administration. In Nairobi, the loyalist presence within the ranks of the rapidly Africanising civil service, central government, and private sector was clear. The son of Chief Josiah, Charles Njonjo, who was appointed Attorney General in 1963, had first joined the Government's legal team in 1955.[108] Joseph Gachathi, a former student at Alliance, Kagumo, and Makerere had worked in the Provincial Administration in Kiambu in 1954 before leaving to take up work in the private sector. He returned to the Provincial Administration as a district assistant in 1957, and in 1962, became assistant secretary to the Treasury. The following year, he served briefly as under secretary in the Ministry of Lands before being appointed as the permanent secretary in the same ministry.[109] Simion Kamunde, deputy chief government whip at independence, was educated at Alliance High School and Kagumo Teachers' Training College. He worked as a teacher between 1953 and 1957, before becoming the marketing manager of the Meru Coffee Union for three years.[110] Loyalists had additional protection in their own localities.

Local structures of power were filled with loyalists across Central Kenya. Throughout the Emergency, the Kenya Police training centre at Kiganjo had graduated hundreds of African constables, with an increasing proportion being drawn from Central Province's loyalist community.[111] The Provincial Administration had moved quickly to capitalise on the growth of the Tribal Police and had fought for a far more formalised and powerful force than had existed prior to the Emergency.[112] Villages

---

[108] Surveys, *Who's Who in East Africa 1963–1964*, 44.
[109] Ibid., 15.
[110] Ibid., 23.
[111] See Ministry of Defence monthly reports in KNA AH/6/4–9 for further brief details. Explicit recruitment of loyalists into the Kenya Police via the Tribal Police ended in July 1957 (see KNA VQ/5/1, minutes of Central Province DCs' Meeting, 4–6 July 1957).
[112] See correspondence in KNA PC/GRSSA/2/19/12 for discussions of the expanded range of offences the Tribal Police could investigate and prosecute and attempts to define the role of the force.

FIGURE 10. Charles Njonjo after appointment as assistant registrar general, 1958.
Reproduced with permission of Kenya National Archives.

were under the control of individuals like Eliud Mahu, headman in the
Ragati sub-location. Mahu had served in the army for seven years until
1949. At the outbreak of the Emergency, he had joined the Home Guard
and had been appointed as a headman of Gaikuyu sub-location in 1955,
from where he moved to Ragati.[113] Above the headmen, the position of
chief remained reserved for loyalists until independence. The successful
applicant for the vacant chief's position in Mahiga location in September
1962, Hezron Mwai, had attained all the trappings of a successful member
of Nyeri's loyalist elite. Mwai was a member of the African District
Council, the Mahiga Presbyterian school committee, and the locational
council. He owned 54 acres of land, spread across two farms, and 2,000
coffee trees.[114] However, as thoughts turned from the defeat of Mau Mau
and the prevention of any recurrence towards preparing a new nation-
state for independent rule, concern began to be raised about the nature
of rule in Central Province.

However hypocritical it may have been, anxiety grew among the outgoing British colonial administrators regarding the nature of the Provincial

[113] KNA VP/1/71, Eliud Mahu to PC Central, 8 December 1960.
[114] KNA VP/1/104, DC Nyeri to PC Central, 20 September 1962.

Administration. In February 1963, Raynor, then the district commissioner in Kiambu, argued that the entire Provincial Administration, including chiefs, headmen, and Tribal Police, should be converted into a more politically acceptable and accountable model of local government to lose the trappings of imperialism.[115] Johnson, district commissioner in Thika, agreed with Raynor. The Tribal Police, he argued, 'as they are at present should go.' Tainted by their role in the Emergency, the force had to be remodelled, 'and even if the bulk of them are absorbed into some new body, the name and the red jersey must be altered.'[116] Underlying such sentiments was awareness that an institution developed to defeat an insurgency was an unsuitable foundation for a pluralistic post-colonial society.

It was the future rulers of the post-colony that vetoed any move towards substantive reform. The most vocal supporter of the Tribal Police was not one of the expatriate officials, but instead John Michuki, by then, district commissioner in Nyeri. Eulogising the Tribal Police's 'unofficial, liberal outlook,' he argued that the force should 'achieve the same results as the Kenya Police, if not more.' He concluded, 'I suggest that we should dig our toes into the ground against any suggestions that would amount to total annihilation of the Tribal Police Force.'[117] A new generation of Kenya's rulers became rapidly convinced of the virtues of a force accountable only to the Provincial Administration and which straddled hazy legal and political boundaries. Although Oginga Odinga later described loyalists as 'despicable collaborators,'[118] he was as responsible as any other individual for their protection in localities into the post-colonial period. On the eve of independence, as Minister for Home Affairs, Oginga argued that responsibility for appointment of chiefs should remain with central government.[119] Furthermore, he reversed the disbandment of the Tribal Police that had been agreed on during the final rounds of constitutional negotiations. Like the chiefs, the reprieved force was to remain the responsibility of central government.[120] Although concerned primarily with sabotaging the devolution of power to the newly established local authorities, Oginga had ensured continuing protection for loyalists

---

[115] KNA VP/1/111, DC Kiambu to PC Central, 25 February 1963.
[116] KNA VP/1/111, DC Thika to PC Central, 5 March 1963.
[117] KNA VP/1/111, DC Nyeri to PC Central, 7 March 1963.
[118] Oginga Odinga, *Not Yet Uhuru* (Nairobi, 1967), 125.
[119] KNA WC/CM/1/13, Minister for Home Affairs, 'Future of Chiefs and Sub-Chiefs,' 21 November 1963.
[120] KNA WC/CM/1/13, Minister for Home Affairs, 'Future of the Tribal Police,' 21 November 1963.

and preserved the Tribal Police force that had long provided a source of employment and patronage for many loyalists and a protection service for others.[121]

The Political Economy of Decolonisation

Although colonialism came to an end in December 1963, the interests that it had sustained survived Kenya's transition to independent rule. The loyalist politicians were the beneficiaries of the doubling of the output of African farms, from £5.5 million in 1956 to £11.6 million in 1966.[122] Although this growth had been visible since 1945[123] and lay at the heart of Mau Mau,[124] its perpetuation into the 1960s was the result of a reorientation of state assistance away from European mixed farming towards African production of cash crops. This policy shift was first set out in the Swynnerton Plan of late 1953.[125] Private land titles were issued to African farmers to provide them with mortgagable assets against which loan capital could be secured. Private land ownership, therefore, became an integral component of the intensification and expansion of African agricultural production. However, as discussed in the previous chapter, this process was manipulated to reward loyalists and punish Mau Mau because of its implementation by the Provincial Administration during the counterinsurgency campaign. A loyalist, landed class was the outcome, although most loyalists did not belong to this group.

As the interests of what Swainson terms indigenous capitalism expanded, it diversified into manufacturing and services. Critically, indigenous capitalists began to form alliances with the representatives of foreign capital, itself an increasingly significant part of the post-1945 Kenyan economy as the stimulant of industrialisation.[126] The interests of both were intertwined by agreements such as that struck by British American Tobacco with the government in 1954, which granted it the status of

[121] For the relevant sections of the constitution contravened by Oginga, see Government of Kenya, *Constitution of Kenya* (Nairobi, 1963), 111 (for establishment of single police force), and 135 (for sole responsibility of Public Service Commission for appointment of government servants).
[122] John de Wilde, *Experiences with Agricultural Development in Tropical Africa*, 2 vols., vol. 2 (Baltimore, 1967), 30–1.
[123] Nicola Swainson, *The Development of Corporate Capitalism in Kenya 1918–77* (London, 1980), 175.
[124] Throup, *Economic and Social Origins*.
[125] Swynnerton, *Plan to Intensify*.
[126] Swainson, *Corporate Capitalism*, 130–2.

FIGURE 11. Chief Commissioner Robin Wainwright (fourth from right) greets nine new district commissioners, Nairobi, 1962. Reproduced with permission of Kenya National Archives.

the sole purchaser of tobacco produced by smallholders.[127] The terms of exchange steadily became more favourable to Kenyans. The interpenetration of international and indigenous capital accelerated after 1963 as the new political elite steadily consolidated its economic strength.[128] It would be wrong, though, to ascribe too much importance to this relationship between loyalists and foreign capital. Politics trumped economics in Kenya's decolonization. The attraction of elite loyalists to the outgoing colonial government lay in the likely political moderation of loyalists. There was no conspiratorial agreement between loyalists, the late colonial state, and capitalists, as the flight of capital between 1960 and 1963 demonstrates.[129]

Nevertheless, the independence-era politicians had few incentives to disrupt the relationship between state and private capital. As that relationship changed in the context of the war and the flight of European

---

[127] Ibid., 132.
[128] Ibid., 285–90.
[129] Robert Tignor, *Capitalism and Nationalism at the End of Empire: State and Business in Decolonizing Egypt, Nigeria, and Kenya, 1945–1963* (Princeton NJ, 1997), 327–86.

capital described by Tignor,[130] loyalist political leaders were among those who benefited. Jeremiah Nyagah's economic fortunes were transformed in a short period of time after his return to Kenya in October 1954. He cast envious glances towards his friends' cars and complained of being 'a simple schoolmaster.'[131] By the end of the same year, he purchased 400 acres of land on which to plant coffee.[132] He bought another 140 acres the following month, enough, Nyagah thought, to make him 'just better than a peasant native *shamba* [smallholder] man.'[133] Nyagah, too, soon joined the ranks of the car-owners,[134] and five years later, could write of passing through London on his way back to Kenya from Switzerland.[135] Even the most left-leaning of the cohort, Oginga Odinga, owned £50,000 worth of property by early 1962.[136] Although Oginga remained committed throughout his political career to the substantial redistribution of resources to Kenya's poor, his contemporaries were less convinced.

At the second Lancaster House constitutional conference of 1962, African representatives accepted the European demand for the purchase rather than seizure of the land of those settlers who wished to leave Kenya.[137] In acquiescing, the legitimacy of colonial land policy was accepted in totality. Ergo, redistribution of land held under titles issued before 1963, particularly that acquired illegally by loyalists during the 1950s, was ruled out. The Lancaster House negotiations had established 'a free-enterprise economy based on the sanctity of private property.'[138] It would be incorrect to view this outcome as solely the last breath of settler politics, a forced imposition by London, or the expression of the nefarious and shadowy influence of international capital. Instead, the political economy of post-colonial Kenya reflected the concerns of the country's 'Founding Fathers,' particularly those hailing from Central Province and their elite constituents. There is no evidence to suggest that Kiano, Nyagah, or Mate personally gained land in an illegal or immoral fashion. However, it is indisputable that they, initially at least, relied on

---

[130] Ibid.
[131] RHL Mss Afr s 1727, Nyagah to Foote, 23 October 1954.
[132] RHL Mss Afr s 1727, Nyagah to Foote, 19 December 1954.
[133] RHL Mss Afr s 1727, Nyagah to Foote, 18 January 1955.
[134] RHL Mss Afr s 1727, Nyagah to Foote, 19 June 1956.
[135] RHL Mss Afr s 1727, Nyagah to Foote, 14 March 1961.
[136] Kyle, *Independence of Kenya*, 148.
[137] Ibid., 152–6.
[138] Patrick Asingo, 'The Political Economy of Transition in Kenya,' in *The Politics of Transition in Kenya: From KANU to NARC*, eds. Walter Oyugi, Peter Wanyande, and Crispin Odhiambo Mbai (Nairobi, 2003), 18.

the support of those who had and those whose newly issued land titles enabled eventual entry into the economic elite in partnership with foreign investment. This political context neither encouraged the redistribution of land nor the support for nationalisation of foreign-owned assets, which already totalled one-third of the private assets held in the colony in 1958.[139]

In many respects, Kiano best represents the loyalist triumph of the system during decolonisation. He was one of the beneficiaries of an early example of elections that 'were deliberately structured to ensure that they could not have a very far-reaching impact on the character of the regime.'[140] However, Kiano's modernist credentials and demands for an accelerated handover of power stand in stark contrast to prevailing depictions of loyalists and were essential to persuade a loyalist electorate to support his candidature. Kiano proceeded to play, along with Mate and Nyagah, an important role in the constitutional negotiations that led to independence.[141] This provided Kiano and the other loyalist leaders with the capital required to remain in power once ex-detainees entered the political arena in 1961.[142] This legitimacy also enabled Kiano to join with other representatives of the new national elite to restrict the redistribution of resources, particularly land, to the poor. In so doing, the national elite consolidated the position of private domestic and international capital within the Kenyan economy.

The Counterinsurgent Path

Political contests of the decolonisation period, such as those described here, are not merely diverting historical sideshows but the first act of the theatre of post-colonial politics. The fault lines between individuals, ideologies, and identities that surfaced in this period remained visible throughout the subsequent decades. In her study of the resolution of conflicts in El Salvador and South Africa, Wood describes what she terms an 'insurgent path to democracy.' In both cases Wood examines, lower class actors were able to force the pace of peace settlements and the transition towards democracy: 'the transition to democracy would not

---

[139] Swainson, *Corporate Capitalism*, 130.
[140] Goran Hyden and Colin Leys, 'Elections and Politics in Single-Party Systems: The Case of Kenya and Tanzania,' *British Journal of Political Science* 2 (1972), 419.
[141] Kyle, *Independence of Kenya*, 102–6, 145–50, 189–92.
[142] Bennett and Rosberg, *Kenyatta Election*.

have taken place in either country when it did, as it did, and with the same consequences in the absence of sustained popular mobilisation.'[143] Wood explains the ability of the lower classes in El Salvador and South Africa to forge this 'insurgent path' as a consequence of the inter-dependence through class of the contending forces within the conflict that made all amenable to seeking a democratic resolution.[144] Kenya was distinctively different.

Rather than an 'insurgent path to democracy' emerging out of the conflict, a counterinsurgent path towards a bureaucratic-authoritarian, capitalist post-colonial state was laid.[145] Agricultural reform consolidated loyalist economic preeminence without the reciprocal requirement for insurgent labour. Political reforms produced representatives who, initially at least, had no need to court the votes of Mau Mau supporters. Finally, appointments to the civil service were made by a colonial government submerged in a crisis of legitimacy and soon to depart Kenya, in any case. The resolution of the war thus created an elite without any formal institutional reciprocal ties to the insurgents and gave loyalists no incentives to seek compromise with insurgents, as seen in El Salvador and South Africa. A temporary consensus among Kenya's African political actors from 1960 onwards on the issue of rapid independence failed to mask for very long the tensions produced by the 1950s. The vociferous refusal after independence of loyalist and other elite politicians to redress land alienation, the foremost grievance of the poor, hastened the collapse of the nationalist coalition in 1966. The seeds of a fragmentary democracy[146] were not merely sown prior to transition but had already germinated.[147]

---

[143] Elisabeth Jean Wood, *Forging Democracy From Below: Insurgent Transitions in South Africa and El Salvador* (Cambridge, 2000), 5.
[144] Ibid.
[145] See also Bates, *Beyond the Miracle*, 11–40.
[146] Samuel Nolutshungu, 'Fragments of a Democracy: Reflections on Class and Politics in Nigeria,' *Third World Quarterly* 12 (1990); Gavin Williams, 'Fragments of Democracy: Nationalism, Development and the State in Africa' (Cape Town, 2003).
[147] Elisha Stephen Atieno Odhiambo, 'Democracy and the Ideology of Order in Kenya,' in *The Political Economy of Kenya*, ed. Schatzberg (New York, 1987), 187.

6

Eating the Fruits of *Uhuru*

Loyalists, Mau Mau, and the Post-Colonial State

Forgive and Forget

Kenyan decolonisation, Jomo Kenyatta promised to his supporters ahead of independence in 1963, was to be much more than a neat inter-elite transfer of power or constitutional event. Political freedom (*uhuru*) from colonial rule was 'not enough.' 'Our people,' the soon-to-be prime minister asserted, 'have the right to be free from economic exploitation and inequality.' Decolonisation provided 'the opportunity to work unfettered for the creation of a democratic African socialist Kenya.[1] Similar words were (of course) at that time being uttered by countless politicians across the African continent. In Kenya, these sentiments carried added weight. Kenyatta was addressing a country that would by the end of year be independent, but which had spent much of the previous decade at war with itself and its outgoing colonial ruler. To overcome the bitterness engendered by loyalist support of the colonial counterinsurgency campaign and the fears of majority rule held by the members of smaller ethnic groups and by European and Asian owners of capital, Kenyatta had no better advice than to look to 'the future, to the good new Kenya, not to the bad old days.'[2] These words had little effect. In April 1967, more than three years after independence and more than a decade since the military defeat of Mau Mau, the district commissioner of Nyeri wrote

---

[1] Kenya African National Union, *What a KANU Government Offers You* (Nairobi, 1963), 1.
[2] From speech given on 3 June 1963, two days after the establishment of self-rule. Quoted in Jomo Kenyatta, *Harambee! The Prime Minister of Kenya's Speeches, 1963–1964* (Nairobi, 1964), 8.

that 'although the President's call to forget the past is repeated often – the feelings are still there.'[3] Kenya after 1963 should then be understood as much a post-conflict society as a post-colonial state. Its politics were dictated in large part by the divisions created by the Mau Mau war, as embodied by Kenyatta himself.

Born in the very first years of British rule in East Africa, Kenyatta owed some of his later prominence to his Church of Scotland mission education. Like many of his generation, his politicisation began with the arrest of Harry Thuku and the subsequent protests. Kenyatta joined the newly formed KCA in 1924, rising quickly within the organisation and gaining particular prominence by virtue of his role as editor of its newspaper. The paper's title, *Muigwithiana* (*The Reconciler*), was apt. During the pre-Mau Mau period, Kenyatta strove to reconcile, first, Kikuyu custom with the demands of the colonial variant of modernity and, second, the colonial state with the grievances of the Kikuyu people. Following an extended absence in Britain, during which time he wrote *Facing Mount Kenya*, Kenyatta had to turn his hand to a very different form of reconciliation. He had left Kenya in 1931 when Kikuyu politics remained the preserve of the elite. He returned in 1946 to find that elite beginning its struggle to retain that monopoly.

In the face of the challenge led mainly by the young radicals of the city, Kenyatta aligned with the constitutionalist faction. But Kenyatta also attempted to reign in what he considered to be the excesses of what would become Mau Mau. Preaching the need for non-violent protest, Kenyatta spent much of the six years between his return and the beginning of the war slowly expending the political capital he had built up while in self-imposed exile. His absence in Britain had allowed the politicians who remained behind to project an idealised image onto him and had distanced him from the many petty squabbles that dogged the KCA. On his return, Kenyatta was greeted as a hero across ethnic and class lines. The mass appeal he derived from his status as the one nationalist leader was based more on the stylised Kenyatta than the real one. As he increasingly swam against the tide of Kikuyu politics, Kenyatta found himself in an unenviable but far from unusual position. On one hand, he was suspected by the colonial government of leading the militant faction towards rebellion. On the other, that same militant faction was fearful that Kenyatta would undermine their support. Kenyatta thus was

[3] KNA VP/9/102, DC Nyeri, 'Handing Over Report Nyeri District: J. H. Kahara to A. C. Kangethe,' 27 April 1967, 2.

confronted by the same dilemma as the great mass of the Kikuyu people: how to stay alive and at liberty in the ever more dangerous setting of Central Kenya in the early 1950s. Again, in common with most Kikuyu, Kenyatta's dilemma was resolved for him by one of the warring parties. Arrested on the first night of the Emergency, Kenyatta was tried and jailed for his alleged leadership of Mau Mau.

Kenyatta's incarceration and the civil war served only to underline in his own mind his prior misgivings about radicalism. The rise of militancy within Kikuyu politics had, it appeared, brought only suffering. Independence, as Kenyatta would explicitly argue later, was won by the efforts of politicians, not by a bedraggled guerrilla army. Kenyatta's own personal experience of the war was no less important in consolidating his suspicion of the radicals. Confined to northern Kenya, the so-called 'Kapenguria Six' – the group accused by the colonial government of leading Mau Mau – were no more united than society outside of the colony's rapidly expanded penal institutions. Bildad Kaggia, Paul Ngei, and Fred Kubai, all prominent militants, formed their own faction, disrespectful to Kenyatta and quick to mock their older colleague. Kenyatta allied himself instead with Kung'u Karumba and Achieng Oneko.[4]

Whatever the circumstances from which it arose and the suffering entailed over its course, imprisonment consolidated Kenyatta's position as the preeminent political figure in Kenya. His leadership of the nationalist cause after his release was accepted as fact long before his return home in 1961. In this almost unchallenged return to preeminence, Kenyatta's status as an ex-detainee was critical. He shared this label with tens of thousands of Kikuyu who understood their own arrest and detention to denote sacrifice for the cause of national liberation. For many ex-detainees caught up in the waves of indiscriminate arrests of the first period of the war, this equating of detention with support for Mau Mau was an act of retrospective politicisation. No doubt, the detention camps and prisons of Kenya were like the 'prison universities' of other conflicts. Behind the wire, the previously uncommitted arrested on trumped up charges lived cheek by jowl alongside the ideologues and militants. Individuals who may have been arrested in the first two years of the war as the result of false evidence provided by a loyalist informer left the prisons and camps as committed supporters of the radical cause. There was then no more fitting a post-war leader than Kenyatta. To question his right to leadership was to call into doubt the credentials of the hundreds of ex-detainees

4 Jeremy Murray-Brown, *Kenyatta* (London, 1974), 255–95.

who dominated the local structures of the nationalist movement. The ex-detainees believed Kenyatta to be the leader to right the wrongs committed against them during the counterinsurgency campaign.

As this chapter makes clear, the grievances held by the ex-detainees did not readily dissipate under Kenyatta's leadership. Much of the archival material on which this chapter is based relates to Nyeri district, which with Fort Hall (known as Murang'a after independence), had witnessed the worst of the fighting during the civil war. With that war viewed as one of national liberation, Murang'a and Nyeri were thought of by Mau Mau veterans from both as the two districts that shed the most blood for independence. However, resentment grew in both districts because of Kenyatta's assumed refusal to spread the fruits of independence equally among the people of Central Province. Instead, Kenyatta consolidated power and influence within an inner circle made up of the Kiambu elite, which included a large number of loyalists. Political activity in Nyeri after independence was thus framed by two cleavages. The first was between loyalists and Mau Mau in Nyeri itself. The second was that between sympathisers of the insurgency and the central government, within which elite loyalists had claimed a disproportionately large influence. Both demonstrated that the divisions of the 1950s were not easily erased.

The Return of the Detainees

In the final years of the 1950s, tens of thousands of detainees returned to their homes from the camps. From a daily average of 71,346 detainees and convicts in the colony's penal institutions in December 1954, just 1,306 remained by August 1959.[5] The ex-detainees found everyday life very different from that which they had left earlier in the decade.[6] The residual effects of the counterinsurgency campaign provided the state with a significant presence in areas that had been only lightly administered prior to the emergence of Mau Mau. The ranks of chiefs, headmen, policemen, and other administrative officials were significantly larger than they had been before 1953 and were used to restrain any group that appeared to the government likely to resume the insurgency. As the district officer in Mathira remarked in September 1956, ex-detainees 'found it impossible

[5] Anderson, *Histories*, 356.
[6] For the experiences of returning detainees, see ibid., 332–3; Elkins, *Imperial*, 277–96 & 457–61.

to ask questions from people like the headman without being told to "shut up."'7 Despite this subjugation, the returned Mau Mau supporters expected to find redress for their suffering during decolonisation. They were, though, willing to wait. With constitutional negotiations progressing rapidly and the steady realisation that independence was imminent by the end of the 1950s, the ex-detainees did little to concern the colonial authorities.8 As a consequence of the resulting climate of relative peace and order, curfews were relaxed in the villages,9 the release of detainees was speeded up,10 and following a controversy over the killings of Mau Mau suspects by their guards at the Hola detention camp,11 the State of Emergency was declared over in January 1960.12 Yet, beneath this transition towards peace and independence, the tensions created by the civil war remained all too real.

Some felt they had no choice but to act according to Kenyatta's pleadings. In many cases, the responsibilities of kinship survived the war. Wanga Mubithe was released from detention in October 1958. Mubithe, a Mau Mau supporter from Mdunyu in the Othaya division of Nyeri, took into his home the wife and children of his brother, a loyalist Home Guard killed during an ambush by Mau Mau in April 1954.13 But many others could not help but look 'to the bad old days' as they attempted to understand their existence in the new Kenya. Mau Mau had murdered Philip Gatuguta Nderi's wife in May 1954. He found the return of her murderers to his home in Nyeri difficult to comprehend, complaining that government appeared to have 'forgiven the offenders while I have not done so.' 'It is very hard for me,' wrote Nderi in April 1960, 'to forget and forgive known and boasting murderers who do not show any sign of repentance.'14 Although many loyalists no doubt shared Nderi's

7 KNA ARC(MAA) 2/5/198 I, DO Mathira to DC Nyeri, 18 September 1956.
8 'Emergency in Second Phase Now: Government Comments on Unrest,' *Sunday Post*, 23 February 1958, 16; KNA DC/KBU/1/45, Kiambu District Annual Report 1956, 2; KNA DC/EBU/1/1/16, Embu District Annual Report 1957, 1; KNA DC/MRU/4/5, Meru District Annual Report, ii; KNA DC/EBU/1/1/18, Embu District Annual Report 1959, 1.
9 KNA DC/EBU/1/1/17, Embu District Annual Report 1958, 1.
10 KNA VP/9/102, PC Central, 'Handing Over Notes: Brigadier M. Hughes to Mr. F. R. Wilson,' 8 September 1960, 3.
11 Anderson, *Histories*, 326–7; Elkins, *Imperial*, 311–53.
12 RHL Mss Brit Emp s 22/G543, 'Proclamation Ends State of Emergency in Kenya,' 12 January 1960.
13 KNA VP/6/2, Wanga Mubithe to PC Central, 25 January 1960.
14 KNA VP/6/2, Philip Gatuguta Nderi to DC Nyeri, 10 April 1960.

frustrations, grievances were most keenly felt by those who had supported the Mau Mau rebellion and who swiftly appropriated the language of
the war to express their dissatisfaction with decolonisation.

The most sustained attack on the loyalist ascendancy came, predict-
ably, from the phalanx of ex-detainees. Initial discontent with the theft
of land during land consolidation in the mid-1950s, voiced by the *Kiama
kia Muingi* (Council of the Masses), was crushed rapidly by the colonial
government.[15] The more long-lived attempt to reverse loyalists' gains
began in the village committees, locational councils, and African District
Councils that collectively made up local government. The village committees and locational councils were both instituted during the Emergency to
formalise various local loyalist institutions established to regulate Home
Guard recruitment, oversee land consolidation, and process loyalty certificate applications. The locational council in Iriaini was the first in the
division of Mathira in the Nyeri district to be formally instituted in the
first months of 1953. It played a crucial role in the formation of the local
Home Guard unit and, led by Chief Eliud Mugo, its partisan commitment to the counterinsurgency made it a target of Mau Mau aggression.
A number of council members were killed during the war, and Chief
Eliud's camp was attacked. During that assault, the Chief's clerk and
four other loyalists were killed. As the war progressed, the Iriaini council firmly supported land consolidation.[16] Iriaini remained dominated by
loyalists up to the end of the decade, as did the other local councils.

Once participation in local government elections was opened up to the
freed detainees, the makeup of these institutions changed accordingly.
Following the Nyeri African District Council elections of 1958, the body
was uniformly loyalist. The four representatives from the North Tetu
divisions, for example, were Rubiro Muita, former headman; Johanna
Kunyhia, president of the North Tetu court; Elias Mukundi, loyalty certificate holder; and David Wanjuki Theuri, a teacher at Muthuaini and
holder of a loyalty certificate.[17] The 10 nominated positions that were in
the gift of the district commissioner were filled by Chiefs Muhoya, Paulo,
Stephen, Eliud, and Wilson Ikamba; Stanley Ngunjiri, a headman; Dedan
Neritu, a schoolmaster; Reverend Charles Muhoro from the Tumutumu

[15] Maloba, *Mau Mau and Kenya*, 147; Ng'ang'a, 'Loyalists and Politics,' 376; Monone
    Omosule, 'Kiama kia Muingi: Kikuyu and Land Consolidation,' *Transafrican Journal
    of History* 4 (1974), 115–34.
[16] KNA VP/1/85, Members of the Iriaini Location Committee to DC Nyeri, 27 July 1955.
[17] KNA VP/1/17, DO North Tetu to DC Nyeri, 6 September 1958.

mission; Leonard Githeri, a farmer; and Nancy Njarua, a midwife.[18] But just as the colonial authorities became aware of the need to make the Legislative Council more representative, so too did they acknowledge the limitations of local authorities monopolised by loyalists once the detainees returned home in large numbers. As early as 1956, Kiambu's district commissioner argued, 'The time has come, I think, to reorganise and strengthen Location Councils, and to base them on the choice of the people.'[19] The councils were 'loyalist yes-men,' the district officer in North Tetu wrote, who 'tend to strengthen the artificial division of the tribe into loyalist and non-loyalist.'[20] Three years before being allowed to vote in legislative elections, ex-detainees were permitted to participate in elections for village committees[21] and the location councils.[22] Over the next five years, ex-detainees would come to dominate the institutions of local government, from village committees to African District Councils.

As the country prepared for independence in 1963, county and area councils were created in readiness for the new constitutional arrangements, which were, theoretically, to devolve considerable powers to local authorities. In Nyeri, candidates for election to these bodies were overwhelmingly either ex-detainees or known to have been Mau Mau sympathisers. Moreover, those same candidates were often important members of KANU, which was founded in 1960 and quickly became the leading nationalist party. The list of candidates from the three locations in the South Tetu division for election to the new Nyeri Area Council in 1963 demonstrates both the grassroots domination of local politics by ex-detainees and their role within local branches of KANU. In Muhito location, Daudi Nyamu, an ex-detainee and a former local Mau Mau leader, was the chairman of the location's KANU office. Of his rivals, Gathio Gichuki had been a Mau Mau oath administrator, a detainee, and subsequently, the chairman of one of the location's sub-locational KANU offices. Kariuki Karaya, too, was an ex-detainee, and Kibuthu Muturi, had been a leading figure among Mau Mau's guerrilla army in the forests. Muturi then became a leader of KANU's Youth Wing, its key mobilising arm, and joined the party's district leadership. Gati Mugo had been a Mau Mau activist in Nairobi, for which he was detained early

---

[18] KNA VP/1/17, DC Nyeri to PC Central, 18 July 1958.
[19] KNA VP/1/85, DC Kiambu to PC Central, 14 August 1956.
[20] KNA VP/1/85, DO North Tetu to DC Nyeri, 4 September 1958.
[21] KNA VP/9/5, DO Othaya to DC Nyeri, 8 October 1958, 2.
[22] KNA VP/9/5, DO Othaya to DC Nyeri, 6 January 1959, 2.

in the Emergency, and after his release, he had joined the *Kiama kia Muingi* and been detained again. Kimaru Kagwe was an ex-detainee and sub-locational KANU chairman.

A similar story was repeated across the South Tetu division in Nyeri. In Githi location, the candidates were again almost all ex-detainees, and most had some formal role within the local structures of KANU. Karebu Kabuga was an ex-detainee and, again, chair of his sub-locational KANU branch. Kamotho Ndwng'u had been a Mau Mau fighter, although he had never been detained. He was, though, by 1963, South Tetu's KANU Youth Wing leader. Wachira Kimani was another former detainee and KANU sub-locational leader, as was Gilbert Nguru Marewa. Kariuki Kabuthi was also an ex-detainee and KANU secretary for Githi. In Gikondi location, a similar pattern emerged. Ndaai Kigutu had been the most prominent local Mau Mau leader, was detained, and then became chairman of the Gikondi location KANU branch after his release. Sylvester Nyaga and Ruchuu Ndoka had both been detainees and were chairman of KANU in their respective sub-locations. Wambugu Kamiru had been a KAU branch secretary prior to the Emergency, was detained during the war, and became KANU treasurer for Nyeri, chairman of a local school, manager of the African District Council beer hall, and sub-locational KANU chairman.[23] Similar lists of candidates were reported from across Nyeri.[24]

In Nyeri and elsewhere, a clear cleavage in local politics formed prior to independence. As we saw in the previous chapter, loyalists dominated the Provincial Administration and the legislature, although their control of the legislature declined once ex-detainees were allowed to vote in 1961. Mau Mau activists, by contrast, steadily assumed control of the local authorities and branches of KANU.[25] Initially, very few loyalists joined the party.[26] Indeed, in Kiambu, loyalists came to be known

[23] KNA VP/1/85, Divisional Assistant, Regional Government Agent (DARGA) South Tetu, 'Short Reports on Candidates for Area Council,' 31 July 1963.
[24] KNA VP/1/85, Chief William, Aguthi Location to DARGA North Tetu, 8 August 1963; Chief Gathaaka, Tetu Location to DARGA North Tetu, August 1963; Chief Harrison Kariuki, Thegenge Location to DARGA North Tetu, 7 August 1963; DARGA to Regional Government Agent (RGA) Nyeri, 20 August 1963; DARGA Othaya to RGA Nyeri, 5 August 1963.
[25] See, for example, KNA DC/EBU/1/1/19, Embu District Annual Report 1960, 5; KNA VP/9/102, PC Central, 'Handing Over Notes: Brigadier M. Hughes to Mr. F. R. Wilson,' 8 September 1960, 2.
[26] KNA VP/9/102, PC Central, 'Handing Over Notes: Brigadier M. Hughes to Mr. F. R. Wilson,' 8 September 1960, 2; KNA DC/MRU/1/1, Nyeri District Annual Report 1960, 2.

as 'KADU,' a reference to KANU's main and more conservative opponent, the Kenya African Democratic Union.[27] KADU was established to
represent the interests of smaller ethnic groups in the country and was
accused by its rival, KANU, of representing the interests of the outgoing
colonial authorities. In contrast KANU, founded in May 1960, provided
the ex-detainees with a focus and a new impetus for their political activities. At the time of the party's founding, Jomo Kenyatta remained in
detention, but he was elected KANU president while still being held at
Kapenguria. Party activists in Central Province organised collections to
assist with the efforts to have Kenyatta freed and to help families of Mau
Mau supporters killed during the war.[28] Local party officials also sold
Kenyatta pin badges in Kiambu.[29] Once Kenyatta was finally released in
1961, the efforts of the former Mau Mau supporters within the ranks
of KANU turned to influencing the shape of the impending post-colonial
state.

KANU's Youth Wing and, to a lesser extent, Women's Wing assumed
responsibility for mobilising the general population in support of the
nationalist cause. Members of the KANU Youth Wing came under suspicion for organising a wide range of subversive activities. In Kiambu,
the chiefs reported that the movement's members were carrying weapons
at night.[30] Although the district officer of North Tetu believed that the
Youth Wing was not a threat to public order,[31] a member there was
arrested for carrying ammunition.[32] A former Youth Wing chairman
from Mweiga was found to have broken into the local district officer's
house in March 1963.[33] One of the tasks apparently carried out by locational Youth Wing leaders was the organisation of public choirs, an
increasingly common phenomenon as independence drew closer. Kibuthu
Muturi and Kamotho Ndwng'u, both leaders of the Youth Wing in South
Tetu, were responsible for the planning of mass singing of protest and cel-
ebration songs in their home locations, Muhito and Githi, respectively.[34]
The choirs sang 'songs at night in villages on suitable occasions, such

[27] KNA DC/KBU/1/47, Kiambu District Annual Report, 5.
[28] KNA DC/MRU/1/1, Nyeri District Annual Report, 1; KNA DC/MRU/2/1/12, Minutes
   of Chuka Division Chiefs' Meeting, 5 October 1961, 2.
[29] KNA VP/2/75, DC Kiambu to PC Central, 7 January 1961, 4.
[30] KNA VP/2/75, DC Kiambu to PC Central, 7 January 1961, 1.
[31] KNA VP/9/102, DO North Tetu, 'Handing Over Report – North Tetu, R. J. H. Chambers
   to I. D. St. G. Lindsay,' 24 January 1962, 13–4.
[32] KNA VP/1/98, DO North Tetu to DC Nyeri, 27 February 1963.
[33] KNA VP/1/98, Officer in Charge Police Department Nyeri to DC Nyeri, 27 March 1963.
[34] KNA VP/1/85, DARGA South Tetu, 'Short Reports on Candidates for Area Council,'
   31 July 1963.

as the release of Kenyatta.'³⁵ Mau Mau's choirs were not just celebratory, but were also used aggressively. John Michuki, for example, found the entrance to his compound blocked 'by a procession whose members' behaviour was not to my liking.' The protestors were singing 'Mau Mau songs.'³⁶ The choice of target of these and other protests was not accidental.

Such actions should be interpreted partly as an expression of discontent with the manner in which Kenya's decolonisation was unfurling. The loyalist influence at the very highest levels of the state was of particular concern to the former insurgents. Loyalists such as Michuki were not just seen as opponents of Mau Mau and friends of colonialism, but also as enemies of the embryonic nation. But the loyalists targeted for harassment were those believed to have transgressed boundaries of acceptable behaviour during the Emergency. Chief Weston Karangi of the Ruguru location in Mathira, Nyeri district, was another figure singled out for aggressive but non-violent agitation. 'He was,' the local district officer admitted, 'one of Mathira's strong men during the Emergency.'³⁷ Chiefs such as Karangi were the most common targets for harassment by former insurgents in the final years and months of colonial rule.

As early as 1957, ex-detainees in Kiambu were using the courts to pursue resolution of their grievances related to land consolidation with chiefs with no great success.³⁸ Ahead of the legislative elections of 1961, the property of chiefs in Kiambu was targeted for vandalism.³⁹ Stripped of the power they had exercised during the war, by the early 1960s, the chiefs of Central Province were finding it almost impossible 'to carry out their instructions without the aid of uniformed assistants.'⁴⁰ This climate of suspicion and distrust culminated in the murder of Sub-Chief Wambugu Kimathi in the Nyeri district during May 1960.⁴¹ Chief Stephen Chorio of Gikondi location, Nyeri, shot himself on 11 April 1961. His suicide was partly the result of financial troubles and worries about the

35 KNA VP/9/102, DO Mathira, 'Handing Over Report: Mr. J. H. Grayburn to Mr. T. H. R. Cashmore, Mathira Division,' 6 December 1961, 2.
36 KNA VP/2/80, RGA Nyeri to ASP SB Nyeri, 19 June 1963, 1.
37 KNA VP/9/102, DO Mathira, 'Handing Over Report: Mr. J. H. Grayburn to Mr. T. H. R. Cashmore, Mathira Division,' 6 December 1961, 3–4.
38 KNA DC/KBU/2/1, DO I, Kiambu, 'Handing Over Report, District Officer I, Kiambu, D. E. Johnston–A. Simmance, June/July 1957,' 20.
39 KNA VP/2/75, DC Kiambu to PC Central, 7 January 1961, 3.
40 KNA VP/1/111, PC Central to Permanent Secretary, Office of the Chief Secretary, 31 July 1961, 2.
41 KNA VP/1/88, PC Central, 'Curfew Order,' 2 June 1960.

health of his wife. However, Chorio was also known to be gravely concerned that land titles he had acquired during the war would be seized at
independence, and he had experienced 'great pressure put upon him by
his local politicians,' a euphemism for harassment by former insurgents
within KANU.[42] KANU activists in Mahiga, Nyeri, conducted a similar
campaign against Chief Jeremiah Ngari in February 1962. The grievances
of local ex-detainees included accusations that Ngari had beaten suspects
and stolen money from Mau Mau supporters during the war. In addition
to these claims were suspicions that Ngari had used public property for
personal gain and that the chief had not encouraged the production of
coffee or educational improvement in his location.[43] While the Provincial Administration anxiously attempted to exonerate the chief, Ngari's
troubles grew over the following few months.[44] On 17 June, Ngari hanged
himself.

With decolonisation impending, the ex-detainees believed themselves
to be on the verge of ultimate victory. Mirroring the development of Mau
Mau's challenge in the forests to the British monopoly on statecraft,[45]
in the final years of colonial rule ex-detainees were busy forming, to
paraphrase Peterson, a counter-state that challenged loyalist claims to
paramountcy.[46] Shadow governments and political courts were established,[47] taxes were not paid, and laws were fragrantly breached.[48] In
Embu, the Youth Wing attempted to assume control of law and order.[49]
Government cars were stopped on the roads and 'donations' taken from
their drivers before they were allowed to continue.[50] Mau Mau supporters
demanded that loyalists in positions of power be replaced by their fellow
former insurgents.[51] Such individuals thought themselves to be shaping

---

[42] KNA VP/1/104, DC Nyeri to PC Central, 12 April 1961; DC Nyeri to PC Central 15
April 1961; DC Nyeri to PC Central, 20 April 1961.
[43] KNA VP/1/104, Mahiga KANU Sub-Branch to Minister of Local Government, Member of Legislative Council Nyeri, DC Nyeri, PC Central, KANU Headquarters Nyeri,
Divisional Chief Paul Murithi, DO Othaya, Mahiga Locational Council & KANU Sub-
Branch Othaya, February 1962.
[44] KNA VP/1/104, DC Nyeri to DO Othaya, 6 February 1962; DO Othaya to DC Nyeri,
February 1962.
[45] Peterson, 'Writing in Revolution,' 88–93.
[46] Ibid., 92.
[47] KNA DC/EBU/1/1/19, Embu District Annual Report 1960, 1; KNA DC/EBU/1/1/20,
Embu District Annual Report 1961, 1
[48] KNA VQ/5/28, Minutes of Meeting of Meru ADC, 8–9 March 1960, 1.
[49] KNA DC/EBU/1/120, Embu District Annual Report, 1961, 2.
[50] KNA VP/2/80, RGA Nyeri to ASP SB Nyeri, 19 June 1963, 1–2.
[51] Kamunchula, 'Meru Participation,' 213.

the nature of the future independent nation. But with the nationalist leadership reluctant to commit to a radical agenda of land reallocation, Mau Mau supporters were fighting the dying light of radical nationalism. The tension caused by the distance between the great expectations of decolonisation and the form independent rule actually took continued to be evident in local politics in Central Province long after independence.

Agitation on the part of former Mau Mau supporters immediately prior to independence thus coalesced on two issues: the loyalist presence within the Provincial Administration and the question of access to land. Both were keenly felt in Nyeri, where over 19 percent of the population was landless in 1969, the highest level in the Mount Kenya region.[52] Agricultural production by African farmers had dramatically increased since 1955, a result of the Swynnerton Plan discussed in Chapter 4. But within the economy as a whole, recession and a 14 percent decline in paid employment levels meant that the significance of land holdings grew. Family smallholdings decreased reliance on other forms of income and brought in much-needed cash to pay taxes, school fees, and other expenses.[53] Those without access to land felt the crunch of the early 1960s particularly harshly. Yet, despite their hardships, from the perspective of many of the new leaders of the post-colonial nation-state and, it must be stressed, many Kikuyu, land was as it always had been, to be earned by labour, not given by government.[54] By contrast, the harassment of loyalist chiefs and headmen was an exercise ridden with far fewer contradictions for nationalist activists seeking grassroots support.

As the country approached independence, many within the outgoing regime feared that the infant post-colonial state would be anointed with the blood of the traitorous collaborators.[55] Long-remembered threats to the lives of loyalists and their families were reinforced as *uhuru* drew closer. Across Central Province, by early December 1963, it was known that 'there are threats of ex-terrorists rising against the loyalists on the independence Day.' In Othaya in the Nyeri district, for example, three headmen 'received some threatening letters that their heads would be

---

[52] Bienen, *Kenya*, 180. This was the highest figure of all comparable districts in Central Province and Embu and Meru, with the exception of Kiambu, where a significant population worked in Nairobi and thus did not rely on income from land.
[53] Ibid., 163.
[54] Gertzel, *Independent Kenya*, 86–7.
[55] RHL Mss Afr s 1915, 'Interview/Discussion on the Mau Mau Emergency in Kenya with Sir Frank Loyd, Robin Wainwright and Dick Wilson – 12th January 1984. Interviewer Anthony Kirk-Greene,' 62.

chopped off on the Independence Day.' What was feared was not the blind justice of a victorious mob, but instead carefully and deliberately targeted retribution towards those felt to have exceeded all acceptable norms in their conduct during the Emergency. Headmen Jimna of Gathera, Taiti of Kagere, and Kariuki of Mahiga were known to 'have some very bitter enemies here.' Indeed, the district officer in Othaya was inclined to see much of the fear of revenge killings as the paranoia on the part of 'those who are guilty-conscious.'[56] The attainment of independence on 12 December 1963 did little to douse the passions of the former insurgents.

Not Yet *Uhuru*

The first New Year of the independence era was heralded by attempts to agitate for the removal of the chiefs and headmen appointed under colonial rule. At a public meeting convened by a group known as the War Council in Karia sub-location of Nyeri, the audience demanded that the Administration to remove Headman Paul Mamo and Sub-Headman Samuel Ndonga from office.[57] The War Council was an underground organisation claiming direct descent from Mau Mau. The group was made up of ex-detainees, and it reappeared frequently in Nyeri as a voice of dissent during the post-colonial period. In an attempt to calm the fires of local disquiet, the Provincial Administration in the district swiftly introduced a number of populist initiatives. Eleven of Nyeri's 17 chiefs, all appointed by the colonial government, were compulsorily retired on the ostensible grounds of old age. At the same time, a very limited programme of land grants to former Mau Mau leaders was introduced.[58] Although no doubt a welcome gesture, this idea fell far short of the wholesale reconsideration of the question of private land tenure demanded by Mau Mau sympathisers. Attempts to enquire if and when an investigation into the land issue would begin were rebuked.[59] At a local KANU meeting in Thegenge, those who had been dispossessed, 'especially those people

---

[56] KNA VP/9/102, DO Othaya, 'Handing Over Report – Othaya Division: Mr. J. N. A. R. Okumali to Mr. D. S. Mwangi,' 2 December 1963, 1.

[57] KNA VP/1/98, D. M. Ndegwa, Chairman War Council, Thigingi Location, General Secretary, War Council & Kinyu Ndegwa, Brigadier, War Council to DC Nyeri, 1 January 1964.

[58] KNA VP/9/102, RGA Nyeri, 'Handing Over Report: Mr. C. K. Koinange to Mr. F. K. Mbugwa,' 12 June 1964, 2–3 & 8; & KNA VP/1/90, Minister for Lands and Settlement to Secretary, Murang'a Freedom Fighters Committee, 17 August 1964.

[59] KNA VP/1/90, Minister for Lands and Settlement to Secretary, Murang'a Freedom Fighters Committee, 17 August 1964.

who had gone to the forest during emergency as Mau Mau,' were told
to detail their grievances in letters to the Provincial Administration.[60]
But such actions were never likely to result in any meaningful restorative
action.

It took only a few more months of independence before these local
voices of dissent began to be heard at the national level. Bildad Kaggia,
one of Mau Mau's radical organisers and fellow detainee with Kenyatta,
resigned his post in the Ministry of Education in June 1964. Kaggia
claimed the government was neglecting 'the freedom fighters who gave
all they had, including their land, for the independence we are enjoying.'[61]
The reverse side of that same argument, namely, opposition towards loyalists within the government, continued to occupy the energy of grassroots activists in Nyeri. Councillors from Ruguru, near Karatina, accused
Administration officers of having been 'home guards,' indicating the
extent to which that label had become pejorative.[62] The loyalist background of district commissioners, district officers, chiefs, and headmen
became the mostly frequently aired grievance in local political meetings.
Dominated by Mau Mau activists, the local branch offices of KANU
instigated the protests against the Administration.[63] In Othaya during
February 1965, a meeting of the local KANU branch demanded the dismissal of all chiefs and headmen inherited from the colonial regime.
Social inequalities between former Home Guards and Mau Mau were bemoaned, and loyalist dominance of local affairs was attacked. More serious threats were also made. One speaker announced, 'Those people
who did not take Maumau oath [are] to be killed immediately. These
are the chiefs, headmen and homeguards.' Another threatened, 'We shall
slaughter headmen and their families.'[64] None were, however, killed.
The absence of retribution can be partly explained through the relative
strength of the state, which of course had a vested interest in protecting its employees, and the relative weakness of institutions controlled by
ex-detainees, most notably, the branch offices of KANU.

[60] KNA VP/1/90, Acting Chief, Thegenge Location, 'Confidential Report: KANU Meeting
at Wamagana Stadium on 25-10-64,' 9 November 1964.
[61] Quoted in William Ochieng, 'Structural and Political Changes,' in *Decolonization and
Independence in Kenya 1940–93*, eds. Bethwell A. Ogot and William Ochieng (London,
1955), 95.
[62] KNA VP/1/90, Wachira Reriani, Chairman KANU Ruguru Location to RGA Nyeri, 24
September 1964, 1.
[63] KNA VP/2/80, Minutes of Nyeri District Security Committee, 23 July 1965, 1; Minutes
of Nyeri District Security Committee, 24 September 1965.
[64] KNA VP/1/98, DO Othaya to DC Nyeri, 16 February 1965.

Although these local branches of the ruling party were dominated by radical former Mau Mau activists, they found the party sidelined in decision making at the state level.[65] As a big-tent party comprising Kenya's many class, regional, and ethnic factions, there was little enthusiasm within the national leadership to pursue radical policies that could disrupt the uneasy harmony within KANU's constituent parts.[66] Within parliament, the party had a very weak structure, making consensus difficult to achieve.[67] In any case, Kenyatta was no party man. To sustain his rule, the president instead relied on, first, his own unquestionable authority as *Baba Taifa* (Father of the Nation), honed over decades of leadership of the nationalist movement and in detention during the 1950s. Second, Kenyatta exerted that authority through the Provincial Administration. By contrast, KANU, the party nominally under Kenyatta's control, was of significantly lesser importance. This lack of importance to the process of policy formation and implementation paradoxically allowed KANU to become the space for dissent with the post-colonial state.[68] Although dissidents in Central Province made use of that space to express their discontent with life under Kenyatta, they also recognised that the party was powerless. This awareness drove the most committed opponents of the regime towards small, subversive, and underground groups, including the War Council, mentioned previously. Although these groups greatly concerned the authorities, attempting to assess their size from local government sources is impossible. The extent to which the Provincial Administration was disconnected from the general population cannot be overestimated, with obvious ramifications for the flow of information. The presence of such groups furthermore suited the purposes of the Provincial Administration and the regime, both of which showed increasing authoritarian tendencies. However, the underground groups were consistently troublesome for the government, if only for the symbolic threat posed rather than any significant physical peril.

One such group was *Ngwataniro*, which means cooperation in both a labouring (working together) and political (acting together) sense. The term would later become associated with the clique of Kenyatta's supporters during attempts to prevent Moi from succeeding to the presidency, but

[65] Bienen, *Kenya*, 66.
[66] Hyden and Leys, 'Single-Party System' 393.
[67] Bienen, *Kenya*, 84.
[68] Daniel Branch and Nicholas Cheeseman, 'The Politics of Control in Kenya: Understanding the Bureaucratic-Executive State, 1952–78,' *Review of African Political Economy* 33 (2006).

it had originally been used in the 1950s during Mau Mau oaths to build support for the insurgency.[69] With the patronage of one local Member of Parliament (MP), the group's initial objective was to bolster support for sympathetic figures during elections for vacant chieftaincies. In this, activists were successful, as two individuals connected to *Ngwataniro* won the polls for chief in the Othaya and Muhito locations in 1965.[70] The choice of the name *Ngwataniro* is revealing. On one level, the label deliberately attempted to draw legitimacy from Mau Mau. However, *Ngwataniro* points to the deeper substance of Kikuyu political debate, namely, the relationship between membership of the ethnic community, access to land, labour, and political authority. *Ngwataniro* was not just a group of war veterans disillusioned with a post-conflict resolution laden with pragmatic compromises interpreted as a betrayal of their ideals and their fallen comrades. Instead, it was a continuation of the condemnation by landless men who could not get access to land to become husbands, fathers, and elders. In the late 1940s, as discussed in Chapter 1, rising land prices, declining soil productivity, and overpopulation of the areas reserved for African farming meant that patrons had evicted their poor tenants from the land. However, those same patrons continued to claim monopoly rights to political leadership, which the poor had always accepted on condition of being allowed access to land. The landless former clients thus contested the patrons' moral entitlement to political domination and instead turned to the radical militant position of Mau Mau.

With the rise of African nationalism in the late 1950s, a new bargain was struck between elites and the alienated sections of society. Since the 1920s, Kikuyu had equated land alienation with colonial rule; each was the expression of the other. This interconnected understanding of political process and economic system led to the widespread assumption that decolonisation necessarily entailed redress of land grievances. Elites were believed to be the right people to lead the charge to independence, as it was recognised that the educated and literate were more likely to achieve this status than the illiterate poor. The moral authority of the elites to lead the nationalist movement was predicated on the assumption that those same elites would deliver land, thus reconstructing the relationship between patrons and clients that formed the basis of Kikuyu social

---

[69] I am grateful to Derek Peterson for his translation of this and his thoughts on its wider significance.

[70] KNA VP/1/120, DC Nyeri to PC Central, 1 July 1965; KNA VP/1/123, Provincial Special Branch Division Central to PC Central, 10 September 1965.

relations for much of the previous century. With most Kenyans unaware
of the ramifications of the pre-independence agreements between the
African nationalist parties and the colonial regime to protect private
property, the realisation that land was not to be delivered to the poor
arrived with a jolt in the mid-1960s.

By laying claim to one side of the intellectual debate of previous decades, *Ngwataniro* was accusing the post-colonial elite of moral bank-
ruptcy and disputed the authority of the country's new leaders in much
the same way Mau Mau had done with the colonial regime in the 1950s.
The Administration rightly recognised that land was still the crucial issue
in Central Province politics.[71] Limited attempts had been made to grant
land to the forest fighters, but they were woefully inadequate. Only 66
plots were allocated in all of Nyeri.[72] As a result, agitation for a review of
land consolidation gathered momentum in the middle months of 1965. In
April, a pamphlet was circulating in Nyeri detailing attempts to organise
a petition of all who felt they had been dispossessed unfairly during the
land reforms of the 1950s.[73] New grievances had been added to those da-
ting back to the 1950s and 1940s, in particular, the corruption of the
distribution of plots in settlement schemes on the former settler farms in
favour of elites.[74] However, this agitation was in vain. With the publication of the Sessional Paper No.10 of 1965, the government committed
itself to development through private enterprise, despite labelling the
policy 'African Socialism.'[75] African Socialism conveyed a very different
meaning in Kenya than it did in many other post-colonial states, such as
Tanzania, for example. Rather than denoting a genuine experiment with
socialism, in the words of Masinde Muliro, in post-colonial Kenya, 'An
African socialist is by nature a capitalist.'[76] Private land tenure was to
form a significant part of the market economy, and the structure of the
colonial economy was to remain intact.[77]

Redress of a different variety was sought by the resurrection of the
Kikuyu Independent Schools Association (KISA). KISA had been the

---

[71] KNA VP/1/90, DO North Tetu to DC Nyeri, 26 March 1965.
[72] KNA VP/9/102, DO I, Nyeri, 'Handing Over Notes: R. A. Rinyamy to J. K. Ndote,'
April 1965, 1.
[73] KNA VP/1/90, DC Nyeri to PC Central, 1 April 1965.
[74] Gertzel, *Independent Kenya*, 45–50.
[75] Government of Kenya, *Sessional Paper No.10 of 1965: African Socialism and its Application to Planning in Kenya* (Nairobi, 1965).
[76] Cherry Gertzel, Maure Goldschmidt, and Donald Rothchild, eds., *Government and
Politics in Kenya* (Nairobi, 1969), 83
[77] Ochieng, 'Structural & Political,' 90 & 96.

heartbeat of Kikuyu politics from the 1930s to the beginning of the Emergency. Formed as a result of the outrage against attempts by certain mission churches to ban attendance at school of those girls who had been circumcised according to Kikuyu custom, a network of independent schools and churches spread across Central Kenya throughout the 1930s. It was among the schools' graduates and teachers that the intellectual opposition to chiefs and the colonial state had been formulated, contested, and discussed.[78] As a result, the schools affiliated to KISA were closed down soon after the declaration of the State of Emergency in October 1952. In 1965, KISA was revived in Nyeri under the management of Jimmy Maina. The group began a campaign intended to reclaim the sites of its schools after they were closed, reissued to mission churches, or taken over by the government during the Emergency.[79] The first site to be targeted in this way was the former independent school at Gikumbo, which had been taken over by the Catholic missions. By October 1965, the KISA campaign had spread to many areas of the district.[80]

The KISA campaign was mirrored by a similar effort of the African Independent Pentecostal Church of Kenya (AIPC, but also written AIPCK). The AIPC had been founded in 1929 following the attempted female circumcision ban and was closely connected to the KISA movement. By 1952, the AIPC had 168 churches and schools, and 6,000 pupils were enrolled in its educational institutions. It, too, was banned shortly after the beginning of the Emergency, but had been re-established after independence in 1963, under the management of Willy Wambugu.[81] During a visit to Kenyatta at his home in Kiambu in December 1964, the AIPC's leadership gained the president's approval for its revival and petitioned for the return of its property seized during the Emergency.[82] In early 1966, the AIPC scored a notable success when it successfully agitated for the return of confiscated property in North Tetu, which

---

[78] Peterson, 'Writing in Revolution,' 76–96; Peterson, *Creative Writing*, 139–58.
[79] KNA VP/2/80, Minutes of Nyeri District Security Committee, 25 June 1965, 1.
[80] KNA VP/2/80, Minutes of Nyeri District Security Committee, 23 July 1965, 1–2; Minutes of Nyeri District Security Committee, 27 October 1965, 1.
[81] KNA VP/2/80, Minutes of Nyeri District Security Committee, 27 January 1967; J. Ndung'u Mburu, 'The Dissemination of Christianity in Nyeri District (1903–1963) with Special Reference to the Work of African Teachers and Evangelists' (MA, University of Nairobi, 1975), 11–15.
[82] Joseph Kariuki, 'Internal Wrangles, State Influence and Schisms: Competing Visions and Struggles in the Africa Independent Pentecostal Church in Kenya,' *Les Cahiers de'IFRA* 25 (2004). (available at IFRA Nairobi website, http://www.ifra-nairobi.net/resources/cahiers/Cahier_25/c25kariuki.pdf – accessed 4 December 2006).

had been handed over to the Presbyterians during the Emergency.[83] The AIPC made no attempt to hide its claim to be 'the legal successor of KISA and Independent Churches.' As a consequence, the church found support from local politicians and was connected to the various underground opposition movements. At an AIPC meeting held at Kimahuri on 13 September 1970, Waruru Kanja, MP, after having been given permission by the AIPC leadership, criticised the government for 'not rewarding the Freedom fighters.'[84] With these allies, the AIPC was able to intensify its campaign to pressure for the return of property seized from KISA and the independent churches during the Emergency.[85]

At two o'clock in the morning on 14 March 1971, AIPC adherents simultaneously stormed church and school buildings in Birithia, Othaya, and at Kabiruini and Gacika, both in Ruguru. After the banning of KISA during the Emergency, the properties had all passed into the hands of the Consolata Catholic missions and the government's District Education Board. Congregations of the invaded churches and parents of pupils were outraged by the invasions. At Kabiruini, parents threatened to demolish the occupied buildings unless their children were not allowed to return. The congregation of the Consolata mission at Birithia promised to use force to regain ownership of the mission's property. However, the AIPC believed that Kenyatta himself had given permission for the seizures.[86] A standoff between the angry parents and the AIPC ensued. After a week, the parents at Kabiruini demolished the disputed buildings. Only the presence of an armed guard prevented a similar occurrence at Birithia.[87]

In an attempt to resolve the situation, Kenyatta issued a ruling giving the AIPC ownership of the property at Birithia on 26 March. This caused 'strong resentment and protest' among local Catholics, who accused Kenyatta of 'making arbitrary decisions without offering an opportunity for them to be heard.'[88] Following intercessions by Catholic leaders, Kenyatta partially reversed his position. The President decreed that both Consolata and AIPC followers were to be prevented from occupying and

---

[83] KNA VP/2/80, Minutes of Nyeri District Security Committee, 27 January 1966; Minutes of Nyeri District Security Committee, 25 February 1966.
[84] KNA VP/2/80, Minutes of Nyeri District Security Committee, 26 September 1970.
[85] See, for example, correspondence relating to storming of two church complexes by AIPC adherents in March 1971 in KNA VP/2/80.
[86] KNA VP/2/80, Minutes of Special Meeting of Nyeri District Security Committee, 15 March 1971.
[87] KNA VP/2/80, Minutes of Nyeri District Security Committee, 23 March 1971.
[88] KNA VP/2/80, Minutes of Nyeri District Security Committee, 26 April 1971.

using the buildings at Birithia. However, after the saga had dragged on for three months, eighty members of the AIPC forced their way into the compound on 13 June. Eleven were arrested, but all were later acquitted. Simultaneously, AIPC followers damaged crops planted on the site of the destroyed buildings at the government school in Kabiruini.[89] Firm action by the Provincial Administration appears to have prevented similar events taking place elsewhere.

Except for a brief revival late in 1972, the AIPC campaign appears to have lost momentum by the end of 1971.[90] Nevertheless, its significance as part of a broader body of protest in Nyeri against the post-colonial state should not be underestimated. The adherents of the AIPC, the management of the new KISA, members of the local KANU, and activists within groups such as *Ngwataniro* used the moral arguments of the 1940s and 1950s to condemn post-colonial patrons they believed to have abandoned them to poverty. Those same patrons could condemn dissenters with the same terms loyalists had used while challenging Mau Mau. In this way, Kenyatta was able to fend off the challenge of radical discontent closely tied to former Mau Mau activists.

The Free Things

In early 1966, Bildad Kaggia launched his fateful campaign to become the party's vice president for Central Province at the upcoming KANU conference. Politicians closely associated with ex-Mau Mau were strong supporters of Kaggia's effort,[91] and a large number from across the Mount Kenya region and beyond gathered for a public rally held in Nyeri on 21 February 1966.

Collectively, the speakers at the rally attacked the loyalist presence within the government and a variety of other issues relating to land. Tom Gichohi, a senator from Laikipia, attacked Kenyatta's Cabinet, which formed policy by listening only 'to civil servants who held high positions during the struggle,' in other words, loyalists recruited into the Provincial Administration during the 1950s, 'and are still holding high positions.' G. G. Kariuki, a Laikipia MP, concurred. Senator Roman Gikuuja, of Kirinyaga, 'thought that land would be given freely after independence and was surprised to see that people are being asked to buy.' Gikuuja

---

[89] KNA VP/2/80, Minutes of Nyeri District Security Committee, 23 June 1971.
[90] KNA VP/2/80, Minutes of Central Province Security Committee, 29 December 1972.
[91] KNA VP/2/80, Minutes of Nyeri District Security Committee, 27 October 1965.

continued by attacking 'civil servants vehemently.' The main speaker was Kaggia, whose attacks on the government, in the words of the Provincial Administration, 'exceeded all' those who had addressed the rally before him. Kaggia repeated the accusation of theft of land belonging to Mau Mau supporters by Home Guard during the Emergency and 'said that land has been bought by ex-home-guards' since independence. He denounced loyalists who monopolised 'big government posts,' thereby 'blocking the way for ex-forest-fighters and youth-wingers.' Kaggia railed against the qualification criteria for jobs and land in resettlement schemes that favoured loyalists over forest fighters and their children. He told his audience that Kenyatta 'had taught him that the land belonged to Africans and will never be bought.' Kaggia promised to 'stick to this to the bitter end.' He concluded by reminding the audience that they had all taken oaths with him and thus, 'they should continue to ask for free land.'[92] Kaggia's speech was one of the last he made from within the ranks of KANU.

Kaggia left the party shortly thereafter and, with Oginga Odinga, formed the KPU. The new party championed populist causes, such as the nationalisation of economic interests owned by European and Asian non-citizens and the introduction of free education. Most significantly, the KPU urged a significant programme of land redistribution, including the cancelling of debts accrued by African smallholders who had joined settlement schemes on former European owned land.[93] Such policies stood in stark contrast to the government's refusal to countenance large-scale land grants and commitment to a capitalist developmental path. Kaggia's advocacy of land redistribution threatened the position of Kenyatta among Kikuyu and brought the social cleavages of Central Province to national politics. Kaggia and Kenyatta's pre-Emergency relationship had been fraught, and their time spent together in detention was not wholly amicable.[94] The two represented very different factions within Kikuyu society.

Both Odinga and Kaggia 'portrayed themselves as the true inheritors of the militant tradition of the fight for independence.'[95] Kaggia drew support from ex-detainees who had resettled in Nakuru in the Rift Valley

---

[92] KNA VP/1/98, Anon, 'Notes on Political KANU Meeting of 21st February [1966] for Provincial Commissioner.'
[93] Gertzel, *Independent Kenya*, 88; Hyden and Leys, 'Single-Party Systems,' 393.
[94] Bienen, *Kenya*, 79.
[95] Clough, 'Contest for Memory,' 257.

and his home district of Murang'a. The KPU could also count on the backing of Nyanza province, from where Odinga originated. Elsewhere in Central Province and the eastern Rift Valley, however, as well as in the remainder of the country, Kenyatta, the conservative elder, could count on the support of most of the population.[96] MPs who had joined the KPU were forced to resign their seats and stand for election once again. Twenty-nine candidates stood for reelection in May 1966, and just nine were returned to Parliament.[97] KANU Youth Wingers were mobilised to attack the homes of KPU supporters, and seven people died during the campaign.[98] The support of the Provincial Administration for the government was apparent, despite the institution's unwillingness to abandon the rhetoric of neutrality.[99] Although the elections marked a triumph for KANU, the declining voter turnout, from 85 percent in 1963 to just 33 percent, indicated the plunging legitimacy of the political process.[100]

Despite the populism of the KPU, it failed to attract the support of a sizeable section of the electorate in Central Province for a number of reasons besides the mobilisation of the state institutions against the new party. Kaggia's personal popularity, although significant, was not sufficient to endanger the President's position as the leading Kikuyu political figure.[101] As one dissident MP remarked just prior to the formalisation of the KPU, 'If Jomo Kenyatta was not leading KANU, and KPU started working under Kaggia and Oginga, I dare say there would be an awful lot of people moving to it [KPU]. But Kenyatta leads KANU.'[102] Kenyatta's well-publicised personal intervention against Kaggia in Kaggia's home constituency asserted the President's dominance.[103] Kenyatta scorned Kaggia's claims to the moral authority and therefore the challenger's right to lead Kikuyu political activity. Kaggia, Kenyatta argued, had been idle since his release from detention in 1961. While his fellow detainees, including Kenyatta himself, Fred Kubai, and Paul Ngei, had prospered as businessmen, Kaggia was still poor. Rather than asking for

---

[96] Ibid., 257.
[97] Bienen, *Kenya*, 70–1; Gertzel, *Independent Kenya*, 73–94; Hyden and Leys, 'Single-Party Systems,' 394.
[98] Lamb, *Peasant Politics*, 44.
[99] Gertzel, *Independent Kenya*, 79; Lamb, *Peasant Politics*, 45.
[100] Bienen, *Kenya*, 90–1.
[101] Gertzel, *Independent Kenya*, 90–1.
[102] Quoted in Gertzel, Goldschmidt and Rothchild, eds., *Government & Politics*, 157.
[103] Lamb, *Peasant Politics*, 44.

the rightful rewards for hard work, Kenyatta termed Kaggia's request for land for Mau Mau veterans as characteristic of a plea by the lazy for 'free things.'[104] One of Kenyatta's closest advisors and one of the first generation of loyalist politicians of the 1950s, Julius Kiano, similarly attacked Kaggia's demands for social equality through a redistribution of land. To Kiano, such a move punished those who had laboured for the benefit of those who had chosen not to. 'Does he mean,' Kiano rhetorically asked, 'that private families may not have private houses or small farmers should be deprived of smallholdings?'[105] Land was to be earned by labour, not given by government.[106] By 1968, the slim likelihood of KPU emerging victorious from its struggle with Kenyatta and KANU was obvious. Kaggia was imprisoned for six months for holding an illegal meeting. Party leaders were unable to build up a network of local offices.[107]

Many Kikuyu benefited greatly from the Africanisation of the economy and the transfer of assets from European and Asian ownership to Africans, in particular, land in the former White Highlands. However, poverty, landlessness, and unemployment remained an ever-present fear for many.[108] Although the economy expanded at a rate of over 6.5 percent per year between 1964 and 1970, the benefits were not evenly distributed throughout the population.[109] The Provincial Administration in Nyeri conducted a survey of its officers on the causes of and possible solutions to social inequality. R. G. Rurua, the district officer in Othaya, wrote, 'the class of haves is increasing their wealth to the expense of have nots; and as the gap between rich and poor people widens, hatred between them too increases.'[110] Generational and gender conflict was also identified as 'affecting the progress of the country.'[111] Furthermore, despite a doubling of the number of schools after independence, tensions between the educated and non-educated remained.[112] It was claimed that in some areas, the younger, educated sections of society 'did not also contribute anything towards the development of their place and kept themselves

[104] Ibid., 36.
[105] Ibid., 37.
[106] Gertzel, *Independent Kenya*, 86–7.
[107] Ibid., 146.
[108] Bienen, *Kenya*, 141 & 182; Robert Maxon, 'Social and Cultural Changes,' in *Decolonization and Independence in Kenya 1940–93*, eds. Bethwell A. Ogot and William Ochieng (Oxford, 1995), 120.
[109] Bienen, *Kenya*, 5.
[110] KNA VP/1/98, DO Othaya to DC Nyeri, 26 April 1968.
[111] KNA VP/1/98, DO Kieni East to DC Nyeri, 18 April 1968, 1 & 23 April 1968.
[112] KNA VP/1/98, DO Mathira to DC Nyeri, 16 April 1968, 1.

aloof and contributed in opposing what was being done by the older groups, and anything done is mostly referred by them [the educated] as "out of date."[113] In all these debates, the divisions of the 1950s could be seen. Dropping the carefully crafted language of his peers when discussing political and social cleavages, the district officer from North Tetu was explicit in his argument:

To my analysis, the whole situation is pertinent to the activities of the past (struggle for Uhuru) in that the former detainees through that they would take key positions in the running of the country, regardless of their background or capability. They still although to a lesser extent, discriminate against the so called loyalists i.e. certain government servants e.g. chiefs, subchiefs etc. To go with this is the discrimination against home-guards.[114]

The underlying problems of disparities of wealth and unequal access to capital were in large part products of the Emergency. The district officer in North Tetu recommended that 'the have nots should be made to realize the need to help themselves by hard work and by forming themselves into groups so as to purchase shambas.'[115] Poverty was still condemned in Kikuyu political thought as an unvirtuous derivative of idleness.

Keeping the Flag

As the proposed date, May 1970, for the next general election approached, the political temperature rose once again. Kenyatta remained concerned that support from his own Kikuyu powerbase might drift again towards the KPU because of the latter's pro-Mau Mau stance. The association of the KPU, AIPC, and other opposition groups with Mau Mau had fixed the rebellion and its legacy as a central part of the discourse of Kikuyu opposition to Kenyatta.[116] Kenyatta, therefore, for the first time decided to embrace the legacy of the insurgency and set aside briefly the war's contradictions and potential for division within Central Kenya. Controversial oathing ceremonies were held at Kenyatta's home at Gatundu and across the Mount Kenya region since May, as the President attempted to meet the challenge of Kaggia by consolidating support for his leadership among Kikuyu. These ceremonies deliberately echoed those of the Mau Mau insurgents during the 1950s and were intended to

---

[113] KNA VP/1/98, DO Kieni West to DC Nyeri, 23 April 1968.
[114] KNA VP/1/98, DO North Tetu, 'Power Struggle,' 16 May 1968, 1.
[115] KNA VP/1/98, DO North Tetu, 'Power Struggle,' 16 May 1968, 2.
[116] Clough, 'Contest for Memory,' 257–8.

appropriate the legacy of the rebellion for Kenyatta. The intention of the oathing ceremonies was twofold. First, they were to dispute the Kikuyu opposition's ownership of the mantle of Mau Mau's descendents. Second, they were to argue that as the Kikuyu had shed most blood in the fight for liberation during the Mau Mau rebellion, Luo communities in Nyanza had no claim to political power. The oaths taken by thousands of Kikuyu included the promise that the Kenyan flag would stay 'in the House of Mumbi,' a reference to the mythical mother of all Kikuyu.[117] Although the opposition posed an insufficient threat to topple the president, the KPU did carry sufficient support, particularly in the Nyanza Province in the west of the country, to challenge his prestige and status as the undisputed Father of the Nation. Moreover, Kaggia still retained enough supporters in Central Kenya to question Kenyatta's claim.

The political scene in Kenya was transformed by the events of the middle months of 1969. On 5 July, the Luo politician Tom Mboya was murdered on a Nairobi street. Mboya was the most significant national political figure besides Kenyatta and was widely assumed to be the heir apparent. His assassination is generally interpreted as having been carried out with the knowledge of Kenyatta, who believed Mboya to be too ambitious, and with the support of Kenyatta's closest Kikuyu advisors, who were concerned about the succession politics as the president's health began to decline. Although Mboya had been a political opponent of the KPU's Odinga for over a decade, his death was interpreted in Nyanza as a Kikuyu-led attack on Luo political figures.[118] Among both the Kikuyu and Luo communities, an extraordinary growth in politicised ethnicity emerged at this time. As the KPU became increasingly associated with the Luo peoples of Nyanza, Kaggia was forced to abandon the party in August 1969. Although the internal debates within Kikuyu society remained preoccupied with the winners and losers of the Mau Mau war, the political value of such arguments now had to be weighed against the new demand made by Kenyatta's government for ethnic unity. The construction of Kenya's new political landscape was completed with the banning of the KPU on 30 October. This followed riots during Kenyatta's visit to Kisumu, the main town in Nyanza, during which his security personnel killed 10 protestors.[119]

---

[117] For a discussion of the various uses of Mau Mau in post-colonial Kenyan politics, see Atieno Odhiambo, '*Matunda ya Uhuru*.'
[118] Hyden and Leys, 'Single-Party Systems,' 394; Ochieng, 'Structural & Political,' 101–2.
[119] Hyden and Leys, 'Single-Party Systems,' 394–5.

Following the banning of the KPU, Kenya became a de facto one-party state. Authoritarian restrictions on opposition politics prevented public and organised expressions of discontent. Instead, dissidents resorted to the well-rehearsed tactics of subterfuge and indirect attacks on government servants to exhibit their frustrations.[120] Moreover, the ostensible ruling party and potential channel of discontent was acknowledged to be moribund, even by its national executive officer.[121] However, elections were still held within KANU, and significant changes in ministerial and parliamentary personnel did take place. It was in this political climate that J.M. Kariuki emerged. During the 1974 election campaign for his Nyandarua North parliamentary seat in the Rift Valley Province, the former junior minister, J.M. Kariuki, asked, 'Now that we have been 10 years independent can we say that the wish or expectations of the majority of the Kenyans have been fulfilled?'[122] Kariuki's response was unequivocal. He asserted that the meaning of independence ought to have been 'justice among all our people.' Yet, he observed that 'it is no justice if some of our children cannot afford education; live in inhuman condition; die before getting to health centres; die of hunger or malnutrition. It is no justice to spread education, health, agricultural, business and other opportunities in certain areas only.'[123] Kariuki reserved particular criticism for post-colonial land policy, which maintained the principles of private tenure and the vast tracts of land for commercial farming that had sustained colonial Kenya's settler economy. 'Such ownership was socially and morally unjust and unacceptable,' Kariuki argued concerning colonial land policy. 'It was wrong then. It is socially unacceptable and unjust today. It is wrong now. I believe firmly that substituting Kamau for Smith; Odongo for Jones and Kiplangat for Keith does not solve what the gallant fighters for our *Uhuru* considered an imposed and undesirable social injustice.'[124] Kariuki was not, though, simply a dissident MP in pursuit of a sound bite during an election campaign.

Kariuki represented the latest and most significant threat to Kenyatta's position as president. Equally important, Kariuki emerged as the foremost challenger to Kenyatta for the affection and loyalty of Kikuyu voters from the country's Central Highlands and Nairobi. Kariuki was the author of

---

[120] See correspondence from 1970 relating to agitation to have Chiefs Hezron Mwai & Gitahi Wachira removed from office in KNA VP/1/126 & KNA VP/1/129.
[121] Bienen, *Kenya*, 59.
[122] Josiah Mwangi Kariuki, *J. M. Kariuki Speaks His Mind* (1974), 11.
[123] Ibid., 3
[124] Ibid., 11.

the best-known memoir of life behind the wire during the British counterinsurgency campaign against the Mau Mau rebels.[125] Yet, after the
war, Kariuki had also preached on the need for reconciliation after independence between loyalists and Mau Mau and across the new nation's
various social, ethnic, and racial cleavages. His nationalist pedigree was
unimpeachable. Despite his wealth, his business interests and race horses,
Kariuki was a champion of the poor and landless, famous for his contributions to fundraising campaigns for the construction of schools and
other public services. But Kariuki was no radical. Indeed, it was his con-
servatism that presented the greatest threat to Kenyatta's position and
explains his appeal to Kikuyu voters. He, too, would argue land was to be
earned through labour. Where he differed from Kenyatta was in his insistence that in fighting the colonial regime, Mau Mau supporters had done
just that – those detained deserved to be given land by the post-colonial
state. Kariuki furthermore levelled at Kenyatta the same accusation that
Kikuyu politicians had made of the colonial government from the 1930s
on: Kikuyu were being denied the opportunity to earn land by the unjust
protection by the state of large-scale commercial farmers over the interests
of peasant smallholders. Kariuki had become a vehicle for the aspirations
of a section of the population disillusioned with decolonisation.

Kariuki could not be defeated easily by Kenyatta. Like the president,
Kariuki had earned his right to political authority through his labour,
as demonstrated by his tangible wealth and his imprisonment during
the 1950s for his opposition to the colonial regime. Unlike Kaggia and
other relatively poor Kikuyu leftist politicians in the 1960s, Kariuki could
not be called to heel by Kenyatta on the basis of the president's greater
social status and thus political authority.[126] An alternative method had
to be deployed to silence Kariuki. Five months after the elections of
October 1974, his corpse was found by school children close to Ngong
town. After having been abducted from the Hilton hotel in downtown
Nairobi, Kariuki had been tortured and shot, and his body was left for
the hyenas. There is little doubt that Kariuki was killed because of the
threat he posed to the position of Kenyatta and to the numerous members
of the president's inner circle jostling for the succession after the ailing
premier's death. Kariuki's assassination or that of other leading political
figures could be represented as the moment at which the reality of post-
colonial political life crushed the expectations of independence. More

[125] Kariuki, *Mau Mau Detainee.*
[126] Lonsdale, 'Jomo Kenyatta,' 49.

tellingly, Kariuki's death should be understood as just the latest episode in a debate within Kikuyu society over labour, wealth, authority, and political virtue.

Class and Ethnicity

With the accession to the presidency of Daniel arap Moi after the death of Kenyatta in 1978, the value of public dispute among Kikuyu declined. Determined to construct his own neo-patrimonial networks and to solidify his core constituency of Kalenjin support, Moi systemically set about the political marginalisation of the Kikuyu elite. Opposition to Moi demanded ethnic unity of the sort Kenyatta attempted to create in 1969. Kikuyu grassroots groups and leaders became the bedrock of the opposition to Moi, which encompassed the full political spectrum from left-wing academics to conservative businessmen and former loyalists.[127]

Nevertheless, the manner of Mau Mau's defeat has had, up to the present, profound effects on the politics of Kenya at every level, from individual households to the State House. The language of decolonisation continues to echo through Kenyan politics and is used to hold political leaders to account for their continuing failure to meet the expectations of the *Uhuru* generation. The public grievances of Mau Mau followers were not addressed by Kenyatta's regime, in particular, those related to land. The methods and rhetoric of protest had obvious roots in the rebellion. The opponents of such groups were also clearly identifiable from the 1950s: loyalists within the Provincial Administration. Nyeri's district commissioner in 1973, Nahashon Muse Ngugi, had been employed by the government in 1956 to supervise land consolidation.[128] The lingering weight of the 1950s suffocated political debate in Nyeri. Through men such as Ngugi, Kenyatta constructed a bureaucratic–authoritarian state based on the ultimate expression of loyalism, the Provincial Administration. As a result, Mau Mau remained in the foreground of political debate for both opponents of the government and its local agents.

The motivations for political activity remained as they had been in 1952, 'to recover stolen lands and to become an adult.' The land in 1975 had been stolen not by European farmers, but by loyalist farmers in the

---

[127] Jennifer Widner, *The Rise of a Party-State in Kenya: From 'Harambee' to 'Nyayo!'* (Berkeley, 1993).

[128] KNA VP/1/101, Annual Confidential Report for 1972: Nahashon Muse Ngugi, 4 January 1973.

late 1950s and by Kenya's new rulers during the parcelling out of the land owned by the departing white farmers. Yet, wealth, most easily obtained through agriculture, remained the precondition for social and political influence. Patrons such as Kenyatta based their right to political domination on their wealth and demanded that the poor both obey and labour if they desired upwards social mobility. Yet, those demands were not matched by the provision of opportunity or recognition of the grievances of the poor. The wealth acquisition of the poor was hampered because of the structural impediments placed in their path by the elite and the unavailability of sufficient land. It is here where the categories of analysis such as class and ethnicity intersect and require much greater and more sophisticated consideration than has hitherto been the case for the post-colonial period. The dichotomies of landed/landless, wealthy/poor, and labourer/idle dictated political debate in post-colonial Central Kenya, in large part, because of the outcome of the civil war of the 1950s.

Conclusion

Loyalism, Decolonisation, and Civil War

Ambiguity and Counterinsurgency

It is impossible to accurately narrate or explain events in Kenya during the 1950s without foregrounding loyalists. Furthermore, the formation of the post-colonial state and local and national politics after 1963 cannot be understood unless the bloody conflict between Mau Mau and loyalists is incorporated into that analysis. Although the war may have emerged out of well-founded grievances against the colonial government, it swiftly changed in form from anti-colonial protest to civil war among the peoples of the Mount Kenya region. The example of Kenya's loyalists demonstrates that violence during irregular civil wars is best conceptualised as the outcome of an alliance between local and supra-local actors. Both groups often have very different sets of motivations for their participation in a counterinsurgency conflict.[1] In other words, the violence of the counterinsurgency effort in Kenya was the product of an alliance of the colonial state, which provided arms and protection, and loyalists, who provided manpower and information.

To date, scholarly explanations for loyalism have either dealt in social categories, based on age and status, or the greed of individuals. The former approach is too broad and fails to capture accurately the diversity of individual experiences of the war. The latter explanation is ahistorical, acultural, and unquantifiable. Certainly, personal economic gain motivated some loyalists, but Kikuyu opposed Mau Mau for many other reasons. These included experience of insurgent violence, the desire for revenge,

---

[1] Kalyvas, *Logic of Violence.*

past connections to the colonial regime, family or clan ties, notions of power and authority, and, perhaps most important, simply a desire to survive the war. What tied these diverse motivations together was a fear or experience of Mau Mau's violence. As we saw in earlier chapters, the cycles of violence that took hold of the Central Highlands created entirely new historical trajectories that had little to do with the grievances that cultivated conditions in which the Mau Mau insurgency took hold.

The motivations of all perpetrators of the violence in Kenya's civil war need to be included in studies of the conflict if the causes of the bloodshed are to be properly understood. The reasons for loyalist participation in the conflict had little to do with the concerns of either European adminis-trators or the white farmers. Instead, loyalist involvement in the conflict was triggered by the experience of the violence of the insurgency. It is not simply that histories of the Mau Mau war are incomplete by excluding loyalists, but that they are profoundly flawed. Any account of the con-flict that ignores entirely the most common targets of the insurgents and the perpetrators of a great proportion of the counterinsurgent violence cannot claim to be explaining the Mau Mau war in any meaningful way.

To explain loyalism, it is necessary to place ambiguity at the centre of our analysis. The story of the civil war is not of two distinct, preexisting camps going into battle. Instead, the critical research question demand-ing explanation is why Kikuyu society became split in two during the war. The answer to that question was located in earlier chapters within the violence and its relationship to allegiances, information, and control, which gave the civil war its structure. The anger and resentment bred as a consequence of the exposure of individuals to violence forced Kikuyu to adopt essentialised identities as they sought protection or revenge. For most, to be a supporter of loyalism or the insurgency initially denoted complex micro-histories of violence during the first stages of the conflict. Steadily, those categories, as we have seen in the later chapters of this book, assumed more permanent political, economic, and social mean-ings. Kenyan and foreign historians alike have uncritically projected that post-war loyalist hegemony backwards on to pre-conflict Kikuyu society, assuming the two factions of the war to reflect pre-conflict divisions. For this reason, the initial ambiguity of the conflict has been lost in the great majority of historical accounts of the Mau Mau war.

Despite the recent reawakening of the memory of the Mau Mau insur-gency within the public history of the Kenyan nation-state discussed in the Preface, the history of loyalism is as silent as ever in those debates. So, too, is ambiguity, buried along with loyalism beneath Mau Mau's memorialisation as a war of liberation. The Church of St James and All Martyrs in Murang'a town is, however, one of the few places where 'the painful past can easily live on, unwanted, in spite of present needs.'[2] The church, the cathedral for the Anglican diocese of Mount Kenya Central, is one of a precious few public monuments to the Kikuyu civil war of the 1950s, albeit an uncomfortable one. The cathedral was built between 1955 and 1958, in the words of Bishop Leonard Beecher of the Anglican Church of Kenya, 'in memory of all those of all races who have lost their lives in the course of duty as loyal citizens, whether in the fighting services or in civilian occupations.'[3] Although the funds for construction were donated through private subscriptions, the Provincial Administration was a keen supporter of the project. Julian Hill, a district officer working in Murang'a during the war, was the architect, and construction was supervised by P. J. Corr, an assistant district officer.[4] The first bishop to take up residence at the cathedral, Obadiah Kariuki, later described the construction work as being carried out in a spirit 'of forced *harambee*.'[5] In practice, this meant that the labour force was made up of Mau Mau detainees. The wrought iron gates, depicting 'a rifle to symbolise the Security forces, a spear to symbolise the Kikuyu Guard, and a Cross to symbolise the cause of decency for which they fought,' were forged in the prison workshop at Kamiti.[6] The cathedral is very much reflective of its time.

These origins are far from obvious inside the church building. A planned book of remembrance containing the name of every person killed by Mau Mau was not realised.[7] Only one brass plaque, close to the rear entrance, belies the original purpose of the church's construction. Put up on the occasion of a clergyman's retirement in 1986, the plaque is a memorial to 47 local Christian victims of Mau Mau. The plaque's legend

---

[2] Jennifer Cole, *Forget Colonialism? Sacrifice and the Art of Memory of Madagascar* (Berkeley, 2001), 26.

[3] Quoted in KNA MSS/124/26, Appeal Committee, the Fort Hall Memorial Church Fund, 'The Foundations Have Been Laid: Help Us to Complete the Building,' 1955.

[4] KNA MSS/124/7, Treasurer, Fort Hall Memorial Church, 'The Memorial Church at Fort Hall,' March 1960, 2–3.

[5] Kariuki, *Bishop Facing*, 71. *Harambee*, meaning 'pull together,' is a method of public fundraising popularised by Kenyatta. The term subsequently became his political slogan.

[6] KNA MSS/124/7, Treasurer, Fort Hall Memorial Church, 'The Memorial Church at Fort Hall,' March 1960, 3.

[7] KNA DC/MRU/2/1/2, PC Central to PCs Southern & Rift Valley, Officer-in-Charge Nairobi EPD, DCs Central, Command Headquarters, Senior Royal Air Force Officer, Commissioner of Police & Commissioner of Prisons, 15 October 1957.

describes those memorialised on it as having been 'murdered during the national liberation in Kenya.' This contradictory depiction of Mau Mau – simultaneously murderers and national liberators – suggests that private memories of the war are (or at least were) far more contradictory and painful than the public memory of a great nationalist struggle suggest.

When discussing their experiences of the 1950s, witnesses to the trauma can speak with any number of identities. The first resident of the Bishopric at Murang'a, Obadiah Kariuki, writes for many:

> When people started actively fighting for their rights in the early fifties, my sympathies were with them. I did not see anything wrong with fighting for one's own freedom in one's own country. What most of us in the church at that time objected to was the violence, coercion and finally forced oathing to make people join the Mau Mau movement. We objected to the brutal killings of those who chose to differ in the political outlook. But such opposition did not blind us to the fact that we had been subjected to a reign of terror during colonial times and we had all suffered together, Christian or non-Christian.[8]

For Kariuki, the apparent contradiction in the words and sentiments of the plaque in what became his cathedral describing Mau Mau's struggle as one of 'national liberation' while memorialising its murdered victims was easily resolved: 'Christians, especially those who faced death rather than take the oath, contributed to the peace to this country: their blood nourished the tree of freedom as much as any other.'[9] It was not just Kenyatta who believed all Kenyans fought for freedom.

The ambiguity memorialised in the cathedral in Murang'a was, in the minds of most, destroyed by the conflict. Anger and resentment drove the population of Central Kenya apart. Kenya is an excellent example of the particularly pernicious, invasive, and divisive nature of counter-insurgency campaigns. Despite the term being widely used in a variety of geographical and historical settings, there have been noticeably few attempts to consider exactly what counterinsurgency actually is beyond the most literal definition of an armed response to insurgency. This portrayal of counterinsurgency in purely reactionary terms is misleading. So, too, is any use of the term intended to denote a form of clean, surgical warfare. To claim, as the editors of one journal have, that we can think about a science of counterinsurgency is fanciful.[10] Counterinsurgency

---

[8] Kariuki, *Bishop Facing*, 71. 77–8.

[9] Ibid., 78–9.

[10] 'Preface: Towards a Science of Counterinsurgency,' *Contemporary Security Policy* 28 (2007).

campaigns are necessitated by the fact that the state does not possess enough information to identify every insurgent. States must instead target sanctions at groups that they believe either support the insurgents or that the insurgents belong to. Conversely, states target rewards at the groups they think do not support the insurgents. Through this programme of sanctions and rewards, counterinsurgency campaigns force populations into polarisation by either escaping punishment by the state or seeking the protection offered by the insurgents. Thus, counterinsurgency campaigns shape society to adhere to the imagination of their architects and exacerbate the already pronounced ability of violence to redraw social and political boundaries during times of conflict.[11]

In seeking to isolate insurgents from host communities, counterinsurgency is 'a particular form of warfare aimed at civilians,' intended to alter relations between the state and society and within communities. Ultimately, counterinsurgency 'domesticates the use of violence.'[12] Counterinsurgency campaigns are not solely waged on the battlefield, if such a thing could be said to have existed in Kenya or in similar wars. Instead, these conflicts are fought in fields, polling stations, markets and, most significantly, homes as populations are coerced into surrendering support for insurgents. Veena Das has written about how in India and Pakistan 'the violence of the Partition was folded into everyday relations.'[13] The same was true in Kenya during the Mau Mau war.

This book begins with an account of how one family, that of Matari Muthamia and her brother-in-law Mugwongo Ruria, were torn apart by the violence of the 1950s. Whereas Matari and Mugwongo were otherwise anonymous figures, the Koinanges of Kiambu were perhaps the single most prominent family in colonial Kenya. The social and political elevation of the Koinange family did not, though, save it from the ravages of the civil war – instead, it was ripped apart by the conflict. The patriarch, ex-Senior Chief, Koinange wa Mbiyu, and two of his sons, Peter Mbiyu and John Westley Mbiyu, were at the forefront of the establishment of the Kenya African Union in the late 1940s. Peter Mbiyu was the leading light of the independent schools movement. John Westley Mbiyu, with the assistance of another brother, Frederick Mbiyu, was the

---

[11] Sen, *Identity and Violence*.
[12] June Nash, *Practicing Ethnography in a Globalizing World* (Lanham MD, 2007), 200–1.
[13] Veena Das, 'The Act of Witnessing: Violence, Poisonous Knowledge, and Subjectivity,' in *Violence and Subjectivity*, eds. Veena Das, Arthur Kleinman, and Pamela Reynolds (Berkeley, 2000), 220.

driving force behind the first wave of oathing in Kiambu in the early
1950s.[14] Although Peter escaped arrest by virtue of being in Britain in
October 1952, John Westley and Frederick Mbiyu were among a dozen
members of the Koinange family, including the ex-Senior Chief, rounded
up in the opening stages of the State of Emergency. To this can be added
Kenyatta, who had married into the family following his return to Kenya
in 1947, and another in-law, Obadiah Kariuki.

Generally considered by colonial officials to belong to the hardcore
faction of Mau Mau's leadership, family members served out their time
in detention in some of the very harshest camps. Conditions took a severe
toll. The chief's daughter, Lilian Wairimu, died in detention in 1955,[15]
and the old man himself wilted while detained and was released only
shortly before he died in July 1960.[16] Although the Koinanges are rightly
remembered among Kenya's nationalist heroes, not all members of the
large family, the ex-Chief having six wives, were committed to Mau Mau.
Another son, Gathiomi, died in a firearms incident at the family house in
Nairobi in 1950. The exact circumstances of his death are unclear. Some
sources suggest that Gathiomi was shot accidentally by a mishandled gun,
whereas other accounts point to his murder as punishment for his refusal
to take an oath or for acting as an informer to the colonial government.[17]
Moreover, Charles Karuga, one of the ex-Chief's sons by his first wife,
was one of Kiambu's foremost loyalists. Having operated a wood mill
with his father prior to the Emergency, Charles Karuga first joined the
government as a headman in the Kiambaa location of Kiambu. Although
he remained loyal throughout the war, Charles Karuga was also thought
by the local district officer in 1955 to be one of the 'ardent nationalists'
among the ranks of loyalists.[18]

Although other members went on to become influential figures within
the public and private sectors after 1963, Charles Karuga and Peter Mbiyu
were the most prominent members of the family following their father's
death and independence. Peter Mbiyu served as minister and advisor to his
long-time close friend and brother-in-law, Kenyatta, until the president's
death in 1978. Peter Mbiyu himself died three years later. Charles Karuga
worked as Provincial Commissioner in Central and Eastern Provinces

[14] Anderson, *Histories*, 30–1.
[15] Koinange, *Koinange*, 95–6.
[16] Ibid., 107–15.
[17] Lonsdale, 'Wealth, Poverty and Civic Virtue,' 435–6.
[18] Sorrenson, *Land Reform*, fn.1, 202.

before entering semi-retirement in 1980, after which he acted as chairman of the Kenya Tea Development Board. It was the consequences of
Charles Karuga's colonial-era employment, however, that were the source
of consternation within the Koinange family.

In the 1980s, a bitter and long-running dispute between Charles
Karuga and 14 of his immediate family members reached the courts and
thus the newspapers. The case centred on the estate of the late ex-Chief
and competing claims to it made by various members of the family. The
land in question totalled approximately 610 acres. Between 1957 and
1958, those land holdings were, as elsewhere in Central Province, consolidated and title deeds issued. At the time consolidation took place,
the ex-Chief and most of his adult family members were in detention or
under some form of restriction. The most notable exception was Charles
Karuga, at that time chief in Kiambaa. Charles Karuga was one of consolidation's strongest proponents, urging the colonial government in 1955
to accelerate the process so that it would be completed while the conditions of the Emergency prevailed.[19] Practicing what he preached, Charles
Karuga was particularly keen to see the consolidation of his family's
holdings completed.

Claiming to be acting under written instructions from his father in
detention, Charles Karuga oversaw the consolidation of the family plots
and the reissuing of title deeds in a fashion that disproportionately
benefited himself, his absent brother Peter Mbiyu, and their mother,
Mariamu Wambui. The other five wives and their children found their
plots to be considerably smaller. With the rest of the family incapacitated
in one way or another by the Emergency and Charles Karuga a powerful
ally of the government, there was little opportunity for an airing of dissent during the 1950s. Even after the ex-Chief was released in 1959, he
was frail and in no condition to adjudicate between the various branches
of his household. In any case, he returned from to detention to stay with
Charles Karuga.

The ex-Chief left no will, in accordance with Kikuyu custom. One of
his contemporaries, Chief Dedan Kimani Mugo, was among an entourage
of family members who visited Koinange in detention to discuss drawing
up a will. 'Koinange never agreed to make a will during the visit,' Mugo
later stated in court. 'He said that according to Kikuyu custom *mundu
ndegoyaga ari muoyo* (a man never makes a will while he is still alive).'
During his testimony in 1985, Mugo told the judge that Koinange had

[19] Ibid., 115 & 153.

told him that 'he was in detention, some of his wives were in detention and some of his sons were also in detention. According to Kikuyu customs, a man cannot distribute his property while his family is scattered.' Koinange died no doubt thinking that the estate would be divided equally between each of the six wives as was customary. However, this reallocation did not occur following the old man's death. 'At the death of our father,' James Njoroge Koinange later recalled, 'we found that 300 acres had been left in the homestead of the first wife, Mrs Miriam Wambui, during land demarcation. I was then in detention in Lamu.'[20]

The remainder of the family was understandably unhappy with Charles Karuga's handling of their father's affairs. However, Peter Mbiyu assumed the position as head of the family after his father's death. With Peter Mbiyu being both highly regarded by his family members and the single most prominent public figure from the Koinanges, there was unwillingness among the family to seek public resolution of the dispute. 'We had a lot of respect for him as a politician and as a Minister and we did not embarrass him,' Leonard Karuga said of Peter Mbiyu. 'What would people say of a man who was not able to solve his family's problem?'[21] The family instead pursued a number of private channels in an effort to find redress for the loss of their rightful inheritance. From 1962 on, various elders from Kiambu and elsewhere in Central Province, including ex-Senior Chiefs Njiri and Njonjo, attempted arbitration. With both sides lacking documentation and supported by contradictory witnesses, all such efforts were to no avail.[22] Whether overburdened by his ministerial commitments or unwilling to reverse a distribution of land that had benefited him and his mother as well as Charles Karuga, Peter Mbiyu showed no great enthusiasm for seeking a permanent settlement of the dispute. Peter Mbiyu eventually withdrew from the negotiations entirely.[23] Once he died in 1981, however, the dispute escalated. Family members no longer felt compelled to keep their dispute private in the same way as they had while their eldest brother was alive. In February 1982,

---

[20] Andrew Kuria, 'Row Erupts Over Letter as Koinange Case Continues,' *Daily Nation*, 19 September 1985.

[21] Andrew Kuria, 'Koinange Son Tells of Being at Mercy of Ex-PC,' *Daily Nation*, 1 October 1985.

[22] Njoroge wa Karuri, 'Koinange Land Case Adjourned,' *Daily Nation*, 10 March 1982; Andrew Kuria, 'Our Husband Didn't Leave a Will, Say Koinange Widows,' *Daily Nation*, 18 September 1985.

[23] Andrew Kuria, 'Witness Relates Rejection of Ex-Minister's Letter,' *Daily Nation*, 20 September 1985.

14 members of the Koinange family sued Charles Karuga in the local courts in Kiambu.[24] With both sides contesting the outcome of the proceedings at every stage, the case moved up through the courts during 1982 and 1984.

Proceedings increasingly centred on the family's experience of the war of the 1950s. In particular, attention was given to the role of Charles Karuga in the consolidation effort in Kiambu and the powers he exercised as the chief of the Kiambaa location that incorporated the Koinange family land. Stephen Kimunio Ng'ang'a, a member of the Kiambu Land Consolidation Board between 1957 and 1958, was a key witness during proceedings at the High Court in Nairobi in 1985. Ng'ang'a testified that Charles Karuga had unduly exploited his position of influence during consolidation to manipulate the processing of the family's holdings. Specifically, Ng'ang'a claimed Charles Karuga assumed responsibility for representing the entire Koinange family during land consolidation to the extent that he drew up a list detailing which members of his family were entitled to which plots. This list, Ng'ang'a and the rest of the Koinange family alleged, included an unfairly large proportion of their father's land for Charles Karuga and Peter Mbiyu.[25] Justice Amin of the High Court agreed with the family members. In May 1986, the dispute was brought to a close by the judge's ruling that the family property should be redistributed equally among each of the deceased ex-Chief's six wives and their children. The judge also awarded five of the wives, which did not include Charles Karuga's mother, 40,000 shillings compensation.[26]

Of all the elements of counterinsurgency that drive families such as the Koinanges apart during such conflict, the most significant is the intensive involvement of non-state actors. Of these, militia groups are perhaps the most significant of all. By their very existence, militia groups such as the Home Guard reveal much about the nature of a counterinsurgency campaign. Kenya is a telling example of how insurgencies escalate into civil wars once civilians are armed by the state and incorporated into the counterinsurgency response. Recent literature on conflict in post-colonial Africa has overwhelmingly focused on the motivations of insurgents and

---

[24] Mutegi Njau, 'Koinange Family in Land Feud,' *Daily Nation*, 23 February 1982, 1.

[25] Andrew Kuria, 'Land Allocation Unfair, Court Told,' *Daily Nation*, 24 September 1985.

[26] High Court, Nairobi, Civil Suit 66 of 1984, Koinange v Koinange, 23 May 1986 (judgement available online at *Kenya Law Reports* website (www.kenyalaw.org/CaseSearch/case_download.php?go=4555175788738126548156&link=- – accessed 30 January 2008).

the armed responses of states to that threat.[27] Militia members such as Home Guards are commonly assumed to be motivated by either the same factors as those that are driving the actions of the state or simply self-interest. As non-state participants in a counterinsurgency campaign, therefore, loyalists are examples of individuals not commonly captured by such studies of irregular civil wars and political violence. The case of Kenya's loyalists suggests that the use of militias in counterinsurgency campaigns is likely to have profound effects on the nature and extent of violence.

The presence of groups such as the Home Guard is indicative of the weakness of regular armed forces and the latter's ability to curb rebel activity. Moreover, militias are used by states conducting counterinsurgency campaigns when internal or external constraints prevent the more extensive use of regular forces.[28] Operating without institutional oversight and firm control from their state sponsors, militias are prone to be 'perverse and destructive.'[29] As Tilly writes:

Pirates, privateers, paramilitaries, bandits, mercenaries, mafiosi, militias, posses, guerrilla forces, vigilante groups, company police, and bodyguards all operate in a middle ground between (on one side) the full authorisation of a national army and (on the other) the private employment of violence by parents, lovers, or feuding clans.[30]

The reliance on militias such as the Home Guard thus facilitates the intensification of irregular civil war by accelerating the privatisation of violence. Put another way, it is through militias recruited from among local populations that states facilitate the transformation of a counterinsurgency campaign into a civil war.

Counterinsurgency as Decolonisation and State-Building

The unwillingness to confront the histories of loyalism has profound implications for efforts to understand the trajectory of the post-colonial state in Kenya. Although the rebellion's vanquishers have largely escaped attention from scholars, without incorporation of them into histories of

[27] See, for example, Christopher Clapham, ed., *African Guerrillas* (Oxford, 1998); Anthony Clayton, *Frontiersmen: Warfare in Africa Since 1950* (London, 1999); George Kieh and Rousseau Mukenege, eds., *Zones of Conflict in Africa: Theories and Cases* (Westport CT, 2002); Weinstein, *Inside Rebellion.*
[28] Batalas, 'Send a Thief.'
[29] Keen, *Conflict and Collusion,* 2.
[30] Charles Tilly, *The Politics of Collective Violence* (Cambridge, 2003), 19.

decolonisation post-colonial political atrophy becomes extremely difficult to understand. Kenya since 1963 has been a post-conflict as well as post-colonial society, at least in its Central Highlands. Civil war and counter-insurgency became exercises in state-building, as the importance of loyalists to the predominant institutions of the late-colonial and post-colonial states makes clear. This is neither surprising nor exceptional. Most modern states, including Britain and the United States, have their origins in conflict and violence.[31] Loyalists did not just provide post-colonial Kenyan state institutions with their personnel, but also the state's predominant 'ideology of order.' Atieno Odhiambo uses that term to show how the post-colonial Kenyan state has attempted to silence dissent from among its citizens and instead prioritise the continuing conduct of capitalist accumulation and patrimonialism.[32] During the colonial conquest, indigenous allies allowed, as we saw briefly in Chapter 1, for the appropriation of precolonial notions of power and authority by the incoming colonial state. Similarly, loyalists provided the ideological bridge between the colonial and post-colonial periods.

The loyalist retention of power preserved the householder ethic within Kikuyu politics and the attendant suspicion of youthful indiscipline that remains visible up to the present. Using the memory of the violence of the Mau Mau war, Kikuyu elders in the 1990s successfully persuaded the youth from taking up arms against the Moi regime.[33] Unsurprisingly, since Moi's retirement and replacement by Mwai Kibaki, who heralds from Nyeri, the ideology of order has remained a critical part of government discourse. Despite leaving Moi's government prior to the 1992 elections and spending the next decade as one of the figureheads of the democratisation movement, Kibaki was closely connected to the regimes of his two predecessors in State House. Kibaki was no loyalist, having spent most of the war as a student at Makerere. Nevertheless, his political ideology contains many of the elements of the same Kikuyu intellectual tradition to which loyalism belongs.

On 1 June 2003, Kibaki made his first Madaraka Day national address as president at the annual national celebrations held to celebrate the anniversary of the attainment of self-rule prior to independence. In the

---

[31] Christopher Cramer, *Civil War Is Not a Stupid Thing: Accounting for Violence in Developing Countries* (London, 2006), 37–39.

[32] Atieno Odhiambo, 'Ideology of Order.'

[33] Mwangi Kimenyi and Njuguna Ndung'u, 'Sporadic Ethnic Violence: Why Has Kenya Not Experienced a Full-Blown Civil War,' in *Understanding Civil War: Evidence and Analysis*, eds. Paul Collier and Nicholas Sambanis (2006), 153.

wake of the dramatic toppling of the KANU regime at the polls the previous December, Kibaki announced his speech as 'a message for the future,' but those listening could not help but hear deafening echoes of the past. Kibaki condemned men who had lost control of their households through drinking. Not only had they left their wives to assume responsibility for the family, but they themselves were transgressing the new moral economy that Kibaki thought he had established by providing free primary education. The lazy drunks, in Kibaki's mind, were not reciprocating his beneficence with their virtuous labour. 'The era of free things is over,' the president warned Kenyans. 'We must work hard together,' Kibaki continued. 'Whoever does not want to work and wants free things must surely be preparing to leave this country.' Kenya was to become 'the working nation' and 'one that recognizes hard work. Hard work to repair our institutions, to revamp our economy, to mend our constitution, and fend for our families.' In the clearest continuity from the discourse of the elites of 50 years before, Kibaki asserted, 'Hard work will guarantee prosperity for future generations.'[34] Such sentiments did not remain merely rhetorical during Kibaki's presidency.

The disdain for the so-called 'mob' that was a central characteristic of the government's response to the protests that followed the 2007 election was one manifestation of the elitist ideology of order. But that was directed against supposed enemies of Kikuyu, namely the Luo, Kalenjin, and Mjikenda. More substantive evidence of the lingering significance of the ideology of order and its use to resolve disputes within Kikuyu society in favour of the elite can be found in the government's crackdown against the Mungiki gang earlier that same year. Mungiki, meaning 'multitude' in Kikuyu, had its origins in a Kikuyu cultural revival movement in the 1980s before changing into a criminal gang and private army during the 1990s.[35] Claiming direct descent from Mau Mau, Mungiki mobilised young unemployed Kikuyu men from the slums of Nairobi and its peri-urban fringe who felt alienated from their elders and political leaders.

Taking on the enforcement of justice and the provision of services, as well as criminal protection rackets and the extortion of taxation from almost every form of commercial transaction, Mungiki became a powerful force in slum neighbourhoods long since abandoned by the state.[36]

---

[34] N. Rugene & D. Mugonyi, 'Work Hard for Kenya,' *Daily Nation*, 2 June 2003.
[35] Anderson, 'Politics of Public Order'; Kagwanja, 'Mount Kenya or Mecca.'
[36] Musambayi Katumanga, 'A City Under Siege: Banditry and Modes of Accumulation in Nairobi, 1991–2004,' *Review of African Political Economy* 32 (2005).

However, once a dispute with drivers and owners of private passenger vehicles on routes controlled by Mungiki's racketeers turned particularly violent in March 2007, the state decided to act against the group. Led by former loyalist and then-minister for internal security, John Michuki, state security forces were accused of having killed up to 500 Mungiki suspects in the subsequent crackdown.[37] When, nearly 50 years after independence, a group claiming descent from Mau Mau engaged in violent struggle with security forces led by an individual first recruited into the government at the height of the counterinsurgency campaign, the importance for Kenya of a history of loyalism and of civil war is self-evident.

Local allies of colonial powers had a profound, although far from identical, effect on decolonisation and the nature of statecraft in a wide range of post-colonial settings. The transfer of power to northern elites contributed significantly to the emergence of civil war in Sudan.[38] Conversely, it was the post-independence loss of influence among Britain's allies in colonial Ceylon, the Tamils, that partly caused the ongoing Sri Lankan civil war.[39] On independence in 1974, African members of Mozambique's colonial forces fled across the border to Rhodesia. There, they were corralled by the Rhodesian security services and sent back across the border as the Mozambique National Resistance, better known as Renamo, and engaged the independent government in one of post-colonial Africa's longest civil wars.[40] In shaping the history of their respective post-colonial state, Kenya's loyalists are far from unique. Yet, despite this readily apparent historical significance, studies of collaboration during the decolonisation period generally and anti-colonial rebellions specifically are rare.

Only the *harkis* of Algeria, Muslim supporters of the French regime during the *Front de Libération Nationale*'s anti-colonial insurgency, have received sustained academic attention.[41] But the *harkis* could not but grasp the attention of scholars. Following Algerian independence in 1962, vast numbers of *harkis* fled to France, and many of those left behind were

---

[37] Cyrus Ombati, 'Police Accused of Executing Suspects,' *The Standard*, 6 November 2007.
[38] Douglas Johnson, *Root Causes of Sudan's Civil Wars* (Oxford, 2003).
[39] Arthur Jeyaratnam, *The Break-Up of Sri Lanka: The Sinhalese-Tamil Conflict* (London, 1988).
[40] Alex Vines, *Renamo: Terrorism in Mozambique* (Oxford, 1991).
[41] See, for example, and for most recent literature review and bibliography, Martin Evans, 'The *Harkis*: The Experience and Memory of France's Muslim Auxiliaries,' in *The Algerian War and the French Army, 1954–62: Experiences, Images, Testimonies*, eds. Martin Alexander, Martin Evans, and John F. Keiger (Basingstoke, 2002).

massacred. When added to the closely entwined histories of Algeria and France and the unique impact of the war in North Africa on metropolitan politics, the *harkis* left an indelible mark on accounts of the conflict.[42] In Britain, during the aftermath of its liberation wars, the imperative to critically examine the role of colonial allies was not so immediate. Only when we incorporate this much-maligned group into our histories of decolonisation can we begin to adequately understand that process and the violence of the end of an empire. But to do so necessitates the final abandonment of the nation as our unit of analysis during the study of decolonisation when viewed from former colonial territories. To overlook indigenous colonial allies during decolonisation, preferring instead to pre-serve with studies of nationalists, is to continue to impose an abstraction on historical subjects that fails to capture alternative imaginings of the future. Attempts have been made recently to critically reassess the position of resistance[43] and decolonisation within African historiography.[44] There is still much ground to be made up.

To pursue a retrospective search for a nation is to continue to impose an abstraction on historical subjects that fails to capture alternative ima-ginings of a future. Where in such approaches is the space for the study of anti- and non-nationalist? Are such actors to be forever ignored and treated with condescension because they were incredulous at the thought of the rapid collapse of empire? And if those individuals were indeed responsible for the collapse of the nationalist dream, for which they are so often blamed, surely this, too, deserves explanations rooted in the same detailed analyses of ideology, class, gender, and community with which we treat those to whom historians are broadly sympathetic. The quest for nationhood was not the only political debate in late colonial Africa or necessarily the most important. 'Politics in a colony,' Cooper writes, 'should not be reduced to anticolonial politics or to nationalism: the "imagined communities" Africans saw were both smaller and larger than the nation.'[45] Even if reframed in the language of nationalism, debates, and disputes that predated or emerged during the decolonisation era and had little or nothing to do with national liberation remained significant.

---

[42] Benjamin Stora, *Algeria, 1830–2000: A Short History*, Jane Marie Todd trans. (Ithaca NY, 2001), 127–8.

[43] Jon Abbink, Mirjam de Bruijn, & Klaas van Walraven, eds., *Rethinking Resistance: Revolt and Violence in African History* (Leiden, 2003).

[44] Frederick Cooper, *Decolonization and African Society: The Labor Question in French and British Africa* (Cambridge, 1996).

[45] Frederick Cooper, 'Conflict and Connection: Rethinking African History,' *American Historical Review* 99 (1994), 1519.

Turning the lens to those commonly ignored by studies of nationalism can be revelatory for those interested in understanding the trajectory of post-colonial states.

Violence and History

This book, to paraphrase Lonsdale, is a study of agency in the tightest of corners.[46] It examines how Kikuyu turned to loyalism in an effort to steer a course through the civil war of the 1950s. Perhaps the lingering inclination of historians generally, and Africanists in particular to attempt to uncover a usable past predisposes us to laud the heroic figures and actions we uncover in our research. In so doing, Kenya's loyalists and other similar groups tend to disappear through the cracks. Historians are noticeably less than eager to describe those in the past that in all likelihood most resemble us. Many of the subjects of this book were risk averse actors that attempted to muddle through great events with only an incomplete understanding of the tumult surrounding them and uncertain of the consequences of their actions. Kikuyu thus attempted to continue their political, economic, and social lives in a context in which agency was strictly regulated. Wrong decisions were liable to be penalised with the harshest of sanctions – death. As a consequence, the time horizons of the subjects of this book were dramatically foreshortened as they looked to simply survive. Some (of course) did a good deal better than mere survival as a result of their opposition to Mau Mau.

Violence was not simply a product of the war, but one of its catalysts. The threat and experience of violence determined allegiances during the conflict, informed a process of social and economic upheaval, and set the agenda for political debate in the Central Highlands for decades after the war's end. Violence was the very substance of war itself, determining the relations between its different actors. It is that transformative effect of violence that has been least understood by historians of the Mau Mau war. Civil war is not politics by other means. Allegiances during times of conflict cannot be assumed to be mere reflections of pre-war political allegiances or social stratification. For decades, the historiography of Mau Mau remained fixated on the question of causation. This was understandable, as the colonial myth of the conflict's origins rightly angered historians who could not but see the very obvious grievances that emerged

---

[46] John Lonsdale, 'Agency in Tight Corners: Narrative and Initiative in African History,' *Journal of African Cultural Studies* 13 (2000).

through Kenya's troubled colonial era. However, one myth was replaced by another. Figures such as Corfield argued that the Mau Mau war in essence had no historical causes besides the inevitable march of progress, which dragged behind it a Kikuyu people unable to cope with modernity. This rejection of history was replaced by another explanation for the conflict which overestimated the power of the past in determining allegiances during the conflict.

For some historians, it was thought enough to explain the historical foundation of the grievances that motivated Kikuyu militant political leaders and their followers up to the moment the war began.[47] Although such work was important, without any serious attempt being made to examine the path of the conflict itself, the deduction readers made was that the dynamics of the war were determined prior to its outbreak. Actors during the conflict, be they insurgents or supporters of the colonial government, were thus merely playing out roles defined by the course of history up to October 1952. From such a perspective, loyalists opposed the rebellion not because their father was murdered by Mau Mau, or because they were press-ganged into service by their chief, or because they believed the insurgents to have no hope of victory. Instead, their loyalism was to be explained by their prior political inclinations, attendance of a particular church, age, wealth, or some other category considered an unimpeachable determinant of action during the war. This book has instead argued that loyalism was much more a reaction to the conduct and direction of the conflict, with a particular importance attached to increasing colonial control of local communities and the violence of the insurgents.

At the outset of the conflict, both the colonial government and the insurgents were convinced of the value of discriminated targeting of their opponents. The strategic costs of indiscriminate violence were acknowledged, as Mau Mau activists eliminated their Kikuyu rivals through the use of gangland-style assassinations and the colonial regime attempted to decapitate the insurgency by arresting those thought to be its leaders. But having instigated the conflict, both sides found violence nearly impossible to control and constrain. Patience and the ability to discriminate friend from foe are imperative for the successful prosecution of either insurgent or counterinsurgent warfare; 'like eating soup with a knife,' T. E. Lawrence famously remarked of the challenge facing the Ottomans

---

[47] Furedi, *Mau Mau War*; Kanogo, *Squatters*; Rosberg and Nottingham, *Myth of Mau Mau*; Throup, *Economic and Social Origins*.

in putting down the Arab revolt.[48] Such patience and discrimination, though, is nearly impossible to sustain in a context of civil war. 'When you're up to your ass in alligators, it's difficult to remember you came to drain the swamp,' American troops learnt in Vietnam.[49] The demand for revenge – the effort 'to keep faith with the dead, to honor their memory by taking up their cause where they left off'[50] – scrambled allegiances. This process was further exacerbated by the privatisation of violence as individual Kikuyu sought to make the best of a terrible situation. In this setting, history was not a determinant of action. Instead, history set the context in which the conflict was fought and provided its witnesses and protagonists with the languages of resistance and accommodation with which they sought to make sense of the bloodshed.[51] No war can be understood until the limits of agency are acknowledged, its violence adequately explained, and all its witnesses and protagonists incorporated into its history.

For too long, loyalists have been derided within Kenya and ignored by historians as a consequence of what Gaddis describes as 'the all too human tendency to attribute behavior one dislikes to the *nature* of those who indulge in it, and to neglect the *circumstances* – including one's own behavior – that might have brought it about.'[52] The consistent failure to give due recognition to the history of loyalism is a contradiction of the single most significant lesson that we can draw from the Kikuyu civil war, namely, what can occur when 'alternative social and moral visions have no place in political debate.'[53] With this book completed in the immediate aftermath of the crisis that grew out of the disputed 2007 Kenyan general election, that message is as good and timely a justification for it as any other.

---

[48] Thomas Lawrence, *Seven Pillars of Wisdom: A Triumph* (London, 2000), 198.
[49] Wade Markel, 'Draining the Swamp: The British Strategy of Population Control,' *Parameters* 36 (2006), 35.
[50] Michael Ignatieff, *The Warrior's Honor: Ethnic War and the Modern Conscience* (New York, 1998), 188.
[51] Mark Leopold, *Inside West Nile: Violence, History and Representation on an African Frontier* (Oxford, 2005), 162.
[52] John Lewis Gaddis, *We Now Know: Rethinking Cold War History* (Oxford, 1997), 21.
[53] Frederick Cooper, 'Mau Mau and the Discourses of Decolonization,' *Journal of African History* 29 (1988), 320.

Bibliography

Primary Sources

Kenya National Archives

Files from the following ministries, offices, and miscellaneous collections of papers were consulted (series reference in parenthesis):

African Affairs (ARC(MAA), MAA)
Agriculture (BV)
Papers of P. Bostock (MSS/129)
Chief Secretary (CS)
Community Development (AB)
Defence (AH)
District Commissioner, Baringo (DC/BAR)
District Commissioner, Embu (DC/EBU, DC/EMB, BG)
District Commissioner, Fort Hall/Murang'a (DC/FH, DC/MUR, XA, XP)
District Commissioner, Kiambu (DC/KBU, MA)
District Commissioner, Kisumu (DC/KSM)
District Commissioner, Laikipia (DC/LKA)
District Commissioner, Meru (DC/MRU)
District Commissioner, Nanyuki (DC/NKI, DC/NYK)
District Commissioner, Nakuru (DC/NKU)
District Commissioner, Nyeri (DC/NYI, VP)
District Commissioner, Thika (DC/THIKA, DC/TKA)
District Commissioner, Turkana (DC/LDW)
Information (AHC)
Kenya Police (AM)
Legal Affairs (MLA)
Office of the President (OP)
Officer-in-Charge, Nairobi Extra-Provincial District (RN)

Bibliography

Papers of J. Murumbi (MAC)
Papers of W. H. Laughton (MSS/124)
Presbyterian Church of East Africa church and hospital, Chogora (ARA)
Prisons (AP)
Provincial Commissioner, Central Province (PC/CP, VQ)
Provincial Commissioner, Northern Province (PC/GRSSA)
Provincial Commissioner, Nyanza Province (PC/NZA)
Provincial Commissioner, Rift Valley Province (PC/NKU)
Provincial Commissioner, Southern Province (PC/NGO)
Secretariat (AE)
War Council & Council of Ministers (WC/CM)

Rhodes House Library, Oxford

The following manuscript collections were consulted:

Papers of Anti-Slavery Society (Mss Brit Emp s 22)
Papers of M. Blundell (Mss Afr s 746)
Papers of European Elected Members' Organisation & Electors' Union (Mss Afr s 596)
Papers of Fabian Colonial Bureau (Mss Brit Emp s 365)
Papers of M. Foote (Mss Afr s 1727)
Papers of Major General R. Hinde (Mss Afr s 1580)
Transcript of interview of Lord Howick (Evelyn Baring) by M. Perham (Mss Afr s 1574)
Papers of O. E. B. Hughes (Mss Afr s 1630)
Papers of L. Leakey (Mss Afr s 1720)
Papers of E. F. Martin (Mss Afr s 721)
Miscellaneous (Mss Afr s 424)
Miscellaneous papers entitled 'Kenya: Mau Mau Emergency, Sir F. Loyd, etc.' (Mss Afr s 1915)
Papers of Njoro Settlers' Association (Mss Afr s 1506)
Papers of M. Perham (Mss Perham)
Papers of W. H. Thompson (Mss Afr s 1534)
Papers of J. Whyatt (Mss Afr s 1694)
Papers of A. Young (Mss Brit Emp s 486)
A further miscellaneous migrated archive, originally from the Kenya National Archives, from Tel Aviv was also consulted. As this deposit is yet to be catalogued at Rhodes House, the prefix used here (TA) is the author's own.

The National Archives (UK), Public Record Office

Correspondence from the following series was consulted:

East Africa, original correspondence (CO 822)
East Africa Command (WO 276)
Papers of General G. Erskine (WO 236)

New York Public Library

The papers of the International League of Human Rights were examined.

Billy Graham Center, Wheaton College

Papers of African Inland Mission's Kenya Field Director (Collection 81) were consulted.

Newspapers

The following newspapers are cited:

The Daily Nation, now known as *The Nation*
The East African
The East African Standard, now known as *The Standard*
The Guardian

Interviews

Richard Kanampiu Githae, Chogoria, South Meru district, Kenya, 15 September 2003
Jotham Kimonde, Chogoria, South Meru district, Kenya, 17 September 2003
Noadia Kimonde, Chogoria, South Meru district, Kenya, 17 September 2003
Celestino Kirengeni, Chogoria, South Meru district, Kenya, 18 September 2003
Kariuki Kiruma, Ihururu, Nyeri district, Kenya 7 February 2004
Pheneas Kithiji, Chogoria, South Meru district, Kenya, 17 September 2003
Reverend Jediel Micheu, Chogoria, South Meru district, Kenya, 18 September 2003
M'Rithaa Mirru, Chogoria, South Meru district, Kenya, 16 September 2003
Duncan Ngatia Muhoya, Ihururu, Nyeri district, Kenya 7 February 2004
Stephen Murocha, Chogoria, South Meru district, Kenya, 15 September 2003
Titus M'Imanene Murong'a, Chogoria, South Meru district, Kenya, 16 September 2003
James Mutgi, Chogoria, South Meru district, Kenya, 15 September 2003
Ephantus N'Dobi, Chogoria, South Meru district, Kenya, 18 September 2003
Sihar Gitahi Ribai, Ihururu, Nyeri district, Kenya, 7 February 2004

Grey Literature and Government Publications

Carothers, John. 'The Psychology of Mau Mau.' Nairobi: Government Printer, 1954.
Humphreys, Macartan and Jeremy Weinstein. 'What the Fighters Say: A Survey of Ex-Combatants in Sierra Leone June-August 2003.' Freetown: PRIDE, 2004.
Kariuki, Joshiah Mwangi. *J. M. Kariuki Speaks His Mind*. Nairobi, 1974.
Kenya, Colony & Protectorate of. An Ordinance to Provide for the Nomination and Election of African Members to the Legislative Council of the Colony and Protectorate of Kenya; and for Matters Connected Therewith and Incidental Thereto. Nairobi: Government Printer, 1956.

_____ *History of the Loyalists.* Nairobi: Government Printer, 1961.

_____ *Report of the Commissioner Appointed to Enquire Into Methods for the Selection of African Representatives to the Legislative Council.* Nairobi: Government Printer, 1955.

_____ *Report of the Commissioner Appointed to Enquire Into Methods for the Selection of African Representatives to the Legislative Council.* Nairobi: Government Printer, 1956.

_____ *The Origins and Growth of Mau Mau: An Historical Survey.* Nairobi: Government Printer, 1960.

Kenya, Government of. *Constitution of Kenya.* Nairobi: Government Printer, 1963.

_____ *Report of the Task Force on the Establishment of a Truth, Justice and Reconciliation Commission.* Nairobi: Government Printer, 2003.

_____ *Sessional Paper No .10 of 1965: African Socialism and Its Application to Planning in Kenya.* Nairobi: Government Printer, 1965.

Kenya, Regional Boundaries Commission. *Kenya: The Report of the Regional Boundaries Commission.* London: H.M.S.O., 1962.

Kenya African National Union. 'What a KANU Government Offers You.' Nairobi: Kenya African National Union, 1963.

Pauker, Guy. 'Notes on Non-Military Measures in Control of Insurgency.' Santa Monica CA: RAND Corporation, 1962.

Swynnerton, Roger. *A Plan to Intensify the Development of African Agriculture in Kenya.* Nairobi: Government Printer, 1953.

Unpublished Secondary Sources

Arjona, Ana and Stathis Kalyvas. 'Preliminary Results of a Survey of Demobilized Combatants in Colombia.' Working paper, Yale University, New Haven, 2006.

Barnett, Donald. '"Mau Mau": The Structural Integration and Disintegration of Abderdare Guerrilla Forces.' PhD dissertation, University of California, Los Angeles, 1963.

Githige, Renison Muchiri. 'The Religious Factor in Mau Mau With Particular Reference to Mau Mau Oaths.' MA dissertation, University of Nairobi, 1978.

Mburu, J. Ndung'u. 'The Dissemination of Christianity in Nyeri District (1903–1963) With Special Reference to the Work of African Teachers and Evangelists.' MA dissertation, University of Nairobi, 1975.

Ndabiri, Margaret. 'A Biographical Essay on Ex-Senior Chief Njiriwa Karanja.' BEd dissertation, University of Nairobi, 1977.

Peterson, Derek. 'The Home Guard in Mau Mau's Moral War.' Paper presented at the African Studies Association annual meeting, Boston, 2003.

Pugliese, Cristiana. 'Gikuyu Political Pamphlets and Hymn Books 1945–1952.' Working paper, Institut Francais de Recherche en Afrique, Nairobi, 1993.

Roelker, Jack. 'The Contribution of Eliud Wambu Mathuto Political Independence in Kenya.' PhD dissertation, Syracuse University, 1974.

Wanjohi, Nick. 'The Politics of Ideology and Personality Rivalry in Murang'a District, Kenya: A Study of Electoral Competition'. Working paper, Institute of Development Studies, University of Nairobi, 1984.
Williams, Gavin. 'Fragments of Democracy: Nationalism, Development and the State in Africa.' Working paper, Democracy and Governance Research Programme, Human Sciences Research Council, Cape Town, 2003.

Published Secondary Sources

Abbink, Jon, Mirjam de Bruijn, and Klaas Van Walraven, eds. *Rethinking Resistance: Revolt and Violence in African History*. Leiden: Brill, 2003.
Adamson, George. *Bwana Game: The Life Story of George Adamson*. London: Collins & Harvill, 1968.
Alam, S. M. Shamsul. *Rethinking Mau Mau in Colonial Kenya*. Basingstoke: Palgrave Macmillan, 2007.
Anderson, David. *Histories of the Hanged: Britain's Dirty War in Kenya and the End of Empire*. London: Weidenfeld & Nicolson, 2005.
———'Surrogates of the State: Collaboration and Atrocity in Kenya's Mau Mau War.' In *The Barbarisation of Warfare*, edited by George Kassimeris, 159–74. London: Hurst, 2006.
———'The Battle of Dandora Swamp: Reconstructing the Mau Mau Land Freedom Army October 1954.' In *Mau Mau and Nationhood: Arms, Authority and Narration*, edited by Elisha Stephen Atieno Odhiambo and John Lonsdale, 155–75. Oxford: James Currey, 2003.
———'Vigilantes, Violence and the Politics of Public Order in Kenya.' *African Affairs* 101, no. 405 (2001), 531–55.
Anderson, David, Huw Bennett and Daniel Branch. 'A Very British Massacre.' *History Today* 2006, 20–2.
Asingo, Patrick. 'The Political Economy of Transition in Kenya.' In *The Politics of Transition in Kenya: From KANU to NARC*, edited by Walter Oyugi, Peter Wanyande, and Crispin Odhiambo Mbai, 15–50. Nairobi: Heinrich Boll Foundation, 2003.
Atieno Odhiambo, Elisha Stephen. 'Matunda ya Uhuru, Fruits of Independence: Seven Theses on Nationalism in Kenya.' In *Mau Mau and Nationhood: Arms, Authority and Narration*, edited by Elisha Stephen Atieno Odhiambo and John Lonsdale, 37–45. Oxford: James Currey, 2003.
———'Democracy and the Ideology of Order in Kenya.' In *The Political Economy of Kenya*, edited by Schatzberg, 177–201. New York: Praeger, 1987.
———'The Formative Years 1945–55.' In *Decolonization and Independence in Kenya 1940–93*, edited by Bethwell A. Ogot and William Ochieng, 25–47. London: James Currey, 1995.
Atieno Odhiambo, Elisha Stephen and John Lonsdale. 'Introduction.' In *Mau Mau and Nationhood: Arms, Authority and Narration*, edited by Elisha Stephen Atieno Odhiambo and John Lonsdale, 1–7. Oxford: James Currey, 2003.
Balch-Lindsay, Dylan, Paul Huth, and Benjamin Valentino. 'Draining the Sea: Mass Killing and Guerrilla Warfare.' *International Organization* 58, no. 2 (2004), 375–407.

Barnett, Donald and Karari Njama. *Mau Mau From Within: An Analysis of Kenya's Peasant Revolt*. London: Modern Reader, 1966.

Batalas, Achilles. 'Send a Thief to Catch a Thief: State-Building and the Employment of Irregular Military Formations in Mid-Nineteenth Century Greece.' In *Irregular Armed Forces and Their Role in Politics and State Formation*, edited by Diane Davis and Anthony Periera, 149–77. Cambridge: Cambridge University Press, 2003.

Bates, Robert. *Beyond the Miracle of the Market: The Political Economy of Agrarian Development in Kenya*. Cambridge: Cambridge University Press, 2005.

———'Ethnic Competition and Modernization in Contemporary Africa.' *Comparative Political Studies* 6, no. 4 (1974), 457–84.

Bayart, Jean-Francois. *The State in Africa: The Politics of the Belly*. Translated by Mary Harper, Christopher Harrison, and Elizabeth Harrison. London: Longman, 1993.

Beecher, Leonard. 'Christian Counter-Revolution to Mau Mau.' In *Rhodesia and East Africa*, edited by Ferdinand Joelson, 82–92. London: East Africa and Rhodesia, 1958.

Bennett, George and Carl Rosberg. *The Kenyatta Election: Kenya 1960–1961*. London: Oxford University Press, 1961.

Berman, Bruce. 'Bureaucracy and Incumbent Violence: Colonial Administration and the Origins of Mau Mau.' In *Unhappy Valley: Conflict in Kenya and Africa*, edited by Bruce Berman and John Lonsdale, 227–64. Oxford: James Currey, 1992.

———*Control and Crisis in Colonial Kenya: The Dialectic of Domination*. London: James Currey, 1990.

———'Ethnography as Politics, Politics as Ethnography: Kenyatta, Malinowski, and the Making of Facing Mount Kenya.' *Canadian Journal of African Studies* 30, no. 3 (1996), 313–44.

———'Nationalism, Ethnicity, and Modernity: The Paradox of Mau Mau.' *Canadian Journal of African Studies* 25, no. 2 (1991), 181–206.

Berman, Bruce, Dickson Eyoh and Will Kymlicka. 'Ethnicity and the Politics of Democratic Nation-Building in Africa.' In *Ethnicity and Democracy in Africa*, edited by Bruce Berman, Dickson Eyoh, and Will Kymlicka, 1–21. Oxford: James Currey, 2004.

Berman, Bruce and John Lonsdale. 'Coping with the Contradictions: The Development of the Colonial State 1895–1914.' In Unhappy Valley: Conflict in Kenya and Africa, edited by Bruce Berman and John Lonsdale, 77–100. Oxford: James Currey, 1992.

———'Louis Leakey's Mau Mau: A Study in the Politics of Knowledge.' *History and Anthropology* 5, no. 2 (1991), 142–204.

Berreman, Gerald. 'Is Anthropology Alive? Social Responsibility in Social Anthropology.' *Current Anthropology* 9, no. 5 (1968), 391–6.

Bienen, Henry. *Kenya: The Politics of Participation and Control*. Princeton: Princeton University Press, 1974.

Blacker, John. 'The Demography of Mau Mau: Fertility and Mortality in Kenya in the 1950s, a Demographer's Viewpoint.' *African Affairs* 106, no. 423 (2007), 205–27.

Blakeslee, Virginia. *Beyond the Kikuyu Curtain.* Chicago: Moody Press, 1956.
Branch, Daniel and Nicholas Cheeseman. 'The Politics of Control in Kenya: Understanding the Bureaucratic-Executive State, 1952–78.' *Review of African Political Economy* 33, no. 107 (2006), 11–31.
Bravman, Bill. *Making Ethnic Ways: Communities and Their Transformations in Taita, Kenya, 1800–1950.* Oxford: James Currey, 1998.
Brett, Edward. *Colonialism and Underdevelopment in East Africa: The Politics of Economic Change 1919–1939.* London: Heinemann, 1973.
Broch-Due, Vigdis. 'Violence and Belonging: Analytical Reflections.' In *Violence and Belonging: The Quest for Identity in Post-Colonial Africa,* edited by Vigdis Broch-Due, 1–40. Abingdon: Routledge, 2005.
Buijtenhuijs, Robert. *Essays on Mau Mau: Contributions to Mau Mau Historiography.* Leiden: African Studies Centre, 1982.
_____ *Mau Mau Twenty Years After: The Myth and the Survivors.* The Hague: Mouton, 1973.
Carruthers, Susan. 'Being Beastly to the Mau Mau.' *Twentieth Century British History* 16, no. 4 (2005), 489–96.
_____ *Winning Hearts and Minds: British Governments, the Media and Colonial Counter-Insurgency 1944–1960.* Leicester: Leicester University Press, 1995.
Cell, John. 'Colonial Rule.' In *The Oxford History of the British Empire,* edited by Judith Brown and Wm. Roger Louis, 232–54. Oxford: Oxford University Press, 1999.
Chesaina, Ciarunji. *Oral Literature of the Embu and Mbeere.* Nairobi: East African Educational Publishers, 1997.
Clapham, Christopher, ed. *African Guerrillas.* Oxford: James Currey, 1998.
Clark, Carolyn. 'Louis Leakey as Ethnographer: On The Southern Kikuyu Before 1903.' *Canadian Journal of African Studies* 23, no. 3 (1989), 380–98.
Clayton, Anthony. *Counter-Insurgency in Kenya: A Study of Military Operations Against Mau Mau.* London: Frank Cass, 1976.
_____ *Frontiersmen: Warfare in Africa Since 1950.* London: University College London Press, 1999.
Clough, Marshall. *Fighting Two Sides: Kenyan Chiefs and Politicians, 1918–1940.* Niwot CO: University Press of Colorado, 1990.
_____ 'Koinange wa Mbiyu: Mediator and Patriot.' In *Biographical Essays on Imperialism and Collaboration in Colonial Kenya,* edited by Benjamin Kipkorir, 57–86. Nairobi: Kenya Literature Bureau, 1980.
_____ 'Mau Mau and the Contest for Memory.' In *Mau Mau and Nationhood: Arms, Authority and Narration,* edited by Elisha Stephen Atieno Odhiambo and John Lonsdale, 251–67. Oxford: James Currey, 2003.
_____ *Mau Mau Memoirs: History, Memory, and Politics.* Boulder: Lynne Rienner, 1998.
Cole, Jennifer. *Forget Colonialism? Sacrifice and the Art of Memory of Madagascar.* Berkeley: University of California Press, 2001.
Comaroff, John. 'Government, Materiality, Legality, Modernity: On the Colonial State in Africa.' In *African Modernities: Entangled Meanings in Current Debate,* edited by Jan-Georg Deutsch, Peter Probst and Heike Schmidt, 107–34. Oxford: James Currey, 2002.

Conrad, Joseph. *Heart of Darkness.* New York: Modern Library, 1999.
Cooper, Frederick. 'Conflict and Connection: Rethinking African History.' *American Historical Review* 99, no. 5 (1994), 1516–45.
_____ *Decolonization and African Society: The Labor Question in French and British Africa.* Cambridge: Cambridge University Press, 1996.
_____ 'Mau Mau and the Discourses of Decolonization.' *Journal of African History* 29, no. 2 (1988), 313–20.
Corum, James. *Training Indigenous Forces in Counter-Insurgency: A Tale of Two Insurgencies.* Carlisle PA: Strategic Studies Institute, US Army War College, 2006.
Cramer, Christopher. *Civil War Is Not a Stupid Thing: Accounting for Violence in Developing Countries.* London: Hurst, 2006.
Danner, Mark. *The Massacre at El Mozote: A Parable of the Cold War.* London: Granta, 2005.
Das, Veena. 'The Act of Witnessing: Violence, Poisonous Knowledge, and Subjectivity.' In *Violence and Subjectivity*, edited by Veena Das, Arthur Kleinman and Pamela Reynolds, 1–18. Berkeley: University of California Press, 2000.
de Wilde, John. *Experiences With Agricultural Development in Tropical Africa.* 2 vols. Vol. 2. Baltimore: John Hopkins Press, 1967.
Edgerton, Robert. *Mau Mau: An African Crucible.* London: I.B. Tauris, 1990.
Elkins, Caroline. *Imperial Reckoning: The Untold Story of Britain's Gulag in Kenya.* New York: Henry Holt, 2005.
_____'The Wrong Lesson.' *The Atlantic Monthly* 296, no. 1 (2005), 34–8.
Engholm, Geoffrey. 'African Elections in Kenya, March 1957.' In *Five Elections in Africa: A Group of Electoral Studies*, edited by William MacKenzie and Kenneth Robinson, 391–461. Oxford: Clarendon Press, 1960.
Evans, Martin. 'The Harkis: The Experience and Memory of France's Muslim Auxiliaries.' In *The Algerian War and the French Army, 1954–62: Experiences, Images, Testimonies*, edited by Martin Alexander, Martin Evans, and John F. Keiger, 117–36. Basingstoke: Palgrave Macmillan, 2002.
Evans, Peter. *Law and Disorder: Scenes of Life in Kenya.* London: Secker & Warburg, 1956.
Fadiman, Jeffrey A. *When We Began There Were Witchmen: An Oral History From Mount Kenya.* Berkeley: University of California Press, 1994.
Fearon, James and David Laitin. 'Ethnicity, Insurgency, and Civil War.' *American Political Science Review* 97, no. 1 (2003), 75–90.
Feldman, Noah. *What We Owe Iraq: War and the Ethics of Nation Building.* Princeton NJ: Princeton University Press, 2004.
Furedi, Frank. 'The African Crowd in Nairobi: Popular Movements and Elite Politics.' *Journal of African History* 14, no. 2 (1973), 275–90.
_____ *The Mau Mau War in Perspective.* London: James Currey, 1989.
_____ 'The Social Composition of the Mau Mau Movement in the White Highlands.' *Journal of Peasant Studies* 1, no. 4 (1974), 486–505.
Gaddis, John Lewis. *We Now Know: Rethinking Cold War History.* Oxford: Oxford University Press, 1997.
Gertzel, Cherry. *The Politics of Independent Kenya 1963–8.* Evanston IL: Northwestern University Press, 1970.

Gertzel, Cherry, Maure Goldschmidt and Donald Rothchild, eds. *Government and Politics in Kenya*. Nairobi: East African Publishing House, 1969.

Girard, Philippe. 'Empire by Collaboration: The First French Empire's Rise and Demise.' *French History* 19, no. 4 (2005), 482–90.

Gonzalez, Roberto. 'Towards Mercenary Anthropology? The New US Army Counterinsurgency Manual FM-24 and the Military-Anthropology Complex.' *Anthropology Today* 23, no. 3 (2007), 14–19.

Green, Maia. 'Mau Mau Oathing Rituals and Political Ideology in Kenya: A Re-Analysis.' *Africa* 60, no. 1 (1990), 69–87.

Harbeson, John. *Nationalism and Nation-Building in Kenya: The Role of Land Reform*. Ann Arbor MI: University Microfilms, 1970.

Harper, Tim. *The End of Empire and the Making of Malaya*. Cambridge: Cambridge University Press, 1999.

_____ 'The Politics of the Forest in Colonial Malaya.' *Modern Asian Studies* 31, no. 1 (1997), 1–29.

Hart, Peter. *The I.R.A. and Its Enemies: Violence and Community in Cork, 1916–1923*. Oxford: Clarendon Press, 1998.

Hauser, Beatrice. 'The Cultural Revolution in Counter-Insurgency.' *Journal of Strategic Studies* 30, no. 1 (2007), 153–71.

Henderson, Ian and Philip Goodhart. *The Hunt for Kimathi*. London: Hamish Hamilton, 1958.

Heyer, Amrik. "Nowadays They Can Even Kill You for That Which They Feel Is Theirs': Gender and Production of Ethnic Identity in Kikuyu-Speaking Central Kenya.' In *Violence and Belonging: The Quest for Identity in Post-Colonial Africa*, edited by Vigdis Broch-Due, 41–59. Abingdon: Routledge, 2005.

Hobsbawm, Eric. 'Could It Have Been Different?' *London Review of Books* 28, no. 22 (2006), 3–6.

_____ *Nations and Nationalism Since 1870: Programme, Myth, Reality*. Cambridge: Cambridge University Press, 1990.

Howard, Michael. 'What's in a Name? How to Fight Terrorism.' *Foreign Affairs* 81, no. 1 (2002), 8–13.

Huggins, Martha, Mika Haritos-Fatouros, and Philip Zimbardo. *Violence Workers: Police Torturers and Murderers Reconstruct Brazilian Atrocities*. Berkeley: University of California Press, 2002.

Hyden, Goran and Colin Leys. 'Elections and Politics in Single-Party Systems: The Case of Kenya and Tanzania.' *British Journal of Political Science* 2, no. 4 (1972), 389–420.

Ignatieff, Michael. *The Warrior's Honor: Ethnic War and the Modern Conscience*. New York: Macmillan, 1998.

Iliffe, John. *Honour in African History*. Cambridge: Cambridge University Press, 2005.

Itote, Waruhiu. *Mau Mau in Action*. Nairobi: Transafrica, 1979.

Jackson, Kennell. "Impossible to Ignore Their Greatness': Survival Craft in the Mau Mau Forest Movement.' In *Mau Mau and Nationhood: Arms, Authority and Narration*, edited by Elisha Stephen Atieno Odhiambo and John Lonsdale, 176–90. London: James Currey, 2003.

Jeyaratnam, Arthur. *The Break-Up of Sri Lanka: The Sinhalese-Tamil Conflict.* London: Hurst, 1988.

Johnson, Douglas. *Root Causes of Sudan's Civil Wars.* Oxford: James Currey, 2003.

Kabiro, Ngugi. *Man in the Middle.* Richmond BC: LSM Information Center, 1973.

Kagwanja, Peter. 'Facing Mount Kenya or Facing Mecca?: The Mungiki, Ethnic Violence and the Politics of the Moi Succession in Kenya, 1987–2002.' *African Affairs* 102, no. 406 (2003), 25–49.

Kalyvas, Stathis. *The Logic of Violence in Civil War.* Cambridge: Cambridge University Press, 2006.

_____ 'The Ontology of "Political Violence": Action and Identity in Civil Wars.' *Perspectives on Politics* 1, no. 3 (2003), 475–94.

Kamen, Henry. *Empire: How Spain Became a World Power.* New York: Harper Perennial, 2003.

Kamunchula, J. T. Samuel. 'The Meru Participation in Mau Mau.' *Kenya Historical Review* 3, no. 2 (1975), 193–216.

Kanogo, Tabitha. *African Womanhood in Colonial Kenya 1900–50.* Oxford: James Currey, 2005.

_____ *Squatters and the Roots of Mau Mau.* London: James Currey, 1987.

Kariuki, Joseph. 'Internal Wrangles, State Influence and Schisms: Competing Visions and Struggles in the Africa Independent Pentecostal Church in Kenya.' *Les Cahiers de'IFRA* 25 (2004), 2–19.

Kariuki, Josiah Mwangi. *"Mau Mau" Detainee: The Account of a Kenya African of His Experiences in Detention Camps 1953–1960.* Nairobi: Oxford University Press, 1975.

Kariuki, Obidiah. *A Bishop Facing Mount Kenya: An Autobiography, 1902–1978. Translated by George Mathu.* Nairobi: Uzima Press, 1985.

Katumanga, Musambayi. 'A City Under Siege: Banditry and Modes of Accumulation in Nairobi, 1991–2004.' *Review of African Political Economy* 32, no. 106 (2005), 505–20.

Keen, David. *Conflict and Collusion in Sierra Leone.* Oxford: James Currey, 2005.

Kelleher, William. *The Troubles in Ballybogoin: Memory and Identity in Northern Ireland.* Ann Arbor MI: University of Michigan Press, 2003.

Kenyatta, Jomo. *Facing Mount Kenya: The Tribal Life of the Gikuyu.* New York: Vintage, 1965.

_____ *Harambee!: The Prime Minister of Kenya's Speeches, 1963–1964.* Nairobi: Oxford University Press, 1964.

Kershaw, Greet. *Mau Mau From Below.* Oxford: James Currey, 1997.

_____ 'Mau Mau From Below: Fieldwork and Experience, 1955–57 and 1962.' *Canadian Journal of African Studies* 25, no. 2 (1991), 274–97.

Kesby, Mike. 'Arenas for Control, Terrains of Gender Contestation: Guerrilla Struggle and Counter-Insurgency Warfare in Zimbabwe 1972–1980.' *Journal of Southern African Studies* 22, no. 4 (1996), 561–84.

Kieh, George and Rousseau Mukenege, eds. *Zones of Conflict in Africa: Theories and Cases*. Westport CT: Praeger, 2002.

Kimenyi, Mwangi and Njuguna Ndung'u. 'Sporadic Ethnic Violence: Why Has Kenya Not Experienced a Full-Blown Civil War.' In *Understanding Civil War: Evidence and Analysis*, edited by Paul Collier and Nicholas Sambanis, 123–56. 2 vols. Vol. 1. Washington DC: The World Bank, 2005.

Kinyatti, Mainawa. *Kenya's Freedom Struggle: The Dedan Kimathi Papers*. London: Zed, 1987.

——— *Mau Mau: A Revolution Betrayed*. New York: Mau Mau Research Center, 1991.

Kipkorir, Benjamin. 'Mau Mau and the Politics of the Transfer of Power in Kenya, 1957–1960.' *Kenya Historical Review* 5, no. 2 (1977), 313–28.

——— 'The Educated Elite and Local Society: The Basis for Mass Representation.' In *Hadith 4: Politics and Nationalism in Colonial Kenya*, edited by Bethwell A. Ogot, 250–69. Nairobi: East African Publishing House, 1972.

Kitching, Gavin. *Class and Economic Change in Kenya: The Making of an African Petite-Bourgeoisie*. New Haven: Yale University Press, 1980.

Koinange, Jeff. *Koinange-wa-Mbiyu: Mau Mau's Misunderstood Leader*. Lewes: Book Guild, 2000.

Kyle, Keith. *The Politics of the Independence of Kenya*. Basingstoke: Macmillan, 1999.

Lacoste-Dujardin, Camille. *Opération Oiseau Bleu: Des Kabyles, des ethnologues et la guerre en Algérie*. Paris: Decouverte, 1997.

Laitin, David. *Identity in Formation: The Russian-Speaking Populations in the Near Abroad*. Ithaca NY: Cornell University Press, 1998.

Lamb, Geoff. *Peasant Politics: Conflict and Development in Murang'a*. Lewes: Julian Friedmann, 1974.

Lambert, Harold. *Kikuyu Social and Political Institutions*. London: Oxford University Press, 1956.

Lathbury, Gerald. 'The Security Forces in the Kenya Emergency.' In *Rhodesia and East Africa*, edited by Ferdinand Joelson, 36–47. London: East Africa and Rhodesia, 1958.

Lawrence, Thomas. *Seven Pillars of Wisdom: A Triumph*. London: Penguin, 2000.

Leakey, Louis. *Mau Mau and the Kikuyu*. London: Methuen, 1952.

——— *The Southern Kikuyu Before 1903*. 3 vols. New York: Academic Press, 1977.

Leary, John. *Violence and the Dream People: The Orang Asli in the Malayan Emergency, 1948–1960*. Columbus OH: Ohio University Center for International Studies, 1995.

Leonard, David. *African Successes: Four Public Managers of Kenyan Rural Development*. Berkeley: University of California Press, 1991.

Leopold, Mark. *Inside West Nile: Violence, History and Representation on an African Frontier*. Oxford: James Currey, 2005.

Lewis, Joanna. *Empire State-Building: War and Welfare in Kenya 1925–52*. Oxford: James Currey, 2000.

Lonsdale, John. 'Agency in Tight Corners: Narrative and Initiative in African History.' *Journal of African Cultural Studies* 13, no. 1 (2000), 5–16.

―――― 'Authority, Gender and Violence: The War Within Mau Mau's Fight for Land and Freedom.' In *Mau Mau and Nationhood: Arms, Authority and Narration*, edited by Elisha Stephen Atieno Odhiambo and John Lonsdale, 46–75. Oxford: James Currey, 2003.

―――― 'Jomo Kenyatta, God and the Modern World.' In *African Modernities: Entangled Meanings in Current Debate*, edited by Jan-Georg Deutsch, Peter Probst, and Heike Schmidt, 31–66. Oxford: James Currey, 2002.

―――― 'Mau Maus of the Mind: Making Kenya Mau Mau and Remaking Kenya.' *Journal of African History* 31, no. 3 (1990), 393–421.

―――― 'Moral and Political Argument in Kenya.' In *Ethnicity and Democracy in Africa*, edited by Bruce Berman, Dickson Eyoh and Will Kymlicka, 73–95. Oxford: James Currey, 2004.

―――― 'Ornamental Constitutionalism in Kenya: Kenyatta and the Two Queens.' *Journal of Imperial and Commonwealth History* 34, no. 1 (2006), 87–103.

―――― 'The Conquest State of Kenya: 1895–1905.' In *Unhappy Valley: Conflict in Kenya and Africa*, edited by Bruce Berman and John Lonsdale, 13–44. Oxford: James Currey, 1992.

―――― 'The Moral Economy of Mau Mau: The Problem.' In *Unhappy Valley: Conflict in Kenya and Africa*, edited by Bruce Berman and John Lonsdale, 265–314. Oxford: James Currey, 1992.

―――― 'The Moral Economy of Mau Mau: Wealth, Poverty and Civic Virtue in Kikuyu Political Thought.' In *Unhappy Valley: Conflict in Kenya and Africa*, edited by Bruce Berman and John Lonsdale, 315–504. Oxford: James Currey, 1992.

―――― 'The Prayers of Waiyaki: Political Uses of the Kikuyu Past.' In *Revealing Prophets: Prophecy in Eastern African History*, edited by David Anderson and Douglas Johnson, 240–91. London: James Currey, 1995.

Louis, Wm. Roger. 'Suez and Decolonization: Scrambling out of Africa and Asia.' In *Ends of British Imperialism: The Scramble for Empire, Suez and Decolonization*, edited by Wm. Roger Louis, 1–34. London: I.B. Tauris, 2006.

Lowe, William. 'The War *Against the R.I.C.*, 1919–21.' *Eire-Ireland* 27, no. 3/4 (2002), 79–117.

Luongo, Katherine. 'If You Can't Beat Them, Join Them: Government Cleanings of Witches and Mau Mau in 1950s Kenya.' *History in Africa* 33 (2006), 451–71.

MacKenzie, A. Fiona D. *Land, Ecology and Resistance in Kenya, 1880–1952*. Edinburgh: Edinburgh University Press, 1998.

Mahone, Sloan. 'The Psychology of Rebellion: Colonial Medical Responses to Dissent in British East Africa.' *Journal of African History* 47, no. 2 (2006), 241–58.

Maloba, Wunyabari. *Mau Mau and Kenya: An Analysis of a Peasant Revolt*. Oxford: James Currey, 1998.

Mamdani, Mahmood. 'The Politics of Naming: Genocide, Civil War, Insurgency.' *London Review of Books* 29, no. 5 (2007), 3–6.

_____ *When Victims Become Killers: Colonialism, Nativism, and the Genocide in Rwanda.* Princeton NJ: Princeton University Press, 2001.

Manning, Patrick. *Francophone Sub-Saharan Africa, 1880–1995.* Cambridge: Cambridge University Press, 1999.

Markel, Wade. 'Draining the Swamp: The British Strategy of Population Control.' *Parameters* 36, no. 1 (2006), 35–48.

Marris, Peter and Anthony Somerset. *African Businessmen: A Study of Entrepreneurship and Development in Kenya.* London: Routledge & Kegan Paul, 1971.

Mason, T. David. "Take Two Acres and Call Me in the Morning': Is Land Reform a Prescription for Peasant Unrest?' *Journal of Politics* 60, no. 1 (1998), 199–230.

Mathu, Mohamed. *The Urban Guerrilla: The Story of Mohamed Mathu.* Richmond BC: LSM Information Center, 1974.

Matiba, Kenneth. *Aiming High: The Story of My Life.* Nairobi: People, 2000.

Maughan-Brown, David. *Land, Freedom and Fiction: History and Ideology in Kenya.* London: Zed, 1985.

Maxon, Robert. 'Social and Cultural Changes.' In *Decolonization and Independence in Kenya 1940–93*, edited by Bethwell A. Ogot and William Ochieng, 110–50. Oxford: James Currey, 1995.

Mazrui, Ali. 'On Heroes and Uhuru-Worship.' *Transition*, no. 11 (1963), 23–8.

McCormack, Richard. *Asians in Kenya: Conflicts and Politics.* Brooklyn NY: T. Gaus, 1971.

McDougall, James. 'The Shabiba Islamiyya of Algiers: Education, Authority, and Colonial Control, 1921–57.' *Comparative Studies of South Asia, Africa and the Middle East* 24, no. 1 (2004), 149–57.

M'Imanyara, Alfred. *The Restatement of Bantu Origin and Meru History.* Nairobi: Longman Kenya, 1992.

Muchai, Karigo. *The Hardcore: The Story of Karigo Muchai.* Richmond BC: LSM Information Center, 1973.

Muoria, Henry. *I, the Gikuyu and the White Fury.* Nairobi: East African Educational Publishers, 1994.

Muriuki, Godfrey. *A History of the Kikuyu, 1500–1900.* Nairobi: Oxford University Press, 1974.

_____ 'Background to Politics and Nationalism in Central Kenya: The Traditional Social and Political Systems of Kenya Peoples.' In *Hadith 4: Politics and Nationalism in Colonial Kenya*, edited by Bethwell A. Ogot, 1–17. Nairobi: East African Publishing House, 1972.

Murray-Brown, Jeremy. *Kenyatta. London: Fontana*, 1974.

Mwangi, Rose. *Kikuyu Folktales: Their Nature and Value.* Nairobi: Kenya Literature Bureau, 1983.

Nagl, John. *Learning to Eat Soup With a Knife: Counterinsurgency Lessons From Malaya and Vietnam.* Chicago: Chicago University Press, 2005.

Nash, June. *Practicing Ethnography in a Globalizing World.* Lanham MD: Altamira, 2007.

Ng'ang'a, D. Makaru. 'Mau Mau, Loyalists *and Politics in Murang'a* 1952–70.' *Kenya Historical Review* 5, no. 2 (1977), 365–384.

Njoroge, Lawrence. *A Century of Catholic Endeavour: Holy Ghost and Consolata Missions in Kenya*. Nairobi: Pauline Publications, 1999.

Nolutshungu, Samuel. 'Fragments of a Democracy: Reflections on Class and Politics in Nigeria.' *Third World Quarterly* 12, no. 1 (1990), 86–115.

Ochieng, William. 'Colonial African Chiefs – Were They Primarily Self-Seeking Scoundrals?' In *Hadith 4: Politics and Nationalism in Colonial Kenya*, edited by Bethwell A. Ogot, 46–70. Nairobi: East African Publishing House, 1972.

_____ 'Structural and Political Changes.' In *Decolonization and Independence in Kenya 1940–93*, edited by Bethwell A. Ogot and William Ochieng, 83–109. London: James Currey, 1955.

Odinga, Oginga. *Not Yet Uhuru*. Nairobi: East African Educational Publishers, 1967.

Ogot, Bethwell A. 'Britain's Gulag.' *Journal of African History* 46, no. 3 (2005), 493–505.

_____ 'Politics, Culture and Music in Central Kenya: A Study of Mau Mau Hymns, 1951–1956.' In *Reintroducing Man Into the African World: Selected Essays 1961–1980*, edited by Bethwell A. Ogot, 237–51. Kisumu: Anyange Press, 1999.

_____ 'Revolt of the Elders: An Anatomy of the Loyalist Crowd in the Mau Mau Uprising 1952–1956.' In *Hadith 4: Politics and Nationalism in Colonial Kenya*, edited by Bethwell A. Ogot, 134–48. Nairobi: East African Publishing House, 1972.

_____ 'The Decisive Years, 1956–63.' In *Decolonization and Independence in Kenya 1940–93*, edited by Bethwell A. Ogot and William Ochieng, 48–79. London: James Currey, 1995.

Okoth-Ogendo, Hastings. 'African Land Tenure Reform.' In *Agricultural Development in Kenya*, edited by Judith Heyer, J. K. Maitha and W. M. Senga, 152–86. Nairobi: Oxford University Press, 1976.

Omosule, Monone. 'Kiama kia Muingi: Kikuyu and Land Consolidation.' *Transafrican Journal of History* 4, no. 1–2 (1974), 115–34.

Osterhammel, Jurgen. *Colonialism: A Theoretical Overview*. Translated by Shelley Frisch. Princeton NJ: Markus Wiener, 1997.

Parsons, Timothy. *Race, Resistance, and the Boy Scout Movement in British Colonial Africa*. Athens OH: Ohio University Press, 2004.

_____ *The African Rank-and-File: Social Implications of Colonial Military Service in the King's African Rifles, 1902–1964*. Oxford: James Currey, 1999.

Percox, David. 'Internal Security and Decolonization in Kenya, 1956–63.' *Journal of Imperial and Commonwealth History* 29, no. 1 (2001), 92–116.

_____ 'Mau Mau and the Arming of the State.' In *Mau Mau and Nationhood: Arms, Authority and Narration*, edited by Elisha Stephen Atieno Odhiambo and John Lonsdale, 121–54. Oxford: James Currey, 2003.

Petersen, Roger. *Resistance and Rebellion: Lessons From Eastern Europe*. Cambridge: Cambridge University Press, 2001.

Peterson, Derek. *Creative Writing: Translation, Bookkeeping, and the Work of Colonial Imagination*. Portsmouth NH: Heinemann, 2004.

_____ 'The Intellectual Lives of Mau Mau Detainees.' *Journal of African History* 48, no. 3 (2008), 73–91.

_____ 'Wordy Women: Gender Trouble and the Oral Politics of the East African Revival in Northern Gikuyuland.' *Journal of African History* 42, no. 3 (2001), 469–89.

_____ 'Writing in Revolution: Independent Schooling and Mau Mau in Nyeri.' In *Mau Mau and Nationhood: Arms, Authority and Narration*, edited by Elisha Stephen Atieno Odhiambo and John Lonsdale, 76–96. Oxford: James Currey, 2003.

Porch, Douglas. 'Imperial Wars: From the Seven Years War to the First World War.' In *The Oxford History of Modern War*, edited by Charles Townshend, 94–116. Oxford: Oxford University Press, 2005.

Posner, Daniel. *Institutions and Ethnic Politics in Africa*. Cambridge: Cambridge University Press, 2005.

_____ 'The Political Salience of Cultural Difference: Why Chewas and Tumbukas are Allies in Zambia and Adversaries in Malawi.' *American Political Science Review* 98, no. 4 (2004), 529–45.

'Preface: Towards a Science of Counterinsurgency.' *Contemporary Security Policy* 28, no. 1 (2007), v–vi.

Presley, Cora Ann. *Kikuyu Women, the Mau Mau Rebellion, and Social Change in Kenya*. Boulder CO: Westview, 1992.

Pugliese, Cristiana. 'Complementary or Contending Nationhoods? Kikuyu Pamphlets and Songs, 1945–52.' In *Mau Mau and Nationhood: Arms, Authority and Narration*, edited by Elisha Stephen Atieno Odhiambo and John Lonsdale, 97–120. Oxford: James Currey, 2003.

Pye, Lucien. *Guerrilla Communism in Malaya: Its Social and Political Meaning*. Princeton NJ: Princeton University Press, 1956.

Redding, Sean. 'Government Witchcraft: Taxation, the Supernatural, and the Mpondo Revolt in the Transkei, South Africa, 1955–1963.' *African Affairs* 95, no. 381 (1996), 555–79.

Robinson, Ronald. 'Non-European Foundations of European Imperialism: Sketch for a Theory of Collaboration.' In *Studies in the Theory of Imperialism*, edited by Roger Owen and Bob Sutcliffe, 117–42. London: Longman, 1972.

Roelker, Jack. *Mathu of Kenya: A Political Study*. Stanford CA: Hoover Institution Press, 1976.

Rosberg, Carl and John Nottingham. *The Myth of "Mau Mau": Nationalism in Kenya*. New York: Praeger, 1966.

Sandgren, David. *Christianity and the Kikuyu: Religious Divisions and Social Conflict*. New York: Peter Lang, 1989.

Seal, Anil. *The Emergence of Indian Nationalism: Competition and Collaboration in the Later Nineteenth Century*. Cambridge: Cambridge University Press, 1968.

Sen, Amartya. *Identity and Violence: The Illusion of Destiny*. London: Penguin, 2006.

Sharkey, Armstrong. *European and Native American Warfare, 1675–1815*. London: UCL Press, 1998.

Sharkey, Heather. *Living With Colonialism: Nationalism and Culture in the Anglo-Egyptian Sudan*. Berkeley: University of California Press, 2003.

Simons, Anna. 'War: Back to the Future.' *Annual Review of Anthropology* 28 (1999), 73–108.

Smith, James. 'Njama's Supper: The Consumption and Use of Literary Potency by Mau Mau Insurgents in Colonial Kenya.' *Comparative Studies in Society and History* 40, no. 3 (1998), 524–48.

Smoker, Dorothy. *Ambushed by Love: God's Triumph in Kenya's Terror*. Fort Washington PA: Christian Literature Crusade, 1994.

Solovey, Mark. 'Project Camelot and the 1960s Epistemological Revolution: Rethinking the Politics-Patronage-Social Science Nexus.' *Social Studies of Science* 31, no. 2 (2001), 171–206.

Sorrenson, M. P. Keith. *Land Reform in the Kikuyu Country: A Study in Government Policy*. Nairobi: Oxford University Press, 1967.

Spencer, Jonathon. 'On Not Becoming a "Terrorist": Problems of Memory, Agency, and Community in the Sri Lankan Conflict.' In *Violence and Subjectivity*, edited by Veena Das, Arthur Kleinman, Mampehla Ramphele, and Pamela Reynolds, 120–40. Berkeley: University of California Press, 2000.

Steinhart, Edward. *Conflict and Collaboration: The Kingdoms of Western Uganda, 1890–1907*. Princeton NJ: Princeton University Press, 1977.

Stora, Benjamin. *Algeria, 1830–2000: A Short History*. Translated by Jane Marie Todd. Ithaca NY: Cornell University Press, 2001.

Surveys, Marco. *Who's Who in East Africa 1963–1964*. Nairobi: Marco Surveys, 1963.

Swainson, Nicola. *The Development of Corporate Capitalism in Kenya 1918–77*. London: Heinemann, 1980.

Swedenberg, Ted. *Memories of Revolt: The 1935–39 Rebellion and the Palestinian National Past*. Fayetteville AR: University of Arkansas Press, 2003.

Tamarkin, Mordechai. 'Mau Mau in Nakuru.' *Journal of African History* 17, no. 1 (1976), 119–34.

_____ 'The Loyalists in Nakuru During the Mau Mau Revolt and Its Aftermath, 1953–1963.' *Asian and African Studies* 12, no. 2 (1978), 247–61.

Throup, David and Charles Hornsby. *Multi-Party Politics in Kenya: The Kenyatta and Moi States and the Triumph of the System in the 1992 Election*. Oxford: James Currey, 1998.

_____ 'Crime, Politics and the Police in Colonial Kenya, 1939–63.' In *Policing and Decolonisation: Politics, Nationalism and the Police, 1917–65*, edited by David Anderson and David Killingray, 127–57. Manchester: Manchester University Press, 1992.

Throup, David. *Economic and Social Origins of Mau Mau 1945–53*. London: James Currey, 1988.

Thuku, Harry. *Harry Thuku: An Autobiography*. Nairobi: Oxford University Press, 1970.

Tignor, Robert. 'Colonial Chiefs in Chiefless Societies.' *Journal of Modern African Studies* 9, no. 3 (1971), 339–59.

_____ *Capitalism and Nationalism at the End of Empire: State and Business in Decolonizing Egypt, Nigera, and Kenya, 1945–1963*. Princeton NJ: Princeton University Press, 1997.

Tilly, Charles. *The Politics of Collective Violence.* Cambridge: Cambridge University Press, 2003.

Townshend, Charles. 'People's War.' In *The Oxford History of Modern War,* edited by Charles Townshend, 177–200. Oxford: Oxford University Press, 2005.

Trench, Charles. *Men Who Ruled Kenya: The Kenya Administration 1892–1963.* London: Radcliffe Press, 1993.

Vines, Alex. *Renamo: Terrorism in Mozambique.* Oxford: James Currey, 1991.

Wakin, Eric. *Anthropology Goes to War: Professional Ethics and Counterinsurgency in Thailand.* Madison WI: Center for Southeast Asian Studies, 1992.

Wanyoike, E. N. *An African Pastor.* Nairobi: East African Publishing House, 1974.

Wasserman, Gary. *The Politics of Decolonization: Kenya Europeans and the Land Issue, 1960–1965.* Cambridge: Cambridge University Press, 1976.

wa Wanjau, Gakaara. *Mau Mau Author in Detention.* Translated by Paul Ngigi Njoroge. Nairobi: Heinemann, 1988.

Weinstein, Jeremy. *Inside Rebellion: The Politics of Insurgent Violence.* Cambridge: Cambridge University Press, 2007.

Weitz, Richard. 'Insurgency and Counterinsurgency in Latin America, 1960–1980.' *Political Science Quarterly* 101, no. 3 (1986), 397–413.

White, Luise. 'Separating the Men From the Boys: Constructions of Gender, Sexuality, and Terrorism in Central Kenya, 1939–1959.' *International Journal of African Historical Studies* 23, no. 1 (1990), 1–25.

Widner, Jennifer. *The Rise of a Party-State in Kenya: From "Harambee" to "Nyayo!".* Berkeley: University of California Press, 1993.

Wipper, Audrey. 'The Maendeleo ya Wanawake Organization: The Co-Optation of Leadership.' *African Studies Review* 18, no. 3 (1975), 99–120.

Wood, Elisabeth Jean. *Forging Democracy From Below: Insurgent Transitions in South Africa and El Salvador.* Cambridge: Cambridge University Press, 2000.

———— *Insurgent Collective Action and Civil War in El Salvador.* Cambridge: Cambridge University Press, 2003.

Young, Marilyn. 'The American Empire at War.' In *The Barbarisation of Warfare,* edited by George Kassimeris, 175–85. London: Hurst, 2006.

Index

Kegonge, 140
Kenya African Democratic Union (KADU),
  187
Kenya African National Union (KANU), x,
  150, 165, 185, 189, 191, 193, 198,
  199, 200, 201, 204, 219
and post-colonial opposition to loyalists,
  192
and prominence of ex-detainees within,
  163, 170, 185–187, 189
detainee strength within, 188
Women's Wing, 187
Youth Wing, 185, 186, 189, 200
Kenya African Union (KAU), 32, 33, 34,
  35, 38, 49, 89, 131, 134, 169, 186,
  212
Kenya Land Commission, 32, 39
Kenya People's Union (KPU), 163,
  199–201, 202, 203, 204
Kenya Police, 55, 61, 67, 81, 90, 117, 160,
  165, 171, 173
expansion of, 90
Kenya Tea Development Board, 214
Kenyatta, Jomo, ix, x, 151, 179, 187, 193,
  198, 199, 200, 201, 202, 203, 204,
  205, 206, 207, 211, 213
and AIPC, 196–197, 228, 234
and arrest and detention of, 49, 162,
  181, 192, 199
and attitudes of towards colonial rule,
  34
and ethnography, 25
and *Mumenyereri*, 131
and political ideology of, 147
and position within pre-Mau Mau
  politics, 132, 134, 180–181
and presidency of, x, xi, 150, 165, 182,
  193, 199, 200, 202, 203, 206
and release of, 181–182, 187, 188
background of, 180
Kerugoya, 47, 103, 111, 234
Kiama, Chief Stanley, 140
Kiamacimti, 87
Kiama kia Muingi, 184, 186
Kiambaa, 214
Kiano, Julius, 150, 161, 162–163, 176,
  177, 201
Kibaki, Mwai, x, xi, xii, xiii, 218, 219
Kibubu, Stephen Mututo, 145
Kiganjo Police Training Centre, 148, 171
Kigumo, 153

Kigutu, Ndaai, 186
Kihumbu, 103
Kikuyu Association, 31, 227
Kikuyu Central Association (KCA), 31, 32,
  36, 38, 39, 180
Kikuyu Guard. *See* Home Guard
Kikuyu Guard Combat Units, 91
Kikuyu Independent Schools Association
  (KISA), 31, 195–198
Kimahuri, 197
Kimani, Matthew, 170
Kimani, Wachira, 186
Kimathi, Dedan, xi, 14, 64, 91, 114, 117,
  118
Kimathi, Sub-Chief Wambugu, 188, 227,
  229
Kimbo, General, 59, 169
Kinaichu, Maina, 138, 139, 141
Kinanjogo, 73
King'ori, Samuel, 144
King's African Rifles (KAR), 49, 56, 62, 98
Kinyoro, George Njoroge, 132, 225
Kioni, Stephen, 156, 158
Kirigi, 142
Kirimukuyu, 68, 94, 230, 234, 236, 240
Kiritu, Parmenas, 22–23, 24, 25, 28, 137,
  234
Kirugami, Wanja, 154
Kiruma, Kariuki, 99, 238
Kiruma, Njugi, 99
Kisou, Shadrack, 90
Kithimu, 103
Koinange, Charles Karuga, 150, 171,
  213–214, 215–216
Koinange, Frederick Mbiyu, 212, 213
Koinange, James Njoroge, 215
Koinange, John Westley Mbiyu, 212
Koinange, Leonard Karuga, 215
Koinange, Lilian Wairimu, 213
Koinange, Miriam Wambui, 215
Koinange, Peter Mbiyu, 212, 213, 214,
  215, 216
Koinange family 225
  land dispute, 212–216
Koinange wa Mbiyu, Chief, 24, 65, 66, 212
Komo, James, 137
Kubai, Fred, 34, 181, 200
Kunyhia, Johanna, 184
Kurdistan, 80
Kuria, Chief Makimei, 56, 57, 58, 99
Kyeni, 89

Njonjo, Charles, 150, 171
Njonjo, Chief Josiah, 65, 171, 215
Njonjo, Lewis Mungai, 65–66
Njuri Ncheke, 156
North Tetu, 62, 64, 114, 122, 154, 167,
    170, 184, 187, 196, 202
Northern Ireland, 230, 232, 234. *See*
    Ireland
Nyachae, Simeon, 150
Nyaga, James, 137
Nyaga, Sylvester, 186
Nyagah, Jeremiah, 1, 2, 51, 139, 150, 156,
    158, 159, 161–162, 176, 177, 237
Nyamu, Daudi, 185
Nyandarua North, 204
Nyanza Province, 64, 154, 200, 203
Nyauhruru. *See* Thomson's Falls
Nyethuna, 125
Nyiah, Alice, 154
Nyoro, Headman, 77

oathing. *See also* Mau Mau
    post-colonial, 202–203
Odinga, Oginga, 150, 173, 176, 227
Ol Joro Orok, 128
Oneko, Achieng, 181
Operation Anvil, 91, 104, 106, 115, 116
Operation Jock Scott, 6, 104
Othaya, 147, 183, 190, 192, 194, 197, 201

Paul, Benson, 55
Paulo, Chief, 184
Pedraza, G. J. W., 168
Peru, 119
police. *See* Kenya Police or Tribal Police
Prideaux, C., 167, 234
Project Camelot, 40
propaganda, 58–59, 64, 73, 109, 125, 138,
    154
Provincial Administration, 21, 49, 64, 107,
    112, 114, 118, 121, 122, 124, 126,
    127, 129, 149, 150, 152, 164, 174,
    186, 189, 190, 191, 198, 201, 206,
    210, 237
    and Africanisation of, 150, 165–173
    and assistance to loyalists seeking work,
    127–129
    and control of chiefs, 61, 66, 225
    and expansion during Mau Mau war,
    164–165
    and management of elections, 152, 155

and recruitment of loyalists into,
    126–127
control of Tribal Police, 111
post-colonial role of, 193, 200

Ragati, 172
Raynor, William, 165, 173
Regional Boundaries Commission, 103
Riakiania, 140
Ribai, Sihar Githai, 118
Rift Valley Province
    and loyalist resettlement, 128
Royal Technical College, 162
Ruck family, 81
Ruguru, 188, 192, 197
Rui, General, 169
Ruria, Mugwongo, 3, 212
Ruringu, 169

screening, 49, 76, 82–84, 88, 89, 104, 123,
    126, 129, 168, 169
Sessional Paper No. 10, 195, 225, 227,
    228, 229, 231, 232, 233, 234, 235,
    237, 238, 240, 241
settlers, 5, 7, 30, 32, 47, 57, 83, 135, 155
Solai, 128
South Africa, 167, 177, 178
South Kinangop, 128
South Tetu, 88, 169, 170, 185, 186, 187
South Yatta
    detention camp, 170, 225
Sri Lanka, 92, 220
Stanford University, 162
Subukia, 128
Sudan, 220
Swann, Anthony, 166
Swynnerton Plan, 121–122, 174, 190

Taiti, Headman, 191
Tanganyika, 83–84, 165
Thailand Controversy, 40
Tharaka, 28
Theuri, David Wanjuki, 184
Thigiru wa Njiri, 62, 64
Thika District, 173
Thirami, Githira, 87
Thirami, Ndirangu, 87
Thirami, Wanderi, 87
Thomson's Falls, 99
Thuku, Harry, 23, 31, 59, 60, 133, 139,
    180

BOOKS IN THIS SERIES

1. *City Politics: A Study of Léopoldville, 1962–1963*, J. S. LaFontaine
2. *Studies in Rural Capitalism in West Africa*, Polly Hill
3. *Land Policy in Buganda*, Henry W. West
4. *The Nigerian Military: A Sociological Analysis of Authority and Revolt, 1960–1967*, Robin Luckham
5. *The Ghanaian Factory Worker: Industrial Man in Africa*, Margaret Peil
6. *Labour in the South African Gold Mines*, Francis Wilson
7. *The Price of Liberty: Personality and Politics in Colonial Nigeria*, Kenneth W. J. Post and George D. Jenkins
8. *Subsistence to Commercial Farming in Present Day Buganda: An Economic and Anthropological Survey*, Audrey I. Richards, Fort Sturrock, and Jean M. Fortt (eds.)
9. *Dependence and Opportunity: Political Change in Ahafo*, John Dunn and A. F. Robertson
10. *African Railwaymenn: Solidarity and Opposition in an East African Labour Force*, R. D. Grillo
11. *Islam and Tribal Art in West Africa*, René A. Bravmann
12. *Modern and Traditional Elites in the Politics of Lagos*, P. D. Cole
13. *Asante in the Nineteenth Century: The Structure and Evolution of a Political Order*, Ivor Wilks
14. *Culture, Tradition, and Society in the West African Novel*, Emmanuel Obiechina
15. *Saints and Politicians*, Donald B. Cruise O'Brien
16. *The Lions of Dagbon: Political Change in Northern Ghana*, Martin Staniland
17. *Politics of Decolonization: Kenya, Europeans, and the Land Issue, 1960–1965*, Gary B. Wasserman
18. *Muslim Brotherhoods in Nineteenth Century Africa*, B. G. Martin
19. *Warfare in the Sokoto Caliphate: Historical and Sociological Perspectives*, Joseph P. Smaldone
20. *Liberia and Sierra Leone: An Essay in Comparative Politics*, Christopher Clapham
21. *Adam Kok's Griquas: A Study in the Development of Stratification in South Africa*, Robert Ross
22. *Class, Power, and Ideology in Ghana: The Railwaymen of Sekondi*, Richard Jeffries
23. *West African States: Failure and Promise*, John Dunn (ed.)
24. *Afrikaners of the Kalahari: White Minority in a Black State*, Margo Russell and Martin Russell
25. *A Modern History of Tanganyika*, John Iliffe
26. *A History of African Christianity, 1950–1975*, Adrian Hastings
27. *Slave, Peasants, and Capitalists in Southern Angola, 1840–1926*, W. G. Clarence-Smith
28. *The Hidden Hippopotamus: Reappraised in African History: The Early Colonial Experience in Western Zambia*, Gwyn Prins
29. *Families Divided: The Impact of Migrant Labour in Lesotho*, Colin Murray
30. *Slavery, Colonialism, and Economic Growth in Dahomey, 1640–1960*, Patrick Manning
31. *Kings, Commoners, and Concessionaires: The Evolution and Dissolution of the Nineteenth-Century Swazi State*, Philip Bonner
32. *Oral Poetry and Somali Nationalism: The Case of Sayid Mahammad 'Abdille Hasan*, Said S. Samatar
33. *The Political Economy of Pondoland 1860–1930*, William Beinart
34. *Volkskapitalisme: Class, Capital, and Ideology in the Development of Afrikaner Nationalism, 1934–1948*, Dan O'Meara
35. *The Settler Economies: Studies in the Economic History of Kenya and Rhodesia 1900–1963*, Paul Mosley